Medieval Islamic Medicine

Comparative Studies of Health Systems and Medical Care

John M. Janzen, *The Quest for Therapy in Lower Zaire*
Paul U. Unschuld, *Medical Ethics in Imperial China: A Study in Historical Anthropology*
Margaret M. Lock, *East Asian Medicine in Urban Japan: Varieties of Medical Experience*
Jeanie Schmit Kayser-Jones, *Old, Alone, and Neglected: Care of the Aged in Scotland and in the United States*
Arthur Kleinman, *Patients and Healers in the Context of Culture: An Exploration of the Borderland Between Anthropology, Medicine and Psychiatry*
Stephen J. Kunitz, *Disease Change and the Role of Medicine: The Navajo Experience*
Carol Laderman, *Wives and Midwives: Childbirth and Nutrition in Rural Malaysia*
Victor G. Rodwin, *The Health Planning Predicament: France, Québec, England, and the United States*
Michael W. Dols, *Medieval Islamic Medicine: Ibn Riḍwān's Treatise "On the Prevention of Bodily Ills in Egypt"*

· MEDIEVAL ISLAMIC MEDICINE ·

Ibn Riḍwān's Treatise "On the Prevention of Bodily Ills in Egypt"

Translated, with an Introduction, by Michael W. Dols

Arabic Text edited by Adil S. Gamal

UNIVERSITY OF CALIFORNIA PRESS
Berkeley • Los Angeles • London

University of California Press
Berkeley and Los Angeles, California
University of California Press, Ltd.
London, England

Library of Congress Cataloging in Publication Data

'Alī ibn Riḍwān, d. ca. 1068.
Medieval Islamic medicine.

(Comparative studies of health systems and medical care)
Text in Arabic and English
Includes bibliographical references and index.
1. Medicine, Arabic—Early works to 1800. 2. 'Alī ibn Riḍwān, d. ca. 1068. Risālah fī daf 'maḍārr al-abdān bi-arḍ Miṣr.
I. Dols, Michael W., 1942– . II. Jamāl, 'Ādil Sulaymān.
III. Title. IV. Series.
R128.3.A4513 1984 610 83-5017
ISBN 0-520-05836-9

1 2 3 4 5 6 7 8 9

Printed in the United States of America

Contents

Preface

I have attempted two things in this book: to describe medieval Islamic medicine[1] and to illustrate my account with a specific medical text, *On the Prevention of Bodily Ills in Egypt* by 'Alī ibn Riḍwān (A.D. 998–1068). In my introductory essay, I have placed Islamic medicine in its historical context by describing the medical profession in medieval Islamic society. The questions that demanded my attention were: What did it mean to be a doctor in medieval Islamic society? What was the nature of the medicine that physicians practiced? And what was the relationship between physician and patient?

My description of Islamic medicine is not—given the present state of scholarship, it could not be—a comprehensive history. Moreover, I have deliberately avoided the more common biobibliographical or purely theoretical approaches to this subject. Instead, I have used Ibn Riḍwān's treatise as a guide to the central features of medical theory and practice in medieval Islamic society. The treatise is a graphic account of medical conditions in Egypt, unlike most medieval medical writings that are largely theoretical. Furthermore, Ibn Riḍwān is an important figure in Islamic medicine because his numerous works are remarkably informative about the profession.

Ibn Riḍwān wrote his treatise to answer the provoking claim of a Tunisian doctor, Ibn al-Jazzār (d. A.D. 980), that Egypt was a particularly unhealthy place, a common and ancient complaint by foreigners. Ibn al-Jazzār's work is lost, save for the excerpts that Ibn Riḍwān quotes in his refutation. The two men disagree, not about

[1]The designation of scientific medicine in Muslim society as *Islamic* seems most suitable for a number of reasons. It is used in the sense of "Islamicate," a neologism proposed by Marshall Hodgson, to describe the nonreligious cultural elements of society in which Islam was the predominant religious faith. *Islamic* has the advantage of encompassing the vast medical literature written in oriental languages and of suggesting the inpingement of religious belief on medical theory and practice. The term, however, has two distinct disadvantages: it should not imply that all medical practitioners were Muslims, nor should it be interpreted as dealing with folkloric or "Prophetic" medicine. The latter was a quasi-medical tradition of religious medicine based on the sayings of the Prophet and his companions, which is discussed in the Introduction. *Arabian* or *Middle Eastern* medicine is simply too restrictive in its geographical connotations. See *Vorlesungen*, pp. 3–4.

methods of treatment, but about the causes of disease in Egypt. Ibn Riḍwān resorts to Greek medical theory to explain his position and criticizes Ibn al-Jazzār both for his lack of experience in Egypt and for his misunderstanding of that theory, particularly of the notion of temperament. To treat patients successfully, Ibn Riḍwān asserts, doctors must understand the unique temperament of Egypt and its people. Ibn Riḍwān's tract is, however, more than a rebuttal of Ibn al-Jazzār. It is a didactic discourse on the proper duties of doctors in the prevention and treatment of endemic and epidemic diseases.[2]

Ibn Riḍwān allows us to see the continuity of the classical Greek or Hippocratic tradition in Islamic medicine and its application in medieval Islamic society.[3] In translation, the Greek tradition was transmitted to the Islamic world in the eighth to tenth centuries A.D. and was incorporated into Islamic culture. From the Hippocratic tradition,[4] Ibn Riḍwān and his fellow doctors learned a naturalistic view of health and illness, which accepted only natural elements and forces and excluded the supernatural or spiritual. In his treatise, Ibn Riḍwān emphasizes preventive over curative medicine and the treatment of the individual over the disease.[5] He follows Hippocratic tradition, too, by his interest in medical topography and gives a valuable description of Egypt and its capital in the mid-eleventh century A.D.[6]

In the elaborate system of Greco-Roman medical theory and practice, which Owsei Temkin has conveniently termed *Galenism*,[7] Islamic physicians found a coherent set of medical concepts, definitions, and techniques. Ibn Riḍwān lets us watch Islamic physicians use the Galenic theory of humoral pathology in their everyday work. He presumes, however, a knowledge of this pathology on the part of the

[2]In this regard, our text is representative of Islamic medical literature on epidemic diseases. See, for example, S. K. Hamarneh, "Ibn al-'Ayn Zarbī and His Definitions of Diseases and Their Diagnoses," *Proceedings of the First International Symposium for the History of Arabic Science* (Aleppo, 1978), 2:310.

[3]A comparable, but more tenuous, continuity of the Hippocratic tradition can be traced in medieval European medicine. See Pearl Kibre, "Hippocratic Writings in the Middle Ages," *BHM* 18 (1946):371–412, and Loren C. MacKinney, *Early Medieval Medicine* (New York, 1979 repr.).

[4]See *EI*[2] *Supplement*, s.v. "Buḳrāṭ" (A. Dietrich).

[5]See Owsei Temkin, "The Scientific Approach to Disease: Specific Entity and Individual Sickness," in his *The Double Face of Janus* (Baltimore, 1977), pp. 441–455.

[6]Concerning Ibn Buṭlān's comparable description of Baghdad, see the discussion below. Manfred Ullmann notes (*MI*, p. 159, n. 2) that Ya'qūb ibn Isḥāq al-Isrā'īlī al-Maḥallī (d. 598/1202) gives a similar account in his *Maqālah fī mazāj Dimashq*.

[7]Owsei Temkin, *Galenism: The Rise and Decline of a Medical Philosophy* (Ithaca, 1973); see also *EI*[2], s.v. "Djālīnus" (R. Walzer).

reader. Consequently, the first part of this book outlines the framework of Galenic medicine as it was conceived by Ibn Riḍwān and Ibn al-Jazzār.

From a wider perspective, the study of medical history makes a significant contribution to our understanding of Islamic society. Medicine may be viewed with an eye to its intriguing relationships, not only with economic conditions, social structures, and religious beliefs but also with Islamic culture in general. For example, medicine appears to have played a greater role in Islamic literature than in Greco-Roman literature.[8] The treatise suggests a world view, which is found in all medical systems, about the nature of man and his relationship with his surroundings.

Finally, my lengthy annotation is intended as a guide to the widely dispersed literature. It should also alert the reader to the fact that the history of Islamic medicine is still imperfectly understood because of the vast amount of poorly edited and unpublished medical material in oriental languages that remains to be studied. This translation and edition of the text are a small contribution to that endeavor.

M. W. D.

San Francisco, 1983

[8] *Vorlesungen*, p. 1.

Acknowledgments

We would like to acknowledge the generous support given to the translation and edition of the text by the Program for Translations of the National Endowment for the Humanities and by the Foreign Currency Program of the Smithsonian Institution. In addition, the award of a John S. Guggenheim Memorial Fellowship to Professor Dols made possible, in part, the final revision of the work. Publication has been facilitated by the University of Arizona, California State University, Hayward, the University of California, San Francisco, and the University of California Press. Our editor at the Press, Karen Reeds, has been of inestimable help in her encouragement, patience, and criticism. We would also like to express our gratitude to those who have read all or part of the manuscript with great care: Professors Franz Rosenthal, William Brinner, Carlo Cipolla, and especially Manfred Ullmann, Felix Klein-Franke, Emilie Savage-Smith, and Charles Leslie.

The following libraries kindly allowed us access to their collections or supplied us with microfilm copies of the text: The Egyptian National Library, The Arab League Microfilm Library, The Vatican Library, The Royal College of Physicians Library, The Chester Beatty Library, and The Baghdad Museum Library. With regard to the last, we would like to thank Ambassador Herman F. Eilts and his associates for their assistance.

Transliteration

The system of Arabic transliteration adopted here follows that of the Library of Congress, the single exception being that the definite article preceding "sun letters" is transliterated as pronounced. Wherever an Arabic word has assumed a more familiar English form than the strict transliteration, such as Cairo for al-Qāhirah, the former has been adopted. For dates, as a rule, we give the Muslim year or century first, then its equivalent in the Christian calendar. In many instances, however, Muslim and Christian dates are cited singly as A.H. (*anno hegirae*) and A.D. (*anno Domini*), respectively.

Abbreviations

Bedevian	Armenag K. Bedevian. *Illustrated Polyglottic Dictionary of Plant Names.* Cairo, 1936.
BHM	*Bulletin of the History of Medicine.* Baltimore.
Darby	William Darby, Paul Ghalioungui, and Louis Grivetti. *Food: Gift of Osiris.* 2 vols. London, 1977.
de Sacy	A. I. Silvestre de Sacy, trans. *Relation de l'Égypte, par Abd-Allatif, médecin arabe de Baghdad.* Paris, 1810.
Dozy	R. Dozy. *Supplément aux dictionnaires arabes.* 2 vols. Leiden, 1881; repr. Beirut, 1968.
EI¹	*The Encyclopaedia of Islam.* 4 vols. Leiden-London, 1913–1934.
EI²	*The Encyclopaedia of Islam.* New ed. Leiden-London, 1960–.
EI² Supplement	*The Encyclopaedia of Islam.* New ed. *Supplement*, Leiden, 1980–.
GAL	Carl Brockelmann. *Geschichte der arabischen Litteratur.* 2 vols. Leiden, 1892–1902; 2d ed., 2 vols. Leiden, 1945–1949; *Supplement*, 3 vols. Leiden, 1937–1942.
Grand'henry	Jacques Grand'henry, ed. and trans. *Le Livre de la méthode du médecin de 'Alī b. Riḍwān (998–1067)*, vol. 1. Louvain-la-Neuve, 1979.
Graziani	Joseph Graziani. *Ibn Jazlah's Eleventh-Century Tabulated Medical Compedium, Taqwīm al-Abdān.* Ph.D. dissertation, University of California, Los Angeles, 1973.

Hippocrates	W. H. S. Jones, ed. and trans. *Hippocrates*, The Loeb Classical Library. 4 vols. Cambridge-London, 1923–1931.
Ḥunayn	Ḥunayn ibn Isḥāq. *Questions on Medicine for Scholars*. Trans. Paul Ghalioungui. Cairo, 1980.
Ibn Bakhtīshū'	Abū Sa'īd ibn Bakhtīshū'. *Risālah fī ṭ-ṭibb wal-aḥdāth an-nafsānīyah (Über die Heilung der Krankheiten der Seele und des Körpers)*. Ed. and trans. Felix Klein-Franke, in *Recherches*, n.s., Orient chrétien, vol. 4. Beirut, 1977.
Ibn Ḥawqal	Ibn Ḥawqal. *Configuration de la Terre*. Trans. J. H. Kramers and G. Wiet. 2 vols. Paris-Beirut, 1964.
Isḥāq	*Isḥāq ibn 'Imrān, Maqāla fī l-mālīkhūliyā (Abhandlung über die Melancholie) und Constantini Africani, Liberi duo de melancholia*. Ed. and trans. Karl Garbers. Hamburg, 1977.
Issa	Ahmed Issa Bey (Aḥmad 'Īsā). *Dictionnaire des nomes des plantes en latin, français, anglais et arabe*. Cairo, 1930.
Kühn	Carolus Gottlob Kühn, ed. *Claudii Galeni Opera omnia*. 20 vols. Leipzig, 1821–1833; repr. Hildesheim, 1965.
Lane	E. W. Lane. *An Arabic-English Lexicon*. 8 vols. London, 1886–1893; repr. New York, 1955–56.
Maimonides	*Moses Maimonides' Two Treatises on the Regimen of Health: "Fī Tadbīr al-Ṣiḥḥah" and "Maqālah fī bayān Ba'ḍ al-A'rāḍ wa-al-Jawāb 'anhā."* Trans. Ariel Bar-Sela, H. E. Hoff, and Elias Faris. In *Transactions of the American Philosophical Society*, n.s., vol. 54, pt. 4 (1964).
MI	Manfred Ullmann. *Die Medizin im Islam*. In *Handbuch der Orientalistik*, vol. 1, no. 6, pt. 1. Ed. B. Spuler. Leiden, 1970.
Nāṣir-i Khusraw	*Sefer Nameh—Relation du voyage de Nasir-i Khusraw*. Ed. and trans. Charles Schefer. Paris, 1881; repr. Amsterdam, 1970.

Schacht and Meyerhof	Joseph Schacht and Max Meyerhof, ed. and trans. *The Medico-Philosophical Controversy Between Ibn Butlan of Baghdad and Ibn Ridwan of Cairo: A Contribution to the History of Greek Learning Among the Arabs*. The Egyptian University, Faculty of Arts, no. 13. Cairo, 1937.
Sontheimer	Joseph von Sontheimer, trans. *Grosse Zusammenstellung über die Kräfte der bekannten einfachen Heil- und Nahrungsmittel von . . . . Ibn Bayṭār*. 2 vols. Stuttgart, 1840.
Vorlesungen	Felix Klein-Franke. *Vorlesungen über die Medizin im Islam*. In *Sudhoffs Archiv, Beihefte*, vol. 23. Wiesbaden, 1982.
WKAS	Manfred Ullmann et al., ed. *Wörtbuch der klassischen arabischen Sprache*. 2 vols. Wiesbaden, 1970–.

• Part I •

MEDIEVAL ISLAMIC MEDICINE

Introductory Essay

Galenism[9]

The dramatic Arab invasion of the Middle East and North Africa in the seventh century A.D. did not destroy the intellectual life of the conquered lands.[10] By a selective process of assimilation, Islamic society came to embody significant elements of Hellenistic culture. This continuity can be seen most vividly in Islamic art and architecture; in a less visible but no less important form, it can be seen in the philosophic and scientific tradition that flourished in medieval Islamic society. Despite an early acquaintance with the scientific achievements of other cultures, notably of India, it was the Greek tradition that was decisive for Islamic learning. The predominance of the Greek tradition was largely due to the Hellenized Christians, Jews, and Persians, who made up the bulk of the population in the newly established empire, and to the persistence of their centers of learning.

The Islamic empire, in its initial expansion, encompassed Egypt, one of the most important centers of Hellenistic learning. The cultural continuity with Islamic learning is well illustrated by the history of the so-called Alexandrian school, which had been famous in antiquity for

[9]For the general theory of Islamic medicine, see: *MI*, pp. 97–100, 108–184; M. Ullmann, *Islamic Medicine* (Edinburgh, 1978), pp. 55–106; M. H. Shah, "The Constitution of Medicine," *Theories and Philosophies of Medicine* (New Delhi, 1962), pp. 92–140; F. E. Peters, *Allah's Commonwealth* (New York, 1973), pp. 373–396; O. C. Gruner, *A Treatise on the Canon of Medicine of Avicenna* (London, 1930), which should be used with caution. A distinction has been made (see n. 1 above) between "Islamic" and "Prophetic" medicine (*aṭ-ṭibb an-nabawī*); regarding the latter, see *MI*, pp. 185–189; J. C. Bürgel, "Secular and Religious Features of Medieval Arabic Medicine," *Asian Medical Systems: A Comparative Study*, ed. Charles Leslie (Berkeley, 1976), pp. 44–62; Cyril Elgood, "Tibb-ul-Nabbi or Medicine of the Prophet. Being a Translation of Two Works of the Same Name . . . ," *Osiris* 14 (1962): 33–192; *Vorlesungen*, chap 1.

[10]The following survey relies on the following works: S. Pines, "Philosophy," in *The Cambridge History of Islam*, ed. P. M. Holt, A. K. S. Lambton, and B. Lewis (Cambridge, 1970), 2:780–784; Martin Plessner, "The Natural Sciences and Medicine," in *The Legacy of Islam*, 2d ed., ed. J. Schacht and C. E. Bosworth, (Oxford, 1974), pp. 425–460; and Max Meyerhof, "Science and Medicine," in *The Legacy of Islam*, 1st ed., ed. T. Arnold and A. Guillaume (Oxford, 1931), pp. 311–355.

its study of medicine. In the centuries before the advent of Islam, the school had lost its former vigor, it had been Christianized, and its medical literature was subjected to condensation and commentary. The institution survived the Arab conquest of Egypt and lasted until the early eighth century A.D. when the school was transferred to Antioch by the Caliph 'Umar (A.D. 717–720), who clearly intended to encourage scientific and medical studies.[11] Medical education continued at Antioch and other cities, and the medical curriculum of the late Alexandrian school became the basis of professional medical education.[12]

The transmission of the Greek scientific tradition during the early Islamic empire was complemented on a more popular level by the infiltration of Greek ideas into Islamic culture via the educated, nonspecialist classes. The nascent Islamic society was quite receptive to the ideas of these newly converted, educated peoples,[13] as can be seen by the infusion of Greek ideas into early Muslim law and theology.[14] Similarly, the Greek philosophical heritage continued uninterrupted "in a more or less underground way," especially skepticism, and, therefore, was never truly revived.[15]

The continuity of Hellenistic learning with Islamic science was also maintained in the Middle East by the Syriac- (or neo-Aramaic) speaking Christians, mainly the Nestorians.[16] The adherents of this persecuted sect were expelled from the Byzantine Empire and migrated

[11]Klein-Franke (*Vorlesungen*, p. 30) has emphasized the importance of Ibn Riḍwān's statement that some of the teachers in Alexandria were persuaded by 'Umar (before he had become caliph) to convert to Islam because it is the first mention of the Alexandrian school in an Islamic source.

[12]See James Longrigg, "Superlative Achievement and Comparative Neglect: Alexandrian Medical Science and Modern Historical Research," *History of Science* 19 (1981):155–200. The history of the late Alexandrian school(s) and its relationship to Islamic learning has been studied by Max Meyerhof in the following publications: "Von Alexandrien nach Bagdad," *Sitzungsberichte der preussischen Akademie der Wissenschaften in Berlin, phil.-hist. Kl.* 23 (1930):389–429; "Le Fin de l'école d'Alexandrie d'après quelques autuers arabes," *Bulletin de l'Institut d'Égypte* 15 (1932–33):109–123; and "Sultan Saladin's Physician on the Transmission of Greek Medicine to the Arabs," *BHM* 18 (1945):169–178. See also *Vorlesungen*, chaps. 1 and 2.

[13]See A. I. Sabra, "The Scientific Enterprise," in *Islam and the Arab World*, ed. Bernard Lewis (New York, 1976), pp. 183–184.

[14]J. Schacht, "Remarques sur la transmission de la pensée grecque aux arabes," *Histoire de la médecine* 2 (1952):11–19.

[15]Josef van Ess, "Skepticism in Islamic Religious Thought," *al-Abhath* 21 (1968):3.

[16]This Christian sect originated in A.D. 428 with Nestorius (d. ca. A.D. 451), patriarch of Constantinople. Nestorianism was the doctrine that there were two separate Persons in Christ, one divine and the other human, as opposed to the orthodox doctrine, which held that Christ was a single Person, at once man and God. The heresy was condemned by the Council of Ephesus in A.D. 431; see F. L. Cross, ed., *The Oxford Dictionary of the Christian Church* (London, 1974), s.v. "Nestorianism."

eventually to Persia, where they were well received by the Sasanian rulers. The Nestorians transferred their scientific center, which included a medical school, from Edessa (Urfa) to Nisibis in Mesopotamia in A.D. 489, and then moved again in the first half of the sixth century A.D. to Gondēshāpūr.[17]

Gondēshāpūr, near ancient Susa, had been established as an imperial city by the Sasanian king Shāpūr (A.D. 241–271). He had enlarged the older settlement to accommodate a large number of prisoners of war after he defeated the Roman Emperor Valerian. Shāpūr married the daughter of the Emperor Aurelian, and among those who accompanied the bride to Gondēshāpūr were two Greek physicians who publicly taught the Hippocratic system of medicine there. The king encouraged these Greek physicians in his provincial capital as well as the physicians and scholars from Persia and India. The city thereafter maintained a tradition of cosmopolitan learning, especially in medicine.

A successor, Shāpūr II (A.D. 306–80), further enlarged the city and founded an academy or university, which included faculties of theology, astronomy, and medicine, and housed both an observatory and a hospital. The movement of Nestorians to Gondēshāpūr augmented the intellectual life of the city, particularly strengthening its Greek orientation. In addition, Greek scholars migrated from Athens to Gondēshāpūr when Justinian closed the Neoplatonic academy in A.D. 529. Consequently, the city became the most important intellectual center of its time. Philosophic and scientific works in Greek and Sanskrit were translated into Syriac and Pahlavi. The literary momentum continued into the eighth century A.D., creating a scientific syncretism that formed the basis for the development of many fields of Islamic thought.[18]

During the Umayyad period (A.D. 661–750), when Syria and Egypt appear to have provided most of the court physicians, Gondēshā-

[17]*EI²*, s.v. "Gondē<u>sh</u>āpur" (Cl. Huart and Aydin Sayili); R. McC. Adams and D. P. Hansen, "Archaeological Reconnaissance and Soundings in Jundī Shāhpūr," *Ars Orientalis* 7 (1968):53–73, including an appendix: "Jundī Shāhpūr: A Preliminary Historical Sketch" by Nabia Abbott; Heinz H. Schoeffler, *Die Akademie von Gondischapur. Aristoteles auf dem Wege in den Orient* (Stuttgart, 1979).

[18]Gondēshāpūr seems to have enjoyed some reputation among the Arabs; the early Islamic sources indicate the existence of scientific education only in the field of medicine. For al-Ḥārith ibn Kaladah (d. A.D. 635), a contemporary of the Prophet, is supposed to have received his medical training at Gondēshāpūr, although it is very improbable. His medical pronouncements, however, bear evidence of Hellenistic influence, so it is likely he received his training secondhand. Although the art of medicine was sanctioned by the Prophet—tradition has it that he referred patients to al-Ḥārith—there were already doubts about its practice among the early religionists. See *MI*, p. 19f.; *Vorlesungen*, pp. 27–29.

pūr made little mark on Islamic culture. When the 'Abbāsids established their new capital in Baghdad, however, the new regime soon recognized the fame of Gondēshāpūr. In A.D. 765 the 'Abbāsid Caliph al-Manṣūr fell ill, and no physician apparently could be found; therefore, he sent for Jurjīs ibn Jibrīl ibn Bakhtīshū', who was chief physician at the well-known hospital at Gondēshāpūr.[19] Al-Manṣūr showed a lively interest in the sciences, providing a suitable intellectual environment for the cultivation of philosophic medicine. Under the caliphate of Hārūn ar-Rashīd (A.D. 786–809), the Bakhtīshū' family was clearly established as court physicians and produced seven generations of distinguished doctors. They were probably responsible for the propagation of Greek medical knowledge in the capital and throughout the empire.[20] Although other medical centers existed at the same time, most of these centers were influenced by Gondēshāpūr, particularly in the organization and administration of hospitals. Not surprisingly, the first important Islamic hospital or *bīmāristān* was founded by Hārūn ar-Rashīd in Baghdad, and it was designed and staffed by Gondēshāpūr physicians.

The greatest impetus to medical studies in Islamic society came from the translation of Greek scientific works into Arabic, the lingua franca of the new empire. The Arabic language thereby became the primary vehicle of medical science, as Latin would be in the West. Even though Arabic was held a sacred language, its scientific tradition remained secular. The translations were sponsored and supported by the 'Abbāsid caliphs and other wealthy patrons. Hārūn ar-Rashīd's successor, al-Ma'mūn (A.D. 813–833) established the House of Wisdom (*Bayt al-ḥikmah*) in Baghdad in A.D. 830 as the central institute for Arabic translations of scientific texts. It is possible that al-Ma'mūn sought in this way to imitate the cultural tradition of pre-Islamic Persia or to rival that of Byzantium. In any case, Islamic society was particularly receptive at this time to Hellenistic culture, particularly to its scientific literature.[21]

The transfer of this knowledge is well represented by Ḥunayn ibn Isḥāq (A.D. 808–873), the most important early translator of the

[19]See *Vorlesungen*, pp. 40–41.

[20]*EI*², s.v. "Bukhtīshū' " (D. Sourdel); *MI*, p. 108; *Vorlesungen*, pp. 44–47.

[21]See the discussion of this matter in *Vorlesungen*, pp. 68–70.

Greek medical works.[22] He was born to an Arab Nestorian family in al-Ḥīrah, in southern Iraq, where his father was a pharmacist. According to one account, the young Ḥunayn studied medicine at Gondēshāpūr. He clearly studied in Baghdad with Yūḥannā ibn Māsawayh (d. A.D. 857), the famous court physician and director of the House of Wisdom.[23] Ḥunayn's teacher eventually sent him away because he asked too many troublesome questions. Ḥunayn left Baghdad for more than two years, during which time he mastered Greek. He also perfected his skill in Syriac, Arabic, and Persian in order to read and translate original texts. Ḥunayn returned to Baghdad and was reconciled with Ibn Māsawayh, who encouraged him to translate Greek works. Under the caliph al-Mutawakkil (A.D. 847–861), Ḥunayn was appointed chief physician to the ʿAbbāsid court.

Ḥunayn translated an immense number of works, frequently from Greek into Syriac and, then, from Syriac into Arabic; he also collaborated closely with other translators and revised their works.[24] His translations were remarkable for their fluency, precision (particularly in the creation of Arabic scientific terminology), and thoroughness. He described his procedure succinctly in comments about his translation of Galen's *On Sects*:

> I translated it when I was young from a defective Greek manuscript; when I was forty, my pupil Ḥubaysh asked me to correct it after I had collected a number of Greek copies of the same work. I therefore arranged these in such a way that I could build up a correct copy. I then compared this work with the Syriac text which I corrected, and this is the method I followed in everything I translated.[25]

Ḥunayn is also credited with translating religious texts and nonmedical scientific works. In his medical treatises, he summarized and explained ancient medicine using the scholastic form of questions and

[22]Ibid., pp. 74–75; *EI*², s.v. "Ḥunayn b. Isḥāḳ al-ʿIbādī" (G. Strohmaier); G. Strohmaier, "Homer in Bagdad," *Byzantinoslavica* 41 (1980):196–200; *MI*, pp. 115–119 et passim.

[23]*EI*², s.v. "Ibn Māsawayh" (J.-C. Vadet); Yūḥannā ibn Māsawayh, *Le Livre des axiomes médicaux (Aphorismi)*, ed. and trans. D. Jacquart and G. Troupeau (Geneva, 1980).

[24]Aside from Ḥunayn's revision of others' translations and his own summaries, he reportedly translated fifty-eight books into Syriac alone; twelve directly into Arabic, and twenty-seven into Syriac and Arabic. On this matter, see Ḥunayn, *Questions on Medicine*, p. xx.

[25]Ḥunayn, pp. xvi–xvii.

answers, following the model of Galen's *Ars parva*.[26] His main work, *Questions on Medicine for Scholars* (*al-Masā'il fī ṭ-ṭibb lil-muta'allimīn*),[27] was an introduction to Galenic teaching set forth in this didactic style and was widely read by medical students.

In the span of about two hundred years—from the time of Ḥunayn until the early eleventh century A.D.—much of the Greek philosophic and scientific literature was rendered into Arabic. The translations were introduced primarily because of the need for practically useful sciences.[28] The medical literature, along with the astrological and alchemical, formed an early and significant part of the translations.[29] Although this massive translation of Greek works had been preceded by earlier translations from before the Arab conquests, mainly into Syriac, the later activity was remarkable for its scope, quality, and wide dissemination. Indeed, this cultural transference seems to represent, as S. Pines has asserted, "the earliest large-scale attempt known in history to take over from an alien civilization its sciences and techniques regarded as universally valid."[30]

Thanks to the translation of classical works as well as to numerous summaries and commentaries, the doctors of the Islamic era had available every work by Hippocrates and Galen that was still being read in the Greek centers of learning during the seventh to ninth centuries A.D.[31] Subsequently, many of these Arabic translations, augmented by the significant additions of Arabic authors, were translated into Latin from the late eleventh century A.D. and had a profound effect on the intellectual life of Europe in the High Middle Ages.[32] The Latin

[26]Strohmaier (*EI*², 3:580) points out that this kind of literature was very common in the biblical exegesis of the Nestorian church at this time.

[27]See the edition of Paul Ghalioungai, Cairo, 1980.

[28]Pines, "Philosophy," p. 784. The Muslims were indifferent, generally, to the nonscientific literature of antiquity, so that a wide range of Graeco-Roman belles lettres were not translated into Arabic.

[29]See the account of this cultural transference in Ullmann, *Islamic Medicine*, pp. 7–40, and more fully in his *MI*, pp. 25–107; concerning Ibn Riḍwān specifically, see Joseph Schacht, "Über den Hellenismus in Baghdad und Cairo im 11. Jahrhundert," *Zeitschrift der Deutschen Morgenländischen Gesellschaft* 90 (1936):526–545, and Schacht and Meyerhof, pp. 7–12. For a succinct account of medieval views about the origin of Greek medicine and its transmission to Arabic culture, see Meyerhof, "Sultan Saladin's Physician," pp. 169–178.

[30]Pines, "Philosophy," p. 782.

[31]*EI*², s.v. "Djālīnus" (R. Walzer).

[32]One might, perhaps, interpret the evolution of modern Islamic society in terms of the transmission, or forceful interjection, of this scientific tradition once again back into Islamic culture, beginning in the nineteenth century.

translations of Arabic medical works transplanted Galenism to the West, where it became deeply rooted until modern times.

Of all the ancient medical authors, Galen ruled over medieval medicine. Both his comprehensiveness and his philosophic interests made his work congenial to medieval philosopher-physicians. Late Hellenistic doctors promoted the works of Galen, seeing in him the highest development of the Hippocratic art and of medical science.[33] Like the contemporary development of Christianity in the religious life of late antiquity, Galenism greatly narrowed ancient tradition: where there had once been lively debate, now there was a single strong voice.[34] Not surprisingly, the works of Galen were conspicuous among Greek medical texts translated during the Islamic era.

Paradoxically, the tradition of Hippocrates only followed in the shadow of Galen.[35] Although medieval physicians greatly esteemed Hippocrates, his works did not attract the interest of translators and their patrons as Galen's did. The Arabic versions of Hippocrates' works were derived almost entirely from the translated works of Galen and other late Hellenistic writers.[36] These secondary works digested the difficult Hippocratic writings in simpler and briefer form and refashioned them in the Galenic spirit. As Ibn Riḍwān said in another treatise, "Galen refined the teaching of Hippocrates and made the art [Ar. *ṣināʿah*] of medicine easy and comprehensible for people of outstanding talent who desire it."[37]

On the one hand, medieval medical literature did not include the entire corpus of Hippocratic and Galenic writings; on the other hand, a number of later pseudonymous works were added to it. The Arabic medical literature, then, encompassed a few major works of both men as well as books falsely attributed to ancient authors and numerous epitomes and commentaries—the last a scholarly enterprise that had developed long before the Arabs adopted ancient medicine. The frequent obscurity of Hippocrates and the prolixity of Galen justified such

[33]Max Neuburger, *History of Medicine*, trans. Ernest Playfair, (Oxford, 1910–1925), 1:302.

[34]See Wesley D. Smith, *The Hippocratic Tradition* (Ithaca, 1979), pp. 61–246; Temkin, *Galenism*; idem, "History of Hippocratism in Late Antiquity: The Third Century and the Latin West," in his *The Double Face of Janus*, pp. 167–177; Heinrich Schipperges, "Die arabische Medizin als Praxis und als Theorie," *Sudhoffs Archiv* 43 (1959):318.

[35]Ullmann, *Islamic Medicine*, p. 11f.

[36]*Vorlesungen*, p. 72.

[37]Albert Dietrich, ed. and trans., *ʿAlī ibn Riḍwān: "Über den Weg zur Glückseligkeit durch den ärztlichen Beruf"* (Göttingen, 1982), p. 12/13.

commentaries. In fact, these learned but not highly original translations stimulated Islamic authors to classify Greek medical knowledge in large encyclopedic works, best exemplified by the enormously influential *Canon of Medicine* (*al-Qānūn fī ṭ-ṭibb*) by Ibn Sīnā, a contemporary of Ibn Riḍwān.[38] Although Ibn Riḍwān did not write this type of encyclopedic work, he stands at the end of a long tradition of Galenic scholarship that had formalized and idealized Galen's work, as Galen himself had done to the works of Hippocrates.[39]

The essence of the Galenic system, humoral pathology,[40] had originated with the Hippocratic school.[41] It had been modified by other medical schools and especially by Aristotle, whose influence on medical theory, such as psychology, was decisive.[42] Galen molded this notion of humors into a comprehensive theory.[43] He conceived of *all* things as composed of the four elements of fire, earth, air, and water, embodying the four qualities of hot, cold, dry, and wet. Food and drink, like everything else, consisted of these basic elements and their qualities; the physician was responsible for knowing their attributes, as well as those of simple and compound drugs.[44] In the process of digestion in the stomach, food and drink were transformed (literally "cooked") by natural heat into different substances (Ar. *banāt al-arkān*, "the daughters of the elements"). Four humors (Ar. *al-akhlāt*) resulted: blood, phlegm, yellow bile, and black bile. Air corresponded to blood, which is hot and wet; water to phlegm, which is cold and wet; fire to yellow bile, which is hot and dry; and earth to black bile, which is cold and dry.[45] After another "cooking" in the liver, a portion of these substances was transported by the blood to the various organs of the body to nourish them,

[38]Arabic ed.: 3 vols. (Cairo, 1877); see *MI*, pp. 152–154. For Ibn Sīnā, see *EI*², s.v. "Ibn Sīnā" (A.-M. Goichen); *MI*, pp. 153–156 et passim. It should be noted that Ibn Riḍwān never appears to refer to Ibn Sīnā in his medical works.

[39]See *Vorlesungen*, pp. 77–80 for an analysis of the structure of the Galenic system according to the *Qābūs-Nāmah* (A.D. 1082–83) of Kai-Kā'ūs.

[40]For a historical survey of the humoral theory, see Raymond Klibansky, Erwin Panofsky, and Fritz Saxl, *Saturn and Melancholy* (New York, 1964), pp. 3–15.

[41]See especially, *Hippocrates, On the Nature of Man*, 4:1–41.

[42]See *Vorlesungen*, pp. 80–83.

[43]See Rudolph E. Siegel, *Galen's System of Physiology and Medicine* (Basel, 1968), pp. 211–215, which discusses morphological pathology and its relation to the humoral theory. Galen was not entirely consistent and did not regard each humor as uniform, nor did he limit the humors to four; see ibid., p. 216.

[44]See Galen, *On the Temperament and Force of Simple Drugs*, ed. Kühn, 11:379 to 12:377.

[45]Siegel, *Galen's System*, pp. 216–241 on the properties of the humors; Ullmann, *Islamic Medicine*, pp. 57–60 on the four humors according to al-Majūsī.

while the rest was excreted. Galen believed that the bodily parts and their actions resulted from varying combinations of these four elements, qualities, and humors. The precise proportions in which the qualities were combined were very important; the proper *krasis* (Ar. *mizāj*),[46] temperament or blending, produced health.[47]

The equilibrium of the four qualities, therefore, created well-being.[48] In Greek medicine this balance was termed *eukrasia*, literally "the state of being well mixed," or *symmetria*; both terms had strong philosophical and ethical connotations.[49] In Arabic medicine this notion was usually translated as *i'tidāl (al-mizāj)* and retained the classical connotations. If there was too much or too little of a humor, the balance was upset, and *eukrasia* was displaced by *dyskrasia* (Ar. *sū' al-mizāj* or *khārij 'an al-i'tidāl*). The result was illness, the particularity of which depended on the affected humor.[50] Sickness was also caused by changes in the normal qualitative makeup of the humors, the tissues and organs, or the spirits.[51] Ibn Riḍwān stresses this influential theme, which can be traced back to ancient Egypt.

[46]Lane, s.v. "mizāj." "The word *mizāj*, or mixture, is to this day the word used in Persian and Turkish, as well as sometimes in Arabic, to denote 'health.' 'How is your noble *mizāj*?' you ask of your friends." (Reuben Levy, "Avicenna—His Life and Times," *Medical History* 1 [1957]:255).

[47]"The association of well-being with proper temperament had complex roots in the pre-Socratic physical doctrine of opposites or contrariety. . . . Medical application of the doctrine of opposites had a complex history in post-Aristotelian thought culminating in the use of the idea by Galen, who devoted one whole treatise of considerable length (*Peri Kraseōn*) to blending, or temperament [see the discussion of this work below], and invoked the subject repeatedly in other treatises as well. Blends—generally of opposed dynamic qualities (hot and cold, dry and moist) rather than elements or humors—differ (a) in different species, (b) in different individuals within each species, (c) in different tissues within each individual, and (d) in the same tissue when sick and when well. It is also the temperament of each tissue that determines its function." (R. J. Pennella and T. S. Hall, "Galen's 'On the Best Constitution of our Body.' Introduction, Translation, and Notes," *BHM* 47 [1973]:284). See also *MI*, p. 39.

[48]Pennella and Hall (ibid., p. 285) state that, according to Galen, the best constitution must comprise both a proper temperament and proper arrangement (*diaplasis*); pathologies can be either temperamental, diaplastic, or both.

[49]"The health of the body is at its very best when the powers and qualities are evenly balanced [*i'tadalat*] and especially when they are intermixed." (Hippocrates, *Kitāb Buqrāṭ fī ṭabī'at al-insān: On the Nature of Man*, ed. and trans. J. N. Mattock and M. C. Lyons [Cambridge, 1968], p. 6/7). For the central idea of *i'tidāl*, see J. C. Bürgel, "*Adab* und *i'tidāl* in ar-Ruhāwīs *Adab aṭ-Ṭabīb*: Studie zur Bedeutungsgeschichte zweier Begriffe," *Zeitschrift der Deutschen Morgenländischen Gesellschaft* 117 (1967):97–102; Bürgel also points out the importance of the related idea of *mesotēs*, the mean between two extremes, in Islamic ethics: "khayr al-umūr awsāṭuhā" (ibid., p. 100f.: Ignaz Goldziher, *Muslim Studies*, ed. S. M. Stern, [London, 1971], 2:360ff.). See also Martin Levey, "Medical Ethics of Medieval Islam with Special Reference to al-Ruhāwī's 'Practical Ethics of the Physicians'," *Transactions of the American Philosophical Society*, n.s., vol. 57/3 (1967):64–65; ar-Rāzī, *Guide du médecin nomade*, trans. El-Arbi Moubachir (Paris, 1980), p. 22 et passim.

[50]Cf. Ibn Bakhtīshū', p. 78v.

[51]Ibid., p. 85v.

The ancient Egyptians assumed that most internal, suppurative, and infectious illnesses were cases of the universally observable corruptibility of organic matter. This seminal idea was widely accepted by Greek doctors and was integrated into the humoral doctrine:

> The Egyptian opinion of the superfluities and their putrefaction was absorbed by the Greeks and modified to form an integral part of almost all their later theories. Even Galen in his elaboration of the humoral doctrine was unable to avoid fusing the more ancient views on putrefaction as the cause of disease with humoral theory.[52]

The etiological agent in Greek medicine was thus considered to be either a quantitative or a qualitative change of a humor; in the latter case, putrefaction rendered the humor pathogenic. Galen distinguishes, therefore, between a superabundance of humors, constituting a plenitude, and a qualitative change in the humors.[53] Ibn Riḍwān follows traditional Galenic views about the need for purging the bodily superfluities that, by putrefying, cause illness. These bodily surpluses could be eliminated by a wide variety of activities aside from normal excretion, such as gymnastics, bathing, coition, purges, and external medications.[54]

Not every deviation from the balance of the humors was considered an illness. Where the Hippocratic school proposed the existence of an ideal equilibrium, Galen argued that there was a wide latitude of health, ranging from the ideal to the chronically sick. Exterior factors, such as climate, occupation, and the season of the year, made one of the four humors dominate in every human body. This gave a man his individual habits and complexion, his disposition, which might be sanguine, phlegmatic, choleric, or melancholic. Thus, the humoral doctrine was applied not only to the causes and course of illness but also to the analysis of the constitutional variations of healthy people.[55]

[52]J. B. de C. M. Saunders, *The Transitions from Ancient Egyptian to Greek Medicine* (Lawrence, Kansas, 1963), p. 32.

[53]Ibid., p. 126.

[54]See, for example, ar-Rāzī, *Guide*, pp. 68–72, 84–89, 92.

[55]See Pseudo-Aristotle, *Problems* 14, ed. and trans. W. S. Hett (Cambridge/London, 1961); for the Arabic version of this work, see F. E. Peters, *Aristotles Arabus: The Oriental Translations and Commentaries on the Aristotelian "Corpus"* (Leiden, 1968), pp. 66–67. Klibansky et al. in their historical account of melancholy (*Saturn and Melancholy*, pp. 99–102) allege that the types of disposition based on the doctrine of the four temperaments were not adopted by Arabic medicine because of their close adherence to Galenism. The preponderance of a primary humor was, consequently, simply a pathological condition. This appears to be mistaken, but the subject has

Galen's interpretation of the temperaments, put forth in his *On Temperaments*,[56] was well known to medieval Arabic doctors[57] and was a basic source for Ibn Riḍwān. In this work Galen states that the qualities coalesce in all living things; they are not composed of one quality exclusively but of the blending of qualities in varying proportions. Bodies are only relatively hot, cold, wet, or dry. Therefore, the mixture of qualities or temperament of living things varies considerably and each is distinguished by the predominant quality or qualities. Yet, he asserts that there is a symmetrical or median temperament proper to the nature of men, animals, and plants, although man is the most well tempered of all things, animate and inanimate.[58] In short, Galen says that there are nine different temperaments,[59] one, the ideal, in which all qualities are well balanced; four in which one of the qualities—hot, cold, dry, or moist—predominates; and four others in which the predominating qualities appear in couples of hot and moist, hot and dry, cold and dry, or cold and moist.[60]

Galen systematically worked out the medical implications of this theory in his *Ars parva*. The treatise outlines medicine under the categories of health and illness. All the principal organs have their own temperament, as has the body as a whole. The diagnostic signs of the various temperaments fill about one-third of the work. Medieval physicians studied the work assiduously, and Ibn Riḍwān is one of many who wrote a commentary on it.[61]

There are causes that maintain good health, those that prevent

---

not been sufficiently studied. The question has been raised anew by Hellmut Flashar in his *Melancholie und Melancholiker in den medizinischen Theorien der Antike* (Berlin, 1966). See also José Luis Pinillos et al., *Constitución y Personalidad. Historia y teoria de un problema* (Madrid, 1966).

[56]Kühn, 1:509–694; *De temperamentis libri III*, ed. Georgius Helmreich (Leipzig, 1904). See *MI*, p. 39; S. Sambursky, *The Physical World of Late Antiquity* (New York, 1962), pp. 38–42. See also Pennella and Hall, "Galen's 'On the Best Constitution,' " pp. 290–296: "The best constitution of the body, then, will be that in which all the homogeneous parts—that, of course, is the name given to the parts that are uniform to our perception—have their own proper temperament, and in which the composition of each of the organic parts out of the homogeneous parts has been achieved with perfect proportion in respect to their size, number, configuration, and arrangement in relation to one another" (p. 292).

[57]See, for example, ar-Rāzī, *Guide*, pp. 53–57.

[58]*De temperamentis libri III*, ed. Helmreich, pp. 41–42.

[59]Ibid., pp. 23, 32, 40.

[60]See Temkin, *Galenism*, p. 19; Ḥunayn, p. 2; ar-Rāzī, *Guide*, p. 54, where the editor mistakenly considers this division of temperaments to have originated with ar-Rāzī (n. 22). Cf. Ullmann, *Islamic Medicine*, p. 57 for this scheme of temperaments according to al-Majūsī; Levey "Medical Ethics of Medieval Islam," p. 49 for this scheme according to ar-Ruhāwī.

[61]Schacht and Meyerhof, p. 41; *MI*, p. 45.

illness, and those that restore the sick body to well-being. The influence of some causes is inescapable. These include the surrounding air, the motion and rest of the body, sleep and wakefulness, food, excretion or retention of superfluities, and the passions of the soul.[62] Eventually, they became known among medieval Galenists as the six "non-naturals," as opposed to the seven "naturals."[63]

The doctrine of the six "non-naturals," along with the temperaments, was one of Galenism's most enduring contributions to medical thought.[64] L. J. Rather defined them as "six categories of factors that operatively determine health or disease, depending on the circumstances of their use or abuse, to which human beings are unavoidably exposed in the course of daily life."[65] According to Galen's *Ars parva*, the six factors are constantly acting on the human body in such a way as to alter the balance of the primary qualities and, thus, affecting the character of the humors and the state of the humoral balance. Therefore, directing an individual's regimen, according to the six factors, was the physician's principal task.[66] Moreover, men's habits with regard to

[62]See Ibn Bakhtīshū', where the pyschic causation of illness is discussed in detail; on the "non-naturals" generally, see pp. 75r–75v.

[63]Temkin, *Galenism*, pp. 101–104; *Vorlesungen*, p. 80. The notion of "naturals" was fundamental to Galenic medical theory; according to Ḥunayn (p. 1), "pathology is deduced by the deviation of the naturals from their normal states." The "naturals" were the elements, temperaments, humors, organs, forces, actions, and spirits or *pneumata* (see discussion below).

[64]Temkin, *Galenism*, p. 180.

[65]L. J. Rather, "The 'Six Things Non-Natural'; A Note on the Origins and Fate of a Doctrine and a Phrase," *Clio Medica* 3 (1968):33.

[66]As a corrective to Rather's discussion, Peter H. Niebyl ("The Non-Naturals," *BHM* 45 [1971]:486–492) has shown that the term *non-naturals* goes back to Galen but that it did not originate with him. The term was used, especially, in Galen's works on the pulse and in chapters dealing with exercise, baths, foods, and drink. "Non-naturals" are identified with causes by virtue of quantity (overeating, overdrinking, etc.). Because the *Book on the Pulse for Beginners* was one of the four Galenic treatises named for beginning students in Alexandria, Galen's threefold classification into natural, non-natural, and praeternatural must have had considerable exposure. This theoretical classification can be found in Paul of Aegina and in Arabic medical writings, especially in Ḥunayn's *Questions in Medicine* (pp. 74–81), al-Majūsī's *Kitāb al-Malakī*, and Ibn Sīnā's *al-Urjūzah* and *al-Qānūn*. Al-Majūsī directly connected the six factors with "things non-natural" several times, and because of his work's early translation into Latin by Constantinus Africanus (before Gerard of Cremona's translation of Ibn Sīnā), it is reasonable to assume that al-Majūsī's terminology of "six non-naturals" was the source of the long-lived Western terminology. Ibn Riḍwān simply refers to the "six causes" (*al-asbāb as-sittah*). Cf. Levey, "Medical Ethics of Medieval Islam," pp. 29–44. See also Ullmann, *Islamic Medicine*, pp. 97–103; Temkin, *Galenism*, pp. 102, 155, 180; S. K. Hamarneh, "Medical Education and Practice in Medieval Islam," in *The History of Medical Education*, ed. C. D. O'Malley (Berkeley, 1970), pp. 46–47; idem, "Some Aspects of Medical Practice and Institutions in Medieval Islam," *Episteme* 7 (1973):15–17; Saul Jarcho, "Galen's Six Non-Naturals: A Bibliographic Note and Translation," *BHM* 44 (1970): 372–377; F. Kudlien, "The Old Greek Concept of Relative Health," *Journal of the History of Behavioral Sciences* 9 (1973):52–59.

the "non-naturals" were important in both the preservation of health and the treatment of illness; the ancient and medieval doctor was expected to investigate thoroughly his patients' customary behavior.[67]

Altogether, the doctrine of elements, humors, qualities, and temperaments served as a basis for a corresponding system of therapy. Therapeutics were based on the allopathic principle of *contraria contrariis* or "contraries"—that is, "hot" diseases could be cured by "cold" remedies, "wet and cold" by "dry and hot," and so forth. Every part of nature possessed such qualities in one degree or another; even the four seasons had specific qualities, as did the successive stages in men's lives. Above all, foods, drinks, and drugs possessed these qualities, and the doctor had to know just how they affected people's health. If a patient's prescribed regimen was ineffective, drugs were administered as correctives to the humoral imbalance. They should be equal in strength but opposite in quality to the imbalanced complexion. To help with this therapy, Galen categorized drugs according to four degrees of potency.[68]

Regarding drugs, Galen considered the *Materia Medica* of Dioscorides[69] a definitive source, and its Arabic translation served as the foundation of Islamic pharmacology. Like the Greeks, Islamic pharmacologists distinguished between simple drugs (Ar. *adwiyah mufradah*) and compound drugs (Ar. *adwiyah murakkabah*).[70] Medieval pharmacology added considerably to classical materia medica; hundreds of names of simple and compound drugs, not known to the Greeks, were added

[67]See F. Klein-Franke, "The Arabic Version of Galen's *περὶ ἐθῶν*," *Jerusalem Studies in Arabic and Islam* 1 (1979):125–150; J. N. Mattock, "A Translation of the Arabic Epitome of Galen's Book *περι ηθων*," in *Islamic Philosophy and the Classical Tradition*, ed. S. M. Stern, A. Hourani, and V. Brown (Oxford, 1972), pp. 235–260. It will be seen that Ibn Riḍwān places considerable emphasis on the influence of habit in the determination of men's health.

[68]See Georg Harig, *Die Bestimmung der Intensität im medizinischen System Galens* (Berlin, 1974); Léon Gauthier, *Antécédents Gréco-Arabes de la Psychophysique* (Beirut, 1938), actually the edition and translation of al-Kindī's work on posology: "Fī Ma'rifat quwā l-adwiyah al-murakkabah"; Siegel, *Galen's System*, p. 236.

[69]*MI*, pp. 257–263 et passim; *EI²*, s.v. "Diyusḳuridīs" (C. E. Dubler); see especially Dubler's "Die 'Materia Medica' unter den Muslimen des Mittelalters," *Sudhoffs Archiv* 43 (1959):329–350. Incidentally, the illustrations to the Arabic translations of Dioscorides' *De materia medica* afford us a vivid representation of the medieval physician in Islamic society; see Hugo Büchthal, "Early Islamic Miniatures from Baghdad," *Journal of the Walters Art Gallery* 5 (1942):18–39, and Esin Atıl, *Art of the Arab World* (Washington, D.C., 1975), pp. 53–60. It may be pointed out that a frequent symbol of the doctor's authority in these miniatures is the book and cross-legged bookstand—a symbol that is often associated with portraits of ancient philosophers and is indicative of a "book intensive" profession.

[70]No branch of Islamic medicine has been so thoroughly investigated as pharmacology; see *EI²*, s.v. "Adwiya" and "Aḳrābādhīn" (B. Lewin) for the relevant literature.

from Persian and Indian sources. The rapid increase in materia medica called for a special group of men and the separation of pharmacology from the medical profession generally.[71] Drugs were bought from the druggist and then compounded by the druggist or physician. The major hospitals had pharmacists on their staffs and fully stocked pharmacies, and pharmacological instruction in the hospitals was very early an important part of medical training.

The keystone of the Galenic system was the maintenance or restoration of *eukrasia*. Man could protect his health by moderation, by conserving symmetry in the different spheres of his life. The doctor's duty was to teach his patients the proper regimen for their bodies according to their individual circumstances.[72] Galen cited Egypt, specifically, as a country with an intemperate climate and, therefore, conducive to a poor bodily constitution.[73] Yet, the constitution could be preserved in good health by a suitable regimen that emphasized diet.[74] Galen said that "one should apply to the healthy the term 'in accordance with nature,' and to the sick the term 'contrary to nature,'[75] since health is a condition that produces functioning in accordance with nature, and disease a condition that produces functioning contrary to nature."[76] This notion is the basis of Ibn Riḍwān's belief in the relativity or sympathy of one's constitution with the environment and the need to attune one's body to it in order to preserve health.

Ibn Riḍwān was keenly aware of the relationship between the physical environment, bodily disposition, and well-being. In all dietary treatises of antiquity, beginning with Hippocrates, great attention had

[71]See *EI²*, s.v. "al-ʿAṭṭār" (A. Dietrich).

[72]See *A Translation of Galen's Hygiene (De Sanitate Tuenda)*, trans. R. M. Green (Springfield, Ill., 1951). For the classical background, see Ludwig Edelstein, "The Dietetics of Antiquity," in *Ancient Medicine*, ed. O. Temkin and C. L. Temkin (Baltimore, 1967), pp. 303–316. On the regimen for health as well as curing illness in Islamic medicine, see the remarks of S. K. Hamarneh, "Ecology and Therapeutics in Medieval Arabic Medicine," *Sudhoffs Archiv* 58 (1974): 165–185.

[73]*A Translation of Galen's Hygiene*, p. 15.

[74]See *Vorlesungen*, pp. 117–118. Maimonides, p. 17, n. 13: "The belief, dating back to Hippocrates, that different foods require different 'digestions' and produce different 'superfluities', accounts for the great emphasis which the ancient physicians placed on proper and selective diet."

[75]Cf. Galen, *On the Doctrines of Hippocrates and Plato*, ed. and trans. Philip de Lacy (Berlin, 1980), 2:362/363. See the expression "khārij ʿan al-amr aṭ-ṭabīʿī" in Ibn Bakhtīshūʿ, p. 51, l. 3 et passim.

[76]*A Translation of Galen's Hygiene*, p. 16. Elsewhere, Galen follows Plato's definition of disease as "the destruction of what is by nature congenial as a result of some dissension." (Galen, *On the Doctrine of Hippocrates and Plato*, [Berlin, 1978], 1:302/303). Galen wrote extensively on the causes of diseases; see the survey of this topic by Pennella and Hall, "Galen's 'On the Best Constitution,' " pp. 287–288.

been paid to physical circumstances and their impingement on one's health. Hippocrates discussed this issue extensively in his treatise, *Airs, Waters and Places*. He concluded that "the bodily constitution and the customs of man depend on the nature of the land."[77] In this important work, Hippocrates asserted that particular physiological and pathological states tend to be associated with particular climatic regions.[78] Unfortunately, the section of *Airs, Waters and Places* that applied this idea to Egypt was lost in antiquity. Ibn Riḍwān was well acquainted with this book, however,[79] and with Galen's commentary on it.[80] In a sense, Ibn Riḍwān "restored" the missing section on Egypt by applying Hippocratic theory in his topographical description of Egypt.

The importance of ecological conditions to health was recognized well beyond the medical profession in medieval Muslim society.[81] In the geographical literature, Yāqūt (d. A.D. 1229) expressed the common belief that geography was written because "men of wisdom and understanding," no less than physicians, needed to be familiar with the airs of various regions and with the salubrity or insalubrity of the land. "Their need to master such knowledge has become absolutely vital, and to reveal its truth, an intellectual imperative."[82] Throughout his work, he frequently noted the climatic conditions of towns and areas and how they affected the inhabitants. The famous writer al-Jāḥiẓ (d. A.D. 868) also stressed the effects of the environment on men's lives; climate played a decisive role not only in determining the physical characteristics of the people of a region but also in shaping their moral standards, breeding, character, and disposition toward good and evil.[83] Al-Jāḥiẓ gives numerous examples of how natural conditions influence all living things.[84]

77Siegel, *Galen's System*, p. 239.

78See also Pseudo-Aristotle, *Problems* 14.

79*Kitāb Buqrāṭ fī'l-amrāḍ al-bilādiyya: On Endemic Diseases (Airs, Waters and Places)*, ed. and trans. J. N. Mattock and M. C. Lyons (Cambridge, 1969).

80See Manfred Ullmann, "Galens Kommentar zu der Schrift *De aere equis locis*," in *Corpus Hippocraticum*, Éditions Universitaires de Mons, Série sciences humaines (Mons, 1977), 4:353–365.

81See André Miquel, *La Géographie humaine du monde musulman jusqu'au milieu du 11e siècle* (Paris, 1973), 1:15 et passim. It is premature to determine the extent to which such topographical descriptions played a significant role in Arabic medical literature.

82Yāqūt, *Mu'jam al-buldān*, ed. F. Wüstenfeld (Leipzig, 1866–1873), 1:4.

83al-Jāḥiẓ, *Kitāb al-Ḥayawān*, ed. Hārūn, 2d ed. (Cairo, 1969), 5:35–36.

84See L. I. Conrad, "*Ṭā'ūn* and *Wabā'*. Conceptions of Plague and Pestilence in Early Islam," *Journal of the Economic and Social History of the Orient*, 25 (1982):268–307; Miquel, *La Géographie humaine*, pp. 37–59.

Life was, then, a constant interplay between the body and the environment. The deterministic aspect of the environment's influence on the body was especially emphasized, for example, in Galen's *That the Mental Faculties Follow the Bodily Constitution.*[85] The reciprocal aspect was also expressed in the ancient works: the body could be fortified against environmental conditions under normal circumstances.

Within this framework, the ancient Greek doctors sought to explain the disruption of the balance between man and his surroundings by the abnormal, that is, by epidemic disease.[86] Generally, three naturalistic theories accounted for the origin of epidemics: miasma, contagion/infection, and astral influence. Although these causes are not easily separable, miasma was, in one form or another, the dominant view from the time of Hippocrates until the nineteenth century.[87] A miasma was a corruption or pollution of the air by noxious vapors. Hippocrates outlined the miasmatic theory on the basis of observations of the effects of climate, season, and locality on the incidence of epidemics.[88]

Galen developed the idea of the miasmatic corruption of the air and added the notion of an energizing spirit or *pneuma* (see below), which is absorbed by the body from the atmosphere; these ideas were put forth in his commentary on the *Epidemics* of Hippocrates and in *De febrium*

[85] *Oeuvres antomiques, physilogiques et médicales de Galien*, trans. Charles Daremberg (Paris, 1854), vol. 1, no. 3; *Galens Traktat "Dass die Kräfte der Seele den Mischungen des Körpers folgen" in arabischer Übersetzung*, ed. and trans. Hans H. Biesterfeldt, in *Abhandlungen für die Kunde des Morgenländes* 40, no. 4 (Wiesbaden, 1973). A. J. Brock, *Greek Medicine* (London, 1929), p. 4; Brock's interpretation of Hippocrates and Galen places considerable emphasis on the environmental factor (pp. 1–34).

[86] See L. Fabian Hirst, *The Conquest of Plague: A Study of the Evolution of Epidemiology* (Oxford, 1953), pp. 22–72; Ullmann, *Islamic Medicine*, pp. 86–96; Dols, *The Black Death in the Middle East* (Princeton, 1977), pp. 85–98 et passim; the important article by Owsei Temkin, "An Historical Analysis of the Concept of Infection," in his *The Double Face of Janus*, pp. 456–471; Mirko D. Grmek, "Le Concept d'infection dans l'antiquité et au moyen age, les anciennes mesures sociales contre les maladies contagieuses et la fondation de la première quarantaine à Dubrovnik (1377)," *Rad Jugoslavenska Akademije Znanosti i Umjetnosti* 384 (1980):9–54.

[87] There was a revived interest in miasma during the nineteenth century that greatly influenced medical treatment and historical writings on epidemics. See, for example, E. H. Ackerknecht, "Anti-contagionism between 1821 and 1867," *BHM* 22 (1948):562–593 for the former, and Charles Creighton, *A History of Epidemics in Britain*, 2 vols. (Cambridge, 1891–1894) for the latter. Regarding the reissue of Creighton's *History* (London, 1965), see R. S. Roberts, "Epidemics and Social History," *Medical History* 12 (1968):305–316.

[88] *Hippocrates, Airs, Waters and Places* and *Epidemics I and III*. The miasmatic theory may be traced back to ancient Egyptian medicine. Saunders (*The Transitions*, p. 33) has asserted: "The essential principle behind putrefaction as conceived by the Ancient Egyptians had definite relations to the conceptions of the nature of odor and thus to views on the particulate nature of matter on the one hand, and the nature of contagion on the other. . . . In Ancient Egypt it is the exhalation of corpses undergoing decomposition which produces pestilence and the thought, although transcendentally conceived, passed onto rational medicine in the theory of miasmas, a theory which was to exist almost to our own day."

differentiis. In this view, epidemic disease resulted from the assimilation of vital air fouled by putrid exhalations of decaying matter, such as unburied corpses or swamps and stagnant waters in summertime.[89] Decay or putrescence of organic bodies—*sepsis*, to cite the Greek word that we still use—was the source of pollution, and its evil smell was an indication of and a guide to its prevalence. The noxious miasma might be carried by the wind from distant areas where putrefaction was in progress. A warm, moist air charged with corruption might brood over a stricken land and affect all living things; among susceptible human beings it caused an epidemic.

Several other factors, aside from poisonous air, entered into Galen's theory of epidemics. Because some people escaped the ill effects of an epidemic, Galen emphasized the aptitude of the body. He believed that the internal state of the human body was even more important than the condition of the air. Galen taught that two factors goverened the body and its vulnerability to disease: temperament and the effects of acquired habits. In addition, he recognized, but did not stress, the role of infection/contagion,[90] and he acknowledged that meteorological conditions affected human health.

Ibn Riḍwān was a strict miasmatist. To explain the interhuman transmission (Ar. *iʿdāʾ*) of disease,[91] he accepts, like many medieval doctors, the creation of a "localist miasma" by diseased individuals. He maintains that the major weakness of the miasmatic theory—the spacial irregularity of the incidence of an epidemic—may be explained by individual predisposition or susceptibility, following Galen's lead. In view of his own background in astrology and the place assigned to it in Hippocratic and Galenic writings, and in contemporary beliefs,[92] it is

[89]Fear of miasma helps to explain the prompt burial that is customary in Muslim society. Moreover, Muslim armies were quick to bury their dead in order to prevent disease; for example, see A. F. Woodings, "The Medical Resources and Practice of the Crusader States in Syria and Palestine 1096–1193," *Medical History* 25 (1971):271f.

[90]As Temkin has pointed out ("An Historical Analysis of the Concept of Infection," p. 460), the concept of contagion among men and animals was known to the ancients but was not studied systematically. See also Vivian Nutton, "The Seeds of Disease: An Explanation of Contagion and Infection from the Greeks to the Renaissance," *Medical History* 27 (1983):1–34. The first systematic enumeration of contagious diseases was made apparently by Thābit ibn Qurra (d. 288/901) in his *Kitāb adh-Dhakhīrah*; see *MI*, p. 136f., and Max Meyerhof, "The 'Book of Treasure,' an early Arabic Treatise on Medicine," *Isis* 14 (1930):61.

[91]On the problem of the transmissibility of illnesses in Islamic medicine, see Ullmann, *Islamic Medicine*, pp. 86–96.

[92]*Vorlesungen*, pp. 53–64. See Ullmann's discussion of al-Majūsī's interpretation of epidemic disease (*Islamic Medicine*, pp. 89–91) and Ibn Buṭlān's account of epidemics in Ibn Abī Uṣaybiʿah, *ʿUyūn al-anbāʾ fī ṭabaqāt al-aṭibbāʾ*, ed. A. Müller (Cairo-Königsberg, 1882–1884), 1:242.

surprising that Ibn Riḍwān omits astrological causes for disease. He appears to go beyond the classical writers in emphasizing that epidemic diseases are caused solely by unnatural changes in air, water, foods, and the human psyche. Although his work is devoted primarily to prophylaxis, Ibn Riḍwān never recommends fleeing from an infected area for protection. This omission does not seem to be prompted by the impracticability of flight for the majority of people, by ethical or religious strictures,[93] or by an ill-defined fatalism. Rather, the omission points to his strong belief in miasma and its all-encompassing nature.[94]

Two other fundamental concepts in Galen's physiology should be mentioned: innate heat and *pneuma.*[95] Galen, following Hippocrates, Aristotle, and other ancients, regarded innate heat as the immortal substance of life. It was to be found primarily in the heart, where it was purest and most intense and where it was nourished by the *pneuma.* Galen repeatedly emphasized its close relationship to the soul.

The *pneuma* or spirit, a complex concept with a long history in ancient and Islamic medical and philosophical thought,[96] was understood as a requisite of life and was of three kinds: (1) the natural or physical *pneuma* (Ar. *ar-rūḥ aṭ-ṭabī'ī*); (2) the animal or vital *pneuma* (Ar. *ar-rūḥ al-ḥayawānī*); and (3) the psychic *pneuma* (Ar. *ar-rūḥ an-nafsānī*).[97] The natural spirit originated in the purest blood in the liver; it was carried by the veins to the bodily organs and nourished them. The animal spirit, which Ibn Riḍwān mentions, was created in the heart from a mixture of the pure vapor of the blood and the inhaled air and reached the organs through the arteries. The airlike substance regulated the innate heat and nourished the psychic *pneuma*. The psychic *pneuma* was located in the ventricles of the brain and reached the organs through the nerves. This psychic spirit was believed to be the specific carrier of nervous and mental activity, the source of movement and reason.[98]

[93]See Dols, *The Black Death*, pp. 22–25 et passim.

[94]Ibid.; cf. D. W. Amundsen, "Medical Deontology and Pestilential Disease in the Late Middle Ages," *Journal of the History of Medicine and Allied Sciences* 32 (1977):403–421.

[95]See M. T. May's Introduction to *Galen, On the Usefulness of the Parts of the Body* (Ithaca, 1968), 1:45–53.

[96]See M. Putscher, *Pneuma, Spiritus, Geist* (Wiesbaden, 1864), p. 46ff. et passim; Qusṭā ibn Lūqā al-Ba'labakkī, *Fī l-Faṣl bayna r-rūḥ wa n-nafs* (*MI*, p. 128), ed. and trans. G. Gabrieli, "La Risālah di Qusṭā b. Lūqā 'Sulla differenza tra lo spirito e l'anima,' " *Rendiconti della Reale Academia dei Lincei, Classe di science morali storiche e filologiche*, ser. v, vol. 19 (1910):622–655.

[97]Siegel, *Galen's System*, pp. 104–106, 184–192; Ullmann, *Islamic Medicine*, pp. 28, 62–68.

[98]These three spirits support the corresponding natural, vital, and psychic forces; see Ḥunayn, p. 4f.

These three *pneumata* were presented by Galen with differing degrees of conviction; it has been said that the natural spirit was "hardly incorporated into his system."[99]

Islamic doctors both simplified and elaborated the Galenic system of humors, innate heat, and *pneumata*, which they inherited through late Hellenistic treatises.[100] They simplified the system by eliminating Galen's inconsistencies, ambiguities, and prolixity and by building on his conceptual foundation. These processes may be seen quite clearly in the development of the central humoral theory. Medieval doctors made the four humors canonical and defined them more precisely, particularly the phlegmatic and sanguine humors, about which Galen had been ambiguous. Exemplifying the elaboration of Galenic theory is the considerable refinement of the idea that insanity was caused by the humors; the discussions of the Islamic doctors greatly influenced the Western interpretation of insanity.[101]

Generally, medieval Galenism perpetuated the view of the Dogmatists, who in ancient medicine had attempted to create an exact science of medicine on the basis of the largely empirical writings of Hippocrates. Through philosophic speculation, the Dogmatists formulated a priori principles or *dogmata* of medical knowledge and deduced treatments from these principles. The Empiricists, conversely, rejected the possibility of a scientific basis for medicine; they relied instead on observation and experience and used the inductive method. Islamic medicine inherited this intellectual contention, and it continued to evoke discussion. In Islamic medicine, however, the Dogmatists and the Empiricists were not two rival schools, but represented complementary orientations or emphases, both of which could be found in the works of Galen.[102]

Although the ancient Empiricist school of medicine may have sur-

[99]Siegel, *Galen's System*, p. 186; Owsei Temkin, "On Galen's Pneumatology," *Gernerus* 8 (1951): 181; L. G. Wilson, "Erasistratus, Galen and the *Pneuma*," *BHM* 33 (1959):293–314.

[100]Temkin, "On Galen's Pneumatology," pp. 188–189, and idem, *Galenism*, p. 107; Ullmann, *Islamic Medicine*, p. 63.

[101]Galenic medicine had held that the melancholic humor was either a corruption of the blood or of the yellow bile. Arabic doctors extended the concept of humoral corruption to the other two humors and assigned different types of mental disturbances to the four corruptions, giving a "generic" foundation to pathological symptoms; see Ibn Sīnā, *al-Qānūn*, 2:68. At the same time, it logically and satisfactorily combined Galen's canonical theory of combustion with the doctrine of the four humors. See Dols, "Insanity in Byzantine and Islamic Medicine," *Dumbarton Oaks Papers*, forthcoming.

[102]See *Paulys Realencyclopädie der classischen Altertumswissenschaft* (Stuttgart, 1958 repr.), 5: cols. 2516–2524; K. Deichräber, *Die griechische Empirikerschule* (Berlin, 1930).

vived at Gondēshāpūr or elsewhere and accompanied the revival of medicine under the 'Abbāsids,[103] the massive translation of Galen's works surely discouraged this tradition. Christian and Muslim aversion to human dissection and to the crude empiricism of folkloric medicine further diminished its appeal. In addition, scientific experimentation was greatly limited by technical and philosophical factors.[104] Yet, empiricism persisted among educated doctors, especially among surgeons, such as Abū l-Qāsim az-Zahrāwī (d. ca. A.D. 1009) of Cordoba.[105] The most famous example is ar-Rāzī (d. A.D. 923), who exercised considerable influence in Islamic medicine. His empiricism came through clearly in his reports of clinical cases[106] and in his well-known monograph on smallpox and measles.[107]

Recently, Felix Klein-Franke has emphasized the strength of the empirical tradition in Islamic medicine.[108] According to him, medical study in Baghdad shifted from a theoretical to an empirical orientation between A.D. 850 and 1100. This shift culminated in an important treatise by Abū Sa'īd ibn Bakhtīshū' (d. A.D. 1058) which argued against medicine's tutelage to philosophy. Although its influence was quite limited, it was "the first work in which an independent status was claimed for medicine and, consequently, its separation from obsolete philosophical theorems."[109]

Ibn Bakhtīshū' criticized the specific errors perpetuated by the philosophic teaching of medicine, such as the doctrine of spontaneous generation (which is found in Ibn Riḍwān's treatise), and the general Platonic notion of the dichotomy of the mind and body.[110] He reverted to the

[103]Van Ess, "Skepticism in Islamic Religious Thought," p. 3f.; cf. Michael Cook, *Early Muslim Dogma* (Cambridge, 1981), pp. 44f., 157.

[104]See *Vorlesungen*, pp. 90–92, 98–100.

[105]See *MI*, pp. 149–151.

[106]Max Meyerhof, "Thirty-three Clinical Observations by Rhazes (circa 900 A.D.)," *Isis* 65 vol. 23 (1935):321–356 and Arabic text (i–xiv); ar-Rāzī, *Guide*, p. 22 et passim. On ar-Rāzī, see *EI*[1], s.v. "al-Rāzī" (Paul Kraus); *MI*, pp. 128–136; *Vorlesungen*, pp. 95–96.

[107]See *MI*, p. 133f.

[108]Unfortunately, Klein-Franke's argument is marred by his failure to recognize the classical precedents for the alleged instances of empiricism in the writings of ar-Rāzī and Ibn Bakhtīshū' and by his overestimation of Islamic achievements, e.g., Caesarean section (*Vorlesungen*, vii–viii) and postmortem autopsies (ibid., p. 114). Elinor Lieber, "Galen in Hebrew: the transmission of Galen's work in the mediaeval Islamic world," in *Galen: Problems and Prospects*, ed. Vivian Nutton (London, 1981), p. 174, has also pointed out the "vocational bias" of the Islamic medical curricula.

[109]Ibn Bakhtīshū', intro., p. 17; see also, *Vorlesungen*, pp. 2, 103f.

[110]Galenic medicine, as it developed in the early Middle Ages, maintained this division and emphasized the somatic causation of illness. This is particularly evident in the interpretation of aberrant behavior, whereby insanity came to be seen as a pathological condition and, thus,

authority of Hippocrates, before the marriage of Platonic philosophy with medicine[111]—a recurrent theme in Western medical history.[112] Ibn Bakhtīshū‘ argued that philosophic theory was incapable of dealing with medical questions, apart from the utility of a preliminary training in logic.[113] He demonstrated this argument, specifically, by pointing out the inadequacy of Platonized medical theory in dealing with mental or psychic illnesses (Ar. *amrāḍ an-nafs*). Drawing directly on his experience in the ‘Aḍudī Hospital in Baghdad, he asserted the holistic view that psychic conditions caused bodily illnesses and vice versa. Consequently, he believed that medical diagnosis and treatment must be directed to both the patient's mind and body. In this manner, Ibn Bakhtīshū‘ anticipated the criticism of Galenic medicine expressed by Islamic doctors, however muted, in the twelfth and thirteenth centuries A.D.[114] This criticism did not, however, entail a repudiation of the underlying humoral theory, but it did temper the influence of the Dogmatists,[115] such as Ibn Riḍwān.[116]

The rigidity of the Galenic tradition in Islamic medicine was not without merit. In comparison with medieval European medicine,[117] the promotion of Galenism helped to establish a nonmoralizing and noncondemnatory interpretation of diseases and their victims in Islamic society. This phenomenon may be seen, for example, in the interpretation of leprosy in professional Islamic medicine and in the relative tolerance of the leper in Muslim communities. While it is impossible to gauge the influence of this naturalistic view of leprosy, it seems reasonable to assume that, through the activity of doctors trained in the

---

attained the status of other illnesses. See Dols, *Majnūn: The Madman in Medieval Islamic Society*, forthcoming.

[111] *Vorlesungen*, pp. 88, 103.

[112] See Smith, *The Hippocratic Tradition*.

[113] Ibn Bakhtīshū‘, pp. 73r–74r.

[114] Ibid., intro., pp. 24–30.

[115] *Vorlesungen*, pp. 73, 84, 106–108.

[116] On the pervasive Muslim fidelity to learned tradition, see *Vorlesungen*, pp. 89–90.

[117] Temkin ("An Historical Analysis of the Concept of Infection," p. 459f.) asserts: "Although all diseases could conceivably be judged as punishment for crime, it appears that there existed a popular classification of diseases into clean and unclean, the latter being 'infectious' par excellence. Of these latter, we mentioned leprosy, gonorrhea, plague, and epilepsy, to which insanity might be added. In the popular mind these types of diseases had and have a moral or religious stigma. The plague as God's wrath at a sinful people, leprosy and venereal disease as filthy, mental disease as a disgrace, are notions very much alive even today. In former times these diseases were popularly considered not only as pollutions but as possibly catching. The superstitious Greek or Roman spit when he met insane or epileptic persons, and people were afraid to eat or drink from a dish an epileptic had used. The pressure of opinion seems to have induced medieval physicians to uphold this belief, at the same time rationalizing it by a natural explanation."

Galenic tradition, it weighed against the selective discrimination and segregation of lepers.[118]

As an intellectual tradition, therefore, Galenism sustained a rational and secular approach to the fundamental questions of health and illness. Like the ancient Greeks, medieval people recognized certain collections of morbid phenomena, called them diseases, associated them with the geographical and atmospheric environment, and expected them to run a certain course. To recover his health, the patient had to modify his ordinary mode of living. Beyond this he knew little and was compelled to explain these events by conjecture.[119]

The Medical Profession

The medical profession in medieval Islamic society may be defined as the vocation of those medical practitioners who adhered closely to the principles of Galenic medicine. This is in fact, how the physicians defined themselves—that is, in terms of the content of Islamic medicine rather than of the discipline's institutional organization.[120] The profession in the medieval period was far less structured than in modern times; it was informal, open-ended, and more dependent on the initiative of the aspirant doctor. Medical education, particularly, was not institutionized and regulated, which helps to explain the obsession of Ibn Riḍwān and others with a thorough education in the Greek medical classics; such familiarity was virtually the only criterion of membership in the profession. In this regard, Islamic medicine shows a continuity with the medicine of late antiquity. As Max Neuburger has stated:

> In consequence of the absolute freedom of educational methods and the absence of state supervision of qualifications there existed between those who claimed position as doctors the greatest difference in knowledge and capacity. . . . It thus depended upon the zeal of the individual and upon the capacities of his teacher whether the student became a genuine physician or an ignorant charlatan.[121]

[118]See Dols, "Leprosy in Medieval Arabic Medicine," *Journal of the History of Medicine and Allied Sciences* 34 (1979):314–333; idem, "The Leper in Medieval Islamic Society," *Speculum* (in press).

[119]General introduction to *Hippocrates*, p. ix.

[120]See Charles Leslie's discussion of medical professionalism in the introduction to his *Asian Medical Systems: A Comparative Study* (Berkeley, 1967), pp. 1–12; Eliot Freidson, *Profession of Medicine* (New York, 1970), pp. 3–22.

[121]Neuburger, *History of Medicine*, 1:279.

In describing, therefore, the features of the medical profession at the time of Ibn Riḍwān,[122] we must be as cautious of modern preconceptions and terminology as we would be about the diagnosis of illnesses in the past.[123]

Education in Islamic society was primarily religious, being devoted to the study of Islam and its ancillary sciences. From its origin in the mosque, Muslim higher education gradually became formalized and

[122]For a survey of medical history in Egypt in the tenth and eleventh centuries A.D., see Lucien Leclerc, *Histoire de la médecine arabe* (Paris, 1876), 1:399–406, 511–538; for science in general, see Aldo Mieli, *La Science Arabe* (Leiden, 1966 repr.), pp. 79–142. It is instructive to compare tenth-century Islamic medicine with contemporary Byzantine medicine; a useful summary of the latter is given by Andrew Sharf in his *The Universe of Shabbetai Donnolo* (Warminster, England, 1976), pp. 94–110.

[123]For the Islamic medical profession, see the following works: Franz Rosenthal, "The Physician in Medieval Muslim Society," *BHM* 52 (1978):475–491; idem, *The Classical Heritage in Islam* (Berkeley, 1975), pp. 182–205; S. D. Goitein, *A Mediterranean Society*, 3 vols. (Berkeley, 1967–1978), Index, s.v. "physicians," "medical" (see especially 2:240–261); idem, "The Medical Profession in the Light of the Cairo Geniza Documents," *Hebrew Union College Annual* 34 (1963):177–194 (which is incorporated in the preceding work); J. C. Bürgel, "Die Bildung des Arztes: Eine arabische Schrift zum 'ärztlichen Leben' aus dem 9. Jahrhundert," *Sudhoffs Archiv* 50 (1966):337–360; idem, "Secular and Religious Features of Medieval Arabic Medicine," pp. 44–62; F. R. Hau, "Die Bildung des Arztes im islamischen Mittelalter," *Clio Medica* 13 (1978):95–123 (with an extensive bibliography), 175–200; 14 (1979):7–25; S. K. Hamarneh, "Medical Education and Practice in Medieval Islam," pp. 39–71; idem, "The Physician and the Health Profession in Medieval Islam," *Bulletin of the New York Academy of Medicine* 47 (1971):1088–1110; idem, "Some Aspects of Medical Practices," pp. 15–31; Gary Leiser, "Medical Education in Islamic Lands from the Seventh to the Fourteenth Century" *Journal of the History of Medicine and Allied Sciences*, 38 (1983):48–75—an important revision of traditional views; E. G. Browne, *Arabian Medicine* (Cambridge, 1962 repr.); Cyril Elgood, *A Medical History of Persia and the Eastern Caliphate* (Cambridge, 1951), pp. 234–301; S. K. Bukhsh, "The Educational System of the Muslims in the Middle Ages," *Islamic Quarterly* 1 (1927):442–472; G. E. von Grunebaum, "Der Einfluss des Islam auf die Entwicklung der Medizin," *Bustan* 3 (1963):19–22; Joseph Graziani, "The Contributions of Arabic Medicine to the Health Profession during the Eleventh Century," *Episteme* 10 (1976):126–143; idem, "Ibn Jazlah's Eleventh-Century Tabulated Medical Compendium, *Taqwīm al-Abdān*," Ph.D. dissertation, UCLA (1973); Ullmann, *Islamic Medicine*; Martin Levey, "Preventive Medicine in Ninth Century Persia," *Studies in Islam* 8 (1971):8–16; idem and Ṣ. Sūriyāl, "The Foundations of Medicine in the Eleventh Century [A.D.]," *al-Mashriq* 63 (1969): 141–156; idem, "Medieval Muslim Hospitals: Administration and Procedures," *Journal of the Albert Einstein Medical Center* 10 (1962):120–127; G. C. Anawati, "La Medécine arabe jusqu'au temps d'Avicenne," *Les Mardis de Dar El-Salam* (Cairo, 1956), pp. 166–206; A. Z. Iskandar, "The Image of the Physician in Medieval Islamic Society: The Shift from the Galenic to the Islamic Ideal," paper delivered at the Colloquium on Biology, Society and History in Islam, University of Pennsylvania, October, 1977; Heinrich Schipperges, "Die arabische Medizin als Praxis und als Theorie," pp. 317–328; idem, "Der ärztliche Stand im arabischen und lateinischen Mittelalter," *Materia Medica Nordmark* 12 (1960):109–118; idem, "Aus dem Alltag arabischer Ärzte," *Deutsche Medizinische Wochenschrift* 82 (1957):1929–1932; idem, "Der ärztliche Stand im arabischen Kulturkreis," *Schweizerische Hochschulzeitung* 31 (1958):80–86; Ernest Wickersheimer, "Organisation et législation sanitaires au Royaume franc de Jérusalem (1099–1291)," *Archives internationales d'histoire des Sciences*, no. 16 (1951):689–705. For further bibliographical references, see R. Y. Ebied, *Bibliography of Medieval Arabic and Jewish Medicine and Allied Sciences* (London, 1971), s.v. "Profession, Medical." Cf. Herbert Hunger, *Die hochsprachliche profane Literatur der Byzantiner*, in *Byzantinisches Handbuch*, 12:5:2 (Munich, 1978), p. 289f.

institutionalized; by the eleventh century A.D., formal education clearly focused on Islamic law and was centered in the *madrasah*, or endowed college.[124] The "ancient" or Greek sciences, such as philosophy, medicine, and mathematics, were studied privately by jurists and theologians and their students, but unlike the Muslim sciences in the *madrasah*, they were not subsidized. On this point, George Makdisi has written:

> Such a mixture of supposedly irreconcilable subjects would not have been possible in a system where there was no easy access to the Ancient Sciences. Not only was access easy, it was in turn concealed, condoned, allowed, encouraged, held in honour, according to different regions and periods, in spite of the traditionalist opposition, the periodic prohibitions, and auto-da-fé.[125]

The science of medicine, specifically, was a bridge between the Islamic and the "ancient" sciences, for it was often taught in the mosques and later in the *madrasahs* by the physician-jurist.[126] The *madrasah*, however, was devoted primarily to the study of Islamic law; between the eleventh and twelfth centuries A.D., *madrasahs* that embraced both Muslim and foreign sciences became extinct. From the end of the twelfth century A.D., cognate institutions were established for the ancillary foreign sciences.[127] This institutional specialization explains the exceptional development of *madrasahs* designated for the study of medicine, for medical education was usually conducted in private or in hospitals. Such medical schools were founded in Baghdad in the twelfth century and in Damascus and Cairo in the thirteenth century A.D.[128] At the same time, *madrasahs* for legal studies were sometimes built in conjunction with a hospital or medical school.[129]

The study of medicine usually presumed learning in the other for-

[124]George Makdisi, *The Rise of Colleges: Institutions of Learning in Islam and the West* (Edinburgh, 1981), pp. 75–77.

[125]Ibid., p. 78.

[126]*EI*[1], s.v. "Egypt" (C. Becker); Carl F. Petry, *The Civilian Elite of Cairo on the Later Middle Ages* (Princeton, 1981), pp. 139, 331, 339. For instances of such teaching, see Makdisi, *The Rise of Colleges*, pp. 11, 78, 87f, 285. A jurisconsult might also be the director of a hospital; for example, see ibid., p. 168.

[127]Ibid., pp. 10, 33f.

[128]Ibid., p. 313, n. 38: Ahmed Issa Bey (Aḥmad ʿĪsā), *Histoire des Bimaristans (Hôpitaux) à l'époque islamique* (Cairo, 1928), p. 16f.

[129]Makdisi, *The Rise of Colleges*, p. 34; A. Süheyl Ünver, "Sur l'Histoire des Hôpitaux Turcs," *Atti del Rimo Congresso Europeo di Storia Ospitaliera (6–12 Giugno, 1960)*, Reggio Emilia, 1960, pp. 1240–1257; see Leiser, "Medical Education," pp. 54–59 for a careful discussion of this topic.

eign sciences—in linguistic and mathematical skills (Ar. *al-ādāb wat-taʿālīm*) or the seven "liberal arts." The course of study reflected the Dogmatists' combination of medicine and philosophy.[130] As in Galen's *That the Excellent Physician Must be a Philosopher*,[131] medicine demanded an intellectual underpinning in philosophy as well as an understanding of other allied sciences.[132] A student's concentration on philosophic-scientific works was well established and was preparatory to medicine.[133] With Arabic translations of the classical texts, medical students could study the Greek works firsthand.[134]

Medieval medical education meant primarily the study of Hippocrates and Galen,[135] a concentration that went back to the medical training in Hellenistic Alexandria. Starting in early Byzantine times, the public teaching of medical writings had become restricted to the Hippocratic and Galenic canons, just as the teaching of philosophy had become limited to a short canon of the works of Aristotle. Drawing up lists of Greek classical texts was a characteristic activity of the Alexandrian school. The Alexandrian canon of twelve Galenic works, which must have existed before the sixth century A.D., was modified by its later Syriac and Arabic redactors. From the ninth century A.D, Islamic writers referred to the selection and partial abridgement of Galen's works as the "Sixteen Books"; they were a reorganized arrangement of the Alexandrian canon, comprising the twelve items of the original

[130]See Schipperges, "Die arabische Medizin," p. 319. Rosenthal has pointed out how this coalescence was a disadvantage to medicine; from the tenth century A.D. Greek philosophy became increasingly suspect among the Muslim masses and endangered the position of the medical profession as well ("The Physician in Medieval Muslim Society," p. 491). See also L. G. Westerink, "Philosophy and Medicine in Late Antiquity," *Janus*, 51 (1964): 169–177; Rudi Paret, *Der Islam und das griechische Bildungsgut* (Tübingen, 1950), p. 19f; John Duffy, "Medicine and Doctors in Early Byzantine Writings, c. 550–650 A.D.," paper read at the annual meeting of the Society for Ancient Medicine, San Francisco, December 30, 1981. Virtually all Islamic philosophers of the medieval period practiced medicine in order to earn a living; in fact, their status was largely due to the practice of medicine (Pines, "Philosophy," p. 784f.). There were, of course, exceptions; al-Fārābī was atypical in not professing medicine. See Gotthard Strohmaier, *Denker im Reich der Kalifen* (Berlin, 1979), p 61f.

[131]Peter Bachmann, ed., *Galens Abhandlung darüber, dass der vorzügliche Arzt Philosoph sein muss* (Göttingen, 1966).

[132]See Bürgel, "Secular and Religious Features of Medieval Arabic Medicine," p. 47f.; *Vorlesungen*, pp. 60, 73, 85–89.

[133]Goitein, *A Mediterranean Society*, 2:172, 210. Goitein also notes that the art of writing was taught to medical students and was a distinctive mark of a person belonging to the professional or higher classes (ibid., p. 179).

[134]The close reading of classical texts did not demand a knowledge of the original Greek texts. Despite Ibn Riḍwān's strong reliance on these works, nothing indicates that he knew Greek, nor does he seem to have been atypical in this regard.

[135]Goitein, *A Mediterranean Society*, 2:249.

Greek canon in Byzantine Alexandria, with the usual addition of Galen's *De sanitate tuenda.*[136] However, the medieval doctors, such as Ibn Riḍwān, added extra Galenic works, particularly on drugs and foods, to the standard list of the "Sixteen Books."

The Islamic ideal of medical education was thus based on the medical curriculum of Alexandria.[137] Its preparatory course included language and grammar, logic, arithmetic, geometry, the compounding of drugs, astrology, and ethics. The main course used four books on logic (the first four books of Aristotle's *Organon*) and twenty books on medicine: Hippocrates' *Aphorisms*, *Prognostics*, *Regimen in Acute Diseases*, and *Airs, Waters and Places* and the "Sixteen Books" of Galen.[138] Completion of this curriculum, particularly the "Sixteen Books," became the criterion for the accomplished physician. Arabic terminology is telling: the *ṭabīb*, according to Ibn Riḍwān, was a doctor educated in the entire course of study, whereas the *mutaṭabbib* was one trained only in the preliminary course.[139]

The selected works of Galen were the mainstay of medical education, but their complexity, disorder, and length presented difficulties. Islamic medicine inherited the tradition of summaries and commentaries of the Galenic canon, and the original works came to be more or less replaced by summaries. As a medieval Muslim scholar said pragmatically, this was done "in order to abridge their rhetoric, to facilitate

[136]For a detailed discussion of the evolution of the Alexandrian canon of Galen's works, see Lieber, "Galen in Hebrew," pp. 171–181.

[137]On the Alexandrian school(s) that lasted until about A.D. 718, see Meyerhof's articles cited in n. 12 above; Ullmann, *Islamic Medicine*, p. 7f.; Grand'henry, p. 11ff.; Owsei Temkin, "Byzantine Medicine: Tradition and Empiricism" in his *The Double Face of Janus*, pp. 202–222; and idem, "Studies on Late Alexandrian Medicine I. Alexandrian Commentaries on Galen's *De Sectis ad Introducendos*," ibid., pp. 178–197. There were other approaches to medical education; see Schacht and Meyerhof, pp. 21–28; Levey, "Medical Ethics of Medieval Islam," p. 84f.; *The Fihrist of al-Nadīm*, trans. Bayard Dodge (New York, 1970), 2:679–683.

[138]A. Z. Iskandar, "An Attempted Reconstruction of the Late Alexandrian Medical Curriculum," *Medical History* 20 (1976):235–258; idem, "The Image of the Physician."

[139]"According to Galen, only he is a perfect physician who is at the same time a philosopher. He only is a real physician (*ṭabīb*), while someone without philosophical education is only a medical practitioner (*mutaṭabbib*). The *ṭabīb* must be learned in the mathematical, natural, theological, and logical sciences" (Schacht and Meyerhof, p. 77). Similarly, Ibn Buṭlān uses the terms *'ammāl* (practitioners) and *'allām* (scientists), ibid., pp. 72, 112f. See Makdisi, *The Rise of Colleges*, p. 34; *Vorlesungen*, pp. 9, 93; Goitein, *A Mediterranean Society*, 2:246; Elgood, *A Medical History of Persia*, pp. 245–246. In the European context, Kristeller has suggested a similar contrast with the introduction of *physicus*, as distinguished from *medicus*, in the twelfth century A.D.; *physicus* "emphasized the need for the medical doctor to have a thorough training in natural philosophy and science, and distinguishes him from the mere medical practitioner who lacks such theoretical training" (P. O. Kristeller, "The School of Salerno: Its Development and Its Contribution to the History of Learning," *BHM* 17 [1945]:160). See also E. J. Kealey, *Medieval Medicus* (Baltimore, 1981), p. 34ff.

their study and understanding, and for ease of transportation."[140] Thus, Arabic collections of summaries based on the "Sixteen Books" evolved and came to be known as the *Jawāmiʿ al-Iskandarānīyīn* or *Summaria Alexandrinorum.*[141] Ibn Riḍwān says that in his time the medical curriculum had given way to these summaries and commentaries (Ar. *al-jawāmiʿ wat-tafāsīr*) as well as to compendia (Ar. *al-kanānīsh*) by later writers.

Ibn Riḍwān believed that these shortcuts to medical education hurt the profession, for they allowed ignorant men to practice medicine. Because of these compendia, he wrote, the public could not distinguish between the truly learned doctor and his imitators, so that the profession was increasingly scorned and considered only as a source of income, "a profession of the poor" (Ar. *ṣināʿat al-fuqarāʾ*).[142] For Ibn Riḍwān, the yardstick of professional competence was the doctor's intimate knowledge of the original classical literature. His stance toward medical education is, therefore, indicative of the general conflict of opinion in the Middle Ages as to whether Galen's works, particularly, should be studied in the original, with or without a commentary, in the form of summaries, or through the medicine of the encyclopedic compilations.[143]

There were generally three methods of obtaining medical education in the Middle Ages. Sons and sometimes daughters were taught by their fathers;[144] several generations of physicians was not uncommon.[145] A physician could also be self-taught, and Ibn Riḍwān was probably the most outspoken advocate of this method.[146] Ibn Riḍwān strongly recommended Galen's own education as a model. If the student had a natural disposition for the subject, was young enough (between puberty and twenty-one), and had a good teacher, he could,

[140]Ibn al-Qifṭī quoted by Lieber, "Galen in Hebrew," p. 171.

[141]Ibid., pp. 176–181; *Vorlesungen*, pp. 75–77, 81f.

[142]Schacht and Meyerhof, p. 22; see also Dietrich, *ʿAlī ibn Riḍwān*, p. 12/13. Cf. Gerhard Baader, "Handschrift und Frühdruck als Überlieferungsinstrumente der Wissenschaften," *Berichte zur Wissenschafts-Geschichte* 3 (1980):7–22.

[143]Lieber, "Galen in Hebrew," p. 181.

[144]On women in the medical profession, see especially Goitein's remarks in his *A Mediterranean Society*, 1:127–130, and 3:64; Issa, *Histoire des Bimaristans*, pp. 8–9; *Vorlesungen*, p. 16f.

[145]See Goitein, *A Mediterranean Society*, 2:245–246.

[146]As Gary Leiser has pointed out ("Medical Education," p. 51f.), this avenue of medical education was possible only after the massive translation of Greek medical works and their dissemination. Then, self-education was not uncommon; for even Ibn Sīnā was self-taught. Yet, Leiser emphasizes the difficulty of Arabic medical manuscripts and the errors that may have arisen from their misreadings by solitary students.

like Galen, acquire the requisite medical learning in three years. If the medical student could not find a competent teacher, Ibn Riḍwān believed that he could study Hippocrates on his own after a training in logic, but this course of study would take longer. In either case, the student must, then, study with the most capable practitioner accessible to him.[147] That was how Ibn Riḍwān got his own training, and his advocacy of it is, of course, a self-justification. As Ibn Abī Uṣaybicah, the famous medieval historian of the profession, said: "Ibn Riḍwān had no teacher in medicine to whom he could have referred; he composed a book on this subject in which he said that learning of the medical science out of books is more profitable than learning from teachers."[148] Self-education, however, was controversial partly because the supervision that would impose some standard of professional training was lacking.

Finally, and most important, medical education in a class, or privately with a tutor, took place in mosques, *madrasahs*, libraries, hospitals, or scholars' homes.[149] Medical theory was usually taught in the traditional lesson-circle (Ar. *ḥalqah*).[150] Ibn Riḍwān describes how each student recited selected classics aloud before the teacher for comment or correction. The other students would follow the recitation in their own texts, if they possessed them. Students often memorized major works in the common belief that knowing a text by heart must precede its understanding. The accomplished physician, like a lawyer, would have to recall passages from authoritative texts accurately and promptly.[151] The physician 'Abd al-Laṭīf al-Baghdādī (d. A.D. 1231) was typical in his advice: "When you read a book make every effort to learn it by heart and master its meaning. Imagine the book to have disappeared and that you can dispense with it, unaffected by its loss."[152]

The medical books, however, required exegesis by an instructor because of the difficult language and subject matter. "Teachers frequently dictated to their students their own works, or those of others, which were read back to verify their accuracy. Regular lectures were also given. The students took extensive notes which they often turned

[147]Dietrich, *'Alī ibn Riḍwān*, pp. 12–15.

[148]Ibn Abī Uṣaybi'ah, *'Uyūn*, 2:101; Makdisi, *The Rise of Colleges*, p. 10.

[149]See Goitein, *A Mediterranean Society*, 2:247–250.

[150]Makdisi, *The Rise of Colleges*, p. 12 et passim.

[151]Ibid., p. 99ff.; E. F. Eickelman, "The Art of Memory: Islamic Education and Its Social Reproduction," *Comparative Studies in Society and History* 20 (1958):485–516.

[152]Quoted in Makdisi, *The Rise of Colleges*, p. 103.

into handbooks."[153] The scholastic method of argumentation was also used orally in class; this method of teaching is reflected in the organization of many medical works, such as Ḥunayn ibn Isḥāq's early primer, *Questions on Medicine for Scholars*, and numerous commentaries.[154] Because of the emphasis on books, which were quite expensive, access to libraries was essential for the well-trained student. Medical texts were available in a variety of places—hospitals, royal libraries, private collections, and from booksellers.

Whatever the source or manner of study, it was customary to have practical training, either by working under a practicing physician or in a hospital.[155] The hospitals, like the *madrasahs*, were charitable trusts and were located in the major cities.[156] The Islamic hospital was a public, secular institution that more closely resembled a convalescent or nursing home than a modern hospital oriented toward interventive medicine. The medieval hospital was not the exclusive center of medical practice. Ibn Riḍwān never mentions hospitals in his description of Egypt; he did not receive any training in the Cairene hospitals, nor does he seem to have practiced in them. Medical care of acute illnesses was usually carried out in the patient's home or in the physician's home or office. Egyptian Jews did not use the hospitals,[157] although Jewish doctors often held prestigious staff positions there.[158] It is unclear to what extent Egyptian Christians used the hospitals, but Christian doctors also served on their staffs. For the Muslim majority, the hospitals attended primarily to the poor and incurable.[159]

[153]Leiser, "Medical Education," p. 60.

[154]Ibid.; Leiber, "Galen in Hebrew," p. 180f.: "The actual philosophical influence [on medicine] was mainly apparent in the commentaries which, in the 6th century A.D., became increasingly confined to a scholastic framework adopted from the teaching of philosophy." See also George Makdisi, "The Scholastic Method in Medieval Education: An Inquiry into Its Origins in Law and Theology," *Speculum* 49 (1974):659; idem, *The Rise of Colleges*, pp. 116, 122. Cf. Charles Talbot, "Medical Education in the Middle Ages," in *The History of Medical Education*, ed. O'Malley, p. 75f.

[155]See 'Alī ibn al-'Abbās's advice to medical students quoted in Heinrich Schipperges, "Zum Bildungsweg eines arabischen Arztes," *Orvostörténeti Közlemények* 60–61 (1971):24. See also *Dictionary of the Middle Ages*, s.v. "Islamic Hospitals and Poor Relief" (Dols), in press.

[156]Makdisi, *The Rise of Colleges*, pp. 27, 38.

[157]This does not appear to be the case in Baghdad in the fourth/tenth century; see Ibn Abī Uṣaybi'ah *'Uyūn*, 1:231, l. 21; Issa, *Histoire des Bimaristans*, p. 10.

[158]See Goitein, *A Mediterranean Society*, 2:133, 250–252, 256–257, 288.

[159]The nursing of the patient has been overlooked in most descriptions of premodern medical care. The function was clearly performed in the home by family members and especially by servants; instruction of the servant *qua* nurse is stressed, for example, in ar-Ruhāwī's ethical treatise (Levey, "Medical Ethics of Medieval Islam," pp. 57–58 et passim).

Apparently, there was keen competition for instruction in these hospitals, which played an increasingly important role in medical education. Despite the opportunities for empirical study, the hospitals mainly promoted the authoritative teaching of Galen. A close association can be seen between the highly developed hospitals and medical education in medieval Islamic society. In Europe, by comparison, such an association was not made until the sixteenth century in Italy.[160] However, universities were developed in Europe during the twelfth and thirteenth centuries and became the institutional home of medicine; the university was crucial to the growth of Western medical professionalism because of its orderly instruction, examination, and certification.[161] A comparable institutional development in higher education did not occur in Islamic society.

There is no evidence to suggest that systematic examinations were given at the end of the course of study or that diplomas were granted. Rather, the student was usually given an authorization (Ar. *ijāzah*) by his teacher to transmit the medical text(s) in turn; this procedure was derived from Muslim legal education.[162] The certificates of audition attest to the "perennial personalism of the Islamic system of education."[163] The only evidence of institutional control was a kind of approbation (Ar. *iṭlāq*) granted by the director of the 'Aḍudī Hospital in Baghdad (founded in A.D. 978–79), but the significance of this innovation is difficult to judge.[164] Licensing of medical practitioners by the government or its appointees,[165] with two notable but dubious exceptions,[166] was not a regular practice.[167]

[160]V. L. Bullough, *The Development of Medicine as a Profession* (Basel/London, 1966), p. 92.

[161]Ibid., p. 108.

[162]*EI*², s.v. "Idjāza" (G. Vajda); Leiser, "Medical Education," p. 72ff.

[163]Makdisi, *The Rise of Colleges*, p. 146. Cf. Kristeller, "The School of Salerno," pp. 171–179, and Amundsen, "Medical Deontology and Pestilential Disease," pp. 406–408; V. Grumel, "La Profession médicale à Byzance à l'époque des Comnènes," *Revue des études byzantine* 7 (1949): 42–46.

[164]*Vorlesungen*, p. 19f.

[165]See Leiser, "Medical Education," p. 67ff.; Bürgel, "Secular and Religious Features of Medieval Arabic Medicine," p. 49f.

[166]The most famous incident of a general examination of physicians occurred in A.D. 931, when a case of malpractice prompted the caliph al-Muqtadir to order the investigation of the profession; the ancedotal account of the examination by al-Qifṭī, however, suggests that it was not very rigorous. A similar examination of physicians appears to have been made by Ibn at-Tilmīdh (d. 549/1154 or 560/1165) when he was chief physician in Baghdad. See Browne, *Arabian Medicine*, p. 40f.; Leclerc, *Histoire de la médecine arabe*, 1:367, and 2:26. It was only in the Crusader Kingdom that certification of physicians was enforced, and this was exceptional with regard to all

A minor branch of medical literature, called *miḥnat aṭ-ṭabīb*, concerned itself with the examination of doctors. Its model was Galen's work on the subject.[168] Both laymen and doctors used these works to test the competency of medical practitioners. For example, a prominent physician, guided by this literature, might be authorized by the market inspector or sometimes by the caliph to grant qualification to an aspiring doctor. The minimum requirement in Egypt during Ibn Riḍwān's lifetime seems to have been a police certificate (Ar. *tazkiyah*) of good conduct for the exercise of the medical profession.[169]

The *ḥisbah* books, which outlined the duties of the market inspector (Ar. *muḥtasib*) for regulating communal activity, frequently prescribed topics of medical education, the ethics of medical practice, and the examination of doctors.[170] According to a late *ḥisbah* book by Ibn Ukhuwwah (d. A.D. 1329), doctors took the *Oath* before the *muḥtasib*.[171] The market inspector was supposed to oversee medical practice and to

---

other vocations. See J. Prawer, *Crusader Institutions* (Oxford, 1981), p. 53; Woodings, "The Medical Resources and Practice of the Crusader States," p. 269.

[167]See the numerous works of S. K. Hamarneh, as well as Issa, *Histoire des Bimaristans*, pp. 16–23; A. A. Khairallah and S. I. Haddad, "A Study of Arab Hospitals in the Light of Present Day Standardization," *Bulletin of the American College of Surgeons* 2 (1936): 176; Schipperges, "Der ärztliche Stand im arabischen Kulturkreis," p. 81ff. Ghada Karmi, "State Control of the Physicians in the Middle Ages: an Islamic Model," in *The Town and State Physician in Europe from the Middle Ages to the Enlightenment*, ed. A. W. Russell (Wolfenbüttel, 1981), pp. 63–84, reiterates the view of these authors about governmental control of medicine in medieval Islamic society; she concludes her article with skepticism, however, questioning whether the various regulations were actually enforced because of the lack of historical evidence. My description of medical supervision and regulation does not accept the customary point of view. In addition, the survey of the civic physician by Vivian Nutton, "Continuity or Rediscovery? The City Physician in Classical Antiquity and Medieval Italy," ibid., pp. 9–46, raises a number of pertinent questions about medical practices in Islamic society.

[168]See *MI*, pp. 52f., 226f.; Leiser, "Medical Education," p. 68ff.

[169]Goitein, *A Mediterranean Society*, 2:246–247, 250; cf. Issa, *Histoire des Bimaristans*, pp. 18–25.

[170]*EI²*, s.v. "Ḥisba" (Cl. Cahen and M. Talbi): a "non-Ḳur'ānic term which is used to mean on the one hand the duty of every Muslim to 'promote good and forbid evil' and, on the other, the function of the person who is effectively entrusted in a town with the application of this rule in the supervision of moral behavior and more particularly of the markets; this person entrusted with the *ḥisba* was called the *muḥtasib*. . . . His competence extended even to professions which we should not nowadays normally consider as being connected with the *sūḳ*: he thus controlled apothecaries and physicians, . . . " See Max Meyerhof, "La Surveillance des professions médicales chez les arabes," *Bulletin de l'Institut d'Égypte* 26 (1944):119–134; S. K. Hamarneh, "Origin and Function of the Ḥisbah System in Islam and its Impact on the Health Professions," *Sudhoffs Archiv* 48 (1964):157–173; Martin Levey, "Fourteenth Century Muslim Medicine and the Ḥisba," *Medical History* 7 (1963):176–182; I. M. Lapidus, *Muslim Cities in the Later Middle Ages* (Cambridge, Mass., 1967), pp. 98–101; R. B. Serjeant, "A Zaidī Manual of Ḥisbah of the 3rd Century (H.)," *Rivista degli studi orientali* 28 (1953):1–34; Issa, *Histoire des Bimaristans*, pp. 23–25; *EI²*, s.v. "Ibn al-Ukhuwwa" (Cl. Cahen); Ibn Bakhtīshū', p. 19f.

[171]*Ma'ālim al-qurbah*, ed. R. Levi (1938), p. 167.

extract penalties for malpractice. Yet, the actual supervision by the *muḥtasib* appears to have been quite ineffectual, if for no other reason than his lack of training in this field.[172] The *ḥisbah* regulations are not an exact reflection of social conditions, especially of medical training and practice, for like all law, they are prescriptive rather than descriptive.[173] The absence of supervision is the reason for Ibn Riḍwān's plea for effective governmental regulation (see Pt. II, chap. 9).

The lack of professional regulation by the state and of self-regulation by doctors is consonant with the social organization of the medieval Islamic world generally.[174] Social relations were fluid, personal, and informal; before the Ottoman period, communal institutions especially were noncorporate in nature.[175] It is logical, therefore, that the medical profession was not tightly regulated. As a consequence, however, protests by medieval doctors against unethical or unprofessional behavior were a common theme in the medical literature. In our text, Ibn Riḍwān is quick to criticize what he considers the ignorance and outright quackery of his colleagues.[176] As in antiquity, the self-proclaimed

[172]*Vorlesungen*, p. 51. Moreover, as Klein-Franke asserts, such inspection by the *muḥtasib* meant a social and professional disdain of the medical profession.

[173]See Hau, "Die Bildung des Arztes," pp. 187–190; *MI*, pp. 225–226. The same may be said for the ethical literature concerning medicine; the intent of this literature was, of course, not unrelated to the *ḥisbah* regulations; see Levey, "Medical Ethics of Medieval Islam."

[174]See R. P. Mottahedeh, *Loyalty and Leadership in an Early Islamic Society* (Princeton, 1980); Lapidus, *Muslim Cities*; and Avrom L. Udovitch, "Formalism and Informalism in the Social and Economic Institutions of the Medieval Islamic World," *Individualism and Conformity in Classical Islam*, ed. A. Banani and S. Vryonis (Wiesbaden, 1977), pp. 61–81; M. G. S. Hodgson, *The Venture of Islam*, 3 vols. (Chicago, 1974).

[175]See Petry, *The Civilian Elite*, p. 324f.; Makdisi, *The Rise of Colleges*, p. 224 et passim.

[176]Ibn Riḍwān's adversary Ibn Buṭlān wrote perhaps the most famous tract against quackery in the form of a symposium of doctors. See Mahmound Sedky Bey, *Un Banquet de médecins au temps de l'Emire Nasr el-Dawla ibn Marwan (Daâwat el-Atibba d'Ibn Batlane)* (Cairo, 1928), Arabic ed. by Bisharah Zalzal (Alexandria, 1901); both the French translation and the Arabic edition are unsatisfactory. Cf. Martin Levey, "Some Eleventh Century Medical Questions Posed by Ibn Buṭlān and Later Answered by Ibn Ithirdī," *BHM* 39 (1965):495–507, which summarizes Ibn Ithirdī's commentary (A.D. 1113–14) on this work by Ibn Buṭlān. See also the reference to Ibn Riḍwān in Rosenthal, "The Physician in Medieval Muslim Society," p. 484. Rosenthal points out, in addition, the small genre of Arabic poetry devoted to the praise of the good physician and the blame of the bad physician (p. 485). As he asserts, there is a significant distinction between medical incompetence and fraud. Concerning charlatanry in Islamic society generally, see ibid., pp. 484–487; H. Schipperges, "Der Scharlatan im arabischen und lateinischen Mittelalter," *Geschichtsbeilage der Deutschen Apothekerzeitung* 12 (1960):9–13; E. Wiedemann, "Über Charlatane bei den Muslimen nach al Gaubarī," *Sitzungsberichte der physikalisch-medizinischen Societät in Erlangen* 43 (1911):206–232; *MI*, p. 227; C. E. Bosworth, *The Medieval Islamic Underground* (Leiden, 1976), 1:90 et passim (it should be noted that Abū Dulaf was himself a physician of dubious reputation); M. Steinschneider, "Wissenschaft und Charlatanerie unter den Arabern im neunten Jahr-

doctor could sell his services at his own discretion to anyone who asked and paid for treatment.[177]

Medieval Galenism, however, retained the strong tradition of professional ethics, perhaps Galen's most enduring legacy to modern medicine.[178] This idealism was conveyed, particularly, in the *Hippocratic Oath*, as well as in the *Nomos* and the spurious *Testament of Hippocrates*. Many Islamic authors recapitulated and discussed the *Oath*. The Hippocratic ethic is clearly reflected, for example, in Ibn Riḍwān's autobiography, where the seven qualities attributed to a doctor are a paraphrase of the *Oath*, and in his other works.[179] He also wrote commentaries on the *Nomos* and the *Testament*.[180] Moreover, the deontological works of the Islamic doctors emphasized the free treatment of poor patients. A concrete expression of professional charity to the poor was the hospital.[181]

The established physician was usually located in an urban area, although he might be compelled to travel if he served the court or army, or if he were called to patients in the countryside.[182] It appears that,

---

hundert," *Virchows Archiv* 36 (1866):570–586; Levey, "Medical Ethics of Medieval Islam," pp. 88–91; A. Z. Iskandar, "al-Rāzī wa Miḥnat aṭ-ṭabīb," *al-Mashriq* 54 (1960):487–492.

[177]See Amundsen, "Medical Deontology and Pestilential Disease," p. 405.

[178]For Islamic medical ethics generally, see Hau, "Die Bildung des Arztes," *Clio Medica* 14 (1979):7–16; *MI*, pp. 223–227; Levey, "Medical Ethics of Medieval Islam"; Heinrich Schipperges, "La Etica Medica en el Islam Medieval," *Asclepio* 17 (1965):107–116. Cf. L. C. MacKinney, "Medical Ethics and Etiquette in the Early Middle Ages: The Persistence of Hippocratic Ideals," *BHM* 26 (1952):1–31.

[179]Ibn Abī Uṣaybi'ah, *'Uyūn*, 2:102; Schacht and Meyerhof, p. 40; *MI*, p. 224. According to Hippocrates, the first condition for a medical student was that he be free by birth. Rosenthal points out, however, that this condition was disregarded by Ibn Riḍwān in his list of necessary qualifications of physicians; see Franz Rosenthal, *The Muslim Concept of Freedom* (Leiden, 1961), p. 83.

[180]M. Steinschneider, *Die arabischen Übersetzungen aus dem Griechischen* (Graz, 1960 repr.), p. 313.

[181]Hau, "Die Bildung des Arztes," 14:8. This attention to the poor appears quite consistent with the influence of Christian charity on medical ethics in late antiquity; see Owsei Temkin, "Medical Ethics and Honoraria in Late Antiquity," in *Healing and History: Essays for George Rosen*, ed. C. E. Rosenberg (New York, 1979), pp. 6–26. It should be recalled that the charitable institution of the hospital, which had been introduced in the Middle East by Christianity, was adopted and developed extensively by Islamic society; see G. E. Gask and J. Todd, "The Origin of Hospitals," *Science, Medicine and History: Essays on the Evolution of Scientific Thought and Practice*, ed. E. A. Underwood (Oxford, 1953), 1:122–130. On the Islamic hospital, see: *EI*², s.v. "Bīmāristān" (Dunlop, Colin, and Şehsuvaroğlu); *Dictionary of the Middle Ages*, s.v. "Islamic Hospitals and Poor Relief" (Dols), in press; Issa, *Histoire des Bimaristans*, and the revised and enlarged edition of this work, *Ta'rīkh al-bīmāristānāt fī l-islām* (Damascus, 1939); Petry, *The Civilian Elite*, pp. 140–141 et passim.

[182]See Goitein, *A Mediterranean Society*, 1:273.

unlike religious scholars, very few medical students traveled great distances for their education. Nor was travel the natural expectation of physicians as it had been in antiquity.[183] Medieval doctors were general practitioners but might also have special skill in ophthalmology, bonesetting, pharmacology, or surgery.[184]

The social status of physicians was ambiguous. On the one hand, they practiced medicine as a livelihood and expected to make money doing so. On the other hand, they claimed for medicine the prestige and pure intellectual motives of the "liberal arts."[185] This ambivalence, which goes back to antiquity, was reflected in the connotations of the Greek classification of medicine as a *techne*, meaning something between a "craft" and an "art,"[186] and the equivalent Arabic term was *ṣināʿah*. We have translated Ibn Riḍwān's use of this term (e.g., fols. 33a, 35a) as both "profession" and "art." Generally, medical practice in Islamic society was more akin to a craft, but doctors were not organized into guilds. There has been considerable controversy in recent scholarship about the existence of guilds in Islamic society before the Ottoman period. The consensus of opinion persuasively argued by I. M. Lapidus and S. D. Goitein is that neither the medieval European nor the Byzantine type of guild existed in the medieval Islamic city.[187] In the later Middle Ages, according to Lapidus, "the so-called corporations of physicians, surgeons, and oculists are so designated only because chiefs called *ra'īses* were appointed by the state to maintain standards of teaching, practice, and discipline in the profession. There is no indication that these functionaries represented guild solidarities."[188] The

[183]Leiser, "Medical Education," p. 61f. Cf. Louis Cohn-Haff, *The Public Physician of Ancient Greece*, Smith College Studies in History, vol. 42 (Northampton, 1956); Hau, "Die Bildung des Arztes," 13:175f.

[184]The bloodletters were rarely full-fledged doctors, and their status appears quite ambiguous; see Goitein, *A Mediterranean Society*, 1:91, and R. Brunschvig, "Métiers vils en Islam," *Studia Islamica* 16 (1962):4–60.

[185]See Temkin, "Medical Ethics and Honoraria in Late Antiquity," pp. 6–26; Fridolf Kudlien, "Medicine as a 'Liberal Art' and the Question of the Physician's Income," *Journal of the History of Medicine and Allied Sciences* 31 (1976):448–459; and Bullough, *The Development of Medicine*, pp. 29–31.

[186]Kudlien, "Medicine as a 'Liberal Art'," p. 448. See also idem, *Der griechische Arzt im Zeitalter des Hellenismus. Seine Stellung in Staat und Gesellschaft* (Mainz, 1979).

[187]Lapidus, *Muslim Cities*, pp. 96–102; Goitein, *A Mediterranean Society*, 1:82f.; see also *Vorlesungen*, p. 83.

[188]Lapidus, *Muslim Cities*, p. 96. The office of *ra'īs aṭ-ṭibb* does not appear to have been comparable to either the public physician in antiquity (see Cohn-Haft, *The Public Physician*) or the community doctor in Renaissance Italy (see C. M. Cipolla, *Public Health and the Medical Profession in the Renaissance* [Cambridge, 1976], p. 87 et passim).

medieval physician's status was more contingent upon his background and his nexus of personal relationships than upon his professional standing.[189]

The physician's learning was a source of prestige. Rulers surrounded themselves with educated doctors both to insure the best medical treatment and to win a reputation as patrons of ancient science. The physician was often called *ḥakīm*, which could mean a wise man or philosopher,[190] and, as such, was regarded as a natural leader. Christians and, especially, Jews in the Islamic world shared this respect for the physician's book-learning.[191] Consequently, Christian and Jewish doctors were invariably leaders of their communities. Regarding the latter, Goitein has observed that "an almost unbroken succession of medical men represented both the actual and official leadership of the Jews of Egypt and the adjacent countries during the whole of the High Middle Ages and far beyond."[192]

Payment for medical services varied according to the status and need of both the doctor and the patient. While the chroniclers report enormous salaries and gifts given to famous aulic physicians, it is very difficult to determine the pay of the ordinary doctor.[193] At the same time, Islam as well as Christianity and Judaism strongly enjoined the charitable treatment of the poor.[194] Ibn Riḍwān personifies the compromise between the Galenic ideal of the philosopher-physician and the practical exigencies of the self-made man: a physician should cultivate an aristocratic indifference to payment that was nonetheless expected.[195] According to Ibn Riḍwān, a man should study medicine

[189]Cf. Gerhard Baader, "Gesellschaft, Wirtschaft und ärztlichen Stand im frühen und hohen Mittelalter," *Medizinhistorisches Journal* 14 (1979):176–185.

[190]See Dimitri Gutas, "Classical Arabic Wisdom Literature: Nature and Scope," *Journal of the American Oriental Society* 101 (1981):51f., 66; *Vorlesungen*, p. 9.

[191]Goitein, *A Mediterranean Society*, 2:241, 345–348.

[192]Ibid., p. 245. See also Moshe Perlmann, "Notes on the Position of Jewish Physicians in Medieval Muslim Countries," *Israel Oriental Studies* 2 (1972):315–319.

[193]Eliyahu Ashtor, *Histoire des prix et des salaries dans l'orient medieval* (Paris, 1969), pp. 68ff., 94, 228, 263f., 378, 532f.; Goitein, *A Mediterranean Society*, 2:256f.; Issa, *Histoire des Bimaristans*, pp. 13–16; Makdisi, *The Rise of Colleges*, p. 163. The subject of medical fees in Islamic medicine has not been systematically investigated.

[194]Rosenthal, "The Physician in Medieval Muslim Society," pp. 487–489; Ibn al-Jazzār may be added to those who refused to enter the service of important personages, described by Rosenthal. See also Schipperges, "Aus dem Alltag arabischer Ärzte," p. 1931, and Elgood, *A Medical History of Persia*, pp. 267–271.

[195]Kudlien, "Medicine as a 'Liberal Art,' " pp. 455–459.

with the intent of acquiring the art and not money, but this did not mean that he would lose the chance of making money:

> When a doctor treats the ailments of the wealthy and they are in severe pain, he can make what financial conditions he likes, and when he knows that his patients will carry out their bargain, it is then his responsibility to produce the cure. The money that he earns should be spent on such useful ends as befits him. I mean on the assistance of relatives, charitable acts and the purchase of drugs suitable for curing disease. Nor should he refrain under any circumstances from tending the poor and associating with them.[196]

While some doctors became affluent and influential, others were less successful.[197] As an occupational group, physicians were renowned for being greedy, as Ibn Riḍwān's criticisms of his colleagues and his own autobiography attest. Their interests were frequently not restricted to medicine. They often engaged in commerce and real estate and were sometimes active as judges and religious scholars.[198] The successful physician might, therefore, achieve a high social status through his wealth, education, and association with the rich and powerful.[199]

The study of medical science was not confined to doctors but was an intellectual discipline that formed part of the "liberal education" of a well-educated man. In the Hellenistic tradition, the teaching of medical theory was often entirely divorced from its practice; there was, however, in the Islamic era, according to Elinor Liber, "an increasing tendency to present the ideas of Galen in a manner specifically adapted to the needs of the practicing physician."[200] Nevertheless, physicians in medieval society could not claim a technical expertise or skill that went

[196] M. C. Lyons, "The *Kitāb an-Nāfi'* of 'Alī ibn Riḍwān," *Islamic Quarterly*, 6 (1961):68–69. Martin Levey's summary, "Medical Ethics of Medieval Islam," p. 12, is instructive: "In regard to the physician's fee, al-Ruhāwī states that he should earn an amount sufficient that he need not be occupied with any other occupation than medicine. The earnings should be large enough so that the physician may afford marriage, the proper food, garments, and housing so that his progeny may be taught the art of medicine. Al-Ruhāwī advocates that the wealthy be just in their fees so that the benefit of the art may be available both for the strong and the weak. Should the wealthy not cooperate, then the physician must turn to other vocations than medicine. Then it is not only the poor but also the wealthy who must lose."

[197] "Most [doctors] chose the practice of medicine as a career that would provide for their livelihood, presumably on a level that by and large did not exceed that of the average shopkeeper" (Rosenthal, "The Physician in Medieval Muslim Society," p. 484). See also Goitein, *A Mediterranean Society*, 1:78.

[198] See the numerous examples given by Goitein in ibid., p. 89 et passim.

[199] See Issa, *Histoire des Bimaristans*, p. 12.

[200] Lieber, "Galen in Hebrew," pp. 169f., 174.

much beyond that of an educated layman. In the long run, it was technical competence that would be the decisive factor in the eventual emergence of the medical profession in the modern sense of the word.[201]

The final course of a medieval patient's treatment was decided by family members rather than by a doctor. Families commonly sought the advice of more than one doctor in serious or chronic cases. Consultations often did not include a physical examination, especially if the patient were female. Medical care was the responsibility of the head of the household, who might be expected to negotiate the treatment from a number of recommendations. This duty of the *paterfamilias* surely goes back to antiquity.[202] As in ancient Rome, it was also customary for the family of the patient to demand copies of the doctor's prescription, so that in the event of the patient's death the doctor's responsibility could be determined.[203]

The inadequacies of Galenic medicine, the lack of rigorous organization, and the expense of professional care moved people to use a wide range of beliefs and practices. Medical pluralism clearly existed in medieval Islamic society and, unlike modern medicine, it directly reflected its social context.[204] As Vincent Crapanzano has remarked about modern Morocco, there was "no single, socially chartered therapeutic system with final authority."[205] In this, medieval medicine followed traditions of late antiquity, of which Peter Brown has observed:

> The individual found himself faced with a choice of therapeutic systems; and, in making his or her choice, the patient would appeal to criteria that reflected a precise social milieu. For the patient would depend on a "support group" of relatives and acquaintances for information about healing and, more generally, would draw on shared attitudes that would designate one therapeutic system rather than another as congruent with the expectations of the group on that occasion.[206]

[201]See Bullough, *The Development of Medicine*. Concerning the modern development of the medical profession in Egypt, see Amira el-A. Sonbol, "The Creation of a Medical Profession in Egypt During the Nineteenth Century: A Study in Modernization," Ph.D. dissertation, Georgetown University (1981).

[202]See John Scarborough, *Roman Medicine* (Ithaca, 1976), p. 19. et passim.

[203]Elgood, *A Medical History of Persia*, p. 265; *Vorlesungen*, p. 51.

[204]For example, several theories for mental illness coexisted with one another in ancient-medieval society; see Bennett Simon, *Mind and Madness in Ancient Greece* (Ithaca, 1978), p. 34f. In the area of nonsomatic illness, medical pluralism has generally persisted to the present day.

[205]V. Crapanzano, *The Ḥamadsha: A Study in Moroccan Ethnopyschiatry* (Berkeley, 1973), p. 133. See, for example, Motoko Katakura, *Bedouin Village* (Tokyo, 1977), pp. 65–69.

[206]Peter Brown, *The Cult of the Saints* (Chicago, 1981), p. 114f.

A major determinant of such attitudes was religion. The relationship of professional medicine to the Muslim religion was ambiguous, if not precarious, because of the fundamental conflict between science and theology.[207] As Franz Rosenthal has said: "It was not altogether possible or desirable for physicians to fit themselves into the dominant religious and legal framework of Islam. They tried not to sell their souls, and they kept medicine, in the words of the eleventh-century Christian physician Ibn Buṭlān 'the most useful of crafts and the most profitable of enterprises,' that is, the craft and science most beneficial for individuals as well as a society somewhat ambivalent about the place it had to assign to it."[208] Tension between professional medicine and Islam appears to have increased markedly during Ibn Riḍwān's lifetime as *ṣūfism* or Islamic mysticism grew in popularity and respectability. Ṣūfism emphasized the view that all health and illness depended on God alone. It is not surprising, therefore, that extraordinary healing powers were imputed to Muslim saints.[209] Prominent *ṣūfī* thinkers, such as al-Ghazālī (d. A.D. 1111), rejected the claims of professional medicine, particularly by denying the basic scientific principle of causation.[210] In turn, the ṣūfīs were strongly criticized by others, such as Ibn al-Jawzī, the famous Ḥanbalī theologian who died in A.D. 1200; Ibn al-Jawzī rejected the asceticism of the ṣūfīs and argued that the Prophet himself had sanctioned medicine.[211] Thus, Islam might be interpreted as being supportive of medical science, a charitable and laudatory pursuit, as exemplified by the life of Ibn al-Jazzār.[212]

[207]See Franz Rosenthal, "The Defense of Medicine in the Medieval Muslim World," *BHM* 43 (1969):519–532; G. E. von Grunebaum, *Islam: Essays in the Nature and Growth of a Cultural Tradition* (London, 1961), pp. 111–126; J. C. Bürgel, "Die wissenschaftliche Medizin im Kräftefeld der islamischen Kultur," *Bustan* 8 (1967):9–19; idem, "Secular and Religious Features of Medieval Arabic Medicine," p. 46; *Vorlesungen*, pp. 87, 108–132; on the broader issue of the relationship between the ancient sciences and Islamic orthodoxy, see the references in Schacht and Meyerhof, p. 9. In Christendom the conflict between medicine and religion was more clearly focused because of the strong belief in supernatural healing based on the New Testament. See Darrel W. Amundsen, "Medicine and Faith in Early Christianity," *BHM* 56 (1982):326–350; idem and G. B. Ferngren, "Medicine and Religion: Early Christianity Through the Middle Ages," in *Health/Medicine and the Faith Traditions*, ed. M. E. Marty and K. L. Vaux (Philadelphia, 1982), pp. 93–131.

[208]Rosenthal, "The Physician in Medieval Muslim Society," p. 491.

[209]On the veneration of saints, see Goldziher, *Muslim Studies*, 2:255–341. See, for example, Rudolf Kriss and Hubert Kriss-Heinrich, *Volksglaube im Bereich des Islam*, (Wiesbaden, 1960)1:35f.

[210]See *Vorlesungen*, pp. 111–113, 123–127; *EI²*, s.v. "al-Ghazālī" (W. Montgomery Watt).

[211]See *Vorlesungen*, p. 127f.; *EI²*, s.v. "Ibn al-Djawzī" (H. Laoust); *MI*, p. 186.

[212]See also Levey, "Medical Ethics of Medieval Islam," p. 14 (with references to ar-Ruhāwī's text).

Medieval medical beliefs and practices were, then, neither monolithic nor static.

Despite these difficulties, medicine was perhaps the most cosmopolitan profession in the Islamic world. Christians and Jews had played a major role in the early development of Islamic medicine, and their share in medical practice during the early Middle Ages was considerable.[213] With the numerous conversions of non-Muslims during the Fāṭimid period, however, the number of Christians and Jews declined; indeed, Ibn Riḍwān and Ibn al-Jazzār reflect the growing ascendency of Muslim practitioners.[214] Nevertheless, on the basis of the Geniza documents, Goitein has been able to depict the detailed workings of the medical profession in the Jewish community in Egypt during the eleventh to twelfth centuries A.D.[215] His description is particularly valuable because it shows that the medical profession transcended the barriers of religion, language, and country.[216] Further study has shown that the Greek tradition of medicine served as a common intellectual framework for professional doctors throughout the medieval Mediterranean world.[217] The dispute between Ibn Riḍwān and Ibn al-Jazzār is a good example of the cosmopolitanism of Galenic medicine.

The medical profession in Islamic society was open to rich and poor, Muslim and non-Muslim. The course of study was not standardized, although it relied very heavily on the works of Galen; nor was the profession closely supervised. The parameters of medical activity were wide indeed and greatly dependent on the status and resources of the doctor and patient. Professional medicine was, however, a sophisticated and respected vocation that fostered and developed the sciences of antiquity. The work of Ibn Riḍwān is a good illustration of what

[213]See N. A. Stillman, *The Jews of Arab Lands* (Philadelphia, 1979), pp. 71–72; A. S. Tritton, *The Caliphs and Their Non-Muslim Subjects* (London, 1970 repr.), pp. 155–164.

[214]See R. W. Bulliet, *Conversion to Islam in the Medieval Period* (Cambridge, Mass., 1979), pp. 94–103; Max Meyerhof, "Notes sur quelques médicins juif égyptiens qui se sont illustrés à l'époque arabe," *Isis* 12 (1929):116–117; idem, "Medieval Jewish Physicians in the Near East from Arabic Sources," *Isis* 28 (1938):432–460.

[215]Goitein, *A Mediterranean Society*, 2:240–261 et passim.

[216]This is not to say that there was not discriminatory legislation prohibiting Muslims from seeking the services of non-Muslim doctors and pharmacists. But as Goitein has asserted, "no discriminatory ruling was less observed than this prohibition." (S. D. Goitein, *Jews and Arabs*, 3d ed. [New York, 1974], p. 70f.) In the later Middle Ages, however, the popular agitation against Jewish and Christian physicians increased and was endorsed by Muslim governments; see Perlmann, "Notes on the Position of Jewish Physicians," pp. 316–319.

[217]Petry, *The Civilian Elite*, p. 79; see also the description of the status of the Jewish physician in the Byzantine Empire in Sharf, *The Universe of Shabbetai Donnolo*, pp. 106–110.

Rosenthal has said about Islamic medicine generally: "Misguided mental acrobatics and arbitrary abstractions are not entirely absent from Arabic medicine, but, on the whole, it lures the student with an entirely satisfactory combination of profound intellectual concern and intimate contact with the realities facing the individual and the society in which he lived."[218]

Egypt in the Fāṭimid Period

The persistence of Galenism as an influential medical system in medieval Islamic society attests to the continuance not only of an intellectual tradition, upheld by professional physicians, but also of social conditions that existed in late antiquity. Galenic medicine survived because the urbanism of late Hellenistic society also survived, though transformed in significant ways. Only the design of the intricate tessellation was changed, not the technique or materials. The medieval Islamic city was economically viable and supported a pluralistic society characterized by its literacy, religiosity, and social tolerance.[219] Cairo at the time of Ibn Riḍwān was such a city.

Ibn Riḍwān lived in Egypt his entire life, and *On the Prevention of Bodily Ills in Egypt* is devoted to the contemporary conditions of that country. During this time, Egypt was ruled by the Fāṭimid dynasty, which had originated in North Africa at the beginning of the tenth century A.D.[220] The Fāṭimids conquered Egypt in A.D. 969 and estab-

[218]Rosenthal, "The Physician in Medieval Muslim Society," pp. 476–477.

[219]Cf. John Boswell, *Christianity, Social Tolerance, and Homosexuality* (Chicago, 1980), pp. 61–136; A. L. Udovitch, "The Jews and Islam in the High Middle Ages: A Case of the Muslim View of Differences," *Gli Ebrei nell'Alto Medioevo (Settimane di Studio del Centro Italiano di Studi sull'Alto Medioevo*, vol. 26) (Spoleto, 1980), 2:655–711.

[220]For historical surveys of the period, see: *EI*², s.v. "Fāṭimids" (M. Canard); H. F. Wüstenfeld, *Geschichte der Fatimiden-Califen* (Göttingen, 1881); C. H. Becker, *Beiträge zur Geschichte Ägyptens unter dem Islam* (Philadelphia, 1977 repr.)—see *Tome quarantième de la chronique d'Égypte de Musabbihī*, ed. A. F. Sayyid and T. Bianquis, pt. 1 (Cairo, 1978); De Lacy E. O'Leary, *A Short History of the Fatimid Khalifate* (London, 1923); Bernard Lewis, "Egypt and Syria," *The Cambridge History of Islam* (Cambridge, 1970), 1:175–201; idem, "An Interpretation of Fāṭimid History," *Colloque international sur l'histoire du Caire* (Cairo, 1972), pp. 287–295; G. E. von Grunebaum, "The Nature of the Fāṭimid Achievement," ibid., pp. 199–215; S. Lane-Poole, *A History of Egypt in the Middle Ages* (London, 1968 repr.), pp. 92–189; H. I. Ḥasan, *al-Fāṭimīyūn fī Miṣr* (Cairo, 1932); Gaston Wiet, *L'Égypte arabe, de la conquête arab à la conquête ottomane 642–1517 de l'ère chrétiene*, in Gabriel Hanotaux, ed., *Histoire de la nation égyptienne* (Paris, 1937), 4:179–254; idem, *Cairo* (Norman, Oklahoma, 1964), pp. 15–42; idem, *L'Égypte musulmane de la conquête arabe à la conquête ottomane*, in *Précis de l'histoire d'Égypte*, ed. M. Z. al-Ibrāshī (Cairo, 1932), 2:173–216; Goitein, *A Mediterranean Society*, 1:29–42; idem, *Letters of Medieval Jewish Traders* (Princeton, 1973); Hodgson, *The Venture of Islam* 2:21–28; and Thierry Bianquis, "Un Crisis frumentaire dans l'Égypte

lished Cairo as the imperial capital. At its height, the Fāṭimid empire encompassed North Africa, Sicily, Palestine, Syria, the Red Sea coast of Africa, Yemen, and the Ḥijāz. The dynasty survived until A.D. 1171, when Saladin put an end to their rule.

During Ibn Riḍwān's lifetime, Egypt evolved from a quiescent province within the 'Abbāsid Empire into an independent state that challenged Baghdad for political and religious leadership. For the Fāṭimids were not just another military dynasty but headed a great religious movement that sought to reform Islam. The Fāṭimid caliphs claimed descent from the Prophet Muḥammad through his daughter, Fāṭimah,[221] and were exponents of the Ismā'īlīyah,[222] a sect that ascribed supernatural faculties to its leaders. The Fāṭimid movement was similar to that of the 'Abbāsids two centuries before, but it was ultimately less successful in reviving the Islamic *oikoumene* under the leadership of a descendent of the Prophet. Yet, the Fāṭimids did create a theocracy, at least in theory, in which the caliph in Cairo headed both the state and the Ismā'īlī sect. From the early eleventh century A.D., theocratic rule turned into military autocracy, with a corresponding decline in religious fervor.

The period from A.D. 969 to 1069 has been called the "high-water mark of medieval Egypt" because of its artistic creativity and economic prosperity. The efflorescence of Egyptian society was due to the stability and probity of its administration, population growth,[223] the influx of gold from the mines of Nubia, and the rich revenues from taxes, dues and tribute. Despite such taxation, the Fāṭimids promoted free trade and fostered the expansion of international commerce in the Mediterranean Sea, where the Christian powers were relatively weak, and in the Red Sea. This trade was effectively extended to Europe and India for the first time. Professor Goitein accounts for the economic "miracle" of the Fāṭimid period by the favorable situation of Egypt and Syria as

---

Fatimide," *Journal of the Economic and Social History of the Orient* 23 (1980):67–101. For further bibliographical information, see Jean Sauvaget, *Introduction to the History of the Middle East*, 2d ed., by Claude Cahen (Berkeley, 1965), pp. 146–150.

[221]See *EI*², s.v. "Fāṭima" (L. Veccia Vaglieri).

[222]See *EI*², s.v. "Ismā'īliyya" (W. Madelung); for further background, see S. H. M. Jafri, *Origins and Early Development of Shī'a Islam* (London, 1979) and Heinz Halm, *Kosmologie und Heilslehre der frühen Ismā'īlīya*, in *Abhandlungen für die Kunde des Morgenländes*, 44/1 (Wiesbaden, 1978). See also Samuel Stern, "Cairo as the Centre of the Ismā'īlī Movement," *Colloque international sur l'histoire du Caire*, pp. 437–450.

[223]M. Clerget has estimated the population of the capital in the 5/11th century as not less than 300,000 (*Le Caire, Étude de géographie urbaine et d'histoire économique* [Cairo, 1934], 1:239).

distribution centers and producers of goods for the growing economic needs of Europe.[224] Recent scholarship has also emphasized the growth of the Egyptian textile industry as the major cause of Fāṭimid prosperity.[225] This sanguine view of the economy should be tempered, however, by the evidence of an increasing number of famines and rebellions in Egypt during the latter half of the eleventh century A.D. The affluence of the Fāṭimid elite belied a fragile domestic economy.

The Fāṭimid court was directly responsible for the development of luxury articles, particularly textiles, metalwork, glass, and ceramics, which reflect a refined and cosmopolitan taste. The Fāṭimids adorned their new capital with mosques, mausoleums, and palaces.[226] Perhaps the act of most lasting importance was the establishment of al-Azhar Mosque as an intellectual center of Islam. Their patronage was also largely responsible for the intense intellectual and literary activity within the capital. The caliphs themselves cultivated poetry and encouraged the study of religion, philosophy, and scientific learning generally. Professor Canard asserts that "the Fāṭimid period is characterized by a burst of intellectual curiosity analogous to that of the 18th century in Europe."[227] Thus, Egypt afforded a congenial environment for distinguished scholars such as the mathematician Ibn al-Haytham,[228] the astronomer Ibn Yūnus,[229] and the physicians, Muḥammad ibn Aḥmad at-Tamīmī,[230] Mūsā ibn Al'azār

[224]Goitein, *A Mediterranean Society*, 1:33.

[225]G. Frantz-Murphy, "A New Interpretation of the Economic History of Medieval Egypt. The Role of the Textile Industry 245–567/868–1171," *Journal of the Economic and Social History of the Orient*, 24 (1981):274–297.

[226]See *EI*², s.v. "Fāṭimid Art" (G. Marcais); Oleg Grabar, "Imperial and Urban Art in Islam: The Subject Matter of Fāṭimid Art," *Colloque International sur l'histoire du Caire*, pp. 173–189; Atıl, *Art of the Arab World*, pp. 39–49; Jonathan M. Bloom, "The Mosque of al-Hākim in Cairo," *Muqarnas* (1983):15–36; Caroline Williams, "The Cult of 'Alid Saints in the Fatimid Monuments of Cairo, Part I: The Mosque of al-Aqma," *Muqarnas* 37–52. Al-Maqrīzī, *al-Mawā'iẓ wal-i'tibār bi-dhikr al-khiṭaṭ wal-āthār* (hereafter referred to as *al-Khiṭaṭ*) (Būlāq, 1854), 1:408f. (cf. al-Qalqashandī, *Ṣubḥ al-a'shā* [Cairo, 1914–28], 3:475f.) describes the extraordinary wealth of the treasuries of the Fāṭimid caliphs, indicating the extent of the luxury industries.

[227]*EI*², s.v. "Fāṭimids" (p. 861).

[228]He was a prominent and prolific Arab mathematician and physicist, born in Baṣra ca. 354/965 and died in Cairo in 430/1039. See *EI*², s.v. "Ibn al-Haytham" (J. Vernet).

[229]One of the most prominent Muslim astronomers, who died in Cairo in 399/1009; his *az-Zīj al-kabīr* constituted the most extensive list of medieval astronomical observations presently known. See *EI*², s.v. "Ibn Yūnus" (B. R. Goldstein); David King, "The Astronomical Works of Ibn Yūnus," Ph.D. dissertation, Yale University, 1972.

[230]At-Tamīmī came from Jerusalem to Egypt in 360/970 and entered the service of Ya'qūb ibn Killīs, wazīr of the first Fāṭimid caliphs; he died in 370/980. See *MI*, pp. 269–270, 315, 332.

al-Isrā'īlī and his sons,[231] Manṣūr ibn Sahlān ibn Muqashshir,[232] as well as Ibn Riḍwān. Christians and Jews played a conspicuous part in this scientific activity as well as in the administration of the empire. Except during the highly eccentric reign of Caliph al-Ḥākim (A.D. 996–1021),[233] the tolerance of Christians and Jews was a salient feature of the dynasty.[234]

Cairo was both the symbol and the center of the new regime, but the new capital was only a northern extension of earlier Muslim settlements, which together formed the greater metropolitan area that Ibn Riḍwān describes.[235] In A.D. 641 the Arab army led by 'Amr ibn al-'Āṣ[236] had captured the Byzantine fortress of Babylon[237] on the east bank of the Nile; it was well situated at the apex of the Delta, commanding the interior of the country. Nearby, 'Amr established a mili-

[231]M. Steinschneider, *Die arabische Literatur der Juden* (Hildesheim, 1964 repr.), no. 55, pp. 96–97 (Moses b. Elasar); Leclerc, *Histoire de la médecine arabe*, 1:403–404.

[232]Ibid., pp. 405–406; Ibn Abī Uṣaybi'ah, *'Uyūn*, 2:89.

[233]Harsh discriminatory measures against Christians and Jews were a striking feature of al-Ḥākim's rule. While such measures were not unprecedented, they were unusual in their severity; yet, they were not strictly enforced. Moreover, this intolerance should be seen within the context of other discriminatory actions by this capricious, if not insane, monarch. See *EI*², s.v. "al-Ḥākim Bi-Amr Allāh" (M. Canard).

[234]See Ibn Ḥawqal, 1:159.

[235]There are a number of descriptions of greater Cairo during the Fāṭimid period by Arabic chroniclers, travelers, and modern historians. With regard to the medieval accounts, see: al-Maqrīzī, *al-Khiṭaṭ*, p. 330ff.; *Description de l'Égypte par Ibn Doukmak*, ed. K. Vollers (Cairo, 1893); al-Iṣṭakhrī, *Masālik va mamālik* (Tehran, 1961), pp. 52–57; al-Muqaddasī, *Aḥsan at-taqāsīm*, ed. de Goeje (Leiden, 1906/1909), pp. 193–200; Naṣīr-i Khusraw, pp. 124–163; Ibn Ḥawqal, s.v. "Fostat;" al-Idrīsī, *Opus geographicum*, ed. E. Cerulli et al. (Napoli-Rome, 1972), 3:322–326; and Else Reitemeyers, *Beschreibung Aegyptens im Mittelalter* (Leipzig, 1903), pp. 162–238 for a compilation of these descriptions. Accounts of the city by modern scholars include the following: Clerget, *Le Caire*, 1:103–143 (for the climate of Cairo, see especially 1:60–87); U. Monneret de Villard, *Ricerche sulla topografia di Qasr aš-Šam'*, *Bull. Soc. Géog. Égypte* 12 (1923–24):205–232; 13 (1924–25):73–94; J. L. Abu-Lughod, *Cairo: 1001 Years of the City Victorious* (Princeton, 1971), pp. 13–27; *EI*¹, s.v. "Cairo" (C. Becker); *EI*², s.v. "al-Fusṭāṭ" (J. Jomier) and "al-Ḳāhira" (M. Rogers); K. A. C. Creswell, *The Muslim Architecture of Egypt*, 2 vols. (Oxford, 1952/1959); P. Ravisse, *Essai sur l'histoire et sur la topographie du Caire d'après Makrizi*, Mémoires de l'Institut Français d'Archéologie Orientale 3 (1887):409–480; P. Casanova, *Description historique et topographie de l'Égypte*, ibid., 13 (1906):1–328; idem, *Essai de reconstitution topographique du la ville d'al-Fousṭaṭ ou Miṣr*, ibid., 35 (1919):1–110; G. Salmon, *Études sur la topographie du Caire*, ibid., 7 (1902):1–135; S. J. Staffa, *Conquest and Fusion: The Social Evolution of Cairo, A.D. 642–1850* (Leiden, 1977), pp. 13–83. See especially the preliminary reports of George T. Scanlon on the American excavation of al-Fusṭāṭ in *The Journal of the American Research Center in Egypt*, beginning with 4 (1965):7–30 to date, and the summary of his work in "Fusṭāṭ: Archaeological Reconsiderations," *Colloque international sur l'histoire du Caire*, pp. 415–428. The earlier excavation of al-Fusṭāṭ is reported in 'Alī Baghgat and A. Gabriel, *Fouilles d'al-Fusṭāṭ* (Paris, 1921) and in *Kitāb Ḥafrīyāt al-Fusṭāṭ* (Cairo, 1928).

[236]See *EI*², s.v. " 'Amr ibn al-'Āṣ" (A. J. Wensinck).

[237]See *EI*², s.v. "Bābalyūn" (C. H. Becker).

tary encampment named al-Fusṭāṭ. The origin of the name is uncertain, but it may be derived from the Arabic *fusṭāṭ*, denoting the "tent" that 'Amr pitched during the siege of Babylon, or from the Byzantine Greek *phossaton*, meaning camp or encampment. The capital was soon transferred from Alexandria to al-Fusṭāṭ, and the settlement gradually developed from a coalescence of the army camp with the nucleus of Babylon.

Al-Fusṭāṭ was built beside the Nile, which at that time followed a more easterly course, and partly on high desert ground that extended for more than four kilometers from north to south. It slowly assumed a more permanent urban character, centering around the Mosque of 'Amr. In the early eighth century A.D., al-Fusṭāṭ expanded and served both administrative and commercial functions. With the accession of the 'Abbāsid regime in A.D. 750, a new suburb called al-'Askar was built just north of al-Fusṭāṭ, and governmental functions were transferred to this new region. This princely town was well planned compared with the original establishment of al-Fusṭāṭ. It also initiated a pattern of urban development northward along the Nile: successive dynasties created a series of planned and well-constructed cities which, over the centuries, slowly fused to form an elongated urban settlement. Such was the case with the founding of al-Qaṭā'i', north of al-'Askar, in A.D. 870 by Aḥmad ibn Ṭūlūn, the independent governor of Egypt, but the Fāṭimids made their most significant extension of the region by establishing the princely city of Cairo. In A.D. 974, the Fāṭimid caliph entered his capital, which was to rival Baghdad.

Al-Fusṭāṭ remained the dominant center for transportation, industry, and commerce, despite the creation of Cairo, which was largely a royal refuge. In fact, al-Fusṭāṭ was invigorated by the advent of the Fāṭimids and appears to have reached the apogee of its growth, being sufficiently removed from the intrigues of the palace and the turbulence of the soldiery. A few years before the birth of Ibn Riḍwān, al-Muqaddasī described al-Fusṭāṭ. He remarked on the five- and seven-story buildings which were "like minarets," and the population that was as "thick as locusts." The most densely settled region was still in the neighborhood of the Mosque of 'Amr. He rated al-Fusṭāṭ superior to Baghdad, and only cursorily described the new city of Cairo. Al-Muqaddasī also mentioned the outlying regions of the city. Specifically, he said that the town of al-Gīzah, the birthplace of Ibn

Riḍwān, had a mosque and a larger population than the island of ar-Rawḍah in the middle of the Nile.[238]

Ibn Ḥawqal, a contemporary of al-Muqaddasī, visited Egypt in the mid-tenth century A.D., and included a description of the country in his geography of the Islamic world. Apart from his sympathy for the Fāṭimid regime, Ibn Ḥawqal, as a merchant, was observant about the economic conditions in Egypt.[239] He depicts al-Fusṭāṭ as a great city, about one-third the area of Baghdad, with a large population. "Its quarters possess large open spaces, enormous markets, impressive commercial centers, extensive private lands, besides a splendid exterior, a sympathetic atmosphere, flowering gardens and parks that are always verdant, whatever the season." The settlement of Arab tribes in distinct quarters in al-Fusṭāṭ was no longer conspicuous.[240] The buildings were as high as seven stories, each containing as many as two hundred inhabitants. Most were built of crude brick, and their ground floor was not usually occupied.[241]

During Ibn Riḍwān's lifetime, Cairo grew considerably, and the Persian traveler Nāṣir-i Khusraw wrote a vivid account of the metropolis when he visited it in A.D. 1046–1049.[242] Cairo was divided into distinct quarters, according to the racial groups that constituted the Fāṭimid army.[243] The numerous houses were built chiefly of brick, so carefully joined that they looked like squared stone, and were often five and six stories high. They were separated by well-cultivated gardens and orchards that were irrigated by wells and waterwheels. All the houses in Cairo were owned by the caliph, and the rents were collected every month. The shops, baths, and caravansaries were also his property. The old wall of the city was no longer standing in A.D. 1046, and

[238]Al-Muqaddisī, *Aḥsan at-taqāsim*, pp. 193–200.

[239]See *EI*², s.v. "Ibn Ḥawḳal" (A. Miquel).

[240]R. Guest, "The Foundation of Fusṭaṭ and the Khittahs of That Town," *Journal of the Royal Asiatic Society* (1907), pp. 49–83. See especially Wladyslaw Kubiak, *Al Fusṭaṭ, Its Foundation and Early Urban Development*, in *Rozprawy Uniwersytetu Warszawskiego*, no. 179 (Warsaw, 1982).

[241]Ibn Ḥawqal, 1:144–145. The usual building material in medieval Cairo was sun-dried or baked brick; stonework became common only at the end of the 8/14th century (Clerget, *Le Caire*, 1:294–296). See also L. I. Conrad, "The Plague in the Early Medieval Near East," Ph.D. dissertation, Princeton University, 1981, pp. 368–371.

[242]Nāṣir-i Khusraw, pp. 110–162. See Henry Corbin, "Nāṣir-i Khusrau and Iranian Ismāʿīlism," *The Cambridge History of Iran*, ed. R. N. Frye (Cambridge, 1975), 4:520–542.

[243]See Clerget, *Le Caire*, 1:128–130, 214, 262ff.

the second wall had not yet been built, but Nāṣir-i Khusraw was struck by the high blank walls of the houses and still more by the Fāṭimid palace, which stood in the middle of the city. He briefly described the ornate interior of the palace, especially the famous throne room. It contained a golden throne decorated with hunting scenes and inscriptions, which was ascended by silver steps. A golden lattice screen surrounded the throne, and the room was furnished with luxurious carpets and tapestries. He was told that the palace contained 30,000 people, including 12,000 servants, and that the guard every night consisted of 1,000 horse and foot soldiers.

The potable water of the city was supplied by the Nile. It was carried by camels from the riverbank in large containers made of animal skins. The number of camels that transported the water for Cairo and al-Fusṭāṭ was estimated at about 52,000. The water was also carried by donkeys and men into the narrow streets of the capital. The well water near the Nile was reportedly sweet, but it became progressively brackish as one withdrew from the river.

According to the Persian traveler, al-Fusṭāṭ was separated from Cairo by a little less than a mile, and the intervening area was covered with villas and gardens. The densely populated area of the city was shaped like a right triangle. Its angles were marked by the three principal gates of the city, while the bank of the Nile formed its hypotenuse.[244] Al-Fusṭāṭ looked "like a mountain" when Nāṣir-i Khusraw saw it from a distance. Some of its houses were seven to fourteen stories high, each standing on a space of thirty cubits square and capable of holding 350 people.

Al-Fusṭāṭ had seven congregational mosques (as compared with eight in Cairo). The most remarkable was the venerable Mosque of 'Amr in the center of the bazaar. It had been recently repaired when Nāṣir-i Khusraw saw it, and he noted the fine marble decoration and inscriptions, the great silver chandelier, the thick matting on the floor, and the numerous lamps that burned throughout the night. Aside from religious services, the mosque was busy with Qur'ān readers, teachers, students, judges, and professional scribes.

On the north side of the mosque was the Market of Lamps, which Nāṣir-i Khusraw believed was unequaled in any country. A number of markets and streets in al-Fusṭāṭ were covered and were, consequently, lit by lamps during the day. In the markets he saw works of art

[244]Ibid., p. 134; see the map of al-Fusṭāṭ, p. 118 (fig. 27).

and rarities from all parts of the world, such as beautiful inlaid work, cut rock crystal, and elephant tusks, skins, and exotic birds from Africa. He was astonished by the profusion of fruits and vegetables in the bazaar and by the abundance of honey and sugar. Nāṣir-i Khusraw described the pottery made in al-Fusṭāṭ, which he said was so delicate that you could see your hand through it; most likely it was a local imitation of Chinese porcelain. He also remarked on the metallic lusterware (which is still found in fragments on the mounds that now occupy the former site of the city) and on the fine transparent green glass made there.

The commercial activity in al-Fusṭāṭ was quite apparent, and the number of *khāns* or warehouses was reckoned at 200. The shopkeepers sold "at a fixed price," and if they cheated, they were put on a camel and paraded through the streets, ringing a bell and confessing their faults. The merchants, including the druggists, sold goods prepackaged in glass bottles, ceramic pots, and paper, showing that one could trust the quality of the material they contained. Tradespeople rode donkeys, which were for hire in every street and were estimated to number about 50,000. Only soldiers and those attached to the army rode horses. Thus, the Persian traveler found al-Fusṭāṭ in a state of the utmost tranquillity and prosperity. Security was so great that the shops of the merchants, jewelers, and money changers were left unlocked, except for a cord or net stretched in front of the shop; apparently, no one had the audacity to steal.

Al-Fusṭāṭ extended along the Nile, where, according to our traveler, there were more boats than at Baghdad or Basra. On its banks were a large number of kiosks and pavillions where water was drawn for the city. Nāṣir-i Khusraw mentioned particularly the large Damascene copper vessels used for the water. Facing al-Fusṭāṭ from the middle of the Nile was ar-Rawḍah Island, which was connected to the city by a bridge of thirty-six boats. On the opposite bank of the Nile was al-Gīzah, which was joined to ar-Rawdah Island by a ferry. Every Sunday a market in al-Gīzah attracted a large concourse of people.

The wealth and security that Nāṣir-i Khusraw observed in Cairo and al-Fusṭāṭ was promoted by the caliph al-Mustanṣir, who reigned from A.D. 1036 to 1094. Our traveler saw the caliph perform the ancient ceremony of cutting the dike of the Red Sea Canal (Khalīj Canal) outside Cairo to mark the annual flooding of the Delta. It was a day of great display and festivities, in which the caliph appeared with an impressive cortege. Following large contingents of the army and cavalry, which were richly equipped, al-Mustanṣir rode a mule; his saddle and bridle were very simple, lacking the gold and silver ornaments of the military. He was a pleasant-looking young man, with shaven face, dressed plainly in a white kaftan over a long rich tunic and wearing a white turban. He held a riding crop of great value. He was accompanied by a high official on horseback who carried the royal parasol, which was encrusted with precious stones and pearls. Three hundred Persians from Daylam followed on foot, armed with halberds and axes. Eunuchs burned incense or ambergris and aloes on either side, and people threw themselves on their faces and called blessings when the caliph passed. The *wazīr*, the chief *qāḍī* or judge, and a crowd of doctors and officials followed the caliph. The ruler's suite also included visiting princes from North Africa, Yemen, Byzantium, Slavonia, Georgia, Nubia, and Abyssinia, and even Tartars from Turkestan and the sons of the king of Delhi. Many poets and men of letters in the caliph's pay took part in the procession. All the people of the metropolis turned out to see the caliph break the dam near the mouth of the canal and then go sailing on the water. The first boatload carried the deaf and dumb. Their presence was believed to be auspicious, and the caliph distributed alms to them.

The decline of this thriving metropolis was soon to take place.[245] The first harbingers of decay were the serious famines and pestilences that began in the mid-eleventh century. These periodic scourges formed the background to the controversy between Ibn Riḍwān and Ibn al-Jazzār, and they were an immediate concern of Ibn Riḍwān in his treatise.

Scarcity and famine were common occurrences because of the fluctuations of the Nile.[246] The Fāṭimid conquest coincided with a period of scarcity that lasted until A.D. 971, and was followed by pestilence in 972. According to the Egyptian historian al-Maqrīzī, scarcity and famine occurred frequently thereafter, especially during the seven years from A.D. 1065 to 1072, when the famine was so terrible that people were reduced to eating dogs and cats and even human flesh.[247]

[245]See the analysis of M. R. Cohen in his *Jewish Self-Government in Medieval Egypt* (Princeton, 1980), pp. 54–60.

[246]Clerget, *Le Caire*, 1:35–39; William F. Tucker, "The Effects of Famines in the Medieval Islamic World," paper read at the 15th annual meeting of the Middle East Studies Association, Seattle, November 6, 1981.

[247]Al-Maqrīzī ("Le Traité des famines de Maqrīzī," trans. Gaston Wiet, *Journal of the Economic and Social History of the Orient* 5 [1962]:14–28) mentions famine in the following years in Fāṭimid

Modern scholars have asserted that no major epidemics occurred in Egypt from the mid-eighth until the mid-eleventh centuries A.D.,[248] but this generally accepted opinion is mistaken.[249] For example, Ibn Buṭlān said in his controversy with Ibn Riḍwān that astrology was Ibn Riḍwān's old profession "before the year of the epidemic (Ar. *wabā'*)."[250] From the mid-eleventh century A.D., numerous pestilences were often associated with famine in Cairo and al-Fusṭāṭ and are well documented by the chroniclers. Pestilence (Ar. *wabā'*) was recorded in the following years: 445/1053, 446/1054,[251] 447–54/1055–1062,[252] 455/1063,[253] and 457–64/1065–1072.[254]

Egypt: 387/997, 395/1005, 398–99/1007–09, 415/1024, 444/1052 and the ensuing five years, especially 447/1055; idem, *al-Khiṭaṭ*, 1:335–337. Concerning this data from al-Maqrīzī and especially the grain shortage and consequent famine in 414–416/1023–1025, see Bianquis, "Une Crisis frumentaire," pp. 67–101. See also the reports of famine in Egypt in the following years: 398–399/1007–1009 (Ibn al-Athīr, *al-Kāmil* [Beirut, 1966], 9:208; O'Leary, *A Short History*, pp. 154–155); 416–18/1025–27 (ibid., pp. 190–191); 448/1056–57 (al-'Aynī, *Ta'rīkh*, Bib. Nat. MS arabe 5761, fol. 185b; Sibṭ ibn al-Jawzī, *Mir'āt az-zamān*, Bib. Nat. MS arabe 1506, fol. 13a); 457/1064–65 (Anon., *Rawḍ al-bāsim*, Bib. Nat. MS arabe 1562, fol. 194a; Anon., *Jawāhir ath-thamīn*, Bib. Nat. MS arabe 1617, fol. 62a); 459–461/1066–1069 (an-Nuwayrī, *Nihāyat al-arab*, vol. 1, Bib. Nat. MS arabe 1577, fol. 59b); and 462/1069-70 (Ibn al-Jawzī, *Ajā'ib al-badā'i'*, Bib. Nat. MS arabe 1567, fol. 57a; Anon., "Fragments of a Muslim History," Bib. Nat. MS arabe 1570, fols. 79b–80a). Professor William Tucker kindly furnished many of these references and those to epidemics below (April 22, 1981).

[248]Alfred von Kremer, "Ueber die grossen Seuchen des Orients nach arabischen Quellen," *Sitzungsberichte der kaiserlichen Akademie der Wissenschaften, phil.-hist. Classe*, 96 (1880):124–125; see also H. P. J. Renaud, "Les Maladies pestilentielles dans l'orthodoxie islamique," *Bulletin, Institut d'Hygiène du Maroc*, 3 (1934):5–16.

[249]See the following references to epidemics in early Fāṭimid Egypt: 396/1005–6 or 397/1006–7 (Eutychius, *at-Ta'rīkh*, ed. Cheiko in *CSCO*, series 3, vol. 7 [Beirut, 1909], p. 191); 398/1007–8 (Ibn al-Athīr, *al-Kāmil* [Beirut, 1966], 9:208); 399/1008–09 (al-Maqrīzī, *Itti'āẓ al-ḥunafā* [Cairo, 1971], 2:77; O'Leary, *A Short History*, p. 155); 425/1033–34 (al-Maqrīzī, *al-Khiṭaṭ*, trans. Paul Casanova [Paris, 1906], 4, pt. 1:26); and 440/1048–49 (Ibn al-Athīr, *al-Kāmil*, 9:552).

[250]Schacht and Meyerhoff, p. 102. In a footnote to this statement the editors say that this epidemic was probably "the great plague of the year 425/1035" and refer to von Kremer's work on epidemics and Lane-Poole's *History of Egypt*. This is problematic because: (1) A.H. 425 is A.D. 1033–34; (2) the reference to page 56 in von Kremer's article is nonexistent; and (3) Lane-Poole refers only to the death of the caliph aẓ-Ẓāhir by "plague" in June, 1036 (p. 136). There is no evidence for any pestilence in Egypt in 425/1033–34, but Ibn Buṭlān may be referring to the serious epidemic and its great mortality in Baghdad, his home, in this year (von Kremer, "Ueber die grossen Seuchen," pp. 121f., 155 [the Arabic text of as-Suyuṭī]), and it would agree with Ibn Riḍwān's career.

[251]Ibn Buṭlān calls the pestilence in 446–47/1054–55 a *wabā' 'aẓīm* (Ibn Abī Uṣaybi'ah, *'Uyūn*, 2:101). He emphasizes the damage of epidemic diseases during his lifetime by listing the deaths of learned contemporaries who died in epidemics—"so that the light of science was extinguished, and minds were left in darkness after their deaths" (ibid., 1:242f.). If the list is accurate, it would indicate a greater prevalence of epidemics than is apparent in the historical sources.

[252]Ibn Buṭlān mentions "qarūḥ sūdāwīyah wa awrām aṭ-ṭihāl" as symptoms of the pestilence (*wabā'*), which spread throughout the Middle East (Ibn Abī Uṣaybi'ah, *'Uyūn*, 1:242). "An Egyptian Christian source states that a smallpox epidemic in Egypt, a few years earlier (around 1062), had claimed the lives of twenty-one thousand young people in less than a month" (Cohen, *Jewish Self-Government*, p. 59). See also M. ibn Qāsim an-Nuwayrī, *Kitāb al-Ilmām*, ed. A. S.

In the fifth and seventh chapters of *On the Prevention of Bodily Ills in Egypt*, Ibn Riḍwān mentions epidemics in Egypt, but unfortunately he is vague about their natures and dates. This lack of clarity is compounded by our uncertainty about the date of the treatise. Ibn Riḍwān wrote that he had seen five epidemics in Egypt in the preceding twenty years and that only one of them was disastrous. That epidemic had raged "several years ago" when together with war, famine, high prices, and an extraordinary inundation of the Nile, it annihilated about one-third of the population. He also wrote that an epidemic occurred at the end of the autumn and winter of the year in which this work was composed. The most serious pestilence or pestilences appear to have taken place in the period from 447/1055 to 454/1062, when they were accompanied by the war, famine, and so forth that Ibn Riḍwān described. Therefore, it may be conjectured that Ibn Riḍwān wrote his tract after 454/1062 but before the severe famine and epidemic that began in 457/1065. If the treatise was written at this late date, however, it is surprising that Ibn Riḍwān did not mention Ibn Buṭlān,[255] for

Atiya (Hyderabad), 4:138; al-ʿAynī, *Ta'rīkh*, Bib. Nat. MS arabe 5761, fol. 185b; Sibṭ ibn al-Jawzī, *Mir'āt az-zamān*, Bib. Nat. MS arabe 1506, fol. 13a; Ibn al-Jawzī, *al-Muntaẓam fī ta'rīkh* (Beirut, A.H. 1359), 8:180.

[253]Ibn al-Jawzī, *al-Muntaẓam fī ta'rīkh*, vol. 8, p. 232.

[254]Von Kremer, "Ueber die grossen Seuchen," pp. 124–125; al-Maqrīzī, *al-Khiṭaṭ*, 1:335–337; Ibn Buṭlān cited in Ibn Abī Uṣaybiʿah, *ʿUyūn*, 1:242; 2:101; al-Manbijī, *Fī Akhbār aṭ-ṭāʿūn*, Dār al-Kutub al-Miṣrīyah MS no. 16 *ṭibb Halīm*, fols. 200b–222b; an-Nuwayrī, *Nihāyat al-arab*, vol. 1, Bib. Nat. MS arabe 1577, fol. 59b; Anon., *Rawḍ al-bāsim*, Bib. Nat. MS arabe 1562, fol. 194a; Anon., *Jawāhir ath-thamīn*, Bib. Nat. MS arabe 1617, fol. 62a; Ibn al-Jawzī, *Ajā'ib al-badā'iʿ*, Bib. Nat. MS arabe 1567, fol. 57a; Anon., "Fragments of a Muslim History," Bib. Nat. MS arabe 1570, fols. 79b–80a; Ibn ad-Dawādārī, *Kanz ad-durar* (Cairo, 1961), 6:387.

[255]Ibn Buṭlān was a Christian physician and theologian, probably a priest. He taught medicine and philosophy in Baghdad, but in 440/1049 he left the city and arrived in Cairo the following year. In Cairo he was attacked by Ibn Riḍwān, and the remarkable medico-philosophical dispute took place; both men exhibited the full range of their erudition, particularly in Greek medicine and philosophy (see Schacht and Meyerhof). After three or four years, Ibn Butlān went on to Constantinople; his arrival there in 446/1054 coincided with the crisis that led to the schism between the Greek and Latin churches. He stayed for a year in the Byzantine capital and then returned to Syria, alternating between Aleppo and Antioch. In 455/1063 he is known to have supervised the building of a hospital in Antioch. At the end of his life he became a monk and retired to a monastery in Antioch, where he died in 458/1066. According to Schacht, his literary production is distinguished by its originality. His main work is the *Taqwīm aṣ-ṣiḥḥah*, a synopsis of hygiene and macrobiotics in the form of tables, an arrangement borrowed from works on astronomy. The topics of his other works include: a sophisticated criticism of medical charlatanism (see above); a book of homely remedies; a treatise on how to buy slaves and detect bodily defects; tracts directed against Ibn Riḍwān; a valuable report of his journey from Baghdad to Cairo; a "Treatise on the Eucharist"; notes for an autobiography; and a discourse on new medical treatment. See *EI²*, s.v. "Ibn Buṭlān" (J. Schacht); *MI*, pp. 110, 157–158, 192, 224; Schacht and Meyerhof, pp. 14f., 18f., 51–66; Levey, "Some Eleventh Century Medical Questions," pp. 495–507.

their controversy in 441/1049–50 touched upon many of the issues raised in the present work. Furthermore, in the course of this controversy, Ibn Buṭlān wrote a brief description of Baghdad, which is comparable to Ibn Riḍwān's account of Cairo in chapter 6; the former appears to contrast Ibn Riḍwān's account of Cairo with Baghdad.[256] This description of Baghdad and the omission of any reference to Ibn Buṭlān in our treatise would lead one to believe that it was composed before 441/1049–50.

In any case, epidemics were a common phenomenon in medieval Egypt. Their frequency can be attributed especially to Egypt's vulnerable position at the crossroads of trade, pilgrimage, and empire. In the case of plague, it is clear that Egypt was not an endemic focus, but because of optimum ecological conditions, it was very susceptible to the disease.[257]

The Arabic chroniclers were usually imprecise in describing epidemics, and it is often difficult to determine the nature of a disease, even when there are clear accounts of the symptoms. Yet, in the early medieval period the terminology was fairly precise: *wabā'*, "pestilence" or "epidemic," was a corruption of the air, land, or water that caused specific diseases to occur, such as plague (Ar. *ṭā'ūn*).[258] This distinction is important in the present translation because Ibn Riḍwān is concerned with epidemics and their relationship to the environment in his attempt to refute Ibn al-Jazzār's allegations about the noxious conditions in Egypt. It is paradoxical that he actually ends up affirming the unhealthy circumstances in Egypt. Ibn al-Jazzār was right, but for the wrong reasons.

Ibn Riḍwān's topographical description of the capital, especially of al-Fusṭāṭ, clearly depicts the insalubrity of the city. The construction of Cairo itself may well have aggravated the poor conditions of al-Fusṭāṭ, which were observed by other writers. Together with the political and economic crises of the Fāṭimid regime from the mid-eleventh century A.D., the baleful health conditions may have been an important factor in precipitating the decline of the Egyptian capital.[259]

[256]Schacht and Meyerhof, p. 89f.

[257]See Dols, *The Black Death*, and idem, "The Second Plague Pandemic and Its Recurrences in the Middle East: 1347–1894," *Journal of the Economic and Social History of the Orient* 22 (1979): 162–189.

[258]See Dols, *The Black Death*, app. 2; Conrad, "*Ṭā'ūn* and *Wabā'*;" and especially idem, "The Plague in the Early Medieval Near East."

[259]Clerget, *Le Caire*, 1:141.

ʿAlī ibn Riḍwān

The life of ʿAlī ibn Riḍwān can be described with unusual fullness. His distinctive traits are quite evident, in contrast to the customary depersonalization of the individual in Arabic literature (except in epic narratives),[260] because of the aggressive and argumentative personality displayed in his writings. The influence of the classical medical literature in which he schooled himself and after which he modeled his life is very apparent. The tone and content of his works resemble classical writing in the way they combine insistent theorizing with acute observation. In particular, the self-consciousness and assertiveness of Ibn Riḍwān's work resemble the personal, novelistic style of Galen.[261] In any case, Ibn Riḍwān's eccentricity affords us the opportunity to draw a fuller picture than usual of a medieval Islamic doctor.[262]

[260]This may reflect the ideal of the individual in Islamic society. As Marshall Hodgson has written in *The Venture of Islam*, 1:474: "The hero was the man who conformed most closely to a moderate pattern of productive common life." See also G. E. von Grunebaum, *Medieval Islam* (Chicago, 1966), pp. 221–257; idem, *Der Islam im Mittelalter* (Zurich/Stuttgart, 1963), p. 344; idem, "The Hero in Medieval Arabic Prose," *Concepts of the Hero in the Middle Ages and Renaissance*, ed. N. T. Burns and C. J. Reagan (Albany, 1975), pp. 83–100.

[261]See, for example, Galen, *On Prognosis*, ed. and trans. Vivian Nutton (Berlin, 1979); Vivian Nutton, "Galen and Medical Autobiography," *Proceedings of the Cambridge Philological Society*, n.s., 18 (1972):50–60. Galen's autobiographical writings were often a model for Islamic scholars; see Franz Rosenthal, "Die arabische Autobiographie," in *Studia Arabica I.*, ed. F. Rosenthal, G. Von Grunebaum, and W. J. Fischel (Rome, 1937), p. 5.

[262]We are unusually well informed about Ibn Riḍwān because of the information in his autobiography and in medieval chronicles. See Ibn al-Qifṭī, *Ta'rīkh al-ḥukamā'*, ed. J. Lippert (Leipzig, 1903), pp. 294, 298–300, 443–445; Ibn Abī Uṣaybiʿah, *ʿUyūn*, 2:99–105; Barhebraeus (Ibn al-ʿIbrī), *Ta'rīkh mukhtaṣar ad-duwal*, ed. Ṣāliḥānī (Beirut, 1890), pp. 331–334; de Sacy, pp. 26, 44, 103f.; Ibn Taghrībirdī, *an-Nujūm az-zāhirah* (Cairo, 1963–1972), 5:69; Ibn al-ʿImād, *Shadharāt adh-dhahab* (Cairo, 1931–32), 3:291. (Concerning some of these primary sources, see S. K. Hamarneh, "Arabic Historiography as Related to the Health Professions in Medieval Islam," *Sudhoffs Archiv* 50 [1966]:2–24.) In addition, Ibn Riḍwān has been the object of study by a number of modern scholars; see the following: M. Steinschneider, *al-Fārābī* (St. Petersburg, 1869), pp. 170–175; idem, *Polemische und apologetische Literatur in arabischer Sprache* (Leipzig, 1877), pp. 96ff., 149, 329; idem, *Vite de matematici arabi tratte da un'opera di Bernardino Baldi* (Rome, 1874), pp. 40–55; idem, *Die hebräischen Uebersetzungen des Mittelalters* (Berlin, 1893), pp. 354, 525ff., 733ff.; idem, *Die arabischen Übersetzungen aus dem Griechischen*, pp. 44, 61, 69, 92, 120, 137, 199f., 202, 206, 310, 313, 318, 331, 361, 369, 377; F. Wüstenfeld, *Geschichte der arabischen Aerte und Naturforscher* (Göttingen, 1840), pp. 80–82; Leclerc, *Histoire de la médecine arabe*, 1:525–530; *GAL*, 1:637–638; *Supplement*, 1:886; Fuat Sezgin, *Geschichte des arabischen Schrifttums*, vol. 3 (Leiden, 1970), s.v. "ʿAlī ibn Ridwān"; H. Suter, *Die Mathematiker und Astronomen der Araber und ihre Werke* (Leipzig, 1900), pp. 103–105; M. Casiri, *Bibliotheca Arabico-Hispana Escurialensis* (Madrid, 1760), 1:347, 350; G. Gabrieli, "Medici e scienziati arabi: ʿAlī ibn Riḍwān," *Isis* 6 (1924):500–506; L. Choulant, *Handbuch der Bücherkunde für die ältere Medizin* (Leipzig, 1841), p. 370; G. Sarton, *Introduction to the History of Science* (Baltimore, 1927), 1:729–730; Franz Rosenthal, "Die arabische Autobiographie," *Studia Arabica* (Rome, 1937), 1:21–24; *MI*, pp. 158–159 et passim; *EI*², s.v. "Ibn Riḍwān" (J. Schacht); *Dictionary of Scientific Biography*, vol. 11 (1975), s.v. "Riḍwān". In 1923 Max Meyerhof published a German translation of chapter six of *On the Prevention of Bodily Ills*

Abū l-Ḥasan 'Alī ibn Riḍwān ibn 'Alī ibn Ja'far[263] was born in 388/998, the son of a poor baker in al-Gīzah, a suburb of Cairo on the left bank of the Nile.[264] His father did not live more than thirty-one years; his mother died when she was forty-three; and he had an older brother and sister.[265]

Ibn Riḍwān tells us in his autobiography, which he composed when he was about sixty years old, that the astrological signs at his birth had indicated that medicine should be his profession.[266]

When I reached my sixth year I began to learn, and when I was ten years old I moved to the capital and urged on my studies. After having completed fourteen years, I began to study medicine and philosophy. I had no fortune with which I could have paid for my education, so that my education was hampered by obstacles and difficulties. Sometimes I earned my livelihood by practicing astrology,[267] again by medical practice, and yet again by giving lessons. So I continued most earnestly my scientific studies until my thirty-second year.[268]

---

in Egypt ("Über Klima und Gesundheit in alten Kairo nach 'Alī b. Riḍwān," *Sitzungsberichte der physikalisch-medizinischen Sozietät in Erlangen* 54 [1923]:197–218) and again called attention to the treatise in 1929 in an English version of the same translation ("Climate and Health in Old Cairo, according to 'Alī Ibn Riḍwān," *Comptes rendus du congrès international de médecine tropicales et d'hygiène*, Cairo, December 1928 [Cairo, 1929], 2:211–235). Subsequently, Meyerhof and Joseph Schacht published *The Medico-Philosophical Controversy Between Ibn Butlan of Baghdad and Ibn Ridwan of Cairo. A Contribution to the History of Greek Learning Among the Arabs*, The Egyptian University, The Faculty of Arts, no. 13 (Cairo, 1937). The translation and edition of the texts were prefaced by a discussion of the transmission and reception of Hellenistic medicine in the Islamic era and by biographical excerpts about the two physicians from medieval sources. Preliminary studies for this topic included: J. Schacht, "Über den Hellenismus in Baghdad und Kairo im 11. Jahrhundert," pp. 526–545; M. Meyerhof, "Une controverse médico-philosophique au Caire en 441 de l'Hégire, 1050 ap. J.-C.," *Bulletin de l'Institut d'Égypte* 19 (Cairo, 1937):29–43; idem, "Über einige Privatbibliotheken im fāṭimidischen Ägypten," *Rivista degli Studi Orientali* 12 (Rome, 1930):286–290. See also J. Schacht and M. Meyerhof, "On the Text of Our Recent Publication," *Bulletin of the Faculty of Arts of the University of Egypt* 4, no. 2 (Cairo, 1938):145–148.

[263]Ibn Abī Uṣaybi'ah, *'Uyūn*, 2:99, l. 18.

[264]Ibid., p. 101

[265]Schacht and Meyerhof, p. 50.

[266]Ibn Abī Uṣaybi'ah, *'Uyūn*, 2:99; the nativity of Ibn Riḍwān is given in detail. Ibn Abī Uṣaybi'ah copied a substantial portion of Ibn Riḍwān's autobiography in his work (pp. 99–106).

[267]"[Ibn Riḍwān] was in the beginning of his career an astrologer sitting at the wayside and earning his living in a non-scientific manner, as is the habit of astrologers" (Ibn al-Qifṭī *Ta'rīkh*, p. 443).

[268]Ibn Abī Uṣaybi'ah, *'Uyūn*, 2:99–100. In one of his mathematical works, Ibn Riḍwān gives the following autobiographical information: "The beginning of wealth was, after I devoted myself to Medicine, because one of my friends took me into his office and I became his substitute, from which I profited also very much for my Medicine. . . . My office was Medicine and Astronomy; in my young years I had other kinds of little lucrative jobs and similar things. Later on my situation began to improve when I began to study Medicine" (quoted in Schacht and Meyerhof, pp. 50–51).

The fact that Ibn Riḍwān never had a master in medical training was a matter of reproach to him later in his life. He tells us that he did not possess the means to pay the apprentice's fee. In one of his books, he describes his training, giving us a valuable description of contemporary medical education:[269]

When I myself was a student I experienced great jealousy and extreme hardship. . . . When I wanted to study medicine, I sought out in Cairo the man whom, as I had seen, the medical students used to try to get as a teacher and whom the laymen praised for his medical skill. I asked him to teach me and he agreed. He then told me to learn by heart Ḥunayn's *Introduction*.[270] I watched how he taught his students, by holding readings where he explained no obscure point and added no single word to whatever it was that was being read, but simply listened as the student read it. Often the reader would make some slip or mistake, but this was never noticed by the teacher, and this was the type of teaching that I saw was given by all the notable Cairo doctors.

A foreigner without any medical knowledge attended the senior of these doctors and saw a man reading out to him Galen's work *On Curative Method*.[271] When more than five pages had been read without comment from the teacher, the foreigner remarked: "You have read out a great deal, but we have heard no explanation from the shaykh, nor any comment on doubtful passages which need to be elucidated. For in this account, master student [*sic*], there are things which you do not understand." The shaykh, however, still kept silent and the foreigner remained in astonishment.

When I heard of that, it occurred to me that these doctors were ignorant of the art of medicine, so I tested them, one after the other, and found that of the works of Galen and Hippocrates, which they kept in their libraries, they knew no more than the names. They simply relied, as I saw, on what was vouched for by their betters. . . . Next I heard that in Iraq there was a man who made a study of medicine, but I was unable to make the journey. So I remained in perplexity, being unwilling to follow the course of the Egyptian doctors and unable to travel.

Then it occurred to me to get hold of the works of Galen and examine them. There came into my possession his tract *On the Theories of Hippocrates and Plato*,[272] which I investigated. There I found him stating that only two types of men can understand what he says. The first are those who have been trained in geometry and have thus acquired for themselves a capacity for proof which

[269]Cf. the description of legal education in Makdisi, *The Rise of Colleges*, p. 142ff.

[270]It is unclear from Lyons's translation whether the work by Ḥunayn ibn Isḥāq is *al-Masā'il fī ṭ-ṭibb lil-muta'allimīn*, ed. Riyān, 'Arab and Mūsā (Cairo, 1978) or *Kitāb al-Mudkhal fī ṭ-ṭibb*; see *MI*, pp. 117–118.

[271]*Fī Ḥīlat al-bur'* (*De methodo medendi*); see *MI*, p. 45.

[272]*Fī Ārā' Buqrāṭ wa Flāṭun* (*De placitis Hippocratis et Platonis*), see *MI*, p. 40; idem, *Orientalische Literaturzeitung* 72 (1977): cols. 194–195. See de Lacy, ed. and trans., *Galen*, *On the Doctrines of Hippocrates and Plato*.

prevents them from accepting erroneous statements. The second type are those with training in logic, who know its rules so that none of their objects escapes them.[273] I then postponed my study of medicine and started to learn geometry[274] and logic, and when I had acquired a capacity for dealing with the particulars of both these sciences, I returned to medicine. There I found that the number of books that had been written was very great indeed, and I saw that everyone gave pride of place to the works of Hippocrates and Galen. So I made a particular investigation of these, together with their epitomes and commentaries, and I found that one could dispense with these latter. Thus, after spending a long time on this study I reached an understanding of the art of medicine.[275]

By the age of thirty Ibn Riḍwān had established himself as a doctor and was able to marry and prosper.[276] Apparently, he had one son and three daughters, but none of them reached maturity.[277] In time he began to acquire a reputation and was appointed as chief physician (Ar. *ra'īs aṭibbā' Miṣr*) by the Fāṭimid caliph al-Mustanṣir.[278] Ibn Riḍwān became "one of the foremost to give information about the branches of knowledge in which he claimed authority."[279] We know that Abū l'Mu'askar al-Ḥusayn ibn Madān, the ruler of Makrān,[280] consulted him when he was stricken by hemiplegia. Ibn Riḍwān appears to have been conscientious in his practice. He said: "When you are called to a patient, give him at first harmless remedies until you know his disease, then begin the real treatment. To know his disease means that

[273]De Lacy, *Galen*, 1:45.

[274]See M. Steinschneider, "Ali ibn Ridhwan's Commentar zu Galens Von den Elementen," *Monatsschrift für Geschichte und Wissenschaft des Judenthums* 38 (1894):Misz. 31.

[275]Lyons, "The *Kitāb an-Nāfi'*," pp. 66–67. On medical self-education, see Rosenthal, "The Physician in Medieval Muslim Society," pp. 482–483.

[276]Ibn Riḍwān's considerable advance in social status was not an uncommon phenomenon; see Goitein, *A Mediterranean Society*, 1:80.

[277]"Steinschneider adds that he had probably many wives 'several of whom were virgins and maidens,' but that he parted from them; he was a great lover of women, but abstinent in conduct. He had a son who died a short time after his birth, and three daughters one of whom did not live more than seven years, another not more than one year. In the same context one reads: 'And my marriage was delayed until the age of thirty . . . (and I had) one son and several daughters, and they all died' " (quoted in Schacht and Meyerhof, p. 51).

[278]Ibid., pp. 12, 38, n. 12; see *EI*[1], s.v. "al-Mustanṣir billāh" (H. A. R. Gibb and P. Kraus).

[279]Ibn al-Qifṭī, *Ta'rīkh*, p. 444.

[280]Schacht and Meyerhof, p. 44, n. 42: Makrān was, in the first half of the eleventh century A.D., a kingdom occupying the coastal region of Baluchistan; it was under the rule of the sultans of Ghazna, King Abū l-Mu'askar is mentioned by Muḥammad Nāẓim in his *The Life and Times of Sultān Mahmūd of Ghazna* (Cambridge, 1931), p. 80.

you know first of all, which humor is the origin of his disease, and secondly, in which organ it has its centre. After that you may treat it."[281]

Despite his reputation and wealth, Ibn Riḍwān never appears to have left Egypt or even the neighborhood of Cairo.[282] He owned a home in the Qaṣr ash-Sham'ah quarter of al-Fusṭāṭ.[283] The house was known by his name down to the time of Ibn Abī Uṣaybi'ah (ca. A.D. 1194–1270), the famous historian of Islamic medicine,[284] but the house had fallen into ruins and only remnants of it remained.[285] Ibn Riḍwān states in his autobiography that he acquired additional real estate in the city and carefully managed it, so that he had a comfortable income in his old age.[286] According to his own account, he was fairly avaricious, and this trait reportedly led to his derangement at the end of his life. He had adopted an orphan girl during the famine and pestilence of A.D. 1053 and had educated her in his home. When he left her alone in his house, she took valuables and gold valued at about 20,000 dīnārs and fled. The shock was said to have affected his sanity.[287]

Ibn Riḍwān furnishes us with an idealized picture of the conduct of his daily life. He states that he read Aristotle's treatise *On Economics*[288] and tried to follow his prescriptions from morning to night. In his leisure hours after finishing his practice, he devoted himself to religious studies and other subjects:

> I made my main recreation the thought of God and His praise, considering the "Kingdom of Heaven and Earth."[289] The ancients and the men of learning wrote many books about these things. I preferred to confine myself in this to the following: five books of literature, ten on religious law, the books of

[281]Ibn Abī Uṣaybi'ah *'Uyūn*, 2:102.

[282]Ibn al-Qifṭī, *Ta'rīkh*, p. 444. As Goitein has noted (*A Mediterranean Society*, 2:257–258, 3:277), competition among doctors was very keen, and they were reluctant to leave their clientele even for a short time. Such sharp competition may also help explain Ibn Riḍwān's virulent criticism of his colleagues.

[283]Casanova, *Essai de reconstitution*, pp. 13, 120, 125.

[284]See *EI*², s.v. "Ibn Abī Uṣaybi'a" (J. Vernet).

[285]Ibn Abī Uṣaybi'ah, *'Uyūn*, 2:101; Ibn Taghrībirdī, *an-Nujūm*, 5:69.

[286]Ibn Abī Uṣaybi'ah, *'Uyūn*, 2:100.

[287] Ibid., p. 101.

[288]Aristotle, *Oeconomica*, trans E. S. Forster (Oxford, 1920). See Peters, *Aristotles Arabus*, pp. 62–63: *Fī Tadbīr al-manzil*, a Pseudo-Aristotelian work that may have been translated by Abū l-Faraj ibn aṭ-Ṭayyib; the Arabic text has been published by I. Malouf in *La Revue de l'Academie Arabe de Damas* 1 (1921):380–385.

[289]Qur'ān vii: 185.

Hippocrates and Galen on the medical art and the like, such as Dioscorides' *Book of Herbs*,[290] the books of Rufus [of Ephesus],[291] Oribasius,[292] and Paul [of Aegina],[293] and *The Comprehensive Book* of ar-Rāzī,[294] four books on agriculture and pharmacopoeia, and of the books of science the *Almagest* and . . . the *Quadripartitum* of Ptolemy.[295] Of the books of philosophers, the works of Plato,[296] Aristotle,[297] Alexander [of Aphrodisias],[298] Themistius,[299] Muḥammad al-Fārābī,[300] and what else may be useful for me. The remainder of my books I sell for any price that I can get or I keep them in cases, but to sell is better than to keep.[301]

There can be little doubt about Ibn Riḍwān's bookish nature, which was not atypical of learned doctors.[302] Ibn al-Qifṭī[303] relates

[290]See n. 69 above.

[291]*MI*, pp. 71–76 et passim; M. Ullmann, "Die arabische Überlieferung der Werke des Rufus von Ephesos," *Proceedings of the First International Symposium for the History of Arabic Sciences* (Aleppo, 1978), 2:348–357.

[292]*MI*, p. 83 et passim.

[293]*MI*, pp. 86–87 et passim.

[294]*MI*, pp. 128–136 et passim.

[295]See *EI*^{2}, s.v. "Baṭlamiyūs" (M. Plessner); Ernst Honigmann, *Die sieben Klimata und die πολεις ἐπίσημοι: eine Untersuchung zur Geschichte der Geographie und Astrologie im Altertum und Mittelalter* (Heidelberg, 1929), pp. 114, 116. Concerning Ibn Riḍwān's commentary on the *Quadripartitum*, see Ibn al-Qifṭī, *Ta'rīkh*, p. 444, and Schacht and Meyerhof, p. 33, n. 1.

[296]*EI*^{2}, s.v. "Aflāṭūn" (R. Walzer).

[297]*EI*^{2}, s.v. "Arisṭūṭālīs" (R. Walzer).

[298]Alexander of Aphrodisias (ca. A.D. 200), a Peripatetic philosopher, was regarded as the most authoritative of the ancient commentators of Aristotle. See *EI*^{2}, s.v. "al-Iskandar al-Afrūdīsī" (G. Strohmaier).

[299]Themistius (ca. A.D. 317–388) was an Aristotelian philosopher, teacher and politician. His chief philosophical concern was with ethics, especially with the questions of toleration and universal philanthropy. He was a successful teacher in Constantinople; in order to make Aristotle intelligible to his students, he paraphrased the philosopher's texts and summarized their philosophical content. Many of the paraphrases were translated into Arabic, and Themistius was frequently quoted by medieval Arabic philosophers. In A.D. 355, Themistius's political career began; he was made senator and tutor to the royal family. He helped the emperor Julian in his attempt to revive the ancient Hellenic religion, but Themistius tended to be tolerant toward Christians. See *Dictionary of Scientific Biography*, 13 (1976), s.v. "Themistius."

[300]An outstanding and influential philosopher, al-Fārābī was born in Turkestan of Turkish parents and died in 399/950 in Damascus. His works are dependent on Christian Aristotelian teaching in Baghdad and on the late Alexandrian interpretation of Greek philosophy. His thought is distinguished by the superiority of reason over religious thought; Greek philosophy, primarily Plato and Aristotle, could explain all the issues raised in contemporary Islamic society. He wrote commentaries on Aristotle's works; monographs on logic, physics, metaphysics, and ethics; refutations of philosophical adversaries; surveys of the sciences, philosophy and politics. See *EI*^{2}, s.v. "al-Fārābī" (R. Walzer).

[301]Ibn Abī Uṣaybi'ah, *'Uyūn*, 2:100–101; cf. Goitein, *A Mediterranean Society*, 2:258.

[302]See *Vorlesungen*, pp. 100–102.

[303]See *EI*^{2}, s.v. "Ibn al-Ḳifṭī" (A. Dietrich).

that "Ibn Riḍwān wrote a mediocre scholar's hand, which was upright and clear. I saw written by his hand the discourse of al-Ḥasan ibn al-Ḥusayn ibn al-Haytham[304] on the light of the moon; he had provided the text with beautiful and correct vowel-marks that proves his intense occupation with this matter."[305] Moreover, Ibn Riḍwān considered the "ability to endure the toil of transcription" a prerequisite for medical students.[306] His library must have been extensive, because in one of his treatises devoted to Hippocrates he says that of the fifty-five works attributed to Hippocrates, he lacked only twelve.[307]

Ibn Riḍwān gives us further details about his daily life:

My activity in my profession every day is sufficient to me as exercise in order to keep myself in good health. Following this exercise, I rest and then eat meals with the purpose of preserving my health. In my professional work, I endeavor to be humble and kind, to help the oppressed, to discover the distress of the afflicted, and to aid the poor. I make it my aim in all this to enjoy the satisfaction which comes from good deeds and sentiments, but at the same time this cannot but bring in money which I can spend. I spend money on my health and on the maintenance of my household, being neither a squanderer nor a niggard, but practice the golden mean, as becomes a reasonable mind, at any time.[308]

After describing various details about his household and his conduct of financial matters, which included real estate and commerce, he continues:

I wear clothes that are adorned by the marks of distinguished people and by cleanliness. I use a delicate perfume, am silent, and hold my tongue where the failings of men are concerned. I endeavor to speak always decently and take care not to swear and not to blame the opinions [of others]. I avoid conceitedness and overweening; I avoid eager desires and covetousness; and if an

[304]See above n. 228.

[305]Ibn al-Qifṭī, *Ta'rīkh*, p. 444; see also Iskandar, "An Attempted Reconstruction," p. 244.

[306]Lyons, "The *Kitāb an-Nāfi'*," p. 68.

[307]Franz Rosenthal, "An Eleventh-Century List of the Works of Hippocrates," *Journal of the History of Medicine and Allied Sciences*, 28 (1973):157.

[308]Ibn Abī Uṣaybi'ah, *'Uyūn*, 2:100. Ibn Riḍwān's self-description is clearly derived from Galen's works. Professor Kudlien has summarized the Galenic view of the doctor's expenditure of his income in the following way: "In the physician Galen we find the moderate Stoic position; he stressed that money should be spent on performing good/honourable deeds such as helping one's relatives and friends. As for oneself, Galen included the provision of adequate food, clothing, and shelter necessary for health, and cultural needs such as the acquisition of books. But this must not degenerate into luxury" (Kudlien, "Medicine as a 'Liberal Art,' " p. 455).

adversity befalls me, I rely on Allāh the Most High and meet it reasonably without faintheartedness nor weakness.[309]

This and further expressions of Ibn Riḍwān's genteel self-image are not confirmed by either his contentious writings or by his biographers.

Ibn Riḍwān was apparently not a good-looking man, and his physical appearance became a subject for recrimination. Ibn Riḍwān criticized Ibn Buṭlān's appearance, and the latter responded by attacking Ibn Riḍwān's ugliness and asking him sarcastically for a legal opinion on his own qualities, to which Ibn Buṭlān then gave a fictitious answer. Ibn Buṭlān said that Ibn Riḍwān would be entitled to his criticism "if Nature had granted him [Ibn Riḍwān], instead of a dark-blackish complexion a rosy white skin, instead of his impotent and inconclusive speech an exact striking manner of expression, instead of his heavy constitution lightness and mobility, and if it had transformed his inconstancy and excitement into dignity and serenity."[310] In addition, Ibn al-Qifṭī reports that Ibn Riḍwān "was not of good looks or appearance."[311] Ibn Abī Uṣaybi'ah states:

> Ibn Riḍwān was dark-complexioned and not of pleasant exterior. He [Ibn Riḍwān] composed a discourse in which he refuted those who scoffed at him on account of his ugly exterior, and in which he maintained the opinion that a perfect physician was not in need of a beautiful face. Most of the attacks directed by Ibn Buṭlān against 'Alī ibn Riḍwān are of this kind. Thus Ibn Buṭlān said about him in a booklet entitled *Conflict of the Physicians*:
>
> When his face appeared to the midwives
> They recoiled in perplexity;
> And said, keeping their words to themselves:
> Alas, had we only left him in the uterus!
>
> Ibn Buṭlān also nicknamed him "the crocodile of the demons."[312]

Thus, a major characteristic of Ibn Riḍwān's career was his conspicuous inclination to acrimonious polemics against his predecessors and contemporaries, both doctors and laymen, which had nothing to do with religious prejudice.[313] His combative disposition may be attrib-

[309] Ibn Abī Uṣaybi'ah, *'Uyūn*, 2:100.

[310] Schacht and Meyerhof, pp. 17, 97–100.

[311] Ibn al-Qifṭī, *Ta'rīkh*, p. 444.

[312] Ibn Abī Uṣaybi'ah, *'Uyūn*, 1:242, l. 12f.

[313] See Schacht and Meyerhof, p. 39, n. 14.

uted to a number of factors: the rigors of a difficult childhood and adolescence, the overly sensitive nature of an autodidact, the model of Galen in many of his writings, and what Ibn Riḍwān perceived to be the deplorable state of medical practice during his lifetime.[314] "He was insolent in his utterings and abused those with whom he held argument."[315] This aspect of his personality is amply borne out by his tracts against Ibn Buṭlān[316] and Ibn aṭ-Ṭayyib,[317] as well as by the present work. Judging from our text, Ibn Riḍwān was highly critical of his associates, often captious, and pessimistic about human nature in general.

Nevertheless, many pupils followed Ibn Riḍwān's lectures and studied under him, and his fame spread abroad. Among his disciples were the Fāṭimid prince, philosopher and bibliophile al-Mubashshir ibn Fātik[318] and the Jewish physician and bibliophile Afrā'īm ibn az-Zaffān.[319] Ibn Riḍwān was also on friendly terms with an otherwise unknown Jewish doctor, Yahūdā ibn Sa'ādah, to whom he addressed two treatises.[320] Ibn al-Qifṭī says, however, that "his pupils used to relate about him ridiculous things concerning his medical argumentation, astrological sayings and logical assertions, if those who have related them are right."[321]

Ibn Riḍwān was a polymath and an unusually prolific writer. Ibn Abī Uṣaybi'ah credits him with more than a hundred works, if one includes a number of duplications under different titles, small tracts, and unfinished notes. The bulk of his output is lost. Most of the items, however, were medical; for example, he wrote short treatises on

314 See the slightly later but comparable criticism of Egyptian medicine by Umayyah ibn Abī ṣ-Ṣalt (d. A.D. 1134), which is quoted in Hamarneh, "Medical Education," pp. 57–58.

315 Ibn Abī Uṣaybi'ah, *'Uyūn*, 2:101.

316 See above n. 255.

317 Ibn aṭ-Ṭayyib was a Nestorian monk, physician, philosopher, and theologian, who died in 433/1043. He studied and worked at the 'Aḍudī hospital in Baghdad, where one of his pupils was Ibn Buṭlān. In medicine he composed abridgements of Hippocrates, Aristotle, and Galen. See *EI*², s.v. "Ibn al-Ṭayyib" (J. Vernet); *MI*, pp. 31, 44, 59, 156f.; Schacht and Meyerhof, p. 63, n. 21.

318 See Franz Rosenthal, "al-Mubashshir ibn Fātik," *Oriens* 13–14 (1961):132–158; idem, *The Classical Heritage in Islam*, p. 28 et passim; F. E. Peters, *Aristotle and The Arabs: The Aristotelian Tradition in Islam* (New York, 1968), pp. 126–128; *GAL*, 1:100, *Supplement*, 1:829; Meyerhof, "Über einige Privatbibliotheken im fāṭimidischen Ägypten," pp. 286–287.

319 Ibn Abī Uṣaybi'ah, *'Uyūn*, 2:105f.; Goitein, *A Mediterranean Society*, 3:157; Meyerhof, "Über einige Privatbibliotheken im fāṭimidischen Ägypten," pp. 287–288; Schacht and Meyerhof, p. 43.

320 See Schacht and Meyerhof, pp. 42 (and n. 29), 45.

321 Ibn al-Qifṭī *Ta'rīkh*, p. 444.

leprosy, hygiene, purgatives, syrups and electuaries, fevers, tumors, asthma, pharmacology, glosses, and medical education. He followed closely the works of Galen and wrote noteworthy commentaries on *De sectis*, *Ars parva*, *De pulsibus*, *Ad Glauconem*, *De elementis*,[322] and especially *De temperamentis*.[323] Altogether, Ibn Abī Uṣaybiʿah records that Ibn Riḍwān wrote fourteen commentaries and epitomes of the works of Hippocrates and Galen.[324] In addition to medical subjects, he wrote on astrology, astronomy, philosophy, natural science, and theology.[325] A number of his works were translated into Latin and Hebrew during the Middle Ages, such as his important commentaries on the *Quadripartitum* of Ptolemy and the *Ars parva* of Galen.[326]

In all of his works, Ibn Riḍwān exhibited a remarkable knowledge of Greek works, and he always insisted on their study.[327] Ibn Riḍwān's erudition and his constant appeal to the classical medical authorities is well illustrated in the unpublished *Kitāb an-Nāfiʿ*, which has been studied by Professors Schacht, Meyerhof,[328] Lyons,[329] and Iskandar.[330] In this work, Ibn Riḍwān gives valuable information about the history of the Greek medical school at Alexandria before its dissolution and a vivid picture of the poor state of medicine in his own time. He attributes this impoverished state, as I have mentioned, to unsatisfactory compendia and commentaries on ancient medicine.[331]

322Steinschneider, "Ali ibn Ridhwan's Commentar zu Galens Von den Elementen," pp. 366–368.

323Ibn Abī Uṣaybiʿah, *ʿUyūn*, 2:103; see Schacht and Meyerhof, p. 41.

324See Manfred Ullmann, "Zwei spätantike Kommentare zu der hippokratischen Schrift 'De morbis muliebribus,' " *Medizinhistorisches Journal* 12 (1977):245–262; M. C. Lyons, " 'On the Nature of Man' in 'Alī ibn Riḍwān's Epitome," *Al-Andalus*, 30 (1965):181–188; Galen, *In Hippocratis de officina medici commentariorum* . . . , ed. and trans. Malcolm Lyons, *Corpus Medicorum Graecorum*, *Supplementum Orientale*, vol. 1 (Berlin, 1963).

325See the annotated list of Ibn Riḍwān's works in Schacht and Meyerhof, pp. 41–49; Grand'henry, pp. 5–7.

326See Heinrich Schipperges, "Die Assimilation der arabischen Medizin durch das lateinische Mittelalter," *Sudhoffs Archiv*, *Beiheft* 3 (1964):34, 49, 89, 127.

327The advocacy of Greek studies by medieval doctors is well attested; see Meyerhof, "Sultan Saladin's Physician," p. 170.

328Schacht and Meyerhof, pp. 20–28.

329Lyons, "The *Kitāb an-Nāfiʿ*," pp. 65–71; idem, " 'On the Nature of Man,' " pp. 181–188.

330Iskandar, "An Attempted Reconstruction," pp. 235–258.

331It should also be noted that Ibn Riḍwān is an important source of information on the works of Hippocrates that were translated into Arabic. In the first chapter of his treatise, *Fī t-Taṭarruq bi ṭ-ṭibb ilā s-saʿādah* (436/1044–45), Ibn Riḍwān gives a list (*fihrist* = Gr. *pinax*) of the writings of Hippocrates. See Rosenthal, "An Eleventh-Century List of the Works of Hippocrates," pp. 156–165; Dietrich, *ʿAlī ibn Riḍwān*, pp. 9, 14–19.

The medical profession could specifically be improved, he asserts, by the direct and thorough knowledge of drugs.[332] Furthermore, Ibn Riḍwān tries to show in this work that learning medicine from books is preferable to learning it from teachers—turning the necessity of his own education into a virtue—but this opinion was not generally accepted.[333] Subsequently, Ibn Riḍwān strongly criticizes Ḥunayn ibn Isḥāq, the eminent Galenic translator, and ar-Rāzī, perhaps the most successful Islamic clinician, for their deviations from the teachings of Galen.

Ibn Riḍwān's ideal is rigid and unmistakable: he exhorts his reader to become "an excellent physician and a perfect philosopher" like Galen. Yet, as Ibn Abī Uṣaybi'ah points out, Ibn Riḍwān was "very given to contradiction." In the *Kitāb an-Nāfi'* he is clearly argumentative despite his censure of others' "contradictory type of logic." While Ibn Riḍwān warned against commentaries and epitomes, he himself wrote a number of such works, in which he did not hesitate to criticize Galen on the grounds that he misunderstood Hippocrates.[334] More generally, inconsistency appears to have been a marked trait of Ibn Riḍwān's personality.

It is, therefore, not surprising that later assessments of Ibn Riḍwān and his works are conflicting.[335] Ibn Abī Uṣaybi'ah called him "a better medical man [than Ibn Buṭlān] and better trained in the philosophical and associated sciences."[336] According to Ibn al-Qifṭī, "he was a man of narrow mind and not of sound judgment."[337] Malcolm Lyons concludes his study of the *Kitāb an-Nāfi'* in the following manner:

> It may be, then, that his picture of himself supporting the lonely role of the true doctor in an age of fools and charlatans errs on the side of self-deception. But there are some details that ring true. His remarks that the works of Hippocrates and of Galen have been neglected in favour of commentaries can be matched in the works of Ibn Rushd, who writes that, in his day, "the

[332]Cf. Levey, "Medical Ethics of Medieval Islam," pp. 59–62.

[333]Specifically, Ibn Buṭlān refuted his belief in self-education: Schacht and Meyerhof, pp. 83–86; see also Goitein, *A Mediterranean Society*, 2:248; Leiser, "Medical Education," p. 52f.

[334]Lyons, "The *Kitāb an-Nāfi'*," p. 70.

[335]These conclusions about Ibn Riḍwān and his works are, of course, provisional. A definitive assessment must await the study and publication of Ibn Riḍwān's entire corpus.

[336]Levey, "Some Eleventh-Century Medical Questions," p. 496: "Although Ibn Riḍwān was the better physician and philosopher, Ibn Buṭlān was distinguished in literary knowledge and was a writer with a flair for satires as well as wit. . . . "

[337]Ibn al-Qifṭī, *Ta'rīkh*, p. 444.

> moderns" had abandoned the works of Aristotle in favour of those of his commentators. In medicine as well as philosophy this appears as a symptom of intellectual decay. More remarkable, and perhaps more significant, is the fact that in his account of medical training 'Alī ibn Riḍwān places the very minimum of emphasis on the need to acquire practical experience. Elsewhere he mentions such operations as the setting of fractured bones, but for the most part the implication of his account is that little more than book-learning is necessary for the would-be doctor. Nor, in view of the check in the development of Arabic medicinal science, does it appear that this theory was confined to him alone.[338]

Schacht and Meyerhof are even more critical in their evaluation of Ibn Riḍwān: his writings show that he was not an original thinker but merely a strong exponent of Hippocrates' and Galen's thought, except for his list of remedies that were unknown to the ancients. "He is the true representative of that scholastic turn of mind which prevailed in medicine and philosophy dating from the Hellenistic period."[339] More charitable is Ibn al-Qifṭī's opinion that Ibn Riḍwān "composed books that are not of the first importance, being mostly compilations and extracts, but they are nevertheless original and well conceived."[340]

Within the scope of the Galenic system as it had developed by the time of our author, *On the Prevention of Bodily Ills in Egypt* does demonstrate a thoughtful and original application of Galenic principles to medical conditions in Egypt.[341] The well-known controversy between Ibn Riḍwān and Ibn Buṭlān, which Schacht and Meyerhof studied intensively, concerns a jejune issue of differences in the constitutions of newborn birds and chickens, which presents Galenic scholasticism and the two medieval doctors at their worst.[342] The issue seems to have arisen because Islamic doctors had come to recognize the contradictions in Galenic medicine, especially in the elaboration of the humoral

[338] Lyons, "The *Kitāb an-Nāfi'*," pp. 70–71.

[339] Schacht and Meyerhof, p. 29. Meyerhof has, however, described Ibn Riḍwān elsewhere as a "savant original et grand connaisseur de la littérature médicale antique" ("La Fin de l'école d'Alexandrie," p. 119).

[340] Ibn al-Qifṭī, *Ta'rīkh*, p. 444.

[341] See Dietrich, *'Alī ibn Riḍwān*, p. 7.

[342] The customary belief was that birds were "warmer" than chickens and that this warm temperament was compensated for in its early stage by a strongly prevalent moisture. This belief was challenged by the opposite opinion, which was based on Aristotle and Galen. Ibn Buṭlān supported the latter but did not agree with it—he considered the issue an "intellectual juggle and gymnastic" in order to test the intelligence of the reader (see Schacht and Meyerhof, pp. 15f., 70, 72).

theory.[343] The polemic turned ultimately on the question of which man was better educated in Hellenistic learning.[344]

Altogether Ibn Riḍwān's medical works are convincing proof that he was an ardent Galenist.[345] There appear to be few, if any, concessions to empirical or religious considerations, which might have modified his views. A striking example of his near idolatry of Galen is reported by Ibn Abī Uṣaybi'ah, who tells us that he copied from Ibn Riḍwān's own handwriting his commentary on Galen's *De sectis*, where Ibn Riḍwān said:

> I was attacked some years ago by severe headaches by an overfilling [*plethora*] of the blood vessels of the head. I made a venesection, but without success; I repeated this several times, but it persisted. Then I saw Galen in a dream, and he asked me to read to him his *Methodus medendi*. I read to him seven parts of it, and when I reached the end of the seventh part, he said to me: "Here! I forgot the kind of headache from which you are suffering." And he prescribed to me cupping at the occipital protuberance. I awoke and did the cupping and got rid of the headache on the spot.[346]

According to Ibn Abī Uṣaybi'ah, Ibn Riḍwān died in 453/1061 or, according to Ibn al-Qifṭī, in the sixties of the fifth century A.H.[347] Modern scholarship places his death in 460/1067–68.[348]

[343]Levey, "Some Eleventh-Century Medical Questions," p. 499.

[344]Schacht, "Über den Hellenismus in Baghdad und Cairo," p. 530. Schacht concludes: "I have placed emphasis on this controversy to show how deeply ingrained Hellenistic knowledge was in both men; it was an essential ingredient of 11th-century culture. It is the last century before the slow and irresistible decline of the Greek scientific spirit in the Arab-Islamic world" (pp. 544–545). From another point of view, Heinrich Schipperges has used the controversy to describe the education of medieval physicians; unfortunately, his article, "Zum Bildungsweg eines arabischen Arztes," *Orvostörténeti Közlemények* 60–61 (1971):13–31, is superficial and misleading.

[345]See Maimonides, p. 6. It is instructive to compare Ibn Riḍwān to his near contemporary Richer, who was similarly dogmatic and who affords evidence as to the state of medical knowledge in tenth-century France; see L. C. MacKinney, "Tenth-Century Medicine as seen in the Historia of Richer of Rheims," *BHM* 2 (1934):347–375.

[346]Ibn Abī Uṣaybi'ah, *'Uyūn*, 1:10. The significance of this anecdote should not be underestimated because of the importance assigned to dreams in the medieval period. See G. E. von Grunebaum and Roger Caillois, ed., *The Dream and Human Societies* (Berkeley, 1966), especially chaps. 1, 16, 17, 21–25; J. S. Hanson, "Dreams and Visions in the Graeco-Roman World and Early Christianity," *Aufstieg und Niedergang der Römischen Welt*, pt. 2, vol. 23/2 (Berlin, 1980), pp. 1395–1427; Fedwa Malti-Douglas, "Dreams, The Blind, and the Semiotics of the Biographical Notice," *Studia Islamica* 51 (1980):137–162; and Ibn Riḍwān's remarks on the medical implications of dreams in Grand'henry, p. 66.

[347]Ibn Abī Uṣaybi'ah, *'Uyūn*, 2:102; Ibn al-Qifṭī, *Ta'rīkh*, p. 444.

[348]*MI*, p. 158.

Ibn al-Jazzār

Abū Ja'far Aḥmad ibn Ibrāhīm ibn Abī Khālid al-Jazzār was a well-known physician of Qayrawān, the medieval capital of Tunisia, during the period of Fāṭimid ascendancy.[349] His father was a doctor, as was his paternal uncle, Abū Bakr. Ibn al-Jazzār received a traditional Muslim education, which was followed by the study of scientific and philosophical subjects. For his medical training, he studied under the famous physician and philosopher Isḥāq ibn Sulaymān al-Isrā'īlī (ca. 243/855–343/955),[350] who was, in turn, the student of Isḥāq ibn 'Imrān (d. 296/908).[351] From his medical education, Ibn al-Jazzār attained a knowledge of classical medical texts fully comparable with that of Ibn Riḍwān. Ultimately, the various works of Ibn al-Jazzār and his teachers were quite important as sources for the development of medieval European medicine. Their works were translated, primarily in Salerno and Toledo, in the late eleventh and twelfth centuries A.D. and disseminated throughout Western Europe.[352]

Ibn al-Jazzār appears to have been a very pious Muslim, assisting at funerals and weddings; every summer he would make a religious retreat to the Rābiṭat al-Munastīr on the Mediterranean coast. Although quite rich, he led an austere life, ministering not only to the wealthy but also to the poor, for whom he composed the *Kitāb Ṭibb al-fuqarā' wal-masākīn* (*Medicine for the Poor*). His consultations in his home were

[349]For the biography of Ibn al-Jazzār, see the following primary and secondary works: Ibn Abī Uṣaybi'ah, *'Uyūn*, 2:37–39; al-Maqrīzī, *Itti'āẓ al-ḥunafā'*, ed. G. Shayyāl (Cairo, 1948), p. 132; Ibn Juljul, *Ṭabaqāt al-aṭibbā'*, (Cairo, 1955), pp. 88–91; de Sacy, p. 43; Ibn Khallikān, *Ibn Khallikān's Biographical Dictionary*, trans. W. M. de Slane, 1 (1843):672–673; Kātib Çelebi, (Ḥājjī Khalīfah), *Kashf aẓ-ẓunūn* (Istanbul, 1945–1947), 2:318; *GAL*, 1:238, *Supplement*, 1:424; Sezgin, *GAS*, 3:20, 61, 63, 65f., 162, 164, 208, 258, 267, 295, 304–307, 317, 413; *MI*, pp. 147ff., 245f., 268f., 293, 333; idem, *Die Natur- und Geheimwissenschaften im Islam* (Leiden, 1972), pp. 25, 118; idem, *Islamic Medicine*, pp. 13, 31, 53, 99, 103; M. Laignel-Lavastine and Ahmed Ben Milad, "L'École médicale de Kairouan aux Xe et XIe siècles," *Bull. Soc. franç. hist. méd.* 27 (1933):235–242; H. R. Idris, *La Berbérie orientale sous les Zīrīdes, X^e–XIIe siècles* (Paris, 1962), 1: xiii-xiv; 2:771, 809–810; *EI*², s.v. "Ibn al-Djazzār" (H. R. Idris); Ahmed Cherif, *Histoire de la médecine arabe en Tunisie*, Ph.D. dissertation, Bordeaux, 1908, pp. 51–53; Leclerc, *Histoire de la médecine arabe*, 1:407, 413–416; Gustave Dugat, "Études sur le traité de médecine d'Abou Dja'far Aḥmad, intitulé: Zad al-Moçafir 'La provision du voyageur,' " *Journal Asiatique*, 5th ser., 1 (1853): 289–353.

[350]He had emigrated from Egypt to Qayrawān about the age of fifty and served as court physician to the Fāṭimid caliph 'Ubaydallāh al-Mahdī. See *EI*², s.v. "Isḥāḳ ibn Sulaymān al-Isrā'īlī" (A. Altmann); *MI*, pp. 137–138.

[351]*MI*, p. 125; Isḥāq, pp. xiii-xiv.

[352]For this cultural transference, see Schipperges, "Die Assimilation der arabischen Medizin durch das lateinische Mittelalter."

free.[353] A helper was installed in the vestibule of his house, which was transformed into a pharmacy, where the helper dispensed medicaments. Ibn al-Jazzār rarely visited his patients and never served officially as an aulic physician. Although he intended to visit Andalusia, he never journeyed outside of Tunisia. Ibn al-Jazzār died at an advanced age in 369/979–80.[354] At his death he left 24,000 dīnārs and twenty-five qintārs' weight of books on medicine and other subjects.

Ibn al-Jazzār's most famous work is the *Kitāb Zād al-musāfir wa-qūt al-ḥāḍir* (*Provisions for the Traveler and the Nourishment of the Settled*).[355] Intended as a small book to fit into a traveling bag, it was to be used in the event of illness when no doctor could be found. The work contains seven sections, which discuss concisely the treatment of illnesses *a capite ad calcem* (with a final chapter on skin ailments) in the classical manner; it contains numerous citations to ancient and early medieval authors. The book was introduced into Spain by his pupil 'Umar ibn Ḥafṣ ibn Barīq, and it was translated into Greek during the author's lifetime. It was also translated into Latin by Constantinus Africanus[356] in Italy and entitled *Viaticum peregrinantis*, and into Hebrew by Moses Ṭibbōn under the title *Zedat ha-derakhīm*.[357] The Arabic text is still unedited.

Although most of his works are lost, we know that Ibn al-Jazzār wrote on many topics, such as hygiene for the aged, stomach maladies, pediatrics,[358] regimens for a prolonged life (which Ibn Abī Uṣaybi'ah esteemed highly), amnesia, gout, leprosy, fevers, simple and compound drugs,[359] oils, general hygiene, poisons, animals, and stones.[360] Unfortunately, his work on the causes, prevention, and treatment of epidemics (*Kitāb Fī na't al-asbāb al-muwallidah lil-wabā'*), which provoked the present work by Ibn Riḍwān, is also lost.[361] Other works

[353] S. K. Hamarneh (*Bibliography on Medicine and Pharmacy in Medieval Islam* [Stuttgart, 1964], p. 64) asserts that Ibn al-Jazzār emphasized urinalysis in his medical practice.

[354] The death date is uncertain; see, however, Ullmann, *Die Natur und Geheimwissenschaften*, p. 25, n. 5.

[355] For an outline of the contents, see Dugat, "Études sur le traité," pp. 340–353 and partial translation, pp. 306–319; *MI*, p. 247; Jutta Schönfeld, "Die Zahnheilkunde im 'Kitāb Zād al-musāfir' des al-Gazzāri." *Sudhoffs Archiv* 58 (1974):380–403.

[356] See above n. 352.

[357] *MI*, p. 148, n. 3.

[358] *Siyāsat aṣ-ṣibyān wa tadbīruhum* (Tunis, 1968).

[359] See Lothar Volger, *Der Liber Fiduciae de Simplicibus medicinis des Ibn-al-Jazzar* (Würzburg, 1941).

[360] Ibn Abī Uṣaybi'ah, *'Uyūn*, 2:38–39 lists twenty-one works by Ibn al-Jazzār.

[361] Ibid., pp. 5f., 39.

that have not survived include several philosophical works; three historical accounts (*Kitāb Maghāzī Ifrīqiyā* on the Arab conquest of North Africa, *Kitāb Akhbār ad-dawlah* on the Fāṭimid dynasty, and *Kitāb at-Ta'rīf bi-ṣaḥīḥ at-ta'rīkh*, a collection of biographies); a geographical work; and probably a biographical dictionary of judges.

Ibn Riḍwān's Medical Description of Egypt

Within the framework of Galenic medicine, Ibn Riḍwān emphasizes at the outset the excessive heat and the exceptional humidity of the summer and autumn, which were caused by the inundation of the Nile. These factors create, according to our author, both the abundance of plants and animals and their special weakness or vulnerability to decay. The warmth and dampness cause widespread putrefaction of all living things that, in turn, corrupts the water and air. Following the Aristotelian theory of generation, the polluted water itself is said to produce various vermin.

Ibn Riḍwān maintains that under normal circumstances Egyptians are accustomed to their exceptional environment. The constitution of their bodies corresponds, or is sympathetic, to the natural conditions of the land. Likewise, the plants and animals are adapted to their environment and are mutually dependent. The general temperament of Egypt, however, is poor; in all things, it promotes a weak nature and a predisposition to corruption and, hence, to illness in human beings. In men the poor temperament of the body directly affects their disposition, and Ibn Riḍwān gives an unflattering picture of the Egyptian character. Consequently, all things in Egypt are more susceptible to decay than they are in other countries that are located in better climes and, therefore, have better temperaments.

Ibn Riḍwān thus argues that Egypt is relatively unhealthy but is ecologically balanced within its own sphere under normal circumstances. Adherence to this balance is crucial with regard to health. Man can preserve his health or, conversely, can cure his sickness by maintaining his sympathy with the environment. The human temperament must match that of its surroundings—in the air man breathes and in the food and drink he consumes—although the Egyptian surroundings are relatively poor and changeable. Deviation from the customary correspondence between man and his environment causes illness, and it may be caused by man or by environmental changes.

The environment in Egypt is balanced, especially in the spring. Disturbances come, however, with the Nile flood, although the native

Egyptians are generally accustomed to the corruption and subsequent illnesses it causes. The customary illnesses that occur primarily at the end of autumn and the beginning of winter are familiar and manageable. The natural surpluses and corruption in the body can be limited by constant attention to the digestive process and can be eliminated by various means of evacuation, especially in the spring and autumn.

It is the marked divergence from the customary that creates epidemic diseases. Epidemics, which afflict many people at one time, are exceptional and may cause a high mortality. They are produced by irregular changes in the air, water, food, or men's psychic well-being. The basic notion is that the unaccustomed change leads, in one manner or another, to a greater corruption or putrefaction of the environment than normal and to a correspondingly greater corruption in men's bodies. It is a disruption of the omnipresent temperament of all things. The more serious the disruption by one or more of these factors, the more intense is the epidemic. Thus, there are customary endemic illnesses as well as epidemic illnesses. The latter are caused by the excessive surplus of humors—particularly phlegm and yellow bile, which are characteristic of the temperament of Egypt—and their greater corruption.

Ibn Riḍwān illustrates these theoretical ideas of sickness and health with numerous examples. He shows specific external circumstances as being major determinants of the health of the Egyptians, which varies according to geography and man-made alterations in the environment. He gives, especially, a detailed description of the capital to exemplify urban health conditions. The account of greater Cairo is unusual because it is historically specific—more characteristic of geographical than medical writings. The author expresses concern for what we would term *public health*: the physical features of the city, the conditions of its air and water, and the disposal of its refuse, particularly its sewerage system. All these factors affect the health of its inhabitants. Historically, the author's description reflects a time when Cairo was newly established and more wholesome than al-Fusṭāṭ. Cairo is less humid and more exposed to favorable winds; its buildings are lower and its streets are broader and cleaner; many of the people drink well water rather than Nile water; and most of its noxious refuse is taken out of the city. In general, the low-lying regions of the metropolis are the most deleterious to good health.

The didactic purpose of the description is to point out the greater insalubrity, the poorer temperament, of urban areas in comparison with the countryside, particularly the urban dwellers' greater vulnerability to epidemic diseases. The city's air, water, food, and location also destroy the inhabitants' strength of character. The author's description attests to a contemporary sensitivity to environmental conditions, a consciousness of the noxious nature of the premodern city, and even an awareness of the antisocial behavior permitted by urban life.[362]

Nevertheless, the environmental conditions are not entirely deterministic; man has the ability to subserve his health. Ibn Riḍwān uses the six "non-naturals" to explain the causes of illness, but they are also cited as the methods by which health can be aided or restored. Proper air, food and drink, exercise, rest, evacuation, and mental activity assist the natural functioning of the body. They are supportive of the body. However, they may be deficient for a number of reasons. It is the principal duty of the physician to know the temperaments of all things, so that he can successfully order men's individual constitutions by suitable regimens. Consequently, Ibn Riḍwān devotes a good portion of his treatise to methods that improve the poor quality of the air, water, and food in Egypt.

In illness, the doctor must determine the qualitative imbalance in the body and then devise the appropriate remedy that contains the opposing qualities of equal strength. The objective is to restore the humoral balance by a beneficial manipulation of the "non-naturals." Treatment assists the innate healing power of the body, particularly by diet but also by drugs and by avoiding whatever has caused the illness. Similarly, at the time of an epidemic, the cause should be ascertained and countered by opposing measures that limit the surplus of the humors and prevent putrefaction. Chapter 14 gives the prescriptions of a number of compound drugs that may be used for these purposes.

A wide spectrum of constitutional types exists, and these in turn vary greatly between ideal health and sickness, according to Ibn Riḍwān. Although the Egyptian has a weak constitution and is susceptible to illness, health can be attained. The doctor should aim at the maintenance and restoration of the approxiate ideal by his knowledge of the temperaments. In this regard, Ibn Riḍwān particularly criticizes doctors who are ignorant about the essential system of temperaments.

Despite the difficulties that impede health in Egypt, Ibn Riḍwān concludes that the illnesses are less serious and are more easily cured than those in other countries. Moreover, it is desirable to live in Egypt because it is a highly civilized and peaceful country.

Finally, the overall intention of Ibn Riḍwān's treatise was the preservation of health. The medical profession was, however, poorly

[362]Cf. Ibn Khaldūn, *The Muqaddimah*, trans. Rosenthal, 2:376f.

equipped to deal effectively with illness, particularly epidemic diseases. Physicians were more successful in promoting health, and, therefore, he believed they should emphasize the proper regimen and prophylaxis rather than remedial treatment. This was the primary thrust of both ancient and medieval medicine. As Ludwig Edelstein has observed:

> Medicine in Hellenistic times, like earlier medicine, is concerned with the dietetics of the healthy. Indeed, at this time the doctrine of health is considered to be not only as important as therapeutics; it seems to be even more important than healing the sick. It is, after all, better not to let people get sick than to cure their diseases; similarly, the helmsman of a ship will be more eager to reach port before a storm than finally to arrive in port after being buffeted by the storm and enduring many perils.[363]

Manuscript Sources

There are seven known manuscript copies of *Kitāb Daf' maḍārr al-abdān bi-arḍ Miṣr*.[364] The present translation is based on an undated manuscript in the collection of the National Library, Cairo (MS no. 18 *ṭibb*). The manuscript is complete, vowelized, and written in *naskh* script. In the same library is a later and almost identical copy of the work (MS no. 36/384 *ṭibb*), which is dated 1099/1688. On the basis of these two manuscripts, Max Meyerhof published in 1923 and 1929 a preliminary study of the work and translated chapter 6.[365] The sixth chapter had its counterpart in Ibn Buṭlān's topographical description of Baghdad,[366] and later the sixth chapter was quoted by al-Maqrīzī in his description of Egypt.[367]

A third manuscript exists in the National Library, Cairo (MS no. 21/470 *ṭibb*), which was copied in 984/1576–77 by Ḥajārī ibn

[363]Edelstein, "The Dietetics of Antiquity," pp. 307–308; quoted from Erasistratus, in Kühn, 14:692. The entire essay (pp. 303–316) is an excellent survey of the subject and is, consequently, very helpful in interpreting Ibn Riḍwān's treatise; *dietetics* should be understood in the broad classical sense of the word.

[364]For bibliographical references, see *MI*, p. 159, n. 1; Ṣalāḥ ad-Dīn al-Munajjid, "Maṣādir jadīdah 'an ta'rīkh aṭ-ṭibb 'anda l-'arab," *Revue de l'Institut des Manuscrits Arabes* 5/2 (1379/1959):258. We are grateful to Professor Ullmann for calling our attention to the Chester Beatty manuscript (April 12, 1977).

[365]Meyerhof, "Über Klima und Gesundheit im alten Kairo," pp. 197–218; "Climate and Health in Old Cairo," pp. 211–235. Meyerhof had sent copies of the two manuscripts to the orientalist Ernst Seidel in 1910 for him to translate; Seidel did not undertake the work, and the copies were returned to Meyerhof at Seidel's death in 1922.

[366]Schacht and Meyerhof, pp. 89–90.

[367]Al-Maqrīzī, *al-Khiṭaṭ*, 1:339–340.

'Umar an-Nahwātī al-Azharī and was attributed to Sarī d-Dīn ibn aṣ-Ṣā'igh al-Ḥanafī.[368] Except for the opening lines and the loss of three full pages, this manuscript and the first Cairene manuscript are very similar; the variations in the text are minor.

The Vatican copy of *Kitāb Daf' maḍārr al-abdān bi-arḍ Miṣr* (MS no. 315, 7)[369] lacks the author's introduction (1a–2b of the first manuscript), the last two prescriptions of chapter 14, and chapter 15 in its entirety (50b–52a). There is no date, but the orthography suggests the twelfth/eighteenth century. Like the Cairene manuscripts, the Vatican one shows no important variations, although it is completely unvowelized.

The fifth manuscript (MS no. 1, 1) in the Library of the Royal College of Physicians, London, is the first of five works dealing with medicine.[370] This collection was in the private library of Dr. Roy Dobbin, and there is evidence that he studied the Ibn Riḍwān text. It came into his possession in or before 1924; previously (1331/1912), it was owned by Aḥmad Muḥammad ash-Sharqāwī. The work is an epitome by an unknown author, which was written in 1307/1889–90. There is no additional information but, rather, a number of omissions from the text.

The sixth copy, the Chester Beatty manuscript (MS no. 5059),[371] is almost completely identical with the first Cairene manuscript, except for a few variations. The only major difference between them is that the former lacks the last line of the final chapter and the entire concluding paragraphs by Ibn Riḍwān. There is no colophon.

Finally, the Iraqī manuscript (MS no. 2042) is undated.[372] The first eleven chapters are identical with those of the first Cairene manuscript, with a few variations. Chapters 12 to 15, however, are drastically abbreviated.

[368]See the *Fihrist al-makhṭūṭāt al-muṣawwarah*, vol. 3, pt. 2, bk. 2 (Cairo, 1398/1978), pp. 93–94. Concerning the three Cairene manuscripts, see also Karl Vollers, "Aus der vicaköniglichen Bibliothek in Kairo, II. Die medizinische Abteilung," *Zeitschrift der Deutschen Morgenländischen Gesellschaft* 44 (1890):386–387.

[369]G. Levi della Vida, *Elenco dei manoscritti arabi islamici della Biblioteca Vaticana, Vaticani Barberiniani Borgiani Rossiani (Studi e Testi 67)* (Vatican City, 1935).

[370]A. S. Tritton, "Catalogue of Oriental Manuscripts in the Library of the Royal College of Physicians," *Journal of the Royal Asiatic Society* (1951), pp. 182–192.

[371]The Chester Beatty Library, *A Handlist of the Arabic Manuscripts*, vol. 7 by A. J. Arberry (Dublin, 1964), pp. 19–20.

[372]Gūrgīs 'Awwād, "A Catalogue of the Arabic Manuscripts in the Iraq Museum Library, Part 3: Medicine, Pharmacology, Veterinary," *Sumer* 15 (1959):no. 25.

• Part II •

IBN RIḌWĀN'S *ON THE PREVENTION OF BODILY ILLS IN EGYPT*

Introduction [1b][1]

In the name of God; the Merciful and the Compassionate.

The book of ʿAlī ibn Riḍwān concerning the ways for preventing bodily ills in Egypt.

ʿAlī ibn Riḍwān said: Our objective is to give a brief account of the ways of preventing physical illnesses in Egypt. It is necessary first to set forth the causes for these maladies, so that we may be able to learn stratagems for their prevention. We ask God for help and for the happy outcome of what we seek. He is the sponsor of fulfillment by His grace and power.

Aḥmad ibn Ibrāhīm, the Tunisian doctor known as Ibn al-Jazzār, wrote a monograph on this subject. His discussion is neither sufficiently thorough in its summation nor exhaustive in the description of local causes of illnesses, their consequences, and the prevention of the damage that they do. It is only natural that his exposition is deficient because he was a Tunisian who had not seen Egypt with his own eyes; thus, he had no practical experience of the country. He had only heard about it, and he stated no more than what he had heard from others.

Our book surpasses his work to the extent of our superior ability in the branches of philosophy and our firsthand experience [2a] of Egypt for many consecutive years. Whoever loves justice and prefers fairness will know the truth of this statement if he compares the two books and considers them without prejudice that blinds the eye of the soul, which is the mind, and extinguishes its light.

If our book is of the kind that we have described, the need for it is imperative for the elite and the common people of Egypt, as well as for the foreigners who come here, in order to maintain the health of their

[1]The pagination refers to the complete Cairene manuscript, Dār al-Kutub al-Miṣrīyah no. 18 *ṭibb*. The following translation, however, is based on the edited text that incorporates the variant readings in the other six manuscripts. The paragraphism of the text is, of course, that of the translators.

bodies and to remove their illnesses. The ones who most need this book are the doctors, for the required treatment cannot be known without a knowledge of the temperament of the country and what particularly occurs in it.

I have divided the work into fifteen chapters. Each chapter deals with a single theme, so that it is easy for one to understand all the ideas in the work. Chapter 1: On the description of Egypt and its temperament; Chapter 2: On the description of the various kinds of air in Egypt and what is generated in the land of Egypt; Chapter 3: On the six causes determining health and illness in Egypt; Chapter 4: On the seasons of the year in Egypt; [2b] Chapter 5: On the incorrectness of most of Ibn al-Jazzār's reasons for the unhealthy air in Egypt;[2] Chapter 6: On the peculiarity of the capital of Egypt today concerning its air and all its conditions; Chapter 7: On the knowledge about the causes of pestilence[3] and all the epidemic diseases;[4] Chapter 8: A summary of what has been said and a commentary on the six causes that determine health and sickness; Chapter 9: On the general stratagem for preserving health and the treatment of illnesses; Chapter 10: On what is necessary for doctors to do for the body in Egypt; Chapter 11: On the prescription of the body's regimen in Egypt; Chapter 12: On the means of improving the badness of the air, water, and food in Egypt; Chapter 13: On the means of preventing injury from epidemic diseases in Egypt; Chapter 14: On the prescriptions used to prevent injury and to preserve the body; and Chapter 15: On the desirability of choosing to live in Egypt although it would have a bad effect on the body. [3a].

[2]Lane, s.v. "wakhamun:" "A tainted condition of the air, engendering pestilential diseases."

[3]*Wabā'*, see Dols, *The Black Death*, pp. 315–316. Conrad, ("*Ṭā'ūn* and *Wabā'*. Conceptions of Plague and Pestilence in Early Islam," pp. 268–307) has persuasively argued that *wabā'* was conceived as a corruption of the air, land, or water, while *ṭā'ūn* was a specific affliction directly attacking man. This is entirely consistent with Ibn Riḍwān's etiology of epidemic illnesses. See also Peter Bachmann, "Quelques remarques sur le commentaire du premier livre des 'Epidemies' par Ibn an-Nafīs," *Actas do IV Congresso de Estudos Árabes e Islâmicos* (Leiden, 1971), pp. 301–309.

[4]*Al-amrāḍ al-wāfidah*, see Ullmann, *Islamic Medicine*, p. 89f.

· 1 ·

On the Description of Egypt and Its Temperament

Miṣr,[1] according to the narrators, is the name of one of the sons of Noah[2] (on him be peace). They report that Miṣr dwelt in this land, raised a family, and made it prosperous. Therefore, the country was called by his name [Miṣr=Egypt]. Today this name designates the land that the Nile inundates.[3]

The country is delimited by four borders. The eastern border is determined by the fact that the sun rises on the most distant habitation in the east eight and one-third hours before it rises over Egypt. The western boundary is determined by the fact that the sun sets on Egypt three and two-thirds hours before it sets on the western end of the habitation. Consequently, this land is in the western half of the inhabited world, according to Hippocrates[4] and Ptolemy.[5] There is less heat and greater moisture in the western half than in the eastern, as the former is allotted to the moon and the latter is allotted to the sun. This is because the sun rises on the eastern half before it rises on the western

[1]A proper name denoting the eponym of Egypt, the ancestor of the Berbers and the Copts. In accordance with the biblical genealogy (Genesis x: 1 sqq.), Miṣr is called the son of Ḥām, the son of Nūḥ (*EI*[1], s.v. "Miṣr" [A. J. Wensinck]); see also al-Mas'ūdī, *Les Prairies d'Or*, trans. A. C. Barbier de Meynard and A.-J.-B. Paret de Courteille (Paris, 1861–77), 2:304f.; Ibn Taghrībirdhī, *an-Nujūm* (Cairo, 1929), 1:48–50; al-Idrīsī, *Opus geographicum* (Rome, 1972), 3:322.

[2]See *EI*[1], s.v. "Nūḥ" (Bernhard Heller).

[3]In the medieval period, "Miṣr" referred as a proper name both to Egypt as a country and to its capital, al-Fusṭāṭ/Cairo. For the discussion of this matter, see *EI*[1], s.v. "Miṣr"; Abu-Lughod, *Cairo*, p. 6, n. 12; A. Grohmann, *Studien zur historischen Geographie und Verwaltung des frühmittelalterliben Ägypten* (Vienna, 1959), p. 7f.

[4]For Ibn Riḍwān's view of the name "Hippocrates" and the division of the world into eastern and western halves, see Dietrich, *'Alī ibn Riḍwān*, pp. 18–21 and 22–25, respectively.

[5]Ptolemy (Claudius Ptolemaeus), astronomer, mathematician, and geographer (fl. A.D. 127–148). His major work, the *Almagest*, is a complete textbook of astronomy and it dominated astronomical theory in the Middle Ages. Ptolemy's *Tetrabiblos*, which was almost as influential in astrology as the *Almagest* was in its field, provided a scientific basis for the various practices of the astrologers. His *Geography* was, on the whole, the most accurate of ancient geographical works and the most comprehensive. His numerous works were translated into Arabic and exerted considerable

half, [3b] while the moon appears in the western half before the eastern half.[6] Some of the Ancients claimed that Egypt was naturally in the center of the civilized world.[7] But by measurement, as we have already described, it is in the western half.

The third boundary is the southern, and it is the closest part of this land to the equator in the northward direction. The best-known city of this region is Aswān,[8] and the distance of this city from the equator is 21½ degrees, on the basis of the full extent of the earth's circumference being 360 degrees.[9] It is clear that the sun is directly over the heads of the people in Aswān twice a year: when it is at the end of Gemini and the beginning of Cancer.[10] At these two times nothing standing in this place at midday casts a shadow at all. Heat, dryness, and burning are, consequently, dominant over the temperament of this city because the sun dries up the moisture there. Thus, the inhabitants' color is black, and their hair is [4a] kinky on account of the scorching of their land.[11]

The fourth boundary is the northern; it is the most distant in Egypt from the equator in the northward direction and is at the Mediterranean

---

influence on Arabic science. Specifically, we know that Ibn Riḍwān was well acquainted with the *Geography* and that he wrote a commentary on the *Tetrabiblos*. See Honigmann, *Die sieben Klimata*, pp. 112–183; E. H. Bunbury, *A History of Ancient Geography* (New York, 1959), 2:546–644; *EI*[1] *Supplement*, s.v. "Djughrāfiyā" (J. H. Kramers). Concerning the division of the inhabited world, Ptolemy made the division of Africa and Asia along a line running from a point on the Mediterranean coast between al-'Arish and Rāfah to the head of the Gulf of Suez; see John Ball, *Egypt in the Classical Geographers* (Cairo, 1942), p. 100.

[6]See Claudius Ptolemaeus, *Tetrabiblos*, trans. J. M. Ashmand (Chicago, 1936), pp. 22, 41f.

[7]See G. Maspero, *The Dawn of Civilization* (London, 1894), p. 16; Ball, *Egypt in the Classical Geographers*.

[8]Aswān is situated at 24° 5′ 3″ N. on the east bank of the Nile to the north of the first cataract; it is the capital of the province of Nubia. See *EI*[1], s.v. "Assuan" (C. H. Becker); al-Maqrīzī, *al-Khiṭaṭ*, 1:197–199; Nāṣir-i Khusraw, pp. 116, 175f.; Ibn Ḥawqal, 1:147, 156; R. B. Serjeant, *Islamic Textiles* (Beirut, 1972), p. 156.

[9]Ibn Riḍwān gives the latitutes only for Aswān, Tinnīs, and al-Fusṭāṭ/Cairo (see below). The latitude for Aswān does not agree with Ptolemy's figure of 23° 50′ (Ptolemaeus, *Geography*, trans. E. L. Stevenson [New York, 1932], p. 104). Apparently, al-Battānī's astronomical work is the only one that gives Ibn Riḍwān's latitudes for all three cities (*Opus astronomicum*, ed. and trans. C. A. Nallino [Rome, 1899–1907], 2:43–45; 3:239). Because al-Battānī's (d. 317/929) astronomical work had considerable influence, it is possible that it or a derivative work was the source for Ibn Riḍwān's data (*EI*[2], s.v. "al-Battānī" [C. A. Nallino]).

[10]Cf. Claudius Ptolemaeus, *The Almagest*, trans. R. Catesby Taliaferro (Chicago, 1952), pp. 14–42.

[11]Cf. Ptolemaeus, *Tetrabiblos*, p. 41; Galen, *De temperamentis libri III*, ed. Helmreich, pp. 68, 74; *A Translation of Galen's Hygiene*, p. 26; Ḥunayn, p. 76; *Avicenna's Poem on Medicine*, trans. H. C. Krueger (Springfield, Ill., 1963), p. 18; de Sacy, p. 5.

Sea. On the Egyptian coast are many cities,[12] such as Alexandria,[13] Rosetta,[14] Damietta,[15] Tinnīs,[16] and al-Faramā.[17] The distance of Tinnīs from the equator is 31⅓ degrees.

This distance is at the end of the third clime[18] and the beginning of the fourth.[19] Therefore, the sun is neither entirely remote from nor entirely near to the people there. Temperateness is their dominant characteristic, with a slight tendency toward hotness, for the most temperate place for good health in the inhabited countries is in the

[12]See William Popper, *Egypt and Syria Under the Circassian Sultans 1382–1468 A.D.: Systematic Notes to Ibn Taghrī Birdī's Chronicles of Egypt*, University of California Publications in Semitic Philology, vol. 15 (Berkeley, 1955), maps 2, 4; Serjeant, *Islamic Textiles*, map 13.

[13]Alexandria was the major seaport of Egypt, lying at the western angle of the Delta (30° 11′ N., 29° 51′ E.); it was founded in 332 B.C. by Alexander the Great. The fortified city was captured by the Arabs in 21/642 and retained its commercial and strategic importance. The international transit trade as well as local industry, particularly cloth manufacture, made Alexandria a cosmopolitan city and an important source of revenue for the state. Under the Fāṭimids, the city was administratively independent, reflecting its ancient status in Roman law. See *EI*², s.v. "al-Iskandariyya" (S. Labib); Ibn Ḥawqal, 1:148–150; al-Maqrīzī, *al-Khiṭaṭ*, 1:144f.; al-Idrīsī, *Opus geographicum*, 3:317–322; Nāṣir-i Khusraw, p. 119f.; de Sacy; p. 3 et passim; Serjeant, *Islamic Textiles*, s.v. "Alexandria;" al-Battānī, *Opus astronomicum*, 2:38, no. 109.

[14]Rashīd or Rashīdīyah is situated at 31° 24′ N., 30° 24′ E., on the western bank of the Rosetta (Baḥr al-Gharb) branch of the Nile (the ancient Bolbitine) about 10 miles above its mouth, which is known as al-Armūsīyah. The fortified city flourished as a commercial and military center until the early nineteenth century. See *EI*¹, s.v. "Rosetta" (A. S. Atiya); Serjeant, *Islamic Textiles*, p. 62.

[15]Damyāṭ is situated on the eastern branch (Baḥr ash-Sharq) of the Nile, near its mouth. An important town before the Muslim conquest, it survived but suffered repeatedly from naval raids. In 238/853 al-Mutawakkil ordered the construction of a fortress at Damietta as part of a general plan to fortify the Mediterranean coast. The city played a particularly important role in the conflicts during the Crusades. The walls and settlements were demolished by the Mamlūks in 648/1250-51. Previously, Damietta was famous for its textile industry. See *EI*², s.v. "Dimyāṭ" (P. M. Holt); Ibn Ḥawqal, 1:150–151, 154; al-Maqrīzī, *al-Khiṭaṭ*, 1:213–226; Serjeant, *Islamic Textiles*, s.v. "Damietta;" al-Battānī, *Opus astronomicum*, 2:43, no. 177.

[16]Muḥammad Ramzī, *al-Qāmūs al-jughrāfī lil-bilād al-Miṣrīyah* (Cairo, 1953), 1:197f.; Ibn Ḥawqal, 1:150f., 154, 158; al-Maqrīzī, *al-Khiṭaṭ*, 1:176–182; Nāṣir-i Khusraw, pp. 109–114; al-Battānī, *Opus astronomicum*, 2:45, no. 194; Serjeant, *Islamic Textiles*, s.v. "Tinnīs."

[17]Or Pelusium. See Ramzī, *al-Qāmūs*, 1:91f.; al-Maqrīzī, *al-Khiṭaṭ*, 1:211f.; al-Battānī, *Opus astronomicum*, 2:45, no. 195; Serjeant, *Islamic Textiles*, s.v. "al-Faramā;" Ibn Ḥawqal, 1:143, 154, 158; Ibn Ḥawqal and others give al-Faramā as the site of Galen's burial place (p. 158).

[18]The inhabited world was divided into seven latitudinal climes (*aqālīm*), beginning at the equator, according to the Greek tradition; this division was largely attributed to Ptolemy in the Islamic era. See Honigmann, *Die sieben Klimata* for a detailed description of the matter; see also *EI*², s.v. "Iḳlīm" (A. Miquel), "Djughrāfiyā" (S. M. Ahmad); *EI*¹ *Supplement*, s.v. "Djughrāfiyā" (J. H. Kramers); Miquel, *Le Géographie humaine du monde musulman*, 1:12, 70 et passim; C. Schony, "Geography of the Muslims of the Middle Ages," *Geographical Review* 14 (1924):257–269; Ziauddin Alavi, "Physical Geography of the Arabs in the Xth Century A.D," *Indian Geographical Journal* 22 (Madras, 1947):53–61. For the division of Egypt into climes, see Ibn Ḥawqal, 1:146, map 6.

[19]See al-Khwārazmī, *Das Kitāb Ṣūrat al-Arḍ*, ed. Hans von Mžik (Leiden, 1926), pl. 3.

center of the fourth clime.[20] The sea is adjacent to this region; its close association creates a balance between the heat and cold, with a slight tendency toward moisture. The humid condition is predominant, but it is neither hot nor cold. Therefore, the inhabitants' color is brown; their manner is mild;[21] and their hair is lank.

If the climate of the southern region of Egypt is characterized by scorching [4b] and the northern region by temperateness with a slight inclination toward warmth, what lies between the two areas is dominated by heat. The strength of its heat is in proportion to its distance from Aswān or, conversely, its nearness to the Mediterranean. Because of this, Hippocrates and Galen said that the dominant temperament of Egypt is heat.[22]

As we have delimited the country and mentioned its temperament, we will now begin with its description. This land is confined between two mountain ranges, which run from south to north and are not high. One is greater than the other, and the greater is the eastern range, known as the Muqaṭṭam Mountains.[23] As for the western range, it is small and discontinuous. The distance between them narrows in some places and widens in others. It is widest in the lowest part of Egypt. These two mountain ranges are barren; no plants grow on them, as they do on mountains in other countries, because the soil is boraxine[24] and saline.[25] The nature of the clay of Egypt is such that it absorbs the moisture, which is necessary for vegetation. [5a] Also, the heat's intensity dissolves the pleasant moisture from the mountains. The moun-

[20]A central theme of the geographical literature, and of *adab* writings generally, is that the fourth clime is the most desirable and represents "moderation in all things." See *EI*², s.v. "Iḳlīm"; *Avicenna's Poem on Medicine*, p. 18.

[21]Dār al-Kutub al-Miṣrīyah MS no. 18 *ṭibb*: "Their eyes are bluish black."

[22]Cf. *Hippocrates*, *Airs, Waters and Places* 18, *A Translation of Galen's Hygiene*, p. 75; Kühn, 17B:597; Ptolemy, *Tetrabiblos*, p. 42; Galen, *De temperamentis libri III*, ed. Helmreich, p. 68.

[23]Al-Muqaṭṭam is the part of the range of hills that lies east of Cairo; from Cairo the hills take a northeasterly direction, bordering the Nile Delta to the southeast. They reach a height of about 600 feet and are composed, as is the greater part of North African mountains, of limestone. The name is neither pre-Islamic nor a true Arabic word; the geographers give different explanations of its meaning. The origin of the name is probably derived from Jewish legendary traditions; it acquired a real geographical identity only after the foundation of al-Fusṭāṭ. Its proximity to the Nile has deeply influenced the territorial expansion of al-Fusṭāṭ and later of Cairo. See *EI*¹, s.v. "al-Muqaṭṭam" (J. H. Kramers); de Sacy, pp. 5–6, n. 11; Ibn Ḥawqal, 1:147f.

[24]*Bawraq* "is natron, sesqui-carbonate of soda, a compound of various salts containing mainly sodium carbonate (soda). Derived from the Persian *būra*, the term does not indicate borax in the modern sense (Natrium biboracicum), but has given its name to it" (*EI*² *Supplement*, s.v. "Bawraḳ" [A. Dietrich]).

[25]Cf. Ibn Ḥawqal, 1:144.

tains do not receive enough rain to make up for this sweet moisture. Therefore, the well water in the two ranges is salty. The mountains burn the animals and other beings that are buried in them, for there is, by nature, little rain in Egypt.[26]

The Muqaṭṭam Mountains in the east hold back the east wind, so that a pure east wind is never seen in al-Fusṭāṭ.[27] But when the east wind does blow, it is a side wind that comes either from the northeast or the southeast. This wind is hot and humid; it is the most balanced and the best wind because of its similarity to the temperament of the bodies of the animals. Generally, Egypt lacks the excellence of the east wind; yet, the places in Egypt where this wind does blow are better than others, such as Alexandria, Tinnīs, and Damietta.[28] These two mountain ranges also impede the radiation of the sun on the land, when the sun reaches the horizon. Therefore, the length of sunlight on this land is less than its normal duration. Similarly, the mountains cause [5b] the stillness and coarseness of the air.

There are a great many animals and plants in Egypt. It is almost impossible to find a place devoid of them. It is a convulsed land, as Afūrus said.[29] The evidence of the cracking can be seen in the condition of the mud when the Nile retreats. When the heat evaporates the moisture in the soil, the earth cracks into great fissures. It was apparent to the Ancients that places with many animals and plants have a great deal of corruption as well. In this land, the heat of its temperament, the weakness to decay, and the large quantity of animals and plants combine; thus, incineration becomes inevitable.[30] As a result, its clay and the earth become black. The soil that is close to the mountains is boraxine or saline. Black and gray vapors also appear in this land in the evening, especially in the summer.

Egypt consists of many distinct parts, each of which is distinguished by something. The cause of the diversity is the country's narrowness, while its length encompasses [6a] the width of the second and third

[26]For the humidity and rains in Cairo, see Clerget, *Le Caire*, 1:74–81. Cf. ath-Tha'ālibī, *The Laṭā'if al-ma'ārif of Tha'ālibī*, trans. C. E. Bosworth (Edinburgh, 1968), p. 121.

[27]Concerning the winds, see Clerget, *Le Caire*, 1:69–73.

[28]*Hippocrates*, 1:75, 77; cf. Levey, "Medical Ethics of Medieval Islam," p. 32f.

[29]Ephorus of Cyme, ca. 405–330 B.C., was the most important Greek historian of the fourth century, apart from Xenophon; see G. L. Barber, *The Historian Ephorus* (Cambridge, 1935). This quotation was apparently taken from Galen; see Kühn, 19:301, ll. 3–6.

[30]For the underlying theory of generation and destruction, especially the decay or putrefaction of living matter by heat, see Aristotle, *Meteorologica*, ed. & trans. H. D. P. Lee (London, 1952), pp. 290–297.

climes. In Upper Egypt there are date palms, acacia, thickets of reeds and papyrus, places where charcoal is made, and very many other things. In al-Fayyūm[31] there are swamps, thickets of reeds, rice, places where flax is left to decay, and many other things.[32] And in Lower Egypt there are varieties of plants, such as the colocasia,[33] bananas,[34] and so forth. On the whole, every place in Egypt has something in which it specializes and in which it is superior to the other regions.[35]

The Nile flows by many peoples from the Sūdān.[36] Then, it comes to Egypt, having washed away the putrid substances and filth in the Sūdān. Passing through Egypt, it cleaves the country in its center from the south to the north, where it enters the Mediterranean. The beginning of the inundation is in the summer, and its highest level is in the autumn.[37]

Much moisture often ascends by invisible dissolution from the Nile at the time of its rising. This therefore lessens the aridity of the summer and autumn. When the river expands, it floods Egypt and washes from

[31]Al-Fayyūm derives its name from the Coptic, *Phiom*, "the Sea." It is a roughly triangular depression, about 35 miles from north to south and about 49 miles from east to west. It is in Middle Egypt, lying in the Libyan Desert, west of the Nile Valley. The cliffs separating it from the river valley are breached at one point, thereby admitting a stream (Khalīj al-Manhā) which branches off from the Nile near Asyūṭ. On entering the Fayyūm, the waters are canalized for irrigation, the surplus escaping to form a permanent lake, now known as Birkat Qārūn. The principal town and provincial capital is Madīnat al-Fayyūm. At the beginning of the Muslim era, the region seems to have been fertile and prosperous; rice and flax were among its chief products, as Ibn Riḍwān mentions. See EI^2, s.v. "al-Fayyūm" (P. M. Holt); Ibn Ḥawqal, 1:145, 157f.; al-Maqrīzī, *al-Khiṭaṭ*, 1:p. 241ff.; al-Idrīsī, *Opus geographicum*, 3:327ff.

[32]For rice cultivation, see Marius Canard, "Le Riz dans le proche orient aux premiers siècles de l'Islam," *Arabica*, 6 (1959): 113–131, and E. Ashtor, "Essai sur l'alimentation des diverses classes sociales dans l'orient médiévales," *Annales*, 23 (1968):1018f. On flax, see Adam Mez, *The Renaissance of Islam* (Patna, 1937), p. 459; Serjeant, *Islamic Textiles*, s.v. "Faiyum"; *WKAS*, 1:54b, ll. 33ff.

[33]*Qulqās, Arum colocasia* L. See de Sacy, pp. 22–26 et passim: "Suivant Ali ben-Redhwan, il n'y a point d'aliment qui se convertisse en bile plus promptement que la colocasie; d'autres médecins Égyptiens assurent que la colocasie est aphrodisique, et possède d'autres vertus, dont l'enumeration est etrangere a cet ouvrage" (p. 26). See also Bedevian, no. 496; Sontheimer, 2:312; Issa, p. 23, no. 3; Darby, p. 655f.; Ashtor, "Essai sur l'alimentation," p. 1024.

[34]See de Sacy, pp. 26–30 et passim.

[35]For a convenient survey of Egyptian agriculture, see R. C. Cooper, "Agriculture in Egypt, 640–1800," in *Handbuch der Orientalistik*, ed. B. Spuler, pt. 1, vol. 6 (*Geschichte der Islamischen Länder*), sec. 1 (Leiden, 1977), pp. 188–204. See also A. W. Watson, "The Arab Agricultural Revolution and Its Diffusion, 700–1100," *Journal of Economic History*, 34 (1974):8–35; idem, "A Medieval Green Revolution: New Crops and Farming Techniques in the Early Islamic World," *The Islamic Middle East, 700–1900*, ed. A. L. Udovitch (Princeton, 1981), pp. 29–58.

[36]The expression *bilād as-sūdān* properly means "land of the blacks." Although it may mean sub-Saharan Africa that was penetrated by Islam, it is used here to refer to the eastern Sūdān or the Egyptian Sūdān, confined to the basin of the Upper Nile. See EI^1, s.v. "Sūdān" (M. Delafosse), *Supplement*, s.v. "Sūdān" (S. Hillelson).

[37]Cf. Kühn, 19:300f.

it the filth, such as animal cadavers, [6b] its refuse, and the surpluses of thickets, plants, and stagnant waters. The river brings down all of this, mixed with a large quantity of clay and soil because of their weakness, along with the eggs laid by the fish that have matured in the swamps. At the beginning of the flood, its color is green because of the large quantity of stagnant and putrid water that contains duckweed[38] and water moss—whose color is very green on account of their corruption. Then, the water becomes turbid until it is finally like sludge. If it is purified, much clay collects in the bottom of a vessel together with a stinking, sticky, and foul-smelling moisture. This is the most convincing reason for the water's ruination and corruption.[39]

Hippocrates and Galen explained that the type of water that is quickly corrupted is that refined by the sun, such as the rainwater.[40] When the Nile water reaches Egypt, it is at the end of its refinement by the strong heat of the Sūdān. Its transformation is increased when the rotten substances of Egypt mix with it. Therefore, a great many kinds of fish are produced in it.[41] The excess of animals [7a] and plants, the corruption of this water, and the eggs of fish—all of them become substances in the creation of these fish, as Aristotle says in his *Book of Animals*.[42] It is also apparent that everything decays, and the animals are generated from the putrefaction. For this reason, many rats, worms, snakes, scorpions, hornets, and others are generated in Egypt.[43]

It is now evident that the dominant temperament in Egypt is the excessive heat and moisture; that the country consists of many distinct parts; and that its air and water are bad.

[38] *'Armaḍ, Lemna minor* L. See Issa, p. 106, no. 15; Lane, s.v. " 'armaḍun." Possibly it is a reference to the Zizyphus family—*Z. Lotus* Lam., see Bedevian, no. 3651; Sontheimer, 2:190; or *Z. Spina Christi* Willd., see Issa, p. 192, no. 8.

[39] See a comparable description of the Nile flood in de Sacy, pp. 329–359.

[40] Cf. Hippocrates, *Kitāb Buqrāṭ fī l-amrāḍ al-bilādiyya*, pp. 47–50, 67–78; idem, *Airs, Waters and Places*, 7; Pseudo-Aristotle, *Problems*, 1. 21; Levey, "Medical Ethics of Medieval Islam," p. 39: ". . . rainwater may be putrid and have a bad odor since it comes from many different kinds of moisture and is mixed with them. As a result, it is the first of waters to stink." On the general subject of water, see Sontheimer, 2:467–475.

[41] See Benjamin ben Jonah, *The Itinerary of Benjamin of Tudela*, ed. and trans. M. N. Adler (New York, 1964 repr.), p. 72.

[42] This is the title by which Aristotle's zoological corpus was most commonly known; see Remke Krut, *The Arabic Version of Aristotle's Parts of Animals: Book XI–XIV of the Kitāb al-Ḥayawān* (Amsterdam, 1979), pp. 15–19; Sezgin, *Geschichte des arabischen Schriftums*, (Leiden, 1970), 3:349–352. See specifically, Aristotle, *Historia Animalium*, 7:10–17; 8:19.

[43] See Aristotle, *Meteorologica*, ed. Lee, p. 296/297. The notion of spontaneous generation based on the teaching of Aristotle was widespread in Islamic thought; see Ullmann, *Die Natur- und Geheimwissenschaften im Islam*, p. 54f.

· 2 ·

On the Description of the Various Kinds of Air in Egypt and What Is Generated in the Land of Egypt

It has been explained in the preceding that heat is dominant in the temperament of Egypt, accompanied by putridity. The Ancients believed that many superfluities dissolve into the air from places where there is much putrefaction; the superfluities do not allow the air to remain the same, depending on the extent that they ascend to the air. It has also been made clear that change is quick to occur to the air in Egypt because [7b] the sun's rays are not constant.[1] Because of these two factors, the diversity of the air changes in one day. At one time it is hot and another cold; at one time dry and at another humid; at one time agitated and at another still; and at one time the sun is shining and at another the clouds hide it.[2] On the whole, the air of Egypt varies greatly on account of what we have said. The air's diversity is not necessarily of one kind. It follows that the animal spirit[3] that is in us, by its connection with this air, is also not necessarily of one kind. Because of this, the bodily humors in the blood vessels and veins are not necessarily of one kind.

The reason for the scarcity of rainfall in Egypt is that the moist vapors, which are dissolved every day, are prevented from meeting in the atmosphere by the diversity of the air, the lowness of the mountains, and the heat of the earth. When the air becomes cold with the chill of night, this vapor descends to the surface of the earth, generating fog that creates dew and dampness. [8a] Sometimes this vapor dissolves

[1]That is, the sun's rays do not last in Egypt, as one would expect from the nature of the climate, because of the presence of the Muqaṭṭam Mountains.

[2]Cf. Prosper Alpin, *La Médecine des Egyptiens*, trans. R. de Fenoyl (Cairo, 1980), 1:19f.

[3]*Ar-rūḥ al-ḥayawānī*, see Part I of this volume.

invisibly. Because the vapor that gathers from the day before dissolves every day, rain clouds very rarely collect over the land of Egypt. It is clear that the air of Egypt is refreshed every day by the moist vapors that ascend to it and by what is dissolved.

Some of the people have said that the fog is formed by the change of the air to the nature of water. If this is added to what we said earlier, the speed of the air's alteration in Egypt and much of its putrefaction are more explicable. It has been explained that in Egypt there is considerable diversity in the air and that corruption rushes to the moist air. The ultimate cause of this is that during the driest time of the year in all other countries, humidity is more abundant in Egypt, for it is refreshed in the summer and autumn by the expansion of the Nile and its flooding, and this is different from other countries.[4]

Hippocrates taught us that the humidity of the summer and autumn is a surplus.[5] By surplus he means what goes beyond the natural course,[6] as rain occurring in the summer. [8b] Because of this, we say that the humidity of Egypt is a surplus. That is, the heat and the dryness are really the natural temperament of Egypt; however, the expansion of the Nile changes the dryness to surplus humidity. Thereby, putrid matters increase in this land. This is the first and greatest cause of Egypt's being the way it is—the poor quality of its soil, the large quantity of its putridity, and the ruination of its air and water.

These things, however, if they occur according to their normal course, do not cause a perceptible transformation in the bodies of Egyptians because they are accustomed to this situation, and their bodies are similar to it. All the plants and animals resemble the temperament of Egypt in the weakness and lack of endurance of their bodies, in the abundance of change, in the swiftness of illness, and in the brevity of life—as wheat in Egypt is doomed to early ruin and is quick to decay. We do not think that the bodies of the people and animals are different from the wheat in its rapid transformation. How could the matter be otherwise, [9a] for their bodies are built from these things. Consequently, the weakness, the abundant surplus, the putrefaction, and the frequent disease of plants and animals in Egypt are parallel to the poor quality of the land, its putridity, its surplus, and its rapid change

[4]Cf. de Sacy, p. 4f.

[5]*Hippocrates, Airs, Waters and Places*, 10.

[6]Cf. Ibn Bakhtīshū', *Risālah fī ṭ-ṭibb*, p. 30, l. 15; p. 49, l. 3; p. 51, l. 4; p. 51, l. 13; etc.

because the relationship is a direct one. Therefore, the life of the animals and plants is possible in it. Inasmuch as this is their relationship and they are close in their similarity, their life is possible. If foreign things come to Egypt, they are changed in their first encounter with this air; however, when they settle down and become accustomed to the air, they become healthy in a way that conforms to the land of Egypt.

· 3 ·

On the Six Causes Determining Health and Illness in Egypt

When God Almighty created all things, He made some dependent on others. He made many causes of health and sickness; some of them happen accidentally, such as earthquakes,[1] beatings, burning, drowning, and so forth. Doctors cannot do anything about these things. Others are inevitable, [9b] and man always has to deal with them. The Ancients considered them to be six in number:[2] (1) the air surrounding people's bodies; (2) food and drink; (3) movement and rest; (4) sleep and waking; (5) retention and evacuation; and (6) psychic events.[3]

We have previously summarized the matter concerning the air in Egypt. It was evident to the Ancients that the air does not cause illness if it adheres to what is customary. There are, however, bodies that deviate from their similarity to the air in some way, and they are susceptible to illness. Sickness afflicts such a body because of its deviation from this correspondence and from its natural predisposition.[4] The principle is the same with regard to the other causes. If they adhere to what is customary, they do not cause illness.[5] If the matter is as we have said, let us now turn to these other causes.

As for food and drink in Egypt, the crops are swift to change and weak in composition, and they spoil in a short time; examples are wheat, barley, lentils, chick-peas, broadbeans, [10a] and rambling

[1]Concerning earthquakes in Cairo, see Clerget, *Le Caire*, 1:56–59. The history of earthquakes in the Middle East is the subject of research by Musṭaphā A. Ṭāhir, including his article entitled "Traité de la Fortification des Demeures contre l'Horreur des Séismes . . .," *Annales Islamologiques*, 12 (1974):131–159.

[2]Cf. Ḥunayn, pp. 13, 25. For the six "non-naturals," see Part I of this volume.

[3]See Part I of this volume. Concerning "psychological accidents" (Ar. *al-aʿrāḍ an-nafsānīyah*), see Bürgel, "Secular and Religious Features of Medieval Arabic Medicine," p. 51.

[4]Ibn Bakhtīshūʿ, p. 88r: "Illness is a condition of the body in which the natural order is lost." See also ibid., pp. 75r, 89r.

[5]Ḥunayn, p. 11: "What is disease? Disease is a condition of the body that deviates from the normal course, and in which actions suffer from immoderation."

vetch.[6] The foods produced from them are not delicious compared with the same foods made in other countries. For example, the bread made from wheat produced in Egypt is not edible if it sits for a day and a night. After that, it is no longer enjoyable and does not hold together in one piece. It is not chewable and becomes moldy[7] in a short time; the same applies to flour. This is different from the breads of other countries.[8] It is the same with all the crops and fruits in Egypt and the products made from them. They are doomed to early spoilage on account of the swiftness of their transformation and alteration.[9]

Clearly, the temperament of imported goods changes according to the difference of the air. Their nature is changed to conform with conditions in Egypt, except that which has arrived very recently and retains its good quality. Thus, this is the state of the produce.

Concerning the animals that the people eat, the temperament of the native animals is similar to that of the people in their weakness [10b] and quickness to change. Consequently, meat is suitable to the people's natures. There are, however, imported animals, such as Cyrenaican rams.[10] Their transportation creates in their bodies aridity, dryness,

[6]For a useful survey of the diet in the classical Islamic period, see *EI*², s.v. "Ghidhā' " (M. Rodinson); see also de Sacy, pp. 311–328. For foods in Egypt especially, see M. A. Ruffer, *Food in Egypt*, *Mémoire presenté à l'Institut Égyptien*, 1 (1919):1–88, and W. J. Darby, P. Ghalioungui, and L. Grivetti, *Food: The Gift of Osiris*, 2 vols., (London, 1977). Ashtor ("Essai sur l'alimentation," p. 1027f.) concludes that oriental taste preferred three kinds of dishes: very sweet, salty, and meats seasoned or served with fruit; he describes the Egyptian diet, noting the widespread consumption of fish (p. 1033f.), which Ibn Riḍwān discourages.

[7]*Yatakarraju*, see *WKAS*, 1:120b, l. 23ff.; 557b, l. 32ff.

[8]The medieval Middle Eastern diet was distinguished by the predominance of wheat or "white" bread, contrary to European and Far Eastern diets. From antiquity Egypt was an exporter of wheat to other countries; the main wheat-growing region was Upper Egypt. See *EI*², s.v. "Khubz" (Ch. Pellat) and "Ḳamḥ" (E. Ashtor); Darby, pp. 55, 501–530; Ashtor, "Essai sur l'alimentation," pp. 1018–1021, 1034–1035, 1044. Ashtor states (p. 1020): "The Arab doctors recommended eating only white bread, and undoubtedly one cannot in this context minimize the influence of these prescriptions. The famous ar-Rāzī (d. A.D. 925) mentions bread made with flour that is not cleaned of bran (*nukhālah*) among the foods that provoke melancholy, and this is why he warns against the consumption of bread made from grits. Ibn Jazlah opposes unleavened bread as less nourishing than bread of the best flour. Similarly, Hibatallāh ibn Jumai' (d. A.D. 1198), private doctor to Saladin, recommended not eating any other than white bread. Maimonides, who lived at this time, gives precise instructions on this subject [see below]." Concerning the way of preparing bread so that it agrees with the eater's temperament, see Klein-Franke, "The Arabic Version of Galen's *περὶ ἐθῶν*," p. 132.

[9]See the remarks about the preparation of bread in Maimonides, p. 18.

[10]"The Berber tribes, the Lawāta, the Hawāra and the Awrigha, intermingled with Arab elements, took increasingly to stock-breeding, which spread at the expense of agriculture; exports to Egypt then consisted of live-stock, wool, honey and tar" (al-Bakrī quoted in *EI*², s.v. "Barḳa" [J. Despois]).

and humors that are not like the temperament of the Egyptians. For this reason, most of the rams get sick when they enter Egypt. After settling down in Egypt for a suitable length of time, their temperament changes and agrees with that of the Egyptians.

The majority of Egyptians drink from the Nile, which we have discussed sufficiently. But some people drink spring water, which is also close to their temperament, and fewer people drink stored water and rainwater. The favored drink among the people is *ash-Shamsī*[11] because the honey in it preserves its strength and does not allow it to change quickly.[12] The beverage is made when the weather is hot, so that the heat brings the drink to maturity. The raisins used in it are imported from a country with better air. Concerning Egyptian wine, it is rare that honey is not added when it is pressed.[13] Because wine is pressed from the native grapes, it resembles their temperament, and therefore the people prefer *ash-Shamsī* to it. With the exception of *ash-Shamsī* and Egyptian wine, [11a] the drinks are bad because of the swiftness of their transformation and the rottenness of their essence,

[11]*Ash-Shamsī*, a strong expensive wine fermented in the sunlight. See Muslim ibn al-Walīd al-Anṣārī, *Sharḥ dīwān Ṣarī' al-Ghawānī*, ed. Sāmī ad-Dahhān (Cairo, 1970), p. 197, l. 13, p. 203, ll. 6–7, and Abū l-'Atāhiyah, *Abū l-'Atāhiyah ḥayātuh wa siruh*, ed. Muḥammad M. ad-Dash (Cairo, 1968), p. 226, ll. 11–12; Mrs. Laylah Ibrāhīm kindly furnished us with these references. See also D. S. Rice, "Deacon or Drink: Some Paintings from Samarra Re-Examined," *Arabica* 5 (1958):22f., 26f.: *ash-Shamsī* or *al-mushammas* indicates naturally fermented wine, as opposed to *maṭbūkh* (see n. 15 below), which is artificially fermented wine.

[12]Despite its prohibition by Islam, Ibn Riḍwān advises the use of wine throughout this treatise, in accordance with the high nutritional value attributed to it by Galenic medicine. Similarly, see ar-Rāzī, *Guide*, pp. 88–91. Maimonides' remarks (Maimonides, pp. 19, 33, 40) on this subject are instructive: the doctor "has not commanded that this ought to be done, but mentions what his Art determines. The lawyers have already known, as the physicians have known, that wine can be of benefit to mankind. The physician, because he is a physician, must give information on the conduct of a beneficial regimen, be it unlawful or permissible, and the sick have the option to act or not to act. If the physician refrains from prescribing all that is of benefit, whether it is prohibited or permissible, he deceives, and does not deliver his true counsel. It is manifest that the Law commands whatever is of benefit and prohibits whatever is harmful in the next world, while the physician gives information about what benefits the body and warns against whatever harms it in this world. The difference between the edicts of the Law and the counsels of Medicine is that the Law commands compliance with what benefits in the next world and compels it, and forbids that which harms in the next world and punishes for it, while Medicine recommends what is beneficial and warns against what is harmful, and does not compel this or punish for that, but leaves the matter to the sick in the form of consultation; it is they who have the choice" (p. 19). On this passage, see F. Klein-Franke, "Der hippokratische und der maimonidische Arzt," *Freiburger Zeitschrift für Philosophie und Theologie*, 17 (1970):442–449.

[13]See *EI*^{2}, s.v. "Khamr" (A. J. Wensinck-J. Sadan); Darby, pp. 597–618; Ashtor, "Essai sur l'alimentation," pp. 1039–1043; J. Sadan, "Vin—Fait de Civilisation," in *Studies in Memory of Gaston Wiet*, ed. M. Rosen-Ayalon (Jerusalem, 1977), pp. 129–160.

such as date wine,[14] cooked wine,[15] and beer made from wheat.[16]

The food of the Egyptians is varied. The inhabitants of Upper Egypt are nourished mostly by the date palm trees[17] and sweetmeats made from sugar cane.[18] The people carry them to al-Fusṭāṭ and other places, where they are sold and eaten. The inhabitants of Lower Egypt are nourished by colocasia and rambling vetch; they carry them to al-Fusṭāṭ and other places, where the produce is sold and eaten. Many Egyptians frequently eat fish, fresh and salted.[19] They often eat sour milk and its products. Among the peasants, there is a type of bread called *ka'k*[20] that is made from crushed wheat; they dry it, so that it is their food during the entire year.

The bodies of the people are nourished by specific foods; they are familiar with these foods and are brought up on them. Yet, Egyptians generally eat bad foods.[21] These foods do not change the people's temperament as long as they follow the normal course. The bad quality of the food is also one of the things that assures the weakness of the people's bodies and the rapid occurrence of illness.[22] [11b]

The people in the countryside are more active than the people in the cities. Therefore, their bodies are healthier because of the exercise that hardens their limbs and makes their bodies strong. Concerning the people of Upper Egypt, their humors are more delicate and more

[14]*Nabīdh*, see Muḥammad M. Ahsan, *Social Life Under the Abbasids* (London, 1979), pp. 111–112.

[15]*Maṭbūkh*, also called *ṭilā'*. See ibid., p. 112; Dozy, s.v. "maṭbūkh;" Rice, "Deacon or Drink," pp. 21f., 26f.

[16]See Nāṣir-i Khusraw, pp. 130, 132, 152; Darby, pp. 56, 63, 533–551.

[17]See de Sacy, p. 32.

[18]See ibid., p. 312; Ashtor, "Essai sur l'alimentation," pp. 1023–1024, 1028; and below, chap. 10, n. 2.

[19]See Darby, pp. 337–404; Ashtor, "Essai sur l'alimentation," p. 1033f.

[20]Dozy, s.v. "ka'k"; *WKAS*, 1:234b, l. 25ff.; Maxime Rodinson, "Recherches sur les documents arabes relatifs à la cuisine," *Revue des Études Islamiques*, 17 (1950): 140, 152.

[21]Cf. *Hippocrates, Regimen in Acute Diseases*, 36.

[22]Cf. Hippocrates, *Kitāb Buqrāṭ fī l-amrāḍ al-bilādiyya*, p. 135/136. Ashtor asserts ("Essai sur l'alimentation," pp. 1035–1039) that the foods of the lower classes of Egyptian society until the end of the Middle Ages were low in calories, proteins, and lipids, but high in gludices. The situation was entirely different for skilled laborers, small merchants, and artisans; at least from the advent of the Fāṭimids, they were able to afford a varied diet with sufficient nutrition. The diet of the rich was marked by an abundance of sweets, wines, and meats, especially lamb. The contrast between the classes and their diets is vividly presented in a popular story that dates from the later Middle Ages. According to the tale, King Mutton declares war on King Honey—the poorman's sugar—who reigns over fish, vegetables, fruits, and milk products—the poorman's diet. See J. Finkel, trans., "King Mutton, a Curious Egyptian Tale from the Mamlūk Period," *Zeitschrift für Semitistik und verwandte Gebiete* 8 (1932):122–148; 9 (1933–34):1–18.

vaporous, dissolvable, and weak because of the intensity of the heat in their land, as compared with the people of Lower Egypt. Regarding the latter, most of the evacuation of their excesses is by excrement and urine because of the moderation of the heat in their land and their use of cold, coarse things, like colocasia.[23]

As for the character of the Egyptians, one man resembles another because the strength of character depends on the temperament of the body,[24] and their bodies are feeble, quick to change, and lacking in patience and endurance. Thus, inconsistency and changeableness dominate their natures, as do timidity and cowardice,[25] discouragement and doubt, impatience, lack of desire for knowledge and decisiveness, envy and calumny, lying and provocation of the ruler against one's own enemy, disparagement of the people, and in general, vile evils that spring from the baseness of the soul. These evils are not common to all Egyptians but are found in most of them. There are some whom God Almighty [12a] has blessed with excellence, a good character, and freedom from evil. Because the land of Egypt generates cowardice and base evils in the soul, lions do not live in this country; if lions are brought to Egypt, they become meek and do not multiply. The dogs in Egypt are less violent than those of other countries. Likewise, everything else in the country is weaker than its equal in other lands, except for what is naturally suited to this condition, such as the donkey[26] and the hare.[27]

[23]What Ibn Riḍwān intends is that the latter do not sweat so much, so that evacuation is brought about by excrement and urine. Regarding sweat, see Pseudo-Aristotle, *Problems* 2.

[24]See *Galens Traktat "Dass die Kräfte der Seele den Mischungen des Körpers folgen" in arabischer Übersetzung*, ed. and trans. Biesterfeldt, or *Oeuvres anatomiques, physiologiques et médicales de Galien*, trans. Daremberg, vol. 1, no. 3. See also Hans H. Biesterfeldt, "Notes on Abū Zayd al-Balḫī's medico-ethical treatise *Maṣāliḥ al-abdān wa-l-anfus*," in *La Signification du bas moyen age dans l'histoire et la culture du monde musulmane*, Actes du 8me congres de l'union europeenne des arabisants et islamisants, Aix-en-Provence, September, 1976 (1978), pp. 29–34.

[25]Cf. Pseudo-Aristotle, *Problems*, 14.

[26]Ath-Tha'ālibī, *The Laṭā'if al-ma'ārif*, p. 120: "The asses of Egypt, and also its horses, are characterized by their fine appearance and spirited temperament. But whereas certain other countries have horses of equally good breeding and pedigree, no other land, in comparison with Egypt, produces such fine asses. The Caliphs would never ride anything else inside their palace precincts and gardens except Egyptian asses. Al-Mutawakkil used to ascend the minaret of Sāmarrā on a Marīsī ass. . . . Marīs is a village in Egypt. . . ." See also de Sacy, p. 140; Ibn Ḥawqal, 1:161; Darby, p. 235f.

[27]See *EI*[2] *Supplement*, s.v. "Arnab" (F. Viré); Darby, p. 260f.

· 4 ·

On the Seasons of the Year in Egypt[1]

Galen believed firmly that spring has a balanced nature, and in his book *On Temperaments*[2] he refuted those who thought that it was hot and moist.[3] It is the nature of this season that bodies are healthy in it. Their digestion is good, and the innate heat spreads throughout the body. The animal spirit becomes clear because of the balance of the air, the equivalence of night and day, and the abundance of the blood. In the balanced air a noticeable coldness is not sensed, nor is heat, moisture, or dryness; the air itself is clear and pure. The animal spirit becomes strong [12b] in this season, and the bodies become healthy. The activity of the animals increases; things grow and reproduce.

If we search in Egypt for something like this air, we would find it only during Amshīr,[4] Baramhāt,[5] Barmūdah,[6] and Bashans[7] when the sun is in the last half of Aquarius and in Pisces, Aries, and Taurus. Only at this time in Egypt would we find balanced, pure, and clear days that are not felt to be especially hot, cold, humid, or dry. On these days the sun is unclouded and the air is calm; in the months of Barmūdah and Bashans, however, the north wind must blow in order to balance by its coldness the heat of the sun.[8] At this time, the movement of the animals increases; they cohabitate; and their sound becomes beautiful. The

[1]See the description of the seasons by Alpin, *La Médecine des Egyptiens*, 1:20–25; Clerget, *Le Caire*, 1:81ff.

[2]Galen, *De temperamentis libri III*, ed. Helmreich, pp. 9–16. Galen argues against the strict assignment of the four conjunctions of the qualities to the four seasons; spring is not characterized by hot and wet but is equally apportioned among the four qualities.

[3]Cf. Lyons, " 'On the Nature of Man,' " p. 185f.; Ḥunayn, p. 78.

[4]The sixth month of the Coptic solar calendar. For this calendar, see M. Chaine, *La Chronologie des temps chrétiens de l'Égypte et de l'Éthiopie* (Paris, 1925), pp. 73–74.

[5]The seventh month.

[6]The eighth month.

[7]The ninth month.

[8]Cf. Alpin, *La Médecine des Egyptiens*, 1:19f.

trees burst into leaves and the flowers bloom. The generative power strengthens, and the sanguine humor[9] predominates.

Clearly, when spring comes earlier than usual, it is curtailed at its end by an equal amount of time. The cause of this is the strength of the heat in Egypt. Days at the beginning of the season, however, may be very cold; [13a] this is in Amshīr, when the north wind blows and the sun is obscured by clouds. The reason for this is the entrance of spring during the winter season. When the north wind blows, it chills the air, causing it to return to being cold after being balanced. Because moist vapor rises from the earth at this time, the air is moistened and returns to its state as in the winter season. Sometimes, this air becomes cold from the blowing of other winds. Although the south wind is the hottest wind, when it blows at this time of year, it takes on the coldness of the earth and water, which the winter air has cooled. Therefore, if the south wind passes by something, it cools it by its accidental coldness; but if the south wind continues to blow for many successive days, its heat returns to it and makes the air hot and dry. The proof that the coldness of the south wind—known by the Egyptians as the *marīsī*[10]—is produced from the coldness of the water and earth of Egypt and is not natural to this wind is that fog does not collect in the atmosphere at the time of its blowing. The fog gathers when the heat dissolves [13b] the moist vapor during the day and the night makes the vapor cold. The heat of the south wind prevents the coldness from accumulating the fog and causes it to disperse in the air.[11] If the blowing of this wind were to continue, it would warm the water and earth, and they would return to their natural condition of heat. If the spring season comes early and varies so much—normally it varies because of the abundance of its transformation and the vapors that ascend to the air—what would you think of the other seasons! Therefore, the winds increase in spring. At this time, the doctors postpone giving purgative drugs until the season comes to rest, when the sun is in Aries and Taurus.[12]

The summer season arrives at the end of Bashans, and is followed by

[9]*Kaymūs*, see *WKAS*, 1:510a, l. 45ff.

[10]See Lane, s.v. "Marīsīyatun"; Dozy, s.v. "marīsīya"; de Sacy, p. 5, n. 15; ath-Tha'ālibī, *The Laṭā'if al-ma'ārif*, p. 121; Ibn Ḥamzah, *Tanbīhāt*, p. 169, l. 11.

[11]Cf. Aristotle, *Meteorologica*, Lee, ed., pp. 68–75; Casimir Petraitis, ed., *The Arabic Version of Aristotle's Meteorology* (Beirut, 1967), p. 35ff.

[12]Generally, emetics were avoided during the changing of the seasons, following ancient beliefs; cf. Pseudo-Aristotle, *Problems* 1.4.

Ba'ūnah,[13] Abīb,[14] and part of Misrā,[15] when the sun is in Gemini, Cancer, Leo, and some of Virgo. The heat and dryness become great at this time; the crops dry and the fruits ripen. Eating them causes many bad substances to collect in the bodies. When the sun enters into Cancer, the Nile begins to increase and to inundate the land. The natural summer temperament is changed by the abundance of moisture produced in the air. [14a]

In the first part of this season, when the sun is in Gemini, there are days whose air resembles the air of spring because the sun is hidden by clouds or the north wind blows. For this reason, many doctors make the mistake of prescribing purgative drugs at this time in the belief that spring has not ended. The more skilled doctors, however, would select the least warm day. Most of the doctors definitely do not know about this matter, and they administer medicines ignorantly and stupidly. They adhere to the sun's being in Gemini, and they neglect the teaching of the learned Galen that the spring is balanced.

At the end of the summer the inundation of the Nile increases. It is clear that when this season comes earlier than usual, it is curtailed at its end by an equal length of time. There is a good deal of disturbance caused by the large quantity of moist vapors that ascends into the air. If it were not for the fact that the people's bodies are accustomed to these differences and conform to them, illness would occur in their bodies. Hippocrates spoke about this and stated that illnesses occur when the summer is damp.[16]

Autumn, whose nature is dry, begins [14b] from the last half of Misrā, followed by Tūt,[17] Bābih,[18] and some of Hatūr,[19] when the sun is at the end of Virgo and in Libra and Scorpio. The Nile reaches its highest point at the beginning of this season and covers Egypt completely. Many vapors, which ascend from the water into the atmosphere, shift the temperament of autumn from dryness to dampness, to the extent that rain sometimes occurs and clouds multiply in the sky. In the first part of this season there are very hot days because it is really

[13]The tenth month of the Coptic calendar.

[14]The eleventh month.

[15]The twelfth month.

[16]*Hippocrates, Airs, Waters and Places*, 10.

[17]The first month of the Coptic calendar.

[18]The second month.

[19]The third month.

summer. When the atmosphere is purified of damp vapors, it returns to its natural state of heat. In it also are days very much like those of spring, when the night is equal to the day and the humidity is equal to the aridity of the air. Yet, in this season the disturbance of the air becomes greater because of the large amount of moist vapor that rises in it. The air may be at one time hot, at another time cold, and at another time dry. Most of the time, however, the air is dominated by humidity and may vary until it is in the end completely dominated by moisture.

A great many fish are caught from the Nile in the autumn. [15a] Their consumption produces a gluey mixture in men's bodies. Often it is transformed into bile if it meets a choleric humor in the body.[20] Because of these things, the animal spirit is disturbed in the body: the humors are upset, the digestion is bad, and the blood vessels and veins are agitated. Consequently, many different bad humors are produced—yellow bile, black bile, viscid phlegm, raw humor, and burnt bile[21]—and often they coalesce. As a result, illnesses increase.

When the Nile recedes at the end of autumn, the earth is uncovered, the air becomes cold, the fish increase, the vapors become congested, and the decayed matter that ascends from the earth becomes stronger. Thus, the disruption of the harmony of nature increases and illnesses intensify. If this land were not accustomed to these things, the maladies that occur in it would be greater.

Winter, whose nature is cold, begins in the last half of Hatūr, followed by Kīhak[22] and Ṭūbah.[23] This is at the time when the sun is in Sagittarius, Capricorn, [15b] and some of Aquarius. Thus, winter comprises less than three months. The cause of this short span of time is the intensity of heat. Men's bodies are disordered in winter.

The uncovering of the land is completed in the first part of this season, and the land is plowed. The land is made putrid, in general, by the quantity of animal dung and its superfluities. Because the earth is poor and like mud at this time, it generates all kinds of rats, worms,

[20]Cf. Darby, pp. 393–397, 399–402.

[21]This list of humors is not entirely clear, but it appears to refer to the various kinds or forms of each humor. For example, Ḥunayn (p. 3) states that there are two kinds of black bile, which are distinguished here and elsewhere in Ibn Riḍwān's treatise. Ḥunayn says: "One is the natural and original; it is like the turbidity and residue of blood; it is called black humour and is in reality cold and dry; the other differs from its natural condition and originates from the combustion of humours; this is the one truly called black bile; it is hotter and drier than the first; it is endowed with sharpness; its quality is bad and destructive."

[22]The fourth month of the Coptic calendar.

[23]The fifth month.

plants, herbage, and innumerable other things. Many vapors are dissolved from the soil into the atmosphere, so that in the early morning the fog is so dense that one cannot even distinguish colored objects that are close by. Many fish are trapped and caught in the stored-up waters. Decay affects them because the water hardly flows. The consumption of these fish produces in the body many gluey excesses that are strongly predisposed to decay. Illnesses intensify at the beginning of this season. When the cold intensifies, however, the digestion becomes strong; the air stabilizes; the natural heat turns inward; the earth is covered with plants; and its rottenness subsides. Then, men's bodies become healthy. This is at [16a] the end of Kīhak and in Ṭūbah.

It is evident from what we have said that the seasons in Egypt, too, are diverse. The worst time of the whole year, when the greatest amount of illness occurs, is at the end of autumn and the beginning of winter, in the months of Hatūr and Kīhak.[24] Because the variations of the seasons are in conformity with the badness of the land, the harm of the seasons to bodies in Egypt is less than it would be to bodies in other countries, if the seasons varied in the same way as in Egypt. It is also evident that the primary cause for this is the expansion of the Nile in the summer and its inundation of the land in the autumn, which is unlike the rivers in the rest of the world. These other rivers expand at the most likely times of precipitation, that is, in the winter and spring. Because the Nile is the most important factor in the prosperity of Egypt, the ancient Egyptians, especially those at the time of the emperor Diocletian,[25] made autumn the beginning of the year, when the Nile inundation reaches its peak. They made the beginning of their months [16b] Tūt, followed by Bābih, Hatūr, and so forth successively, according to the known sequence of these months.

[24]Concerning the seasons in Egypt, ʿAbd al-Laṭīf wrote (de Sacy, p. 4f.): "Aussi pendant ces mêmes saisons il règne des exhalaisons infectes; l'air se corrompt; les maladies putrides, produites par les humeurs bilieuses et flegmatiques, dominent parmi les habitans. Rarement y observe-t-on des maladies bilieuses pures; leur caratère dominant est flegmatique, même chez les jeunes gens et les subjets d'un tempérament porté à l'inflammation: très-souvent une humeur crue est mêlèe avec la bile. La fin de l'automne et le commencement de l'hiver sont les époques où les maladies sont le plus communes; mais elles ont ordinairement une heureuse issue. Les maladies aiguës et les affections sanguines qui occasionnent des morts subites, sont rares parmi les Égyptiens: mais la plupart, dans l'état de santé, sont lâches, nonchalans, d'un teint décoloré et livide; il est très-rare d'y rencontrer des sujets d'un teint vif et où la couleur du san se manifeste."

[25]Valerius Diocletianus (A.D. 245–313), Roman emperor from 284 to 305. Ibn Riḍwān refers here to the adoption in Egypt of the Era of Diocletian or the Era of Martyrs, which began on August 29, 284. This calendar persisted until the Arab conquest of Egypt and was adopted by the Arabs alongside the Muslim calendar. See Chaine, *La Chronologie*, pp. 12–18; Ibn al-ʿIbrī (Bar Hebraeus), *Mukhtaṣar taʾrīkh ad-duwal* (Beirut, 1890), p. 132; aṭ-Ṭabarī, *Taʾrīkh*, de Goeje, ed., 1st ser., vol. 2 (Leiden, 1881–82), p. 778.

• 5 •

On the Incorrectness of Most of Ibn al-Jazzār's Reasons for the Unhealthy Air in Egypt

Ibn al-Jazzār said in the first chapter of his book: "The cause of illness in those who traveled from Tunisia to Egypt is the great variation of the air. The journey exhausted them and made them susceptible to illness. Then, when their air was changed, they fell sick and death was swift." Although this statement is true, it does not follow that Egyptians are afflicted as those arriving in the country, for Egyptian bodies are accustomed to the variation of the air, and they are not exhausted by traveling.

In the second chapter Ibn al-Jazzār said: "The air of Egypt during most of the year is similar to the air of autumn in its coldness, dryness, and variation." [17a] This is different from what is actually perceived during the entire year. The air of Egypt is always damp in the autumn and other seasons as well. Ibn al-Jazzār supported his statement by reports that created an illusion of the truth for the listener. Among these reports is the assertion of Hippocrates: "When there is at any time of the year a day that is at one time hot and another time cold, expect the occurrence of autumnal illnesses."[1] Ibn al-Jazzār said in this chapter: "Most of the illnesses of the Egyptians are autumnal." This is wrong. The air of Egypt changes in one day not only to coldness and heat but also to dryness. Most of the time the air is humid, to the extent that a good deal of dew is found in the early mornings during the summer. And because of this the harvest is not possible for the peasants in the summer except during dewy days.

Also, most of the illnesses of the Egyptians are not illnesses of the black bile.[2] On the contrary, these illnesses are the least frequent; even

[1]See Hippocrates, *Kitāb Buqrāṭ fī'l-akhbāṭ: On Humours; Kitāb al-ghidhā' li-Buqrāṭ: On Nutriment*, ed. and trans. J. N. Mattock (Cambridge, 1971), p. 25/26; idem, *Aphorisms* 3.4. See also Galen, *De temperamentis libri III*, ed. Helmreich, p. 12f.

[2]Black bile was considered the primary cause of melancholy and mental disturbances; see Flashar, *Melancholie und Melancholiker*, and the important treatise of Isḥāq ibn 'Imrān, ed. Karl Garbers

mad dogs are few in this land.[3] It is likely that this mistake occurred to Ibn al-Jazzār [17b] because he did not see Egypt. When the people who visited Egypt told him about the illnesses that occurred to them and about the variation of the air, he deduced that the air was the cause of the outbreaks of pestilence. It has been explained in the preceding that the moisture in Egypt is excessive; therefore, it is clear that the native sicknesses are from this kind of moisture.

I myself have rarely seen native illnesses of all these kinds that were not combined with phlegm and raw humor at the beginning. It is sufficient to consider the epidemic illness at the end of the autumn and the beginning of the winter of this year, for all the fevers were semitertian fever[4] or pleurisy[5] caused by tertian fever.[6] Nevertheless, during the epidemic, many people were afflicted by apoplexy,[7] epilepsy,[8] angina, and sudden death. Among them, some whose blood eventually burned because of the length of their fever were, in the end, subject to quartan fever through the change of the humors, by scorching, to black bile.[9] These, in particular, are few. All the illnesses occur at all times, as Hippocrates said.[10] Most of the people's maladies are caused by superfluities; that is to say, [18a] the putrid illnesses are mostly from yellow and phlegmatic humors, according to what conforms to the temperament of their land.

Ibn al-Jazzār said in the fifth chapter of his book: "The cause for pestilence in Egypt is the fog existing in the air."[11] This statement also is

(Hamburg, 1977). See also Klibansky, Panofsky, and Saxl, *Saturn and Melancholy*, pp. 1–123. Cf. Grand'henry, p. 65f.

[3]For rabies (hydrophobia) in dogs, see *WKAS*, 1:306a, l. 45 to 306b. l. 4; 310a, l. 28 to 310b, l. 14; 311a, ll. 13–31, 311b, ll. 15–17; Graziani, p. 106ff.

[4]*Shaṭr ghibb*, febris semitertiana; see Kühn, index, p. 261f.

[5]See chap. 9, n. 18.

[6]*Ghibb* or *ghabb*. According to Ḥunayn (p. 85), it is a putrefactive fever caused by the putrefaction of yellow bile "that alternates one day on and one day off, and is called in Greek triatos." On putrefactive fevers, see ibid., pp. 85–92.

[7]See Dozy, s.v. "saktah"; Lane, s.v. "sukātun."

[8]There is no systematic study of epilepsy (*ṣar'*) in medieval Islamic medicine. See, however, Owsei Temkin, *The Falling Sickness*, 2d ed. (Baltimore, 1971); Ullmann, *Islamic Medicine*, p. 75; Lane, s.v. "ṣar'un." For European observations of epilepsy in Egypt, see Prosper Alpin, *Histoire Naturelle de l'Egypte*, trans. R. de Fenoyl (Cairo, 1979), 1:122; idem, *La Médecine des Egyptiens*, 1:95, 211; M. H. I. Letts, ed. and trans., *The Pilgrimage of Arnold von Harff*, The Hakluyt Society, ser. 2, vol. 94 (London, 1946), p. 115f.

[9]See Klibansky, Panofsky, and Saxl, *Saturn and Melancholy*, pp. 52f., 86–90.

[10]See *Hippocrates, The Nature of Man* 8.

[11]This opinion appears to have been widespread; for example, al-Ya'qūbī described Egypt as a place "with changeable weather and many plagues, situated between a damp and fetid river, full of

not true. For the generation of this fog in Egypt coincides with the health of the bodies at the end of Kīhak, and then in Ṭūbah and Amshīr. It is the nature of winter that there is much moisture. If the season and the land adhere to their natural order, illness is not created. In the winter, fog, rather than rainwater, moistens the air.

As for the saying of Hippocrates that a little rain is healthier than a lot of rain and reduces deaths, he meant to indicate the consequences of a deviation from nature and habit. If the rain diverges from the ordinary, its scarcity is healthier than its abundance and reduces deaths. If you do not accept this, despite the lengthy discussion of Galen, listen to the statement of Hippocrates. He said: "The changes of the seasons of the year help to produce illnesses."[12] By this he meant [18b] that the seasons of the year, if their natural order is not followed, create illnesses. The moisture of the winter, then, is more laudable and better. The fog in the winter in Egypt is not bad because it, rather than rain, moistens the air. Hippocrates said: "If the seasons of the year follow their natural order and every season of the year has what it should, then, the illnesses that occur in the season have a proper constancy, order, and a good crisis.[13] If the seasons of the year do not follow their normal order, the diseases occurring in them would be unstable and would have an improper crisis."[14] What Hippocrates said shows that it is correct to say that the fog in winter in Egypt is not bad—not to speak of its being infectious, as Ibn al-Jazzār said—because it is a substitute for the rain in other countries. It can be clearly seen from Hippocrates' statement that the adherence of the seasons of the year to their natural order is not an adversity for the Egyptians because the seasons follow their normal course in one constant way all the time.

Galen explained, as did Hippocrates before him, [19a] that if the

---

unhealthy mists that engender disease and spoil food." Quoted in Bernard Lewis, ed., *Islam from the Prophet Muhammad to the Capture of Constantinople* (New York, 1974), 2:72.

[12] *Hippocrates, Aphorisms* 3.1.

[13] *Buḥrān*. "Crisis" is defined in the Hippocratic treatise *On Diseases* as a condition in which a disease suddenly takes a turn for the worse or for the better, changes its character, or ends by being healed. The climax of the illness should witness the elimination of offending humors or excessive matter from the body. This elimination takes place on certain definite days ("critical days") of a disease, by sweating, purging, urination, or even hemorrhaging; thereby, *eukrasia* is restored. See Brock, *Greek Medicine*, p. 10; H. E. Sigerest, *History of Medicine*, (Oxford, 1961), 2:328–329; *Hippocrates*, General Introduction, pp. lii–lv; F. Klein-Franke, "Die Ursachen der Krisen bei akuten Krankheiten, eine wiederentdeckte Schrift al-Kindī's," *Israel Oriental Studies*, 5 (1975):161–188. The works of Rufus and Galen on this subject were known in Arabic translation; see *MI*, pp. 43, 73. For example, see ar-Rāzī, *Guide*, pp. 109–113.

[14] See Hippocrates, *Kitāb Buqrāṭ fī'l-akhlāt: On Humours*, pp. 25–28; idem, *Aphorisms* 3.8.

human body conforms to the air, water, food, land, and soil, health results. If it were not for this fact, it would be impossible to live in Egypt because of the badness of its air, nor in the Sūdān because of the excess of its heat, nor in the land of the Scythians[15] because of the intensity of its coldness.[16] I wish that I knew where Ibn al-Jazzār got the idea that it is the variation of the air in Egypt and the existing fog that cause the occurrence of pestilence, for the two do not depart from the ordinary course of events.[17]

Subsequently, Ibn al-Jazzār asserted: "The water of the Nile is noticeably harmful for everyone who inhabits Egypt." I wish I knew how this were so. The Nile is the greatest cause for the habitation of this land, and the bodies of the Egyptians have become accustomed to it. The Nile's air is not harmful although it is actually bad.

Ibn al-Jazzār was mistaken about the things he used as the basis for his book. If what he said were true, pestilence in Egypt would necessarily be continuous, for these things are endless and uninterrupted. Egypt would be deserted, and all of its people would perish. The statements of Ibn al-Jazzār are contrary to the statements of the Ancients, and this is quite unthinkable. [19b] Also, Ibn al-Jazzār did not distinguish anywhere in his book between indigenous and epidemic diseases;[18] rather, he considered them one thing. This ruined the purpose of his work. His negligence in the matter of the correspondence between the bodies of the Egyptians and these indigenous diseases landed Ibn al-Jazzār in error.

I have lived in Egypt many years, and I have seen pestilence occur in Egypt only five times in about twenty years. Only one of them was disastrous, while the rest were customary illnesses.[19] If it were said that I have mentioned the corruption of this land, its change, and so forth, which cause the great number of illnesses, then, the answer is that everything that I mentioned earlier does indeed cause the frequent occurrence of sicknesses. The correspondence, however, of these fac-

[15]*Ṣaqālibah*, see Gottard Strohmaier, "Völker- und Ländernamen in der Griechisch-Arabischen Übersetzungsliteratur," *Philologus* 118 (1974):266–268; David Ayalon, "On the Eunuchs in Islam," *Jerusalem Studies in Arabic and Islam* (Jerusalem, 1979), 1:92–122 for a review of the literature on this topic.

[16]See Ptolemaeus, *Tetrabiblos*, p. 41f.

[17]Ibn al-Jazzār appears to have derived his ideas from such works as Pseudo-Aristotle, *Problems* 1.21: "Why is it that when considerable vapor arises under the action of the sun, the year is pestilential?"

[18]". . . bayna al-amrāḍ al-baladīyah wa bayna al-amrāḍ al-wāfidah."

[19]For the dating of this pestilence, see Part I of this volume.

tors to one another and their agreement in the same proportion prohibit them from causing illness when they follow the normal course. But if the factors deviate from the customary, they produce illness. Their deviation from the normal in Egypt [20a] is what I consider to be the disease-causing difference, not the variations that characterize them. The Nile does not produce illness in the bodies every year, but if the customary inundation is excessive or deficient, it is a reason for the occurrence of epidemic illness. Ibn al-Jazzār was not aware of this causal relationship and therefore overlooked it, even though it is basic to an understanding of this phenomenon.

Ibn al-Jazzār did not write about every subject that we have dealt with in this book. His book is readily available, and you may learn the truth of this statement if you look at his work attentively and carefully. If it were said that the bodies of the people in Egypt are weak, as I have mentioned, and that they may be chronically ill, then the answer is that this is an irrelevant point. According to Galen and the doctors before and after him, illness is actually what causes perceptible injury directly to the body. For this reason, the bodies of the Egyptians are not chronically ill, but they are very susceptible to illness. [20b]

· 6 ·

On the Peculiarity of the Capital of Egypt concerning Its Air and All Its Conditions[1]

We have said enough about Egypt in general with regard to its air, food, water, and soil. We shall now speak of the capital of this country in particular because it serves as an example of what is found in other cities.

The capital of Egypt consists of four parts: al-Fusṭāṭ,[2] al-Qarāfah,[3] Cairo,[4] and al-Gīzah.[5] The distance of this city from the equator is thirty degrees.[6] To the east of it rises the Muqaṭṭam Mountains,[7] and between the city and the mountains lie the cemeteries of the city. The doctors say[8] that the very worst place to live is where a mountain in the east keeps the east wind from it.[9]

The most important part of the city is al-Fusṭāṭ. The Nile delimits al-Fusṭāṭ on the west. On the western bank of the Nile stand many

[1]The previous translations of this chapter by Max Meyerhof have been reviewed, and his notes have been incorporated into the following annotation.

[2]For the history of al-Fusṭāṭ, see Part I of this volume.

[3]This was the northeastern suburb of al-Fusṭāṭ, established by the tribe of the Banū Qarāfah when al-Fusṭāṭ was founded. It became the principal burial place of the city. See L. Massignon, *La Cité des morts au Caire (Qarāfa Darb al-Aḥmar)*, in *Bulletin de l'Institut Français d'Archéologie Orientale* 57 (1938):25–79; *EI*², s.v. "al-Ḳāhira" (J. M. Rogers). (Al-Maqrīzī gives al-Gazīrah, i.e., ar-Rawḍah Island, as the second region of the city; see n. 9 below.)

[4]For the history of Cairo, see Part I of this volume.

[5]According to Clerget (*Le Caire*, 1:97), riverine al-Gīzah was founded in the fourth century A.D., as opposed to the pharaonic city that was much farther west. It was located on the western bank of the Nile, opposite the fortified island of ar-Rawḍah and the armed camp at Babylon, later al-Fusṭāṭ; al-Gīzah benefited from its association with them. During the medieval period, al-Gīzah was an important commercial center, being the terminus of the North African caravans, and its location attracted the rich (ibid., 1:136). See also Abu-Lughod, *Cairo*, p. 6 et passim; *EI*², s.v. "al-Ḳāhira"; Nāṣir-i Khusraw, p. 153.

[6]*EI*², s.v. "al-Ḳāhira" gives the latitude of the city as 30° 6′.

[7]See chap. 1, n. 23.

[8]See *Hippocrates, Airs, Waters and Places* 6.

[9]This and the following two paragraphs are quoted from Ibn Riḍwān, with minor variations, by al-Maqrīzī in his description of al-Fusṭāṭ (*al-Khiṭaṭ*, 1:339–340).

trees, both high and low. The greatest part of al-Fusṭāṭ is low-lying.[10] [21a] In the east the boundary is formed by the Muqaṭṭam Mountains, in the south by ash-Sharaf,[11] and in the north by the high-lying district of 'Amal Fawq[12] that includes the three districts of al-Mawqif, al-'Askar,[13] and the Mosque of Ibn Ṭūlūn.[14] When you look toward al-Fusṭāṭ from ash-Sharaf or from another elevated place, you see that it lies in a depression.

Hippocrates has shown that low-lying places are hotter than elevated places and that the air in the former is worse because of the accumulation of vapors. The higher districts surrounding them hinder the penetration of the wind.[15] The alleys and streets of al-Fusṭāṭ are narrow, and their buildings are high.[16] Rufus[17] said: "If you enter a city and see that it has narrow alleys and tall buildings, flee from it because the city is contaminated." He meant that the vapors do not dissolve as they should on account of the narrowness of the streets and the height of the buildings.[18]

The people of al-Fusṭāṭ are in the habit of throwing whatever dies in

[10]Its name, which curiously enough Ibn Riḍwān does not mention, was 'Amal Asfal, "lower part of the town."

[11]That is, "the elevated place." Ash-Sharaf was a chain of rocky hills to the south of the city. It was, and still is, the site of the ancient Byzantine city of Babylon.

[12]That is, "the upper part of the town" that encircled 'Amal Asfal in a semicircle to the northeast.

[13]See Abu-Lughod, *Cairo*, p. 14

[14]Aḥmad ibn Ṭūlūn, d. 270/884, founded the Ṭūlūnid dynasty in Egypt, which became independent of the 'Abbāsid caliphate in Baghdad. North of al-Fusṭāṭ, he established a new quarter, al-Qaṭā'i', which was the seat of Ṭūlūnid government and the site of the great mosque. In A.D. 905 'Abbāsid troops destroyed al-Qaṭā'i' except for the great mosque, which still stands, and Egypt reverted to 'Abbāsid control. See *EI*², s.v. "Aḥmad b. Ṭūlūn" (Z. M. Hassan); Nāṣir-i Khusraw, p. 145f.

[15]See *Hippocrates, Regimen* 2.37.

[16]Nāṣir-i Khusraw (p. 146f.) and Ibn Ḥawqal (1:144) speak of the large multistoried buildings in al-Fusṭāṭ. See the discussion of Abu-Lughod, *Cairo*, p. 19, n. 18; S. D. Goitein, "Urban Housing in Fatimid and Ayyubid Times (as Illustrated by the Cairo Genizah Documents)," *Studia Islamica* 47 (1978): 5–23; Clerget, *Le Caire*, 1:317.

[17]Rufus of Ephesus, ca. A.D 110-ca. 180, an important doctor of the Roman Empire, who was equally distinguished as a practitioner and theoretician. Galen appears to have been greatly indebted to Rufus's work, for example in Galen's presentation of melancholy. Of Rufus's many works, only a few manuscripts have survived; however, he is frequently cited by later doctors besides Galen. Some of Rufus's works are known in Arabic translations only. See *MI*, pp. 71–76; Johannes Ilberg, *Rufus von Ephesos, ein griechischer Arzt in trajanischer Zeit*, in *Abhandlungen der Sächsischen Akademie der Wissenschaften, phil.-hist. Kl.*, vol. 41, 1930, no. 1 (Leipzig, 1930); Manfred Ullmann, ed. and trans., *Rufus von Ephesos Krankenjournale* (Wiesbaden, 1978). For this particular quotation from Rufus, see Ullmann, "Neues zu den diätetischen Schriften des Rufus von Ephesos," *Medizinhistorisches Journal*, 9 (1974):36–40.

[18]Cf. Maimonides, p. 27.

their homes—cats, dogs, and other animals that are household companions—out into the streets and alleys where they decay, and their corruption mixes with the air. In addition, they customarily throw into [21b] the Nile, from which they drink, the droppings of their animals and their carrion. The sewers from their latrines also empty into the Nile.[19] Sometimes, when the flow of water is cut off, the people drink this corruption mingled with the water.

In al-Fusṭāṭ there are large hearths for the baths,[20] from which excessive smoke rises into the air. Moreover, there is a great deal of dust because of the fineness of the soil, so that in the summertime the air appears dingy. It affects breathing, and clean clothes become dirty in one day. If a man goes out on a business errand, he does not return without having collected a good deal of dust on his face and beard. On summer days, especially in the evening, a dusty gray and black vapor rises in the town, particularly if the air is free of any winds.[21]

If these things are as we describe them, it is apparent that these conditions harm our animal spirit. In this way, therefore, many excesses and tendencies toward corruption are engendered in the body from these conditions. The inhabitants of al-Fusṭāṭ, however, have accustomed themselves to this state of affairs and have become familiar with it, so that most of the evil is averted from them. [22a] Nevertheless, of all the inhabitants of Egypt, they are the ones who most quickly succumb to illnesses.[22]

The part of al-Fusṭāṭ that is situated along the Nile is necessarily damper than the area adjoining the desert. The inhabitants of ash-Sharaf are in a healthier condition because the winds penetrate into

[19]This was probably true only for areas close to the Nile. In the center of the old town were pits hewn deep into the rocky ground, which received the waste from the latrines. They were probably cleaned out from time to time with casks, which were then emptied into the Nile. See particularly George T. Scanlon, "Housing and Sanitation: Some Aspects of Medieval Islamic Public Service," *The Islamic City*, ed. A. H. Hourani and S. M. Stern (Oxford, 1970), pp. 179–194.

[20]See de Sacy, pp. 297–299; *EI*², s.v. "Ḥammām" (J. Sourdel-Thomine); E. Pauty, *Les Hammams du Caire*, in *Mémoires de l'Institut Français d'Archéologie Orientale*, vol. 64 (Cairo, 1933); Heinz Grotzfeld, *Das Bad im arabisch-islamischen Mittelalter* (Wiesbaden, 1970).

[21]Two centuries after Ibn Riḍwān, the Andalusian Ibn Saʿīd (see *EI*², s.v. "Ibn Saʿīd" [Ch. Pellat]) described in verse a donkey ride that he was obliged to take through the dust-laden atmosphere of Cairo: "In Miṣr I found the worst hell, indeed;/ Of the dust the blackness, of the donkey-ride the speed;/ A veil of dust over my features lay,/ And the dust had hidden the light of day." (Quoted in al-Maqrīzī, *al-Khiṭaṭ*, 1:341.)

[22]It is commonly assumed that the populations of premodern cities could not sustain their numbers without continual immigration from the countryside. In this regard, the high urban mortality of Cairo was not necessarily uncommon, nor did it lead to urban depopulation.

their homes. The same is true of 'Amal Fawq and al-Ḥamrā',[23] except that the drinking water of ash-Sharaf is better because it is drawn from the river before the putrefaction of al-Fusṭāṭ mingles with it.

Al-Qarāfah is the best of these places because the Muqaṭṭam Mountains prevent the vapor of al-Fusṭāṭ from passing through it.[24] But when the north wind blows, it carries many parts of the vapor from al-Fusṭāṭ and Cairo to ash-Sharaf and changes the air in ash-Sharaf. It is evident that the open part of al-Fusṭāṭ as well as the elevated places have healthier air.

Comparable with al-Fusṭāṭ in size and population is Cairo. It lies north of al-Fusṭāṭ; to the east of it are the Muqaṭṭam Mountains, which keep the east wind from the city. The Nile is slightly more distant from it than the Muqaṭṭam Mountains.[25] On the whole, Cairo is exposed to the open air although 'Amal Fawq may block some of that air. Cairo's buildings are not as high [22b] as those of al-Fusṭāṭ but much lower.[26] Cairo's lanes and streets are broader, cleaner, less dirty, and they contain much less putrifying rubbish. Its inhabitants drink mostly well water. When the north wind blows, it pierces the town; when the south wind blows, much of the vapor from al-Fusṭāṭ descends on Cairo. The proximity of the well water of Cairo to the surface of the earth, combined with the thinness of the soil, makes it inevitable that some of the waste from the latrines reaches the underground water by secretion. Between Cairo and al-Fusṭāṭ there are pools filled with the secretion of the earth from the days of the Nile flood. Some of the sewers of Cairo flow into them. The water in these pools is ruined because it is stagnant and because their soil is salty and substances flowing into them are putrid. The vapor that arises from the pools over Cairo and al-Fusṭāṭ considerably increases the bad air in both regions. A good deal of this is cast toward the district of al-Bāṭilīyah to the south of Cairo[27] and also

[23]"The Red" was the name of the middle district in the western part of al-Fusṭāṭ, which was colonized by three Arab tribes and stretched along the shore of the Nile and the Nile Canal as far as Jabal Yashkūr.

[24]This seems hardly possible because al-Qarāfah was situated between al-Fusṭāṭ and the Muqaṭṭam Mountains; the range of mountains could not have kept the vapors of al-Fusṭāṭ from al-Qarāfah.

[25]Although the Nile at that time flowed at least two kilometers farther east than in present-day Cairo, it was certainly a kilometer's distance from the western town wall. The alteration in the position of the riverbed did not take place until the thirteenth century A.D., when the additional land gave rise to the suburb of Būlāq. See Abu-Lughod, *Cairo*, maps I–VII.

[26]See Nāṣir-i Khusraw, p. 132f.

[27]Al-Bāṭilīyah was a district before the southeast gate (Bāb al-Maḥrūq) of Cairo, which was

toward the center of al-'Abīd district.[28] If we consider, however, the condition of Cairo in comparison with al-Fusṭāṭ, the air of the former is better and more suitable, and its condition is healthier because most [23a] of its decaying substances are thrown outside the city and most of the vapor is dissolved. Nevertheless, many of the inhabitants of Cairo also drink from the water of the Nile, especially during the time of its flowing into the Khalīj Canal,[29] and this water is used for drinking after passing by al-Fusṭāṭ and being mixed with the district's refuse.

Al-Gīzah is west of the Nile and is small.[30] It is situated parallel to the low-lying region of al-Fusṭāṭ. In the neighborhood of al-Gīzah, many trees and plants grow. Thickly wooded areas abound in decay, as the Ancients said. The cause of this is the waste that disintegrates from the trees and the vapor that is retained among them. The water that the people of al-Gīzah drink is drawn from the Nile without having been mixed with the corruption of al-Fusṭāṭ. For the flow of the Nile toward al-Gīzah is greater, and the part of it that reaches there does not pass by al-Fusṭāṭ, except when the current of the Nile is interrupted on the side of al-Fusṭāṭ; then, the corruption extends to al-Gīzah. Because of its great proximity to the Nile, al-Gīzah is very damp.

Al-Gizīrah is smaller than al-Gīzah and lies in the middle of the Nile,[31] between al-Gīzah and al-Fusṭāṭ. On it, too, stand many trees,

---

occupied by a Berber tribe that immigrated with the Fāṭimids. The Bāṭilīyah quarter was destroyed by fire in A.D. 1263. The present street of that name is near the Azhar Mosque, far away from the place where these pools were.

[28]Darb al-'Abīd, i.e., the slave quarter, lay to the southwest of the aforementioned district. It should not be confused with Khandaq al-'Abīd, "the slave moat," in the north of Cairo.

[29]The Khalīj Miṣrī or Red Sea Canal was an ancient canal linking the Nile to the Red Sea; it was reopened in the first century A.D. by Trajan. In A.D. 643 the canal was reactivated by 'Amr ibn al-'Āṣ, following the Arab conquest of Egypt. According to al-Maqrīzī (*al-Khiṭaṭ*, 1:141), it originally led as far as the Red Sea in order to take grain from Egypt to Arabia; in A.H. 145 it was partially filled in by order of the caliph al-Manṣūr and, then, only served to irrigate the northern outskirts of Cairo and to supply water to the city. Since pre-Islamic times, religious ceremonies and great festivity have attended the annual cutting of the dike at Cairo, signaling the annual flooding of the delta. The canal was finally filled in at the end of the nineteenth century after the establishment of a modern water supply. See also Abu-Lughod, *Cairo*, p. 5 et passim; Joseph de Somogyi, "The Nile Red-Sea Canal," *Actas do IV Congresso de Estudos Árabes e Islâmicos*, pp. 523–526.

[30]See Nāṣir-i Khusraw's description given in Part I of this volume.

[31]Nāṣir-i Khusraw p. 152, n. 1: "The island of ar-Rawḍah was designated under the Fāṭimid caliphs as Jazīrah, Jazīrat Miṣr (the Island of Miṣr) or Jazīrat al-Ḥiṣn (the Island of the Fortress)." Al-Gazīrah or ar-Rawḍah no longer lies in the middle of the Nile but near the eastern bank, separated only by a 60- to 70-meters wide canal, while it is separated from the western shore near al-Gīzah by the main stream, 500 meters wide. At the time of Ibn Riḍwān, the eastern arm of the Nile may have been 300 meters wide, for Nāṣir-i Khusraw saw a bridge of thirty-six boats over it (p. 153), but it dried up, as Ibn Riḍwān informs us, when the Nile was low. In consequence of this,

[23b] and it is naturally damper than these places because the Nile surrounds it.

It is evident that the healthiest parts of the city are al-Qarāfah, Cairo, ash-Sharaf, 'Amal Fawq with al-Ḥamrā', and al-Gīzah. The northern part of Cairo is the healthiest of all these on account of its distance from the vapor of al-Fusṭāṭ and its nearness to the north. The worst place in the city is the district around the Old Mosque,[32] extending to the shores of the Nile. Al-Khandaq,[33] in the northern region of Cairo, is equally bad because it is situated in a depression. For this reason, its air is altered. Finally, al-Maqsim[34] is damper on account of its proximity to the Nile.

In the winter and early spring, many fish are brought from the sea to this city. Often they spoil and diffuse a detestable smell. They are sold in Cairo, and its inhabitants and those of al-Fusṭāṭ eat them. Then, many putrid residues from the fish collect in their bodies. If their temperaments were not well balanced and if their bodies were not healthy at this time, it would produce in them many fatal diseases, but their fortitude [24a] prevents that.

Sometimes, the Nile is cut off from the region of al-Fusṭāṭ at the end of spring and in the early summer. The remaining water becomes foul with all that is thrown into it, until its corruption reaches the point that an abominable smell arises from it. It is obvious that this water, when it is in such a condition, makes a marked change in the people's temperament.

---

masses of mud settled on the eastern shore, upon which present-day "Old Cairo" (Miṣr al-Qadīmah or Miṣr al-'Atīqah) was founded, as the riverside quarter, while al-Fusṭāṭ meanwhile declined and became a dumping ground for rubbish. At the south end of ar-Rawḍah Island, there still exists the famous Nilometer (al-Miqyās), constructed in A.D. 716 and later restored several times.

[32]Al-Jāmi' al-'Atīq or Jāmi' 'Amr was established in A.D. 643 by 'Amr ibn al-'Āṣ (d. ca. 42/663). Originally measuring 50 by 30 cubits, it was close to the then course of the Nile in al-Fusṭāṭ and formed the center of the new garrison city. There grew up around the mosque a bazaar quarter with narrow streets. Since the seventh century, the mosque has been continually rebuilt and enlarged; it attained its present dimensions in 212/827. It served simultaneously as a place of prayer, council chamber, courtroom, post office, and as lodging for travelers. The mosque is still venerated as the oldest mosque in North Africa—at least in situation—and as one of the oldest in the Islamic world. See K. A. C. Creswell, *A Short Account of Early Muslim Architecture* (Baltimore, 1958), s.v. " 'Amr."

[33]Of the three districts of this name, there is no doubt that here is meant the one outside the north wall of Cairo, which was near the moat built in A.D. 969 by the Fāṭimid general and administrator Jawhar (d. 381/991) (see *EI*², s.v. "Djawhar al-Ṣiḳillī" [H. Monés]); it was colonized by purchased slaves (*'abīd ash-shirā*); hence its name, Khandaq al-'Abīd ("slave moat").

[34]Al-Maqsim, i.e., "the water works," also corrupted to al-Maqs or Maks, was the harbor of Cairo on the Nile, outside the northwest corner gate of Bāb al-Baḥr ("river gate"), where today the Mosque of Awlād 'Inān stands.

To the south of this city, at a great distance from it, is a place called al-Fayyūm, in which the water of the Nile is stored up. The people there sow crops several times a year. It is observable that when the water is released, a change occurs in the color and taste of the Nile. This condition, felt most strongly during the rising of the Nile in al-Buḥayrah,[35] Saft, Nahyā,[36] and farther upriver in the lands close to al-Fayyūm, increases the bad state of the inhabitants of the capital, particularly when the south wind blows. On account of their close proximity to one another, al-Fusṭāṭ, Cairo, al-Gazīrah, and al-Gīzah share together in the air, food, water, and epidemic diseases. Yet, in some of them, the disease may be less intense than in others.

Clearly, the inhabitants of the Egyptian capital fall a swifter [24b] prey to diseases than do all other inhabitants of this land, except for those of al-Fayyūm, which also abounds in pestilences for the reasons mentioned above.[37] The worst quarter of the capital is the low-lying district of al-Fusṭāṭ. Thus, cowardice and a lack of generosity characterize its inhabitants; rarely does one of them help another or afford shelter to the stranger. Envy predominates among them, and they are intriguers and slanderers to a high degree.[38] Their cowardice is so great that only five officials are needed to drive a hundred or more of their men before them, while in countries whose people are accustomed to combat, five officials are necessary to drive only one man. It is apparent,

[35]Buḥayrah (Beḥerah) is the name of the western province of the Egyptian delta. At the time of the division into provinces in Fāṭimid times, Buḥayrah was an extensive region, situated west of the Rosetta branch and reaching from the point of the delta right up to, but excluding, Alexandria. The capital was Damanhūr. See *EI*², s. v. "Buḥayra" (G. Wiet).

[36]Saft and Nahyā or Nāhyā are the names of at least a dozen villages in Egypt. Here the two places Saft al-Laban, 6 kilometers, and an-Nahyā, 9 kilometers to the northwest of al-Gīzah are doubtlessly meant. They lie in the inundation district of the Nile but not close to the river itself.

[37]Cf. Ibn Ḥawqal, 1:158. Meyerhof noted that al-Fayyūm was still considered particularly unhealthy in the early twentieth century. The official rates of mortality and blindness were among the highest in Egypt.

[38]Ibn Riḍwān's unfavorable judgment pronounced on the inhabitants of al-Fusṭāṭ is not confirmed by Arabic travelers. Al-Muqaddasī (ca. A.D. 985) certainly described them as dirty, immoral, and addicted to drink, but also as amiable and generous (*Aḥsan at-taqāsīm*, de Goeje, ed., pp. 193–200). The Persian Nāṣir-i Khusraw in no way complained of a bad reception in al-Fusṭāṭ (pp. 145–159); nor did Ibn Ḥawqal (1:144). And al-Idrīsī (ca. A.D. 1154) says: "Its inhabitants are high-minded and pious; they possess great wealth, which is always increasing, and the most beautiful merchandise; they are neither bothered by cares nor devoured by worry, for they enjoy great security and perfect tranquility, since public authority protects them and justice reigns among them. Al-Fusṭāṭ is generally well populated, and its bazaars are well furnished with all sorts of food, drink, and beautiful clothing. The inhabitants enjoy affluence and are distinguished by their elegance and the gentleness of their manners (*Opus geographicum*, 3:323). Regarding this latter account, see Roberto Rubinacci, "La Ville du Caire dans la geographie d'al-Idrīsī," *Colloque international sur l'histoire du Caire*, pp. 405–411. See also Clerget, *Le Caire*, 1:231ff.

then, why the people of the capital of Egypt succumb most quickly to illnesses and have the weakest spirit. Perhaps it was for this reason that the Ancients chose their capital to be in another place. Some of them established it in Memphis[39]—it is ancient Miṣr—others in Heliopolis,[40] others in Alexandria, and still others in different places, as their ruins prove.

[39]Memphis is located about 12 miles south of modern Cairo on the west bank of the Nile. It flourished between 5000 and 2500 B.C., reaching its zenith when the Southern Kingdom extended its hegemony over the delta and united the two regions. Memphis was centrally located and the logical capital. In the Christian era the city declined. According to the description of Egypt by al-Muqaddasī, Memphis in the tenth century A.D. (then called 'Azīzīyah, "which used to be al-Miṣr in olden times") had completely disintegrated. See Abu-Lughod, *Cairo*, p. 4 et passim; Ibn Ḥawqal, 1:158–159.

[40]See Ibn Ḥawqal, 1:158f.; *EI*², s.v. " 'Ayn Shams" (C. H. Becker).

· 7 ·

On the Causes of Pestilence

As for the indigenous Egyptian illnesses, [25a] we have said enough about the people and the causes of their illnesses. It is clear that most of their diseases are diseases of superfluities, and yellow and raw biles combine with the superfluities.[1] The rest of the illnesses occur among the people quickly and in close succession, especially at the end of autumn and the beginning of winter.

As for epidemic illnesses, we have not discussed anything of this matter until now. The meaning of an epidemic illness is that it encompasses many people in one land at one time. One type is called *al-mawtān*,[2] in which the mortality rate is high. Epidemic diseases have many causes that may be grouped into four kinds: a change in the quality of the air, a change in the quality of the water, a change in the quality of the food, and a change in the quality of psychic events.

The quality of the air is changed in two ways: first is its normal variation, and this does not produce an epidemic illness. I do not call this a sickness-inducing change. [25b] Second, when the change does not follow the normal course, it creates epidemic illness. It is the same with the other causes. If they change according to habit, they do not create illness. If the change is irregular, however, epidemic illness occurs. A deviation that changes the air from its customary nature takes place when the air becomes hotter, colder, damper, drier, or when a corruption mixes with it. The state of corruption may occur from a nearby or faraway place. Hippocrates and Galen said that it is not impossible that an epidemic disease may occur in the land of the Greeks because of a corruption that accumulated in Ethiopia, ascended to the atmosphere, then descended on the Greeks, and caused epidemic illness among them.[3] The temperament of the air may also be changed

[1]Cf. Grand'henry, p. 62.

[2]See Dols, *The Black Death*, p. 316f.; *MI*, p. 245; Bachmann, "Quelques remarques," p. 305.

[3]See Galen, *De differentiis febrium* l. 6.

from the normal when a large group of people arrives, whose long journey has ruined their bodies and whose humors have thus become bad. Much of their humors mixes with the air, and it is transmitted to the people, so that epidemic disease becomes evident.[4]

The water may create epidemic illness if the water is excessive in [26a] its increase or decrease, or if a corrupt substance mixes with it. The people are forced to drink it, and the air surrounding their bodies is corrupted by the water as well. This corrupt substance may mix with the water, either in a nearby or distant place, when the water's course passes by a battlefield where many dead bodies are found. Or the river passes by polluted swamps, and it carries and mixes with this stagnant water.

Foods produce epidemic illness. If blight attacks the plants, prices rise and most people are forced to change their foods.[5] If most of the people increase their consumption of these foods at one time, as at the festivals, dyspepsia increases and the people become ill. And if the pastureland and the water of the animals that we eat are corrupted, it will cause epidemic illness.

Psychic events create epidemic disease when a common fear of a ruler grips the people. They suffer prolonged sleeplessness and worry about deliverance or the possibility of trouble. As a result, their digestion becomes bad and their natural heat is changed. Sometimes, people are forced to violent action [26b] in such a condition. When they expect a famine in some years, they increase their hoarding. Their distress intensifies because of what they anticipate may happen.[6]

All of these things produce epidemic illness in human bodies when many people in one country and at one time are subjected to them. It is evident that if an illness increases at one time in one city, a good deal of vapor arises from the ill bodies and changes the temperament of the air. When this vapor meets a body that is susceptible to illness, it makes that body sick, even if it were not directly subjected to what the other people had been exposed to. For example, if an epidemic illness occurs among the people because there is a rise in prices and a lack of food and there is among them someone who does not change his habit in what he eats and

[4]For the miasmatic theory of disease transmission, see Part I of this volume.

[5]Ibn Riḍwān's reasoning here should be noted: it is not the scarcity and high prices of food that produces epidemic illnesses but the forced change in the individual's customary diet. See Klein-Franke, "The Arabic Version of Galen's *περὶ ἐθῶν*," pp. 125–150.

[6]See Tucker, "The Effects of Famines in the Medieval Islamic World." Cf. Ibn Bakhtīshū', *Risālah fī ṭ-ṭibb*, p. 30: "The physician has to observe the psychic events because they are one of those causes that necessarily effects diseases."

drinks, and if the rotten vapor of the sick reaches his body, which is susceptible to disease, he falls ill as well.

As set forth, epidemic illnesses take place in Egypt on account of a corruption that is not customary and befalls the air, regardless of whether the substance of this [27a] corruption is from the land of Egypt itself or from the lands that border it, such as the Sūdān, the Ḥijāz,[7] Syria, or Barqah.[8] Epidemics may result also from what befalls the Nile when its increase is excessive, whereupon the increase of moisture, as well as the decay, is greater than usual. When its inundation is very inadequate, the air becomes drier than usual, and the people are obliged to drink the bad water. A rottenness may also mix with the water that results from a war in Egypt, the Sūdān, or another place where many men die, and a vapor rises from their corpses into the air and putrifies it. The air's decay reaches the people of Egypt, or the water flows and carries the decay with it. In addition, epidemics may happen when prices become excessive and cause a change in diet, when blight besets the crops, injury occurs to the rams, or general fear or despair seizes the people.

Every one of these reasons produces an epidemic illness. The intensity of the illness is related to its originating cause. If more than one cause occur together, the illness is stronger, more intense, and swifter in its killing, as appeared in Egypt several years ago. Many wars took place then, killing a large number of the enemy as well as our own people. A great fear of the enemy and high prices befell the Egyptians. [27b] Furthermore, the inundation of the Nile was extraordinary in both its increase and decrease. Considerable decay from the dead mixed with the water, and the air surrounding them was contaminated by the decay of these things. Famine increased, and a high mortality occurred among the people. About a third of the people died from it.[9]

The principle that we have related concerning the deviation of these things from their normal course each year escaped the attention of Ibn al-Jazzār, so that he mistakenly considered the things that conform with the temperament of Egypt to be the cause for the occurrence of epidemic illness.

[7]Northwestern Arabia, see *EI*², s.v. "al-Ḥidjāz" (G. Rentz).

[8]Barqah designated both the town (now al-Marj) and the region that belonged to it, i.e., Cyrenaica, a broad African peninsula jutting out into the eastern Mediterranean between the Gulf of Bomba and that of the Great Syrtis. To the east begins the Marmarica, while the vast eastern Libyan Sahara stretches away to the south. See *EI*², s. v. "Barḳa" (J. Despois).

[9]This imprecise account appears to describe the severe famine and pestilence, as well as the other circumstances in Egypt, in 447–454/1055–1062. See Part I of this volume.

· 8 ·

A Summary of All That Has Been Said and an Addition to the Commentary on the Six Causes that Determine Health and Illness

The temperament of Egypt is hot and moist and includes an excessive humidity. The southern region of the country is the hottest, and less corruption exists in the southern water of the Nile than in the northern, especially north of al-Fusṭāṭ. An example is the people of al-Bushmūr;[1] their disposition is grosser, and stupidity is dominant because they [28a] eat very coarse foods and drink bad water. As for Alexandria, Tinnīs, and similar places, their closeness to the sea, their mildness of heat and cold, and the blowing of the east wind improve their natures and enhance their ambitions, freeing them from the coarseness and asininity of the people of al-Bushmūr. The fact that Tinnīs is surrounded by the sea imposes a predominant humidity on the city and causes the effeminate character of its people. It is evident, therefore, that Egypt possesses many regions; each one is distinguished by special characteristics.

The reasons for pestilence in Egypt that Ibn al-Jazzār related are incorrect. The actual reason is the occurrence of a deviation from the normal, as we have stated. The bodies of the Egyptians and everything in their land are weak and quickly fall victim to illness. The end of autumn and the beginning of winter are the worst seasons of the year, when illness is most frequent. The capital is actually worse off than other cities in the rapid incidence of sicknesses. The customary illnesses are many, and most of them are illnesses of superfluity [28b] and putrefaction, accompanied by yellow bile and phlegm.

If these things are as we have described, it is desirable that we add a brief excursus on the six causes. The state of the body's temperament is good in the balanced air; the digestion improves because the light animal spirit that is in us becomes clear; and the natural heat spreads

[1]Ramzī, *al-Qāmūs*, 1:31f.; Yāqūt, *Muʿjam al-buldān*, 1:634, 1.16ff.

through the body in moderation. The air that deviates from the balance changes the bodies that are not accustomed to it but does not harm the bodies that are used to it, unless they are greatly susceptible to disease or are liable to deviate immoderately from their normal functioning.

Likewise, concerning the statement about what is eaten and drunk, if people become accustomed to specific foods and their bodies grow up with them, they fall ill when these foods are not available.[2] Also, customary physical exercise may be a reason for good health because it dissolves the superfluities and smoky vapors that collect in the body. The limbs of one who has become habituated to physical exercise are firmer and stronger. Therefore, the peasants and all other workmen have greater strength and spirit [29a] than the people of leisure and luxury; the superfluities in their bodies are less. Moderate quiet makes bodies healthy and strong. Being excessively sedentary, however, does not allow the vapor to evaporate, so that congestion of the superfluities occurs, which causes harm to the body. For this reason, sedentary bodies become much more susceptible to illnesses. Consequently, quiet and leisured Egyptians more readily fall victims to illness. Excessive physical exercise also harms the bodies because it exhausts them and generates smoky superfluities in them.[3]

If sleep and wakefulness are balanced, they produce and preserve health. When asleep, digestion improves because of the descent of heat to the interior; wakefulness dissolves the superfluities of digestion because of the ascent of heat to the exterior. Excessive sleep cools the body, and the superfluities increase in it; excessive wakefulness makes the body dry and spoils its digestion.

The teaching about retention and evacuation is similar, for if the superfluities retained in the body are excessive, they spoil digestion and decay rushes to them. If what is evacuated is more than what is retained, it is inevitable that this surplus is from the essence [29b] of the humors of the body itself, which are very vital to the body; consequently, their evacuation causes illness to occur. Therefore, what is retained should be equal to what is evacuated. Galen and other physicians said that in the winter many viscid, phlegmatic substances and filth gather in the body and stick fast[4] in the stomach, the vessels, and the veins, as viscid and filthy substances stick fast in the watercourses of

[2]See Klein-Franke, "The Arabic Version of Galen's περὶ ἐθῶν."

[3]Cf. Maimonides, pp. 16–18.

[4]*Talḥaju*, see *WKAS*, 2:276b, 1.28ff.

canals and drains.[5] When spring begins, it dissolves these phlegmatic, viscid humors; then, it increases the amount of blood. The filth that accompanies the humors putrefies them; therefore, it is necessary to evacuate these before they change the blood. The vessels and veins should be cleansed of their recurring filth by purgative medicines.[6]

Likewise, in the summer fierce humors and harmful filth collect in the body and remain in the bottom of the stomach, vessels, and veins. When autumn begins, the change of the air stirs them up and burns many of them. Because of this, it is necessary that they be evacuated [30a] before they cause harm to the body. Thus, it is desirable that every year the bodies be emptied in the spring and autumn, so that the vessels are cleansed of their filth and purged of the bad things that persist in them. There is one kind of purgative that should be used in the autumn and another kind that should be used in the spring. The desirable medication for evacuation in the spring should purge, to a great extent, much of the phlegm and viscid substances. The medication for emptying the body in the autumn should purge, to a great extent, much of the yellow bile and the fierce filth, because of what we have presented earlier. It is necessary that the medication of autumn also evacuates the moisture peculiar to Egypt, especially because the moistures produced in people's bodies at that time are great. These two evacuations—one in the spring and the other in the autumn—eliminate the filth that becomes congested in the bodies between the two seasons.

The psychic events, such as anger, sadness, [30b] and joy, do not create illness if they do not go beyond the proper bounds.[7] It is desirable that the people of Egypt increase their gaiety and joy in order to strengthen the natural heat of their bodies, for the digestion improves, and the congestion in their bodies lessens.

It is evident from what we have said that every one of the six factors produces and sustains good health if its quantity and quality are well balanced. When they deviate from what is appropriate, they bring about illness.[8] Therefore, the customary and epidemic illnesses of Egypt, and other illnesses as well, increase and decrease according to the degree of one's awareness of these factors and his negligence or

[5]*Hippocrates, A Regimen for Health* 5.

[6]On the subject of purgatives, see Grand'henry, pp. 72–78, 101–109.

[7]This topic is discussed extensively in Ibn Bakhtīshū', pp. 75v–76r.

[8]Ḥunayn, p. 13: "If duly apportioned in quantity, quality, time, and order, the six conserve and engender health. If used otherwise, either in quantity, manner, time, or order, they engender and maintain disease."

attention to them. For example, whoever increases the consumption of food that produces black bile, his body is susceptible to melancholic illnesses. This is the case with the other causes. These six factors may change the temperament of man, his aging, his physical constitution, and his habits; they may affect the influence of the current season and the temperament of male and female. What we have said of these important things is sufficient.

• 9 •

On the General Stratagem for Preserving Health and the Treatment of Illnesses [31a]

Philosophers and doctors have taught us this stratagem. They advised us to imitate nature in what it does to the body.[1] Thus, Hippocrates said: "If what must be cleansed from the body is the kind that may be evacuated by voluntary bowel movement and vomiting, it is beneficial and easy to endure. If it is not natural, the matter would be the opposite. It is desirable also that you consider the current season, the country, the age, and the illnesses in determining whether an evacuation that you have in mind is necessary or not."[2] Hippocrates also stated: "It is necessary that what is given as medication to evacuate the body should be of the type that causes a natural evacuation; it would be beneficial. But if the evacuation is contrary to that, it should be stopped."[3] He said: "The things that are desirable to be evacuated should be evacuated from the appropriate limbs."[4] Furthermore, he stated: "Whatever illnesses occur from corpulence, its cure is by evacuation; [31b] whatever illnesses occur from evacuation, its cure is corpulence. The remedy of the rest of the illnesses is by 'contraries'."[5] About the preservation of health, Hippocrates said that it is desirable to preserve everything as it is.

If we consider all that we have heard from Hippocrates and Galen about this and other things, we find it contains what the philosophers and the Dogmatists[6] among the doctors agreed upon. Namely, it is

[1]See *Vorlesungen*, p. 66.

[2]*Hippocrates, Aphorisms* 4. 1–3; see also 1. 25.

[3]Ibid., 4. 2.

[4]Ibid., 1. 21; see also Hippocrates, *Kitāb Buqrāṭ fi'l-akhlāṭ*, p. 13/14.

[5]*Hippocrates, Aphorisms* 2. 22; *The Nature of Man* 9. Cf. Grand'henry, p. 62f.

[6]*Aṣḥāb al-qiyās* (as opposed to the *aṣḥāb at-tajribah* [the Empiricists]), emphasized analogical reasoning in their diagnosis. See the discussion of the Dogmatists in Part I of this volume as well as in *Vorlesungen*, pp. 87, 95 and in M. Neuburger, *Geschichte der Medizin* (Stuttgart, 1906), 1:236ff.

desirable that we follow nature in what it does to the body, for nature (which God Almighty created as a support for managing the body, if He chooses) preserves the health of the body by the foods that it supplies and by the superfluities that it eliminates every day. The superfluities are eliminated by respiration, perspiration, urination, vomiting, spitting, nosebleed, menstruation, and by hemorrhoids; the elimination is according to the appropriate organ, the temperament of one's body, the current season of the year, the country, and one's age, external appearance, and habits.

This should be our procedure in the foods, medication, and different [32a] kinds of treatment that we administer to the body.[7] Just as nature evacuates the harmful humor from the appropriate limb, as in the crisis of an illness, our procedure is to empty the harmful humor that collects in the body from the appropriate limb. For example, if we observe the condition of the sick—his temperament and appearance, the temperament of his country, the current season, the nature of the illness, its causes and symptoms—and we choose the suitable foods and remedies and we consider everything that he needs, it is possible for us to preserve his health and to remove what is harmful from him. Therefore, we are compelled to know the natures of foods and remedies, the anatomy, and the rest that the Dogmatists practice.

The things that the doctor needs to count, memorize, and know in order to cure every disease and to preserve health are twenty-five, aside from other details: (1) the temperament of the country; (2) the indigenous illnesses; (3) the current season; (4) the temperament of this season; (5) the epidemic illnesses; (6) the disease existing in the body and in what limb; (7) the cause of the illness; (8) the degree of strength of the illness; (9) the symptoms of the illness; (10) the intensity of the symptoms; [32b] (11) the strength of the patient; (12) the temperament of the patient;[8] (13) the age of the patient; (14) the temperament of the limb affected by the illness and the limb's functioning, form, and position; (15) the external appearance of the patient; (16) the nature of the patient, whether male or female; (17) his habits in times of health;[9] (18) the nature of the foods

See also Galen, "On the Medical Sects: For Beginners," in *Greek Medicine*, ed. Brock, pp. 130–151; idem, "De la meilleure secte, à Trasybule," in *Oeuvres*, ed. Daremberg, 2:398–467; idem, *On Medical Experience*, ed. R. Walzer (Oxford, 1944), p. 87ff.

[7]See Ibn Riḍwān's *Kitāb Kifāyat aṭ-ṭabīb*, which has been edited and translated by Grand'henry, for his detailed discussion of therapeutics.

[8]See Ḥunayn's rules for treatment according to the temperament of the patient (Ḥunayn, pp. 30f., 37).

[9]See Klein-Franke, "The Arabic Version of Galen's *περι εθων*."

and medicines; (19) his usage of them in times of health and illness; (20) the foods and medicines that are desirable for the doctor to select at times of health and illness; (21) what the treatment should be; (22) what is the proper time for treatment; (23) what is the proper limb for administering treatment; (24) the patient and whoever cares for him should follow the instructions of the doctor; and (25) the circumstances of the patient should be conducive to recovery.[10]

These are the things that the doctor follows in order to assist nature in performing its task of preserving health and treating the sick. The study, practice, and understanding of these things are very difficult and require a good deal of work, toil, lengthy experience, training, and no lack of attention or neglect of anything, either great or small. Today, I do not know [33a] any doctors who promote these sureties of the profession. I do not know in this great city anyone who concerns himself with a knowledge of the temperament of the Egyptians, not to mention other things. This is a matter without which treatment is impossible. It suffices to say that Ibn al-Jazzār, despite his stature in the profession, wrote a book about Egypt in which he failed to explain its temperament or its condition. In addition, mistakes appear in many passages of his work. If these twenty-five things are as difficult as we have described, one can master them only after long nights of reading the books of the Ancients, contemplating their meaning, and exerting one's mind and body, night and day, as far as is humanly possible.

Hippocrates and Galen described the difficulty of medical practice. Hippocrates said: "Life is short; the art is long; the time is limited; the testing is risky; and the decision is difficult."[11] Galen described the rigors of the medical profession in many of his books. Whenever man neglects those things that are inescapable, depends on hopes and [33b] vanities, and prefers leisure, death overtakes him. The goodness and beauty of life's fruits elude him. In the hereafter he suffers loss and terrible pain. When one works hard, however, for what is needed, good fortune in this world and the next comes to him. If the prosperity of this

[10]Inexplicably, Ibn Riḍwān does not mention the examination of the patient's urine or taking the patient's pulse, which were common diagnostic tools. Neither subject in Arabic medicine has been systematically studied; see, however, ar-Rāzī, *Guide*, pp. 101–107; *MI*, p. 82f.; O. Spies and H. Müller-Bütow, "Drei urologische Kapitel aus der arabischen Medizin," *Sudhoffs Archiv* 48 (1964): 248–259; Loren MacKinney, *Medical Illustrations in Medieval Manuscripts* (London, 1965), pp. 9–14; Ḥunayn, pp. 70–72, 95–107.

[11]"Al-'umar qaṣīr wa ṣ-ṣinā'ah ṭawīlah wa l-waqt ḍayyiq wa t-tajribah khaṭar wa l-qaḍā' 'asir:" *Hippocrates, Aphorisms*, 1. 1. See Franz Rosenthal, " 'Life is Short, the Art is Long': Arabic Commentaries on the First Hippocratic Aphorism," *BHM* 40 (1961):226–245; and idem, *The Classical Heritage in Islam*, p. 186f.

world escapes him, the good fortune of the hereafter will not fail him. The punishment of the ignorant doctor is not small in the hereafter because of the great harm that he caused to people. His punishment is much greater than for those who steal and commit murder. Oh doctor, beware of neglecting your art for the delights of animals—eating, drinking, intercourse, accumulating riches, glorious deeds, love of bragging about mounts, clothing, and other things in which one prides oneself. You deceive the common people by associating with those who have wealth, letting your beard grow long, and having gray hair. Being obsessed by all of these things prevents you from becoming clever in the art of medicine. They are what Galen and other philosophers and doctors condemn, but they are coveted by the Egyptian doctors more than anything else, for I am well acquainted with them.[12] [34a]

An Egyptian doctor came to me once and asked me about potions that lengthen the hair of his beard and produce grayness in it. I was astonished, and I asked him to tell me the truth about his condition. He said: "It is useful in the profession of medicine in Egypt today to have a long gray beard, fine clothes, mounts, and similar objects of pride. Don't you see that the people extol the man who possesses these qualities, and they do not consider anything else?" I said to him: "You speak the truth. This is what has made the druggists[13] more skilled and knowledgeable about drugs than the doctors. Some of them have become the most famous doctors of the city."[14] Then, I admonished him about what he should do and warned him against being foolish. I informed him of what Galen said; namely, that the ignorant doctor is more harmful to the body than a current pestilence or thieves. For thieves desire only money while the ignorant doctor takes away one's soul. I do not think that he accepted my advice.

Some time ago one of the well-known doctors of al-Fusṭāṭ met me. He took me by the hand and rebuked me for my failure to attend the

[12]See the references to charlatanry in Part I of this volume. The same theme is treated by Ibn Riḍwān in his *Kitāb an-Nāfiʿ*. See Lyons, "The *Kitāb al-Nāfiʿ* of Alī ibn Riḍwān," p. 67f.; Schacht and Meyerhof, p. 25f.; *MI* p. 224. See also A. Z. Iskandar, "Galen and Rhazes on Examining Physicians," *BHM* 36 (1962):362–365. A comparable criticism of Egyptian medical practice is given by Ibn Jamīʿ; see Meyerhof, "Sultan Saladin's Physician," pp. 174–175.

[13]See the description of the drug trade in Egypt by Albert Dietrich, *Zum Drogenhandel im islamischen Ägypten*, in *Veröffentl. aus der Heidelberger Papyrus-Sammlung, Neue Folge, hsgb. von der Heidelberger Akad. d. Wiss., phil.-hist. Kl.*, no. 1 (Heidelberg, 1954), pp. 16–20.

[14]Ibn Riḍwān complains about the common habit, which has persisted until the present day, of sick people's resort to a pharmacist instead of a doctor, without a proper understanding of the illness or the drugs that are dispensed. Cf. Lyons, "The *Kitāb al-Nāfiʿ*," p. 69f.; see also Elgood, *A Medical History of Persia*, p. 254f.

notables; for not collecting my fees; for my preoccupation [34b] with reading the books of the Ancients, practicing with them, and gaining experience; and for my negligence of the pleasures of this world and its dirhams.[15] I said to him: "Galen does not even call the doctors who devote themselves assiduously to the houses of the nobles 'doorkeepers' because they are baser than that. I do not allow myself this kind of behavior."[16] He chided me and said: "This is an ill fate, and, like an incurable illness, I do not think that it will relinquish you." He departed, leaving me alone. Another man said: "If you see a man looking into a book, he is ill-fated."

One of the senior doctors also met me some time ago, and he began to ask me about the crisis in illnesses.[17] It turned out that he did not know about it and did not understand it except for its name. He stayed with me part of a day, and I instructed him on the meaning of the crisis of an illness. I do not think that he understood.

One day I visited a notable, and I observed him breathing heavily because of the pressure in his lungs. One of the family remarked to me: "Someone," and he named him to me (and the man is one of the best and most prominent doctors in the country), "stated: 'Your sick man has pleurisy [*shawṣah*].' " I was astonished at this. I said to them: "Know that pleurisy [*shawṣah*] is accompanied by a constant fever, a pain in his side and a cough; these [35a] are the symptoms of true pleurisy [*dhāt al-janb*]. This is not the case with your sick relative."[18]

I shall tell you some stories about these doctors, their deceit and ignorance, so that you will be cautious of them. The government might examine their affairs in order to prevent their being in a position to profit by this profession unless they are skilled. The government could determine the best doctors, and the rest could emulate them. Examination by the authorities could bring about the disappearance of this

[15]The silver unit of the Islamic monetary system from the rise of Islam down to the Mongol period. See *EI*², s.v. "Dirham" (G. C. Miles), and chap. 14, n. 2 below.

[16]Galen said: "If any examiner wants to distinguish an eminent physician from an imposter, he should first enquire what are the activities to which a person has dedicated most of his time? Is it the perusal of books and the treatment of patients; or has he simply been dancing at the doorsteps of wealthy people, rambling from house to house, accompanying rich people on their travels? There will be no need to examine such people, for they will be found to possess no more knowledge than charlatans, doorkeepers, and boon companions" (Iskandar, "Galen and Rhazes on Examining Physicians," p. 364). See also Lyons, "The *Kitāb al-Nāfi*'," p. 66; Galen, *Methodus medendi*, l. 1; Kühn, 10:4; Temkin, *Galenism*, p. 36; Schacht and Meyerhof, p. 25.

[17]See chap. 5, n. 13 above.

[18]A distinction should be made here between *shawṣah* and *dhāt al-janb*. See Ullmann's discussion in *Rufus von Ephesos Krankenjournale*, p. 125. Cf. Levey, "Medical Ethics of Medieval Islam," p. 62.

calamity.[19] For example, one of the most famous doctors of al-Fusṭāṭ acquired renown because he used to ride with a pillow on the saddle under him, and did not consider someone's illness until he took out an astrolabe from his sleeve and looked at it.[20] Because of this, the common people thought that he was an outstanding physician. I swear by God, I do not think this man understood a thing about the science of medicine.

Among them also is a senior doctor with a great beard. He is unable to copy or write, let alone anything else. He deceived the people about himself by talking to the women about what is proper for them in the matter of sexual intercourse. Likewise with the men, he would relax his speech and display a cheerful mien. He would do that by joking and being playful with them, and they recommended him to others. [35b] He gained a great reputation and excellent earnings.

I am acquainted with another senior doctor among them, and I do not know another man in the world more ignorant than he is in every respect. This is a description of him: he is well built, having a large, lean physique with a small head and a long beard. This man deceives the people and the notables by the display of conceit and rage. He gained a great position by showing that he was in the service of the authorities. One of our friends told me that he had himself announced to this man one summer, when the heat was intense. Our friend was not permitted to enter until the man dressed in five gowns,[21] put on long turbans, and wrapped his body with many garments. My friend said: "When I entered and he was in this condition, I saw a madman who could not talk to me because of the intense heat from which he was suffering. He scolded me and exclaimed: 'Go away for I am busy treating myself and evacuating my body by perspiring.' He thought that it was something that would deceive me. I said to him: 'The bath is better for you than this.' "[22]

[19]See the discussion of this in Part I of this volume. If Ibn Riḍwān were the chief physician of Cairo, he would have been directly involved in the certification of physicians and knowledgeable about its procedure; from his statement here, this does not appear to be so. Similarly, Ibn Jamīʿ proposed, presumably to the sultan Saladin, that the medical profession be improved by an examination imposed on medical practitioners by the government; as far as we know, Saladin did not take such action. See Meyerhof, "Sultan Saladin's Physician," p. 175.

[20]It was not uncommon for a doctor to consult a "calculator" (*ḥāsib*) in order to determine the position of the stars before medical treatment; see *Vorlesungen*, p. 54.

[21]Dozy, s.v. "jubbah"; L. A. Mayer, *Mamluk Costume* (Geneva, 1952), pp. 15, 52, 58, 62; Edward Lane, *The Manners and Customs of the Modern Egyptians* (London, 1966 repr.), p. 30; R. Dozy, *Dictionnaire détaille des noms des vêtements* (Amsterdam, 1845), pp. 107–117; Serjeant, *Islamic Textiles*, s.v. "Djubba;" *EI*², s.v. "Libās" (Y. K. Stillman).

[22]Ibn Riḍwān appears to refer here to the same doctor that is mentioned in his *Kitāb an-Nāfiʿ*; see Iskandar, "An Attempted Reconstruction," p. 255.

I met this doctor at a notable's house. I saw him sitting [36a] at the feet of a sick person. He ordered the person to stand up before him, although the sick person was in great distress. Then, he took his pulse. I saw him also when he visited an old man who was hemiplegic, and he prescribed for him the dripping of milk on his head on very cold days.[23]

As for the surgeons and oculists, they treat the old man and the small boy, man and woman, rich and poor, townsman and villager with the very same medicines.

This is the state of the Egyptian doctors today. The practice of none of them is praiseworthy, with the exception of four or five. Now, I end the report about them and return to what I was saying. Concerning the stratagem for preserving the health and treating the sick, we have spoken sufficiently about it in the general discussion. As for the summary of these things, it is a matter that Hippocrates has summarized and Galen has elaborated.

[23]See Ullmann's discussion of this practice in *Rufus von Ephesos Krankenjournale*, p. 122f.

· 10 ·

On What Is Necessary for Doctors To Do in Egypt

Whereas Egypt and everything in it are weak in their substance [36b] and change and decay are rapid, it is necessary for the doctor to choose foods and remedies that are very fresh because they are still strong and have not yet been completely changed. The doctor's treatment should be adapted to the bodies in Egypt. He should work hard to make the sick more inclined in the opposite direction from the illness. He should avoid medicines that strongly relieve the constipated bowels and everything that has an excessive strength. The harm of such drugs is rapid in the body, especially in the Egyptians, whose bodies are quick to incur injury. He should select from the purgative drugs and others the gentlest in strength, so that there is no discomfort or harm to the bodies of the Egyptians. He should not prescribe the drugs found in the medical books of the Greeks and Persians, for most of them are aimed at bodies with strong constitutions and coarse humors. These are rarely found in Egypt. Likewise, it is indispensable for the doctor to examine carefully these drugs and to choose the gentlest one. He should reduce the dosage and replace much of it with substitutes that are gentler.[1] For example, sugary oxymel[2] is a substitute [37a] for honey, and julep is a

[1]Substitute drugs were discussed in all pharmacological works and gave rise to a small literature (*kutub al-abdāl*); see *MI*, p. 292ff.; Martin Levey, *Substitute Drugs in Early Arabic Medicine* (Stuttgart, 1971).

[2]*As-sakanjabī as-sukkarī*, see G. C. Anawati, *Drogues et médicaments dans l'antiquité et le moyen age* (in Arabic, Cairo, 1959), p. 108; Maimonides, p. 43; Graziani, p. 322. Before the introduction of sugar in the Middle Ages, oxymel was a sweet mixture prepared from water, vinegar, and honey that was commonly drunk as a beverage; prescriptions for its preparation are given in Galen's treatise on *Hygiene* (Kühn, 6:271ff.); see also *Hippocrates, Regimen in Acute Diseases*, p. lviii–lx. J. Ruska (*EI*[1], s.v. "Sukkar") gives Bengal as the original home of sugarcane (*qaṣab as-sukkar*). The purification of sugar was first known in India in about A.D. 300; the first certain mention of the product west of India was in A.D. 627 in connection with the conquest of Dastagird, the capital of the Persian king Khusrū II, when sugar is mentioned among the Indian treasures of the king. It is assumed that the manufacture of sugar and the cultivation of sugarcane reached Persia about the

replacement for honey. Also, it is necessary to know that the air of Egypt makes the electuaries[3] and the rest of the drugs weak in strength. If the matter were as we have recounted, the lives of the medicines—simple, compound, and electuaries of these and others—are shorter than their lives outside of Egypt.[4]

The doctor needs to evaluate and distinguish these things, so that nothing escapes his attention. If he is not satisfied with the cleansing of the body by a purgative remedy one time, there is no harm in its repetition after a few days. This is more commendable than taking a strong remedy once. Indeed, don't you see that a heavy object, if it is divided and carried piece by piece, is easier and lighter than carrying it whole. Therefore, it is desirable to extract the humors existing in the limbs repeatedly because the extraction of these by a gentle purgative remedy is difficult the first time.[5] Do not be deceived by these remedies, but compare them with everything that is needed for the patient. Remedies that are used often in the body wear it out, as a great deal of washing wears out [37b] good cloth.

In every season give those foods and remedies that are agreeable to the temperament of the season and to what is produced in that season in the bodies.[6] Allow the people to follow their habits, and do not keep them from it unless something else prevents it.[7] Order constant exercise

---

same time. At first cultivated only to a small extent for medical purposes or as a valuable sweet, sugarcane was very rapidly spread by the Arabs after the conquest of Persia to wherever the climatic conditions were suitable to the plant, notably in Egypt. See. E. O. von Lippmann, *Geschichte des Zuckers* (Leipzig, 1890); Sontheimer, 2:35f.; J. H. Galloway, "The Mediterranean Sugar Industry," *The Geographical Review*, 67, no. 2 (1977):177–194; Finkel, "King Mutton," 9:5; E. Ashtor, "Levantine Sugar Industry in the Late Middle Ages—A Sample of Technological Decline," in *The Islamic Middle East, 700–1900*, pp. 91–132; Ahsan, *Social Life Under the Abbasids*, pp. 100–103. Ibn Riḍwān wrote a "Discourse on the temperament of sugar"; see Schacht and Meyerhof, p. 48.

[3]*Ma'jūn*, see Graziani, p. 315; Lane, s.v. "ma'jūnun: . . .an electuary; any drug, or drugs, mixed with honey or inspissated juice or sirup; generally applied to such as contains opium, or some other intoxicating ingredient." On the therapeutic use of electuaries, see Grand'henry, p. 77.

[4]This was one matter that was at issue between Ibn Buṭlān and Ibn Riḍwān. The former was reproached, presumably by Ibn Riḍwān, for prescribing remedies that were inappropriate to the Egyptian climate (Schacht and Meyerhof, pp. 17, 89f.).

[5]*Hippocrates, Aphorisms* 2.51.

[6]Hippocratic medicine demonstrated a keen awareness of the influence of the seasons on men's constitution; the manipulation of the diet was intended, as shown by Ibn Riḍwān, to offset the unfavorable effects of the seasons. See *Hippocrates, Regimen in Acute Diseases*, 2:57–125 (*MI*, p. 29; *Kitāb Tadbīr al-amrāḍ al-ḥādda li-Buqrāṭ*, ed. and trans. M. C. Lyons [Cambridge, 1966]) and *On Humors*, 4:61–95 (*Kitāb fī'l-akhlāṭ*; *MI*, p. 30). Cf. Grand'henry, p. 61.

[7]Cf. Levey, "Medical Ethics of Medieval Islam," p. 46f.

to strengthen the limbs; then, illness does not hasten to them. Treat everyone with what suits him.

The general principle is that you should consider at every instant what is needed, mix some of the medicines with others until you know entirely what is right, and use it. And this is your duty.

· 11 ·

On the Prescription of the Body's Regimen in Egypt

All bodies are of five types: (1) the body with an excellent constitution, which is the norm for the medical profession; (2) the body with a constitution opposite to the first, which is the sick body; (3) the body with a constitution close to the excellent type, which is a healthy and cured body; (4) the body with a constitution close to the sick type, [38a] which is one susceptible to illness; and (5) the body with a constitution in the middle between health and illness.

Because Egypt produces in bodies a weakness and a high susceptibility to illness, there are necessarily only a very few bodies in Egypt that have an excellent constitution. As for the other bodies, there are many. Good health is found among them, and it is close to the excellent constitution. It was clear to the Ancients, I mean the Dogmatists, that the treatment of every one of these bodies should be different because of the individuality of the bodies, even though they are equally united in four methods of treatment.

First, all things are to be done in the most balanced manner for those who possess a perfect constitution. Second, all things are to be done on the basis of their correspondence to healthy bodies. Third, all things are to be made close to balance in bodies susceptible to illness, which are neither healthy nor sick. And fourth, all things are to be done opposite to the condition of sick bodies.

The first method, by which the bodies in excellent condition are managed, [38b] needs the planning of the air, water, food, and other things in the most balanced manner. The remaining methods require comparison with the perfect constitution and close examination of what is needed from these things. Such things that I have mentioned are the basic support and the greatest source for the preservation of health and the treatment of the sick. I have neither seen nor heard of one of the doctors of Egypt who understands this matter, not to speak of acting according to it.

Because digestion, as well as the animal spirit, is often bad in Egypt, you should turn your attention to the consideration of the heart, the brain, the liver, the stomach, the vessels, the veins, and the rest of the interior organs for the improvement of the digestion,[1] the restitution of the animal spirit, and the cleansing of the existing filth. Know also that the balance in all things by no means produces a harmful effect on one of these matters. If you are not able to do what is necessary, consider the objective of balance in every case and improve the air, water, and food in accordance with what is suitable to the temperament of each man, his habits, and his ability. Do not neglect any of these matters. [39a]

[1]On the physiology of nutrition, see Part 1 of this volume.

· 12 ·

On the Means of Improving the Badness of the Air, Water, and Food in Egypt

The first thing that is necessary in this matter is that the houses and living rooms be spacious, so that much of the vapor is dissolved. The buildings should have an opening[1] in order that the vapor may escape and the rays of the sun may enter. It is desirable that these houses and living rooms are tiled with marble, paved, or plastered with gypsum.[2] The floors should be cleaned regularly, and when it is hot they should be covered with cool mats and coverings,[3] such as reed mats[4] and *Ṭabarī*[5] and *ʿAbbādānī* mats.[6] In cold weather they should be covered with *Ḥumrānīyah* carpets,[7] *Maysānī* carpets,[8] *ṭinfisah* carpets,[9] felts,

[1]*Al-makhārīq*, see Clerget, *Le Caire*, 1:329–331. Cf. *EI²* *Supplement*, s.v. "Bādgīr" (C. E. Bosworth); de Sacy, p. 295; Alpin, *Histoire Naturelle de l'Égypte*, 1:22f.; Alexandre Lézine, "La Protection contre la chaleur dans l'architecture musulmane d' Égypte," *Bulletin d'Études Orientales*, 24 (Damascus, 1971):7–17; Franz Rosenthal, "Poetry and Architecture: The Bādhanj," *Journal of Arabic Literature* 8 (1977):1–19. Could not the term *bādhanj* have been introduced by the relevant medical literature?

[2]On the construction of buildings in Cairo, see de Sacy, p. 295f.

[3]See J. Sadan, *Le Mobilier au Proche Orient Medieval* (Leiden, 1976), pp. 25–31.

[4]*As-sāmān*, see Serjeant, *Islamic Textiles*, pp. 159, 212.

[5]Mats and textiles from Ṭabaristān, especially its capital Amul, were exported throughout the Middle East and were highly prized; see ibid., p. 79; Sadan, *Le Mobilier*, pp. 25, 108.

[6]In the medieval period ʿAbbādān was a prosperous port on the island of the same name, located on the left bank of the Shaṭṭ al-ʿArab; see Serjeant, *Islamic Textiles*, p. 58, and *EI²*, s.v. " ʿAbbādān" (L. Lockhart). Serjeant (*Islamic Textiles*, p. 212) quotes Abū l-Qāsim, who satirizes the Iṣfahānīs: "Nor have you Sāmān or ʿAb-badānī mats (*ḥuṣr*) which fold in two as cloth does, lovelier than carpets (*zurbīya*), and softer than Sūs *kh*azz-silk, of fine workmanship, perfect craftsmanship and fine weave. . . . "

[7]Possibly carpets from Ḥumrān, see Yāqūt, *Muʿjam al-buldān*, 2:333, l. 13ff. Or from Ḥawrān: "In the Hawran (Ḥawrān) district of Damascus lay Aʿnāk, and Yāḳūt said: 'Carpets (*busuṭ*) and fine robes (*aksiya*) are made in it which are named after it' " (Serjeant, *Islamic Textiles*, p. 118).

[8]"The district of Maisān in southeastern Iraq is famous for the type of cloth which derives its name from that locality. Even in pre-Islamic times, if one can trust Azrakī's sources, it supplied the Arabs with precious stuffs, for he said that the mother of Zaid ibn Thābit saw on the Kaaba, when the prophet was there, 'various coverings of striped Yemen stuffs (*waṣāʾil*), carpets (*anṭāʿ*), stuffs called *kurr* (pl. *kirār*), silk (*khazz*), and Iraqi carpets (*namāriḳ*), that is to say Maisānī' " (ibid., p. 33; see also pp. 35, 63, 213). See also Sadan, *Le Mobilier*, p. 108.

types of silk brocade, and wool. Those who cannot afford these things may use tattered mats and pelts of rams. Prescribe for every man to the extent of his ability, so that you prescribe for some of them sand and permissible cool grasses[10] in place of marble and cool coverings. And for others, prescribe permissible warm grasses in place of warm coverings. Appoint for every man what he needs to the extent of his ability, [39b] his temperament, and his way of life.

If the air is hot, you should advise the sprinkling of cold water, fountains, and the pouring of water into pools, waterskins, pots, and tubs of silver, china, lead, ceramic, and earthenware made especiallyin the month of Ṭūbah. Recommend many fans and the use of canvas tents in the outdoors. The living rooms should face north,[11] and their furnishings should include cooling aromatics, such as violets, rose, nenuphar, and delicate scents of wild thyme, mandrake, and similar things.[12] Use perfume,[13] camphor, rose water, sandalwood; use oils, such as oils of rose, violets, and nenuphar. If these are unavailable, furnish the living room with myrtle leaves, branches of grapevine and its leaves, Egyptian willow, and all kinds of willow, houseleek tree, duckweed,[14] watermoss, and black nightshade. If none of these fresh things can be found, you may take the dried plants and sprinkle them with a little water. For meals make kid[15] and lamb, orache, spinach, purslane, endive, lettuce, gooseberry, sumac, white poppy, cucumber, pumpkin, [40a] melon, snake cucumber, squirting cucumber, and what is made from barley, such as *kishk*[16] and *sawīq*.[17] For clothing, make

[9]Serjeant, *Islamic Textiles*, pp. 35f., 63, 132, 205; Lane, s.v. "ṭinfisatun."

[10]*Ḥashīsh*, see Serjeant, *Islamic Textiles*, p. 173. The sense of "permissible" is unclear; it may mean free, being found everywhere, or legal. Regarding the latter, see Franz Rosenthal, *The Herb: Hashish versus Medieval Muslim Society* (Leiden, 1971), pp. 21, 101–130.

[11]Lézine, "La Protection contre la chaleur," p. 9: "Sauf dans un cas, il n'en est pas de même à Fustat où la salle principale est unique et orientée dans une direction se rapprochant du nord. Cette observation s'accorde avec ce qu'avait écrit Ibn Duqmaq sur les habitations égyptiennes, toujours conçues en premier lieu, selon lui, en fonction de leur utilisation estivale."

[12]For the literature on perfumes, see *MI*, pp. 313–316.

[13]*Ṭīb*, see Lane and Dozy, s.v. "ṭīb"; Rodinson, "Recherches," pp. 132, 152 (*aṭrāf aṭ-ṭīb*); Serjeant, *Islamic Textiles*, s.v. "tīb." Possibly *ṭīb al-ʿarab*, *Andropogon schoenanthus* L. (Sontheimer, 2:165).

[14]See chap. 1, n. 38.

[15]See Ashtor, "Essai sur l'alimentation," p. 1021f.

[16]A dough made of bulgar and sour milk; see *WKAS*, 1:221a, l. 24ff.; Rodinson, "Recherches," pp. 137, 140, 147; Maimonides, p. 21.

[17]Meal of parched barley (*shaʿīr*), sometimes wheat; it is generally made into a kind of gruel, being moistened with water, clarified butter, fat of sheep's tail, etc. See Lane, s.v. "sawīqun"; *EI*², s.v. "Ghidhā' " (M. Rodinson).

robes of honor[18] with *Dabīqī* stuff;[19] gowns[20] and the rest of the clothing should be light, free, and clean. Perfume them with camphor, sandalwood, and rose water. Drink sour milk and the juice of unripe and sour grapes. Cook the acidic and sour, such as whey, the juice of unripe and sour grapes, lemon juice, sour pomegranate juice, tamarind juice, sour milk, sea buckthorn, and barley flour, broad bean flour, ground roses, and ground sandalwood. Eat fruits, such as apple, quince, prune,[21] pomegranate, peach, and the fruit of Christ's thorn.[22] Use the sweetmeat that is made with camphor, rose water, sugar, julep, and starch. Employ the remedy of tamarind, oxymel, barley broth, dried fruit, prune juice, and other things that cool the body. Drink the pure white wine and the acrid fresh wine. Altogether, make use of all those things that are inclined to coldness.

If the air is cold, put stoves in the living rooms and furnish them with branches, leaves, and warm flowers, [40b] such as narcissus, gillyflower, sweet basil, wild thyme, citron, camomile leaves, sweet marjoram, sticks of balsam and its leaves, lily of the valley, jasmine, musk rose and its branches and leaves, leaves of Abraham's balm, soft-haired basil, wormwood, southernwood, dog's fennel, camomile, and aquatic mint. Perfume the air with *nadd*,[23] ambergris, aloeswood, and spices[24] made from cardamom, *aflanjah*,[25] lotus of India, Arabian costus, compound perfume,[26] frankincense,[27] mastic, bark of frank-

[18]See *EI*², s.v. "Khil'a" (N. A. Stillmann).

[19]Serjeant, *Islamic Textiles*, s.v. "Dabīkī"; Ibn Ḥawqal, 1:150; Mez, *The Renaissance of Islam*, p. 460f.; ath-Thaʿālibī, *The Laṭāʾif al-maʿārif*, pp. 46, 143; Sadan, *Le Mobilier*, p. 108; *EI*², s.v. "Dabiḳ" (G. Wiet): Dabīq was "a locality in the outer suburbs of Damietta, noted for the manufacture of high quality woven material, which it exported to the whole of the Muslim empire. . . . Fine cloths embossed with gold were made there, and during the Fāṭimid period, turbans of multicoloured linen. These textiles were so sumptuous that *dabīḳī* soon became known, and its fame grew to such an extent that the word came to designate a type of material."

[20]*Ghalāʾil* (pl.), see Dozy, s.v. "ghalālah"; idem, *Dictionnaire détaille*, pp. 319–323; Serjeant, *Islamic Textiles*, s.v. "ghalāla."

[21]See Henri Leclerc, "Histoire du pruneau," in *International Congress of the History of Medicine, Proceedings, 1921* (Paris, 1922), pp. 421–425.

[22]For various fruits, see Ashtor, "Essai sur l'alimentation," p. 1025ff.

[23]A certain kind of perfume of aloeswood, compounded with ambergris, musk, and frankincense; see Rodinson, "Recherches," p. 130f.; Lane, s.v. "naddun."

[24]*Afāwīh*, see *EI*² *Supplement*, s.v. "afāwīh" (A. Dietrich).

[25]See Dozy, s.v. "iflunjah"; as-Samarqandī, *The Medical Formulary*, trans. Martin Levey and N. al-Khaledy (Philadelphia, 1967), p. 176; M. Moʿīn, *An Intermediate Persian Dictionary* (Tehran, 1964), s.v. "falanja"; Sontheimer, 2:261.

[26]*Sukk*, see Lane, s.v. "sukk: . . . a sort of perfume, prepared from *rāmak* or from musk and *rāmak*, the former being bruised, or pounded, sifted, kneaded with water, and wrung hard, and wiped

incense, storax, perfume, musk, ambergris, *ghāliyah*,[28] saffron, warm *lakhālikh*,[29] aloeswood, clove, clove juice, and juice of camomile flower. Use oils of mahaleb, ben, narcissus, sesame, nard, Arabian costus, mastic, radish, and castor.[30] Cloths: silk, cotton,[31] and wool. Foods: meat of sheep[32] and sparrows, chick-peas, beets, asparagus, carrots, turnips, mint, fennel, celery, garlic, onions, leeks, rue, mustard, ginger, [41a] and elecampane. Pepper should be put in the foods, as should long pepper, cinnamon, cinnamon bark, galangale, caraway, anise, sea buckthorn, schoenanthum, cyperus, melilot, saltwort that is sold in Egypt, chick-pea flour, and lupine flour. Fruits: figs, raisins, honey, sugar, walnuts,[33] almonds, hazelnuts, pistachios, and the rest of the sweetmeats as well. Remedies: rose honeys, electuaries,[34] and everything that warms the body. Drinks: *ash-Shamsī* and aged wine. Assign to everyone what he can afford, to the point that you may have to prescribe the dirt in the rams' legs, which is lanolin.[35]

If the air is dry, you should moisten it by constantly pouring and spattering water. You should use dried things, such as the smoke from aloeswood, *nadd*, ambergris, frankincense and its bark, storax, and sandarac. If the air is stagnant, agitate it with fans. If it is agitated, calm it with curtains and close the doors. If the air is putrid, dry it and

---

over with oil of the *khīrīya* in order that it may not stick to the vessel, and left for a night; then musk is pounded, or powdered, and put into it by degrees, and it is again wrung hard, and cut into small, round, flat pieces, and left for two days, after which it is perforated with a large needle, and strung upon a hempen string, and left for a year; and as it becomes old, its odour becomes the more sweet." See also Sontheimer, 2:38f.

[27]See Nigel Groom, *Frankincense and Myrrh. A Study of the Arabian Incense Trade* (London, 1981).

[28]Perfume composed of musk and ambergris; see Manfred Ullmann, "Beiträge zum Verständnis der 'Dichterischen Vergleiche der Andalus-Araber,' " *Die Welt des Orients* 9 (1977):109: Sontheimer, 2:233; P. Guigues, trans., "La Guérison en une heure de Razès," *Janus*, 1903, p. 368, n. 4.

[29]A kind of perfume; see Rodinson, "Recherches," p. 131; *MI*, p. 316.

[30]See Ashtor, "Essai sur l'alimentation," p. 1022f.

[31]Cotton clothing appears, by this passage, to have become commonplace in Egypt after cotton's introduction into the country in the early Islamic period; see Watson, "The Arab Agricultural Revolution," p. 26, and *EI*², s.v. "Ḳuṭn" (E. Ashtor).

[32]Ashtor, "Essai sur l'alimentation," p. 1021f.; Ashtor notes the preference for sheep, as opposed to beef, by Arab doctors. See also Finkel, "King Mutton," 8:136f.

[33]*EI² Supplement*, s.v. "Djaz" (A. Dietrich).

[34]*Jawārishāt*, see Max Meyerhof, "Über eine arabische Krankenhaus-pharmakopöe aus Kairo (um 1200 n. Chr.)," *Max Neuburger Festschrift* (Vienna, 1948), p. 342f.

[35]*Az-zūfā' ar-raṭb*, wool fat or lanolin; see Maimonides, *Sharḥ asmā' al-'uqqār (L'Explication des noms de drogues; un glossaire de matière médicale composé par Maïmonides)*, ed. Max Meyerhof (Cairo, 1940), n. 136; Ibn al-Bayṭār, *al-Jāmi' li-mufradāt al-adwiyah* (Cairo, 1874), 2:173, l. 10 to p. 174, l. 1; Isḥāq, p. 202, no. 68; Sontheimer, 1:546f.: Anawati, *Drogues*, p. 96.

remove its moisture by the burning of French tamarisk, oriental tamarisk, grapevines, oak, Christ's thorn, acacia, and the bark of [41b] frankincense. These things improve the air.

As for water, Nile water should be drunk from places where the current is strongest and the rottenness is least. An example in al-Fusṭāṭ is the area parallel to the famous al-Kūm al-Aḥmar[36] near al-Gīzah. Everyone should purify this water to the extent that it is agreeable to his temperament. For irascible people, in the summer use *ṭabāshīr*,[37] Armenian clay,[38] red earth,[39] crushed Christ's thorn, crushed azarole, and vinegar to purify the water. For placid people, in the winter use bitter almonds, the pith of apricot pits, wild thyme, and dill to purify the water.

It is desirable to skim the purified water and, then, to drink it. Clarification is accomplished by putting the liquid in ceramic vessels, earthenware, or skins, and removing what is filtered from it by secretion. If you wish, you may heat the liquid by fire, place it in the night air until it is pure, and skim what is clarified. If it appears to you that it has a noticeably bad quality, cook it on a fire, cool it outdoors in the cold of the night, and purify it with one of the potions that I have mentioned. [42a] This water is made better by clarifying it several times. For

[36]"The Red Hill," see Casanova, *Essai de reconstitution*, plan 1, G5.

[37]*Ṭabāshīr* may have two meanings: Isḥāq, p. 204, no. 93: "1. Kreide; in Persien asserdem Magnesia und Talkerde. 2. Bambuskonkretionen, auch Bambuszucker genannt." In the present context, the former, chalk, is almost certainly meant. Regarding the latter, see von Lippmann, *Geschichte des Zuckers*, p. 76ff.; Maimonides, p. 41; Sontheimer, 2:149f. Ar-Ruhāwī mentions the deception of an apothecary who sold alum as *ṭabāshīr* (Levey, "Medical Ethics of Medieval Islam," p. 60); Graziani, pp. 190, 326f.

[38]This was a compact clay, reddish because of its iron content, and an astringent. According to Galen, it was used externally and internally for wounds, ulcers, pestilence, and poisons. See Dols, *The Black Death*, pp. 102–104; Gilbert Watson, *Theriac and Mithridatium: A Study in Therapeutics* (London, 1966), p. 68; Sontheimer, 2:174f.; Guigues, "La Guérison en une heure de Razès," p. 412 and n. 6. This last citation, a translation of a minor work by ar-Rāzī, refers to "du grenadier sauvage de la terre d'Arménie." This is quite unclear without the Arabic text, but it may refer to the pomegranate-shaped ceramic containers for such commodities as Armenian clay. These vessels, sometimes called *aeolipiles* or *grenades*, are a minor mystery of Islamic archeology. See Richard Ettinghausen, "The Uses of Sphero-Conical Vessels in the Muslim East," *Journal of Near Eastern Studies* 24 (1965):218–229; J. M. Rogers, "Aeolipiles Again," *Forschungen zur Kunst Asiens im Memoriam Kurt Erdmann*, ed. Oktay Aslanapa and Rudolph Naumann (Istanbul, 1969), pp. 147–158.

[39]*Maghrah, Rubica sinopica*. See Lane, s.v. "maghratun;" Sontheimer, 2:522f. The whole subject of earth-eating is exhaustively treated by Berthold Laufer in his monograph, "Geophany," *Field Museum of Natural History Publication* no. 280, Anthropological Ser., vol. 18, no. 2 (Chicago, 1930), pp. 101–198, especially pp. 150–155 for this phenomenon among the Persians and Arabs. See also M. Mohaghegh, "The Title of a Work of Rāzī with Reference to al-Ṭīn al-Nīshābūrī," *Proceedings of the First International Symposium for the History of Arabic Science*, 2:338ff.

example, heat or cook it and cool it in the night air; then, cook what is purified again and clarify it with some potions. Take what is pure and put it in vessels that filter it in the cold of night. Then, you can take the filtered water and drink it.

In summer, for this water, use ceramic vessels and earthenware made in the month of Ṭūbah, Ḥijāzī vessels and waterskins, and others that cool the liquid. During the winter, use glass and oiled vessels and earthenware and ceramics made in the summer. Its storage in the summer should be in underground passages and in places exposed to the north wind; in the winter it should be placed in warm areas. Cool the water in the summer by mixing it with rose water. Or take a clean rag and tie in it *ṭabāshīr*, purslane seed, white poppy, Armenian clay, or red earth and drop the bag into the water, so that the water takes the coldness from it but does not mix with the concoction. In summer, clean the containers with crushed pottery and barley flour, broad beans, and sandalwood, and perfume them with camphor [42b] and sandalwood. In the winter, clean the containers with saltwort and cyperus, and perfume them with mastic and aloeswood.

As for the water from wells, it should be heated, cooled in the night, and then drunk. The worst is the Nile water during its inundation and the halting of its movement.[40] Then, it must be cooked and one's utmost be done to purify it with the marrow of apricot pits and other things that break up its viscidity. The best water is in Ṭūbah, when the cold is most intense. Because of this, the Egyptians know by experience that the water of Ṭūbah is the best water.[41] Thus, many of them begin to store it in thin waterskins and china, and they drink it all year and claim that it does not change. Also, they do not purify the water at this time because of their belief that it is of the utmost purity. As for you, do not rely on that belief and purify it in any case. The stored-up water certainly will change.

As for the foods, eat a lot of what is new, what is fresh, firm, and solid. Their firmness and solidity in Egypt is comparable to their softness and weakness in other countries. [43a] Assign the best of them to a person whose temperament is best and can afford to have the best, like the high-quality manufactured bread whose dough has been well

[40]See Ibn Ḥawqal, 1:146.

[41]Al-Masʿūdī, *Les Prairies d'Or*, 2:296: "Pendant le mois de *ṭubeh* et après le fête du Bain (ʿĪd al-Ghuṭās), qui tombe le 10 de même mois, on prépare, avec l'eau du Nil, le vin nommé *shubrāwī*, parce que jamais ce fleuve n'est plus limpide, et les habitants en vantent lors la pureté. A la même époque, on fait provision d'eau à Tennis, Damiette, Tūna et dans les autres villages du district de la Buḥayra."

kneaded. Its salt and leaven are set exactly, and it is baked in an oven with a gentle fire, whose heat penetrates all its parts equally. The wheat from which it is made is carefully selected, and its flour is recently ground. Then, it is eaten when it cools a little and up to two-thirds of the day after it is cooked because the bread in Egypt is no good if it sits overnight.

Feed the people capons, young chickens, francolin, partridge,[42] larks, and egg yolks.[43] Reduce these recommendations for the people according to the capacity of each person. Put into the bread some spices that help its digestion and make its taste pleasant. Caution the people against overeating and overindulgence.

As for meat, it is desirable that it be from young animals that graze on suitable grasses and are healthy in body. Before slaughter they should be put into roomy places, [43b] which have good ventilation and where the animals can move freely, so that the collected superfluities of their bodies dissolve. Of meats, the best is that which has most recently been slaughtered. Select the fish that have been most recently caught, and avoid what is excessively large. Because most people usually get meat from the market, it is necessary for them to choose the best and the freshest. Then, they improve it by cooking or grilling with spices and other things, which they add if they want the restoration of their bodies and the maintenance of their health.

All these things should be done in a way that is agreeable to the body of the eater and to the type of food that is eaten. The drinks should be matured wines and *zabīb*[44] from recently collected sweet grapes. In this way, everything that is eaten and drunk should be suitable. A thorough discussion of this topic would take a long time. Many of the doctors have written monographs specifically on it, as the book that Abū Bakr ar-Rāzī composed, *On the Prevention of Harm in Foods*.[45] You can learn from there what is needed. [44a] Perhaps, we will write a useful book on this subject if God Almighty grants life and leisure.

[42]*Ṭayhūj*, a species of small partridge; see *WKAS*, 2:362a, l. 37ff.; Sontheimer, 2:165; Joseph Somogyi, "Medicine in ad-Damiri's Ḥayāt al-Ḥayawān," *Journal of Semitic Studies* 2 (1957):79.

[43]On poultry, see de Sacy, p. 135 et passim; Rodinson, "Recherches," pp. 132–135. Cf. Maimonides, p. 18.

[44]A strong colorless liquor made from raisins; see Isḥāq, p. 202, no. 65; Sontheimer, 1:515ff.

[45]Ar-Rāzī, *Daf' maḍārr al-aghdhiyah* (Cairo, 1305/1888); see *MI*, pp. 134, 200.

· 13 ·

On the Means of Preventing Injury from Epidemic Diseases in Egypt

It is desirable at this point that you learn what Hippocrates and Galen recommended. As for Hippocrates, he said: "It is necessary to preserve the regimen in its usual manner, unless it is itself the cause of illness." If the normal regimen causes illness, he instructed that the accustomed amount of food and drink be diminished gradually and gently. After this, it is advisable that one be disposed toward the opposite of the cause of the illness. Beware of its having the effect of weakening the body. He also instructed that efforts be made to alter the cause that produces the illness as far as possible, so that what reaches the body is completely opposite to the cause that initially altered the body. Galen stated: "It is desirable to refrain from exertion and to be cautious of thirst, overeating, and overdrinking."

If you [44b] remember what we said at the beginning, you may easily understand the reasons for epidemic illness in Egypt and know what prevents its damage. Concerning the air, when it becomes hot, it is desirable for you to sit in the rooms that are far away from the glare of the sun, and vice versa. In general, if the weather deviates from the customary in its heat, coldness, moisture, dryness, or corruption, the way to prevent its harm is to have the rooms in the houses and living rooms furnished with what is contrary to that condition.

Likewise, concerning water, if it differs from the ordinary, you should not risk drinking much of it. Water is improved by boiling; it should be boiled if it is spoiled or if much corruption is mixed with it. Then, it is purified by what opposes this corruption, and it should be protected from the putrid air. Its containers should be fumigated with mastic and washed with cyperus and sandalwood. You should put into the water Armenian clay and *ṭabāshīr* if the temperament is hot. If it is cold, you should splash the rim of the vessels with tar. Garlic should be dropped into the water because garlic is beneficial for the drinking of bad water. If the occurrence of epidemic illness is due to [45a] bad foods, beware of those foods. If it is because of a general fear, it is desirable that the people hearten one another and enjoin one another to relinquish their fear and despair.

When an epidemic disease results from more than two of these matters, you should combine the regimen of the one with the other. It is apparent that the air is affected by all these changes, as are the things that are surrounded by the air. It is also apparent that if the water is altered and is plentiful, as the waters of the Nile, this changes the air. Equally, the breathing of the people changes the air when illness spreads among them. Because of this situation, care should be taken in every epidemic to improve the air.

We have said that when the air becomes excessively hot, it can be improved by pouring out cold water, furnishing the rooms with roses, violets, myrtle, and Egyptian willow; drinking sweetened oxymel, nenuphar, Egyptian willow, prune, rose water, sour and sweet pomegranate juice, tamarind juice, and prune juice; and smelling cool oils, like the oils of roses, nenuphar, and violets. Similarly, the following are useful: camphor, sandalwood, and rose water; [45b] and making use of astringent things like apples, quince, the bark of trees, and cold grasses; and bandaging for the chest made with the oil of violets, rose water, and sandalwood.[1] For the meals, make the *sawīq* of barley with sugar and all the cooling things, and add to the cooked foods the seeds of sour pomegranates, the juice of unripe and sour grapes, vinegar, sumac, tamarind juice, lemon or citron juice, and their like. In this situation, foods and other things having a hot temperament should be avoided. Sexual intercourse and fasting are to be guarded against. One should face the north wind and be seated in underground passages. If you see tht the body is full, evacuate it with gentle laxatives, as tamarind, *taranjubīn*,[2] and purging cassia. If one has need of bloodletting, you should bleed him immediately on the spot. If bloodletting is not possible because of youth or old age, then use cupping.[3] Do your best, so that everything that is eaten and drunk is cold and constricting. Be cautious of physical exercise and bathing in such a condition.

[1]On bandaging, see Grand'henry, pp. 69, 89; Galen, *In Hippocratis de officina medici commentariorum*, ed. and trans. Lyons.

[2]A vegetable purgative; see Isḥāq, p. 199, no. 26; Ullmann, *Die Natur- und Geheimwissenschaften im Islam*, p. 93; Maimonides, p. 43: "manna: the solidified sweet, yellow, juice that exudes from incisions made in the bark of several trees. The manna of *Fraximus ornus*, the manna-ash"; Sontheimer, 1:207.

[3]See *EI²* *Supplement*, s.v. "Faṣṣād, Ḥadjdjām" (M. A. J. Beg). On the legal and social status of the *ḥajjām*, see R. Brunschvig, "Métiers vils en Islam," *Studia Islamica* 16 (1962):46–50.

If the air becomes excessively cold, you should ignite fires [46a] and furnish the rooms with sweet basil, narcissus, bitter orange, sweet marjoram, gillyflower, jasmine, and wild thyme. Also, use musk, ambergris, aloeswood, saffron, mastic, frankincense, Arabian costus, and all the hot spices. Increase the hot remedies of a delicate substance, so that its heat combats the coldness of the air and the gentleness of the substance combats the density produced by the air. Use rose jam, electuaries, honey, drinks, physical exercise, perspiration in the bath, and everything that opens the pores of the body and diminishes the coldness of the air.

If the humidity of the air is excessive, it may be sufficient to use fires and dried foods, such as fried and roasted things. Use ambergris, musk, narcissus, and sweet marjoram. If the air is excessively dry, then pour out water constantly and use wet things. If the air becomes polluted—and this is more frequently what produces epidemic disease—try to dehydrate the body little by little with the decrease of foods, drink, and gentle evacuation. [46b] Try to improve the digestion. Refrain from movement in the air, and advise staying in homes where French and oriental tamarisks and grapevines are burned, and where the rooms are furnished with myrtle, Egyptian willow, roses, and branches and leaves of grapevines. The houses should be sprinkled with vinegar mixed with water. Make the meals more inclined to coldness and constriction. All of these things act against corruption. You should take the theriac Mithridatium[4] and similar things. The smelling of tar,

[4] *Al-Mithrūdayṭūs* = ἡ Μιθράτειος ἀντίδοτος, see Grand'henry, p. 78; Isḥāq, p. 70/115b; Maimonides, p. 44. The term *theriac (theriaca)* originated in the fourth to third century B.C. and is first attested in Alexandrian medical works. Derived from *therion*, "a wild or venomous animal," theriac was the name given to an antidote meant to counteract the bite of venomous animals but was later extended to other purposes. (See the explanation of theriacs by Ḥunayn, p. 59f.) Theriac was always characterized by a large, variable number of ingredients, including herbs, animal substances, minerals, and usually the flesh of vipers. The ingredients were customarily pulverized and reduced with wine or honey to an electuary. Mithradatium was a notable antidote attributed to Mithridates VI, King of Pontus in Asia Minor from 114 to 63 B.C. Specifically, it included lizard (skink) as an ingredient and was intended initially to be used against poisons. Galen is unclear about the composition of Mithridatium but advised the use of a number of theriacs for internal use against poisons, venoms, and general ailments. To counteract the harmful air, Galen advised the use of the theriac Galene, as an air cleaner or disinfectant. Although Mithridatium was not recommended for this purpose by Galen, it appears from our text that it was used in the same manner as Galene and other theriacs. Ibn Riḍwān says: "On the whole, [the theriac] fortifies the constitution and is useful when the air is polluted and an epidemic [*wabā'*] occurs" (Grand'henry, p. 14/78). Finally, theriacs should be seen as the application of the general principle of healing by contraries: their constituents possessed qualities opposite to noxious substances. See Watson, *Theriac and Mithridatium*, p. 3 et passim; *MI*, p. 321f.; G. W. Corner, "Mithridatium and Theriac, The Most Famous Remedies of Old Medicine," *Johns Hopkins Hosp. Bull.* 26 (1915):222–226; Georg Harig, "Die antike Affassung von Gift und der Tod des Mithridates," *Schriftenreihe für*

incense with mastic, aloeswood, laudanum, storax, myrrh,[5] and frankincense and its bark is beneficial in this situation. Likewise, the wearing of gems is advantageous, such as sapphire, emerald, pearl, gold, silver, high-quality carnelian, and all the precious stones.[6] In general, all the things that bring happiness are beneficial; the best of them are the cold and constrictive ones. Coldness and constriction act against the state of corruption, which is from the heat and excessive moisture of decaying things.

Galen stated that he witnessed, in an epidemic, people who used to drink Armenian clay every day with vinegar mixed with [47a] water; thereby, they rid themselves of the harm of the epidemic. All those who were not treated with it perished.[7] One of the Ancients stated that he took a portion of aloe and the same amount of myrrh and saffron, and he crushed all of it. Every day he drank from it a mithqāl's[8] weight with a ūqīyah's[9] weight of a mixed drink, and he profited by it a good deal. He said: "Everyone who takes this remedy during the epidemic will escape its harm."

It is desirable that you drop into the drinking water, during times of an epidemic, Armenian clay, *ṭabāshīr*, and red earth and that you protect the water from the corrupt air. Be on your guard against excessive drudgery and sexual intercourse. Likewise guard against excessive fasting, thirst, and all things that generate bad excesses in the body, such as all the fruits and cooked things that are difficult to digest. It is not desirable to eat a lot in this condition. If you have need for bloodletting, bleed. Pay attention to the strengthening of the chest, the organs of digestion, and the principal limbs by bandaging soaked in barley flour, roses, sandalwood, rose water, quince juice, and apple juice. [47b]

Geschichte der Naturwissenschaften, Technik und Medizin 14 (1977): 104–112; Bishr Farès, "Le Livre de la Thériaque," *Art Islamique*, vol. 2 (Cairo, 1953); Penelope Johnstone, "Galen in Arabic: The Transformation of Galenic Pharmacology," in *Galen: Problems and Prospects*, pp. 207–209.

[5]See Groom, *Frankincense and Myrrh*.

[6]For the use of minerals in Islamic medicine, see Ullmann, *Die Natur- und Geheimwissenschaften im Islam*, pp. 138–144; idem, "Neues zum Steinbuch des Xenocrates," *Medizinhistorisches Journal* 8 (1973):59–76; idem, "Der literarische Hintergrund des Steinbuches des Aristoteles," *Actas do IV Congresso de estudos Árabes e Islâmicos*, pp. 291–299; *EI*², s.v. "hadjar" (M. Plessner).

[7]Cf. Kühn, 12:189f.

[8]*EI*¹, s.v. "Ḳirāṭ" (E. von Zambaur); Walther Hinz, *Islamische Masse u. Gewichte*, in *Handbuch der Orientalistik*, ed. B. Spuler, vol. 1, pt. 1 (Leiden, 1955), p. 4: 4.68 g. For medical weights and measures, see *MI*, pp. 316–320.

[9]Popper, *Systematic Notes* 16:40; Hinz, *Islamische Masse*, p. 35: 37.5 g.; *MI*, p. 317.

Give the remedies that are cooling and constricting and that obstruct the corruption of the humors. Give what is cold and diuretic, like spices. And give a diluent for the disposition, such as drinking prune juice and herb juice, for it is beneficial in this case. Work hard in preserving the temperament and opposing the cause of the disease to the utmost of your ability, if God Almighty wills.

· 14 ·

On the Prescriptions for Compound Remedies That Are Useful in Preventing Injury and Preserving Health

You should select the most useful remedies in this chapter; so, choose what best suits your condition.

A prescription of a potion that I composed strengthens the liver and the stomach for digestion. Take a raṭl[1] of sour quince juice and sour apples, a similar amount of acrid wine, and four raṭls of sour and sweet pomegranates, and put it on the fire. In a clean cloth tie a half-dirham's[2] weight of each of the following: ginger, mastic, spikenard, musk, and saffron. This is cooked until it becomes the proper consistency for drinking.

A prescription for a drink that as-Sāhir[3] composed has the same effects as the first. [48a] Take one part Irāqī roses and soak them in four times as much hot water for three days. Boil them in water until the water is reduced by half and is clear. Drop into the water one part sugar and one part honey whose foam has been removed. Boil a second time until the potion thickens. Remove its froth and take it off the fire.

As-Sāhir mentioned another prescription for a drink; with it he improved the stomach of 'Ubaydallāh ibn Ṭāhir.[4] Take one part each of quince juice, apple juice, and rose water, half a part each of sugar and

[1]A unit of weight that dates from pre-Islamic times, varying according to country and period. In medieval Damascus it equaled 600 dirhams and in Aleppo 720 dirhams. See *EI*[1], s.v. "Raṭl" (A. Atiya); Hinz, *Islamische Masse*, p. 28ff.: 437.5 g.

[2]A unit of weight derived from the Greek δραχμή. Traditionally the *dirham kayl or shar'ī* weighed from 50 to 60 average-sized, unshelled *sha'īrah* or *ḥabbah* and was theoretically divided into 6 dānaq, the latter being calculated variously between 8 and 10 *sha'īrah*. See *EI*[2], s.v. "Dirham" (G. C. Miles); Hinz, *Islamische Masse*, pp. 2–8: 3.125 g.

[3]Yūsuf al-Qass, who lived during the caliphate of al-Muktafī (289–295/902–908); see *MI*, p. 124.

[4]'Ubaydallāh ibn 'Abdallāh ibn Ṭāhir (d. 300/912), governor of Baghdad; see Ibn Khallikān, *Wafayāt al-a'yān*, 3:120–123.

honey, and six parts wine. Boil all of it until it thickens; then, remove it from the fire.

A prescription for a drink that I composed preserves the body in the time of a pestilence. Take one part each of the following: rose water, sour quince juice, sour apple juice, sour citron juice, sweet and sour pomegranate juice; and white wine or sweet basil juice that is not very old like the rest. Boil all of it until it becomes the proper consistency for drinking. Drink it with julep, and it is salutary.

The prescription of oxymel that I composed is for this condition: it opens obstructions and makes the urine flow. Take seven dirhams' weight of each of the following: the seeds of endive, white clover dodder, fennel, and celery. [48b] Soak them in four raṭls of wine vinegar for four days. Then, take one part of acrid quince juice and one part of unripe and sour grape juice. Boil the mixture with ten raṭls of water and an equal amount of sugar until it becomes the consistency of julep. Then, the vinegar mixture is dropped into the concoction and is blended until it is well done.

A prescription for a drink that Ibn Māsawayh[5] composed is useful for high fevers in an epidemic and opens obstructions; it is wonderful in its effect. Take five raṭls of wine vinegar, two ūqīyahs' weight each of the skin of celery and fennel, a ūqīyah each of asrabacca, flower of the schoenanthum, and celery seed, and half a ūqīyah each of anise and spikenard. Put this together and soak in vinegar a day and a night. Boil it until it is reduced by half. Then, take sour pomegranate juice and boiled quince juice and mix the whole with an equal amount of molasses and boil it once more until it is blended and clear. Then, remove it from the fire. The amount of the concoction to be drunk at one time is a ūqīyah with cold water.

The following is a prescription for a prune drink, which ar-Rāzī said is beneficial for the colic and pain in the joints and promotes evacuation by stool: Take some resinous pulp of prunes, [49a] and put it into a cooking pot that is not greasy and cover it with water to the height of four fingers. Boil it on a moderate flame and keep the amount of water and fire constant. Increase the water when the decoction is reduced, until the prunes are boiled to shreds. Then, clarify it after it is macerated, purified, and left overnight, so that it settles and the drink is clarified of the foul sediment. Cast into the potion an amount of lump

[5]Ibn Māsawayh (161–243/777–857) was a famous physician at the 'Abbāsid court; see *MI*, pp. 112–115, and Part I of this volume.

sugar[6] equal to the weight of the mixture. Boil it and skim its foam until it is done. Put the mixture in a bottle when it is cold. Its proper consistency is like julep. If something soothing for the stomach is desired, a raṭl of it is drunk with the like amount of water, little by little, as wine drinkers do. It is drunk in the summer in early mornings, for it extinguishes the heat, cools and quenches the thirst, soothes the stomach, and reduces the yellow bile.

Ar-Rāzī gives a prescription for a fig drink that is used in the winter. It promotes evacuation by stool, makes the kidneys strong, gives the body a good physical condition, benefits a person with hemorrhoids, and prevents colic unless it is a serious condition. Take the very sweet, juicy pulp of yellow figs, and make the prescription in the same manner as the prunes. Combine its pure juice with an equal amount of *fānīd* sugar.[7] [49b] I say: "If this *fānīd* cannot be found, it is advisable to substitute *Sulaymānī* sugar."[8] Ar-Rāzī said: "If a hot excess is needed, put in every raṭl of the drink a dirham's weight each of cinnamon, galangale, pepper, and ginger. Crush everything, tie it in a cloth, throw it into the mixture while boiling, and mix it well. Then, it does wonders and helps the digestion. It is good for those who do not drink wine, old people, and those who need to keep their stomachs and bodies warm."

The prescription of a drink that Ibn al-Jazzār composed is astonishing in its effect during a pestilence and for erysipelas,[9] smallpox, and measles. He said: "I do not know anyone who used it whom it did not protect from the corruption of the air and the acute diseases." Take a raṭl of the juice of sour pomegranates and a raṭl and a half each of quince juice, sour apple juice, unripe and sour grape juice, the frothy extract of endive juice, and a raṭl of rose water. Put all of this into a cooking pot

[6] *As-sukkar aṭ-ṭabarzadh* is sugar that is brought to a boil three times with a tenth of its bulk being fresh milk, which has been added to the sugar; when it solidifies, it is called *ṭabarzadh*. The name, meaning "chopped with an axe," is also given to rock slate; the sugar made in this way must have been so hard that it had to be smashed into small pieces. See *EI*[1], s.v. "Sukkar" (J. Ruska); Lane, s.v. "ṭabarzadh," "sukkarun"; D. N. MacKenzie, *A Concise Pahlavi Dictionary* (London, 1971), p. 81; Isḥāq, p. 204, no. 94; Sontheimer, 2:152.

[7] When sugar has been boiled twice and poured into a mold shaped like a pineapple (*qālib ṣanawbarī*), it is called *fānīd*; the name came into Persian from the Sanskrit *phāṇita*. See *EI*[1], s.v. "Sukkar" (J. Ruska); Sontheimer, 1:244; ath-Tha'ālibī, *The Laṭā'if al-Ma'ārif*, p. 146; al-Kindī, *The Medical Formulary*, s.v. "fanīdh;" Dozy, s.v. "fānīd"; Charles Pellat, trans., *Le Livre des avares de Ğāḥiz* (Paris, 1951), p. 44; Grand'henry, pp. 8, 23–25/69, 91–93; Isḥāq, p. 205, no. 101.

[8] When sugar is boiled twice and purified by being poured into a vessel where the impurities are deposited, it is called *Sulaymānī*. This name is probably a trademark, from the name of the town of Sulaymānān in Khūzistan. See *EI*[1], s.v. "Sukkar"; Dozy, s.v. "sulaymānīya."

[9] According to Ḥunayn (p. 94f.), a tumor caused by yellow bile.

with three raṭls of lump sugar. Boil it over a moderate fire until it has [50a] the right consistency. And put a dāniq's weight[10] of camphor into it. Then, remove it from the fire and use it.

Ibn al-Jazzār composed the prescription of a drink that he had tested. He found it beneficial for making the urine flow, cleansing the veins, opening obstructions, and warding off the harmful air from the respiratory organs. It has many advantages. Take from the bark of the endive root, the bark of the fennel root, and the bark of the celery root—from each twenty dirhams' weight; the highest part of the peeled licorice root, flower of the schoenanthum, red rose blossoms, and white clover dodder—from each ten dirhams' weight; seeds of endive, fennel, and maidenhair—from each four dirhams' weight; and barberry, *ṭabāshīr*, white sandalwood, and mastic—from each a dirham's weight. These ingredients are combined and soaked in twelve raṭls of boiled fresh water for one night. Then, it is cooked over a moderate fire until only four raṭls remain; it is mashed and purified. Forty dirhams' weight of *taranjubīn* is added and mashed thoroughly. It is clarified a second time. It is returned to the pot; a raṭl of sour pomegranate juice, sour apple juice, or sour citron juice is added to it on hot days. If these things cannot be found, use a raṭl of very acid wine vinegar and four raṭls [50b] of lump sugar; it is thickened on a moderate fire until it becomes the consistency of julep. It is cooled and drunk. It maintains health, opens obstructions, and hinders the causes of pestilence.

The following is a prescription of an electuary[11] that strengthens the stomach, arouses the appetite, and is wholesome; as-Sāhir related it. Take two raṭls of selected Syrian apples[12] and soak them in a similar amount of acrid wine for two days. Boil it until it is well cooked. Then, grind it and add ginger, cardamom, cinnamon bark, and *nārmashak*[13]—from each a mithqāl's weight; cinnamon and aloeswood—from each half a mithqāl's weight; saffron—a dirham's weight; and musk—a dāniq's weight.

[10] *EI*[1], s.v. "Dānaḳ" (Cl. Huart); Hinz, *Islamische Masse*, p. 11: one-sixth dirham.

[11] Cf. Grand'henry, pp. 31/77f. on electuaries.

[12] *Tuffāḥ Shāmī*, see Dozy, s.v. "tuffāḥ"; ath-Tha'ālibī, *The Laṭā'if al-Ma'ārif*, pp. 29, 118, 145: "The specialties of Syria include apples, whose excellence and wholesomeness are proverbial. Each year, the Caliphs used to have brought for them 30,000 apples in containers. It is said that they have a stronger fragrance when in Iraq than when they are in Syria" (p. 118); Mez, *The Renaissance of Islam*, p. 434.

[13] A kind of small pomegranate, see Dozy, s.v. "nārmashak"; Manfred Ullmann, "Die Schrift des Badīgūras über die Ersatzdrogen," *Der Islam* 50 (1973):241; Sontheimer, 2:546.

Another prescription of an electuary that fortifies the stomach: Take peeled quince and Syrian apples and boil them with wine until they are well cooked. Then, add foamless honey to them, as it is needed. Cook all of it over a moderate fire until it thickens. Take it from the fire, and put ground ginger, long pepper, mastic, and saffron into it. The dosage is a mithqāl.

The prescription of quince jam that strengthens the stomach, the liver, and the heart, which I composed: Take quince, [51a] peeled and spliced, and soak it in an acrid wine with a little borage for four days. Then, pour foamless honey into the juice, as it is needed. Boil it over a moderate fire until it is well cooked. The quince are put into it, and it is scented with musk.

The prescription of a cerate[14] that is beneficial against the hot weather and for burning in the heart, the stomach, and all the intestines: Take white pure wax and melt it with oil of roses. Then, mix it in a mortar with pumpkin juice, houseleek juice, purslane juice, lettuce juice, and cucumber juice or juice of nightshade or whatever of these is available, and some camphor, white sandalwood, and rose water. Now, it is ready to be used.

[14]*Qīrūtī*, a wax-salve or cerate, from *κηρωτή*; see *MI*, p. 299, l. 1; Graziani, p. 320.

· 15 ·

On the Desirability of Choosing To Live in Egypt although It Would Have a Bad Effect on the Body

It is desirable to live in Egypt for reasons that will be explained in this chapter. We have said that the elimination of the illnesses that befall bodies in Egypt is possible. [51b] It is also evident that men's dispositions can be treated, as is said in the books on ethics. The evils of the Egyptians are easily treated because their evils are weak, simple, and not difficult to cure. What is detested in living in Egypt may easily be eradicated.

Egypt has many buildings and people. Such a place is more civilized, and man by nature is surely a social being. His dwelling, then, is most appropriate in places that suit him best; he needs the many things that he finds in the city for the proper condition of his life. Also, Egypt has little discord and war because of the acquiescence of its people to whoever governs them and the weakness of their resistance.[1] Therefore, living in Egypt is preferable, even though its prices are high, for the benefits in dwelling here are many.[2]

The book is completed. Many thanks be to God. [52a]

* *

'Alī ibn Riḍwān said: After I had completed this book, a man of a distant country studied it under me. He began to apply the contents of this book to Egypt and its inhabitants, and he thought that I censured them in my description of their natural dispositions. I responded: "The matter is not as you think. The evils of the Egyptians are simple and

[1] *EI*², s.v. "Djihād" (E. Tyan).

[2] Regarding the urban bias of Islamic society, see von Grunebaum, *Medieval Islam*, pp. 173–174; Bulliet, *Conversion to Islam in the Medieval Period*, pp. 54–56.

uncomplicated. Therefore, their treatment is easy and their consequences are not so bad. Their evils do not get them into distressing and dangerous situations. As for the evils of peoples other than the Egyptians, they are harmful, vicious, and wicked, and their consequences get the peoples into distressing and dangerous situations, long wars, misfortunes, and murder. Their treatment is hard and difficult. Evil is the dominant nature in people, with the exception of the unusual among them. This being so, the simple evils that quickly and easily admit to treatment are more commendable, and their outcome is surer than harmful evils whose treatment is especially difficult. The people of Egypt, therefore, are better in their natural dispositions and mode of living." I record it here, so that it will be attached to what preceded, if God Almighty wills.

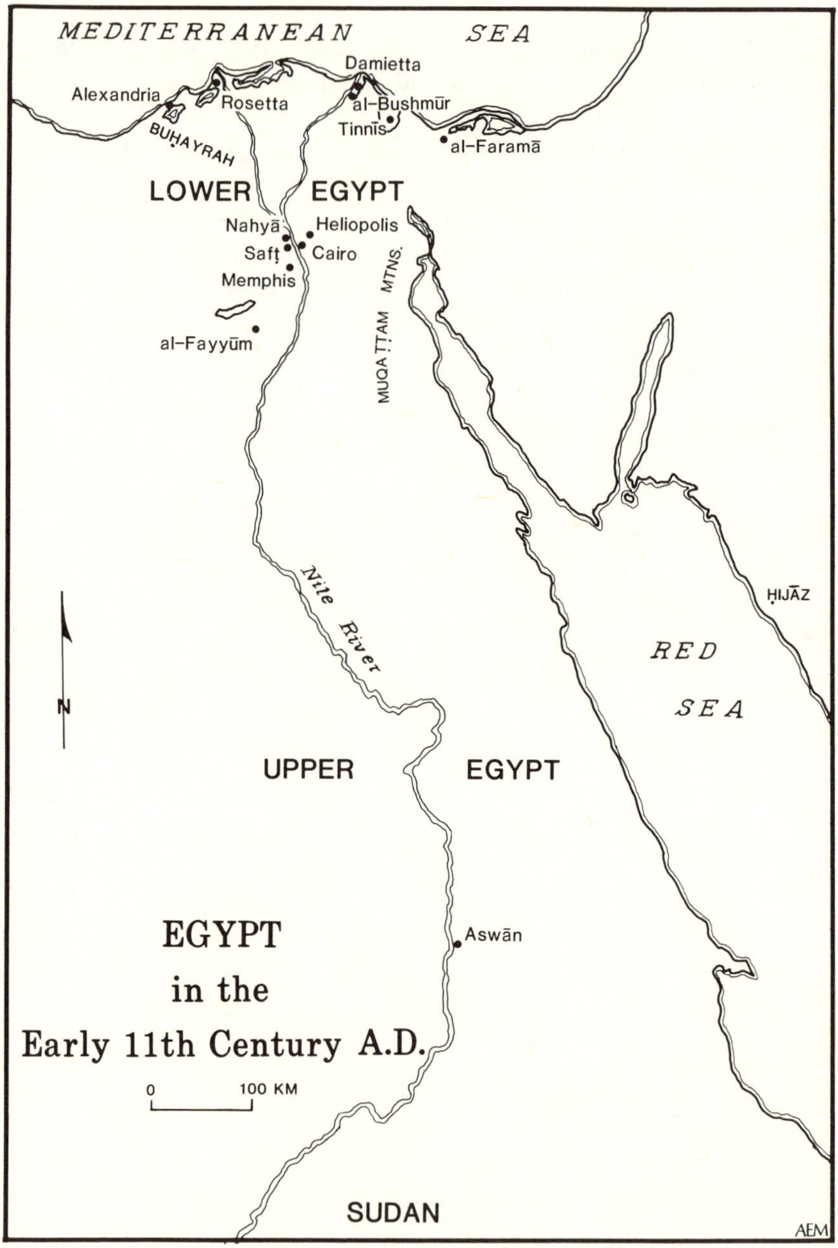
MEDITERRANEAN SEA
Damietta
Alexandria
Rosetta
al-Bushmūr
Tinnīs
al-Faramā
BUḤAYRAH
LOWER EGYPT
Nahyā
Heliopolis
Saft
Cairo
Memphis
MUQAṬṬAM MTNS.
al-Fayyūm
Nile River
ḤIJĀZ
RED SEA
N
UPPER EGYPT
Aswān
EGYPT
in the
Early 11th Century A.D.
0 100 KM
SUDAN
AEM

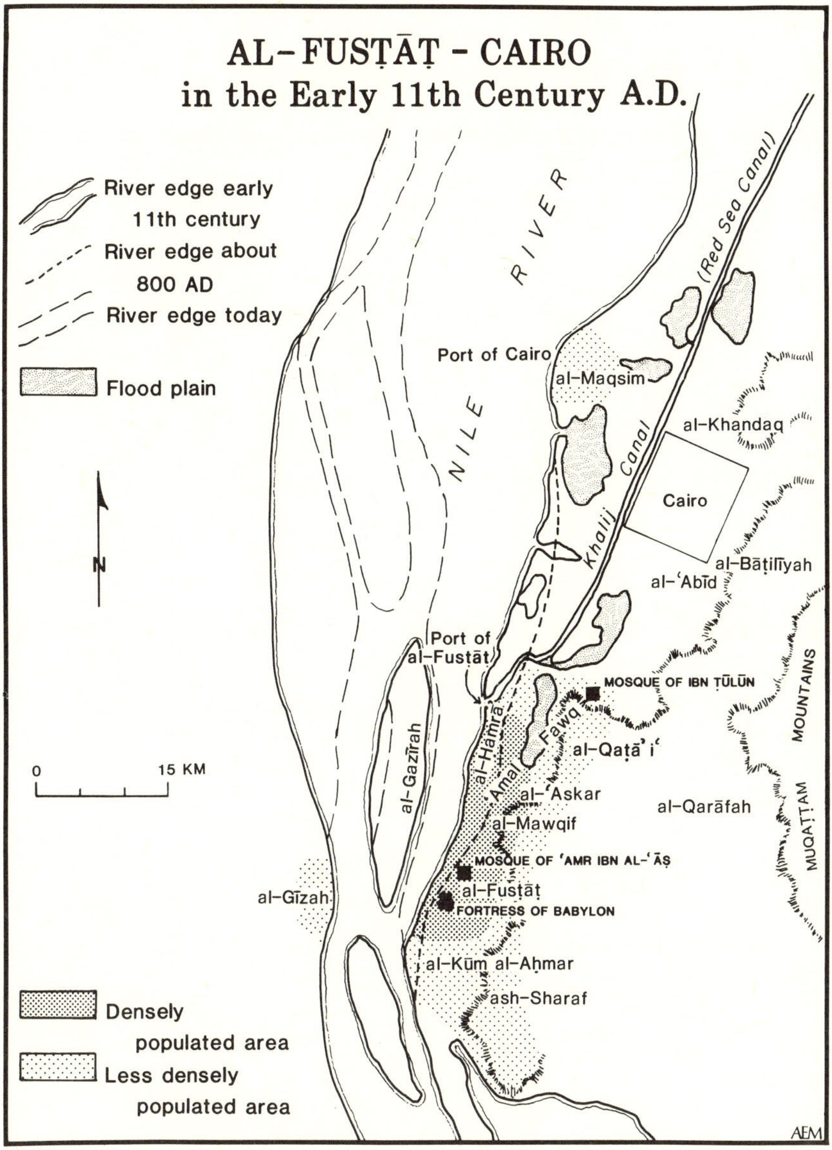
AL-FUSṬĀṬ - CAIRO
in the Early 11th Century A.D.
River edge early
11th century
River edge about
800 AD
River edge today
Flood plain
N
0
15 KM
Densely
populated area
Less densely
populated area
NILE RIVER
(Red Sea Canal)
Port of Cairo
al-Maqsim
al-Khandaq
Khalij Canal
Cairo
al-Bāṭilīyah
al-ʿAbīd
Port of
al-Fusṭāṭ
MOSQUE OF IBN ṬŪLŪN
MOUNTAINS
al-Qaṭāʾiʿ
al-Ḥamrāʾ
Amal Fawq
al-Gazīrah
al-ʿAskar
al-Qarāfah
al-Mawqif
MUQAṬṬAM
MOSQUE OF ʿAMR IBN AL-ʿĀṢ
al-Fusṭāṭ
al-Gīzah
FORTRESS OF BABYLON
al-Kūm al-Aḥmar
ash-Sharaf
AEM

Glossary to the Translation

This glossary contains the names of the drugs, herbs, vegetables, fruits, animals, and minerals mentioned in the translation of the Arabic text. No detailed explanation is made of familiar terms. The Arabic terms are transcribed in parentheses; when the Arabic text uses more than one term in designating the same object, all such terms are listed.

Abraham's balm (*shajarat Ibrāhīm*), *Vitex agnus-castus* L. See Bedevian, no. 3610; Sontheimer, 2:86; Issa, p. 190, no. 1.

Acacia (*sanṭ*), *Acacia Arabica* Willd. See de Sacy, pp. 33–34; Anawati, *Drogues*, p. 46; Bedevian, no. 33; Issa, p. 2, no. 2.

Aflanjah. See chap. 12, n. 25.

Almonds (*lawz*), *Prunus amygdalus* Stock. See Isḥāq, p. 207, no. 126; Bedevian, no. 2834; Sontheimer, 2:442–443; Issa, p. 148, no. 15; Nāṣir-i Khusraw, p. 154; Darby, p. 751f. Bitter almonds (*lawz murr*), *Prunus amygdalus* var. *Amara*. See Bedevian, no. 2835; Issa, p. 148, no. 16.

Aloe (*ṣabir*, *ṣabr*), *Aloe vera* L. See Bedevian, no. 227; Lane, s.v. "ṣabirun;" Sontheimer, 2:120–125; Issa, p. 10, no. 9.

Aloeswood (*'ūd*), *Aloexylon Agallochum* Lour. See Isḥāq, p. 205, no. 98; Bedevian, no. 228; Sontheimer, 2:224–224; Issa, p. 10, no. 10.

Ambergris (*'anbar*). Maimonides, p. 41: A morbid secretion from the intestine of the sperm whale found floating in some tropical seas. It is a waxlike substance of ashy color used primarily in perfumery. It was used formerly as a stimulant and an antispasmodic. The name ambergris is a derivative of *amber grisea*. See also Lane, s.v. " 'anbarun;" Sontheimer, 2:210–211; Graziani, p. 298.

Anise (*anīsūn*), *Pimpinella Anisum* L. Maimonides, p. 41: An umbilplant, a native of the Levant, cultivated chiefly for its aromatic and carminative seeds, known as aniseed. See also Bedevian, no. 2683; Sontheimer, 1:86f. Issa, p. 140, no. 5; Darby, p. 793ff.; Graziani, p. 298f.

Apple (*tuffāḥ*), *Pyrus Malus* L. See Bedevian, no. 2899; Sontheimer, 1:208ff.; Issa, p. 151, no. 17; de Sacy, pp. 31f., 36; Darby, p. 697ff.

Apricot (*mishmish*), *Prunus armeniaca* L. See Maimonides, p. 41; de Sacy, p. 132; Anawati, *Drogues*, p. 93; Bedevian, no. 2863; Issa, p. 148, no. 17; Sontheimer, 2:517f.; Darby, p. 747.

Arabian costus, Kust-root (*qusṭ*), *Costus speciosus* SM. See Isḥāq, p. 206, no. 113; Anawati, *Drogues*, p. 90; Bedevian, no. 1207; Issa, p. 58, no. 15; Sontheimer, 2:297–299; Graziani, pp. 220ff., 321. Oil of Arabian costus: Sontheimer, 1:459.

Asarabacca (*asārūn*), *Asarum europaeum* L. See al-Kindī, *The Medical Formulary*, s.v. "asārūn"; Bedevian, no. 507; Issa, p. 23, no. 15.

Asparagus (*halyawn*), *Asparagus officinalis* L. var *altilis* L. See Isḥāq, p. 209, no. 151; Bedevian, no. 519; Issa, p. 24, no. 4; Darby, p. 660f.; Graziani, p. 308.

Azarole (*zu'rur*), *Crataegus azarolus* L. Maimonides, p. 41: The fruit of the Neapolitan medlar, *Cratageus azarolus*, a spiny shrub related to the hawthorn, the fruit of which resembles a small brown apple. The English azarole is derived from Arabic. See also Bedevian, no. 1217; Sontheimer, 1:532f.; Issa, p. 59, no. 5; Graziani, p. 331.

Balsam or balsam of Mecca (*balasān*), *Commiphora opobalsamum* Engl. Maimonides, p. 41: An aromatic, oily, resinous exudation of various trees of the genus *Balsamodendron*, especially the greenish turbid exudate of *B. opobalsamum*, the balsam of Mecca, which was used as a soothing ointment and for anointing. See also Isḥāq, p. 198, no. 20; Anawati, *Drogues*, p. 90; Bedevian, no. 1140; Issa, p. 55, no. 7; de Sacy, pp. 20–22; Nāṣiṛ-i Khusraw, p. 143. 'Ayn Shams was considered the unique source of balsam (*EI*², s.v. " 'Ayn Shams" [C. H. Becker]; Ibn Ḥawqal, 1:159).

Banana (*mawz*), *Musa paradisiaca* L. See Bedevian, no. 2344; Sontheimer, 2:535–536; Issa, p. 121, no. 5; de Sacy, pp. 26–31; Darby, p. 755.

Barberry (*amīrbārīs*), *Berberis vulgaris* L. See Dozy, s.v. "amīr bāris;" Sontheimer, 1:79–80; Maimonides, *Sharḥ*, no. 17; Bedevian, no. 640; Issa, p. 30, no. 18; Maimonides, p. 41.

Bark (*qishr*, *liḥā'*).

Barley (*sha'īr*), *Hordeum vulgare* L. See Bedevian, no. 1864; Sontheimer, 2:97–98; Darby, p. 55 et passim.

Basil, sweet (*rayḥān*), *Ocimum Basilicum* L. See Isḥāq, p. 202, no. 64; Bedevian, no. 2430; Maimonides, p. 41; Sontheimer, 1:509.

Beer (*mizr*), *Zythum*. See Lane, s.v. "mizrun"; Sontheimer, 2:512–513.

Beet or Swiss chard (*silq*), *Beta vularis* L., var. *Folliosa*. See Lane and Dozy, s.v. "silq"; Isḥāq, p. 203, no. 78; Bedevian, no. 646; Issa, p. 30, no. 22; Sontheimer, 2:41–43.

Ben-oil (*bān*), *Moringa aptera* Gaertn. See Bedevian, no. 2335; Sontheimer, 1:115–116; Maimonides, p. 41. Oil: Issa, p. 120, no. 18; Anawati, *Drogues*, p. 91; Sontheimer, 1:451; Darby, p. 784.

Borage (*lisān ath-thawr*), *Borrago officinalis* L. See Bedevian, no. 677; Sontheimer, 2:437–438; Issa, p. 32, no 1.

Branches (*aghṣān*).

Bread (*khubz*).

Broad bean (*bāqillā'*), *Vicia Faba* L. See Bedevian, no. 3590; Issa, p. 189, no. 1; Sontheimer, 1:112ff.

Broth (*ḥisā'*).

Camomile (*bābūnaj*), *Matricaria Chamomilla* L. See Dietrich, *Zum Drogenhandel*, pp. 51–55; Isḥāq, p. 197, no. 10; Bedevian, nos. 983, 986, 2229; Sontheimer, 1:106–108; Issa, p. 115, no. 12; *EI*² *Supplement*, s.v. "Bābūnadj" (A. Dietrich).

Camphor (*kāfūr*), *Cinnamomum Camphora* Nees & Eberm. Maimonides, p. 41: The bitter, aromatic, white crystalline substance distilled from the bark and wood of the evergreen camphor tree. The English *camphor* is derived from the Arabic. See also Bedevian, no. 1036; Sontheimer, 2:333–336; Issa, p. 49, no. 2; Graziani, p. 311.

Caraway (*karāwiyā, karawyā*), *Carum carvi* L. See Bedevian, no. 880; Sontheimer, 2:368–369; Issa, p. 41, no. 2.

Cardamom (*hāl*), *Amomum Cardamonum* L. See Dietrich, *Zum Drogenhandel*, pp. 26–29; Bedevian, no. 289; Sontheimer, 2:568; Issa, p. 13, no. 6. Java cardamom (*qāqullah*), *Amomum maximum* Roxb. See Maimonides, p. 41; Bedevian, no. 293; Sontheimer, 2:273; Graziani, p. 319.

Carnelian (*'aqīq*). See Lane, s.v. " 'aqīqun"; Sontheimer, 2:201.

Carpets (*busuṭ*). See *EI*² *Supplement*, s.v. "Bisāṭ" (F. Spuhler).

Carrot (*jazar*), *Daucus Carota* L. var. *sativa*. See Bedevian, no. 1371; Maimonides, p. 41; Sontheimer, 1:247–248; Issa, p. 69, no. 5.

Cassia, purging (*khiyār shanbar*), *Cassia fistula* L. See Maimonides, p. 41; Isḥāq, p. 201, no. 54; Bedevian, no. 898; Issa, p. 42, no. 12; Sontheimer, 1:401–403; de Sacy, p. 36.

Castor oil plant or Palma Christi (*khirwa'*), *Ricinus conmunis* L. See Isḥāq, p. 200, no. 49; Bedevian, no. 2981; Sontheimer, 1:357f., 449; Issa, p. 159, no. 17; Darby, p. 782f.

Cats (*sanānīr*).

Celery (*karafs*), *Apium graveolens* L. var. *dulce* DC. See *WKAS*. 1:135b, l. 27ff., p. 560a, l. 30ff.; Bedevian, no. 411; Issa, p. 19, no. 5; Sontheimer, 2:352–356; Darby, p. 670.

Ceramic (*khazaf*).

Charcoal (*faḥm*).

Chicken (*farūj*, pl. *farārīj*). See Maimonides p. 43; de Sacy, pp. 135–140 for the hatcheries in medieval Egypt; Darby, pp. 297, 301, 305, 309.

Chick-pea (*ḥimmiṣ*, *ḥimmaṣ*), *Cicer arietinum* L. See Bedevian, no. 1029; Sontheimer, 1:322–324; Issa, p. 48, no. 10; Darby, pp. 654, 685–687.

China (*ṣīnī*).

Christ's Thorn, jujube, or Nabk tree (*nabq*, *sidr*), *Zizyphus spina Christi* Willd. See Bedevian, no. 3653 (not 3765); Maimonides, p. 43; Sontheimer, 2:5f., 550; Issa, p. 192, no. 8; de Sacy, pp. 17, 36; Darby, p. 702f.; Graziani, p. 317.

Cinnamon (*dārṣīnī*, *qirfah*), *Cinnamomum Zeylanicum* Nees. See Maimonides, p. 42; Isḥāq, p. 201, no. 55; Bedevian, no. 1039; Sontheimer, 1:404–408; Issa, p. 49, no. 5; Rodinson, "Recherches," p. 154; Darby, pp. 782, 791ff., 797f.; *EI*[2] *Supplement*, s.v. "Dār Ṣīnī" (A. Dietrich).

Citron (*utrujj*), *Citrus Medica* L. var. *cederata* Risso. See Bedevian, no. 1072; Maimonides, p. 42; ath-Tha'alibī, *The Laṭā'if*, p. 130, no. 85; Sontheimer, 1:11ff.; Issa, p. 51, no. 19; de Sacy, p. 31; Darby, p. 703f.; Graziani, pp. 213f., 328f.

Clay (*ṭīn*). Armenian clay (*aṭ-ṭīn al-armanī*), see chap. 12, n. 38.

Clove (*qaranful*), *Caryophyllus aromaticus* L. See Bedevian, no. 885; Maimonides, p. 42; Sontheimer, 2:281–282; Graziani, p. 321.

Clover dodder, white (*kashūth abyaḍ*), *Cuscuta Epithymum* Murr. See *WKAS*, 1:204b, l. 29ff.; Bedevian, no. 1290; Sontheimer, 2:380–381; Issa, p. 63, no. 6.

Colocasia (*qulqās*), *Arum colocasia* L. See chap. 1, n. 33.

Cooking-pot (*burmah*).

Cotton (*quṭn*).

Coverings (*farsh*, pl. *furush*). See Serjeant, *Islamic Textiles*, s.v. "fursh."

Cucumber (*khiyār*), *Cucumis sativus* L. See Isḥāq, p. 201, no. 54; Bedevian, no. 1267; Sontheimer, 1:400–401; Issa, p. 62, no. 10; Darby, p. 694f. Snake cucumber (*faqqūs*), *C. sativus* L., var. *Flexuosus* Nand. See Bedevian, no. 1268; Sontheimer, 2:260; de Sacy, p. 34. Squirting cucumber (*qiththā'*), *Ecballium elaterium* A. Rich. See Dozy, s.v. "quththā' "; Isḥāq, p. 206, no. 109; Bedevian, no. 1477; Maimonides, p. 44; Sontheimer, 2:276–280; Issa, p. 73, no. 6.

Cyperus (*sa'd*), *Cyperus longus* L. See Anawati, *Drogues*, p. 90; Bedevian, no. 1331; Sontheimer, 2:21–22: Graziani, p. 325.

Date palm (*nakhl*), *Phoenix dactylifera* L. See Bedevian, no. 2642; Issa, p. 138, no. 16; Darby, pp. 722–730.

Dill (*shibith*), *Anethum graveolens* L. See Isḥāq, p. 203, no. 72; Bedevian, no. 368; Sontheimer, 2:79–80; Issa, p. 17, no. 10; Darby, p. 800.

Dogs (*kilāb*).

Dog's fennel (*uqḥuwān*), *Anthemis Cotula* L. See Bedevian, no. 384; Lane, s.v. "bābūnaj"; Sontheimer, 1:69–70; Issa, p. 18, no. 1, p. 115, no. 12.

Donkey (*ḥimār*). See chap. 3, n. 26.

Dough (*'ajīn*).

Duckweed (*'armaḍ*). See chap. 1, n. 38.

Earthenware (*fakhkhār*). See Serjeant, *Islamic Textiles*, p. 84; Lane, s.v. "fakhkhārun."

Egg yolks (*muḥaḥ al-bayḍ*). See Lane, s.v. "muḥḥun."

Elecampane (*rāsin*), *Inula Helenium* L. See Bedevian, no. 1924; Sontheimer, 1:476–478; Issa, p. 99, no. 4.

Electuary (*jawārish*). See Lane, s.v. "jarasha"; Isḥāq, p. 199, no. 33; *MI*, p. 297. *Ma'jūn*, see chap. 10, n. 3.

Emerald (*zumurrad*), *Smaragdus*. See Lane, s.v. "zumurrudhun"; Sontheimer, 1:537.

Endive (*hindibā'*), *Cichorium endivia* L. See Bedevian, no. 1030; Maimonides, p. 42; Sontheimer, 2:575–578; Issa, p. 48, no. 12; Darby, p. 672f.; Graziani, p. 309; *EI*[2] *Supplement*, s.v. "Hindibā'" (A. Dietrich).

Fans (*marāwiḥ*).

Felts (*lubūd*). See Serjeant, *Islamic Textiles*, s.v. "lubūd"; Lane, s.v. "libdun."

Fennel (*rāziyānaj*), *Foeniculum vulgare* Mill. See Isḥāq, p. 201, no. 60; Dozy, s.v. "rāzyānaj"; Maimonides, p. 42; Sontheimer, 1:486–488; Issa, p. 84, no. 11.

Fig (*tīn*), *Ficus Carica* L. See Bedevian, no. 1617; Maimonides, p. 42; Sontheimer, 1:221–225; Issa, p. 83, no. 4.

Fish (*samak*). See de Sacy, pp. 145–147.

Flax (*kattān*), *Linum* Tourn. See Bedevian, no. 2107; Sontheimer, 2:348; Graziani, p. 314.

Flour or meal (*daqīq*).

Francolin (*durrāj*), *Tetrao francolinus*. See Maimonides, p. 42; Sontheimer, 1:419–420; Darby, pp. 55, 309–314.

Frankincense (*lubān, kundur*), *Boswellia Carterii* Birdw. See Bedevian, no. 680; *WKAS*, 2:172a, l. 9ff.; 1:553b, l. 2ff.; Lane, s.v. "lubānun," "kundurun"; Sontheimer, 2:397–402, 428; Issa, p. 32, no. 4.

Galangale (*khūlanjān*), *Alpinia Galanga* Willd. The aromatic, medicinal rhizome of certain plants of the ginger family, especially *Alpine officinarum*, a native of India, the odor and taste of which are gingerlike. The English term is derived from the Arabic, which in turn is a derivative of the Chinese *Ko-Liang-Kiang*—mild ginger from Ko. See Bedevian, no. 234; al-Kindī, *The Medical Formulary*, s.v. "khūlanjan"; M. Ullmann, "Die Schrift des Badīġūras über die Ersatzdrogen," *Der Islam* 50 (1973):243; Sontheimer, 1:399; Issa, p. 10, no. 13; Graziani, p. 313.

Garlic (*thūm*), *Allium sativum* L. See Isḥāq, p. 199, no. 28; Bedevian, no. 214; Maimonides, p. 42; Sontheimer, 1:230–233; Issa, p. 9, no. 15; Darby, pp. 656–660.

Gem (*jawhar*).

Ghāliyah, see chap. 12, n. 28.

Gillyflower (*khīrī*), *Matthiola incana* R. Br. See Bedevian, no. 2232; Sontheimer, 1:403–404; Issa, p. 115, no. 15.

Ginger (*zanjabīl*), *Zingiber officinale* Rosc. See Bedevian, no. 3645; Maimonides, p. 42; Sontheimer, 1:537–538; Issa, p. 191, no. 11; Graziani, p. 330.

Glass (*zujāj*).

Gold (*dhahab*), *Aurum*. See Sontheimer, 1:474.

Gooseberry (*rībās*), *Ribes Grossularia* L. See ath-Thaʻalibī, *The Laṭā'if*, p. 131, n. 93; Bedevian, no. 2978; Sontheimer, 1:508; Graziani, p. 321.

Grape or grapevine (*karm*, pl. *kurūm*), *Vitis vinifera* L. See Bedevian, no. 3614; Sontheimer, 2:356–357; Issa, p. 190, no. 6; Darby, pp. 711–715. Unripe and sour grapes (*ḥiṣrim*), see Sontheimer, 1:309–311; Lane, s.v. "ḥiṣrimun"; Rodinson, "Recherches," p. 136.

Grasses (*ḥashā'ish*). See Lane, s.v. "ḥashīshun."

Grease or lanolin. See chap. 12, n. 35; greasy (*dasim*), see Lane, s.v. "dasimun."

Gypsum (*jiṣṣ*). See Lane, s.v. "jiṣṣun"; Sontheimer, 1:249.

Hare (*arnab*). See Lane, s.v. "arnabun."

Hazelnut (*bunduq*), *Corylus Avellana* L. or *C. Colurna* L. See Bedevian, nos. 1199, 1200; Sontheimer, 1:177–178; Issa, p. 58, no. 13.

Herbage (*ʻushb*), *Medicago ciliaris* Hook. See Bedevian, no. 2238; Lane, s.v. " 'ushbun"; Issa, p. 115, no. 20. Herb (*baql*), see Lane, s.v. "baqlun."

Honey (*'asal*). See Lane s.v. " 'asalun"; Sontheimer, 2:190–193; Darby, p. 55 et passim; Finkel, "King Mutton," p. 137f.

Hornets (*zanābīr*). See Lane s.v. "zunbūrun."

Houseleek (*ḥayy al-'ālam*), *Sempervivum arboreum* L. See Bedevian, no. 3144; Sontheimer, 1:341; Issa, p. 167, no. 1; Graziani, p. 308.

Incense (*bakhūr*). See Lane, s.v. "bakhūrun."

Jasmine (*yāsmīn*), *Jasminum officinale* L. See Bedevian, no. 1966; Sontheimer, 2:591; Issa, p. 101, no. 10; de Sacy, p. 35f.

Julep (*jullāb*). Maimonides, p. 42: A sweet medicated drink prepared usually from rose water. The English term is derived from the Arabic, which in turn is derived from the Persian *gullāb*—a combination of *gūl* (rose) and *ab* (water).

Kid (*jadī*). See Maimonides, p. 42.

Kishk. See chap. 12, n. 16.

Lakhālikh. See chap. 12, n. 29.

Lamb (*ḥamal*, pl. *ḥumlān*). See Lane, s.v. "ḥamalun."

Larks (*qanābir*). See Lane, s.v. "qunburun."

Laudanum (*lādhin*), *Cistus ladaniferus* L. See Bedevian, no. 1053.

Lead (*raṣāṣ*), *Plumbum*. See Sontheimer, 1:494–496.

Leaven (*khamīr*). See Lane, s.v. "khamīrun"; Sontheimer, 1:383–384; Anawati, *Drogues*, p. 96.

Leek (*kurrāth*), *Allium Porrum* L. See Isḥāq, p. 207, no. 117; Bedevian, no. 211; Maimonides, p. 42; Sontheimer, 2:363–367; Issa, p. 9, no. 11; Darby, p. 673ff.

Lemon (*laymūn*), *Citrus Medica* L., var. *limonum* Ris. See Bedevian, no. 1073; Sontheimer, 2:452–459; Issa, p. 52, no. 1; de Sacy, pp. 31, 36; Darby, p. 705.

Lentil (*'adas*), *Lens esculenta* Moench. See Bedevian, no. 2065; Sontheimer, 2:185; Issa, p. 107, no. 1.

Lettuce (*khass*), *Lactuca sativa* L. See Isḥāq, p. 201, no. 50; Bedevian, no. 2002; Sontheimer, 1:264–267; Issa, p. 103, no. 26; Darby, pp. 675–680.

Licorice (*sūs*), *Glycyrrhiza glabra* L. See Isḥāq, p. 203, no. 81; Bedevian, no. 1732; Maimonides, p. 43; Sontheimer, 2:66–67; Issa, p. 58, no. 6; Graziani, p. 326.

Lily of the valley (*sawsān*), *Lilium candidum* L. See Isḥāq, p. 203, no. 82; Bedevian, no. 2091; Sontheimer, 2:68–71; Issa, p. 109, no. 2; Graziani, p. 326.

Lion (*asad*).

Lotus of India (*fāghirah*), *Xanthoxylon Avicennae* DC. See Bedevian, no. 3625; Sontheimer, 2:241; Issa, p. 191, no. 4.

Lupine (*turmus*), *Lupinus termis* Forsk. See Bedevian, no. 2158; Sontheimer, 1:203–205; Issa, p. 112, no. 13; Darby, p. 689f.; Graziani, p. 328.

Mahaleb or perfumed cherry (*maḥlab*), *Prunus mahaleb* L. See Bedevian, no. 2845; Sontheimer, 2:490–491; Issa, p. 149, no. 4.

Maidenhair (*kuzburat [al-] bi'r*), *Adiantum Capillus veneris* L. See *WKAS*, 1:564b, l. 5ff.; Bedevian, no. 114; Maimonides, p. 43; Sontheimer, 2:379; Issa, p. 6, no. 1.

Mandrake (*luffāḥ*), *Mandragora officinarum* L. See Bedevian, no. 2206; Sontheimer, 2:440; Issa, p. 114, no. 13; Graziani, p. 329.

Marble (*rukhām*). See Lane "rukhāmun"; Sontheimer, 1:493.

Marjoram, sweet (*marzanjūsh*), *Origanum majorama* L. See Isḥāq, p. 208, no. 134; Bedevian, no. 2481; Sontheimer, 2:494–496; Issa, p. 130, no. 2; Darby, p. 802f.; Graziani, p. 316.

Marrow (*qulūb*).

Mastic (*maṣṭakā'*, *maṣṭakā*), *Pistacia lentiscus* L. Maimonides, p. 43: The gum that exudes from the bark of *P. lentiscus* and some other related trees. The English *mastic* is probably derived from the Arabic. See also Isḥāq, p. 208, no. 137; Bedevian, no. 2719; Sontheimer, 2:518–521; Graziani, p. 316. Oil of mastic, see Issa, p. 141, no. 12; Sontheimer, 1:448.

Mats (*ḥusur*). See Serjeant, *Islamic Textiles*, s.v. "ḥaṣīr."

Melilot (*ḥandaqūq*), *Trigonella caerulae* Ser. See Isḥāq, p. 200, no. 44; Bedevian, no. 3465; Sontheimer, 1:335–338; Issa, p. 183, no. 2; *EI*[2] *Supplement*, s.v. "Iklīl al-Malik" (A. Dietrich).

Melon (*biṭṭīkh*), *Citrullus vulgaris* Schrad. See Bedevian, no. 1060; Sontheimer, 1:145–148; Issa, p. 50, no. 12; de Sacy, p. 34f.; Darby, p. 717f.

Milk (*laban*). Coagulated sour milk (*albān*). See Sontheimer, 2:413–426; Darby, pp. 760–772.

Mint (*na'nā'*), *Mentha sativa* L. See Isḥāq, p. 209, no. 147; Bedevian, no. 2271; Sontheimer, 2:556–558; Issa, p. 117, no. 14; Darby, p. 803. Aquatic mint (*fūdanj*), *M. pulegium* L. or *M. aquatica* L. See Isḥāq, p. 206, no. 108; Dozy, s.v. "fūdhanj"; al-Kindī, *The Medical Formulary*, s.v. "faudanaj"; Sontheimer, 2:267–270; Graziani, p. 305; EI[2] *Supplement*, s.v. "fūdhandj" (A. Dietrich).

Mithridatium (*Mithrūdayṭūs*). See chap. 13, n. 4.

Molasses (*'asal as-sukkar*).

Musk (*misk*). Maimonides, p. 43: The secretion obtained from a sac under the abdominal skin of the male musk-deer; it is an odiferous reddish-brown substance. The English term is derived from the Arabic *misk* or the Persian *muskh*. See also Sontheimer, 2:513–516; Graziani, p. 316.

Mustard, white (*khardal*), *Sinapis alba* L. See Isḥāq, p. 200, no. 48; Bedevian, no. 3204; Issa, p. 169, no. 16; Darby, p. 803f.; Graziani, p. 312f.

Myrrh (*murr*), *Commiphora myrrha* Engl. See Isḥāq, p. 208, no. 132; Bedevian, no. 1139; Sontheimer, 2:496–500; Issa, p. 55, no. 6; Graziani, p. 317.

Myrtle (*ās*), *Myrtus communis* L. See Bedevian, no. 2374; Maimonides, p. 43; Sontheimer, 1:38–41; Issa, p. 122, no. 19; *EI*[2] *Supplement* s.v. "Ās" (A. Dietrich); Graziani, p. 299f.

Nadd. See chap. 12, n. 23.

Narcissus (*narjis*), *Narcissus poeticus* L. See Bedevian, no. 2382; Sontheimer, 2:552–553; Issa, p. 123, no. 3; Graziani, p. 318. Oil of narcissus, see Sontheimer, 1:434; Anawati, *Drogues*, p. 91.

Nard (*nārdīn*), *Nardus stricta* L. See Isḥāq, p. 209, no. 143; Anawati, *Drogues*, p. 91; Bedevian, no. 2388; Sontheimer, 2:546. Oil of nard, see Sontheimer, 1:437–438; Graziani, p. 326.

Nārmashak. See chap. 14, n. 13.

Nenuphar (*nīlūfar*), *Nymphaea alba* L. See Ishāq, p. 209, no. 149; Sontheimer, 2:564–565; Graziani, p. 318. Oil of nenuphar, see Sontheimer, 1:443.

Nightshade, black (*'inab ath-tha'lab*), *Solanum nigrum* L. See Issa, p. 171, no. 17; Bedevian, no. 3243; Sontheimer, 1:212–215.

Oak (*ballūṭ*), *Quercus* L. See Bedevian, no. 2907; Sontheimer, 1:164–166.

Onion (*baṣal*), *Allium Cepa* L. See Bedevian, no. 209; Sontheimer, 1:142–144; Issa, p. 9, no. 7; Darby, pp. 477, 660–663.

Orache (*qaṭf*), *Atriplex hortensis* L. See Bedevian, no. 575; Maimonides, p. 43; Lane, s.v. "baqlun"; Sontheimer, 2:307–308; Issa, p. 27, no. 4.

Orange, bitter, or Seville orange (*naranj*), *Citrus Aurantium* var. *amara* L. See Bedevian, no. 1062; Sontheimer, 2:545–546; Issa, p. 51, no. 9.

Oxymel. See chap. 10, n. 2.

Papyrus (*bardī*), *Cyperus papyrus* L. See Bedevian, no. 1334; Issa, p. 66, no. 11; Sontheimer, 1:127–129; *EI*[2], s.v. "Ḳirṭās" (R. Sellheim); Darby, pp. 244–249.

Partridge (*ṭayhūj*). See chap. 12, n. 42.

Peach (*khawkh*), *Prunus persica* Stokes. See Bedevian, no. 2847; Issa, p. 149, no. 5; Sontheimer, 1:400; de Sacy, p. 36; Darby, p. 733ff.

Pearl (*durr*). See Lane, s.v. "durrun."

Pelts (*firā'*).

Pepper (*fulful, filfil*), *Piper nigrum*, L. See Bedevian, no. 2714; Sontheimer, 2:261–263; Darby, p. 804. Long pepper (*dārafilfil*), *Piper Chaba* Hunter. See Dozy, s.v. "dārfilfil"; Isḥāq, p. 201, no. 56; al-Kindī, *The Medical Formulary*, p. 266, no. 97; Bedevian, no. 991; Sontheimer, 1:409.

Perfume (*ṭīb*) and compound perfume (*sukk*). See chap. 12, ns. 13 and 26.

Pistachio (*fustuq*), *Pistacia vera* L. See Isḥāq, p. 205, no. 105; Bedevian, no. 2722; Maimonides, p. 43; Sontheimer, 2:255–256; Nāṣir-i Khusraw, p. 154; de Sacy, p. 312f.

Pit (*nawan*).

Pomegranate (*rummān*), *Punica Granatum* L. See Isḥāq, p. 202, no. 61; Bedevian, no. 2880; Anawati, *Drogues*, p. 93; Maimonides, p. 43; Sontheimer, 1:499–503; de Sacy, p. 36; Darby, pp. 703, 740–744.

Poppy, white (*al-khashkhāsh al-abyaḍ*), *Papaver somniferum* L., var. *album*. See Bedevian, no. 2541; Maimonides, p. 43; Sontheimer, 1:367–369; Issa, p. 134, no. 8; Graziani, p. 313.

Prune (*ijjāṣ*), *Prunus domestica* L. Maimonides, p. 43: The Arabic *ijjāṣ* is now used to designate "pear" rather than "prune." This usage probably originated in the Maghrib, where the term *ijjāṣ*, or *injāṣ*, was always employed to designate the pear. Formerly, however, the term *ijjāṣ* was used to designate the prune. See also Sontheimer, 1:16–18; Issa, p. 149, no. 1; de Sacy, p. 36.

Pulp (*samīn*). See Lane, s.v. "samīnun."

Pumpkin or gourd (*qar'*), *Cucurbita*. See Bedevian, nos. 1270–1273; Maimonides, p. 43; Sontheimer, 2:284–287; de Sacy, p. 35; Graziani, p. 319.

Purslane (*rijlah*, *al-baqlah al-ḥamqā'*), *Portulaca oleracca* L. See Maimonides, p. 43; Sontheimer, 1:155, 492; Issa, p. 147, no. 10; Dozy, s.v. "al-baqlah al-ḥamqā' "; Darby, p. 681; Graziani, p. 301.

Quince (*safarjal*), *Pyrus cydonia* L. See Isḥāq, p. 203, no. 75; Rodinson, "Recherches," p. 131 et passim; Bedevian, no. 1304; Sontheimer, 2:25–27; de Sacy, p. 36.

Radish (*fujl*), *Raphanus sativus* L. See Isḥāq, p. 205, no. 102; Bedevian, no. 2937; Sontheimer, 2:246–248. Oil of radish, see Sontheimer, 1:452–453; Darby, p. 663f.

Raisins (*zabīb*). See Sontheimer, 1:515–517; Darby, pp. 715f., 794; and chap. 12, n. 44.

Rambling vetch (*julubbān*), *Vicia peregrina* L. See Bedevian, no. 3593; Sontheimer, 1:252; Issa, p. 189, no. 5.

Rams (*kibāsh*). See Lane s.v. "kabshun."

Rats (*fa'r, fār*). See Lane, s.v. "fa'run"; *EI*[2] *Supplement*, s.v. "Fa'r" (F. Viré).

Reeds (*qaṣab*). See Isḥāq, p. 206, no. 114; Bedevian, nos. 502, 2649, 3023; Sontheimer, 2:302–303.

Resin (*'ilk*). See Sontheimer, 2:206–209; Lane, s.v. " 'ilkun," "kundurun."

Rice (*aruzz*), *Oryza sativa* L. See Bedevian, no. 2495; Sontheimer, 1:24–25; Darby, p. 492f.

Roosters, castrated (*khaṣīy ad-duyūk*).

Root (*aṣl*).

Rose (*ward*), *Rosa* Tourn. See Bedevian, no. 2987; Sontheimer, 2:582–585; de Sacy, p. 35; Graziani, p. 329. Rose oil, see Sontheimer, 1:440–442; Anawati, *Drogues*, p. 91. Musk-rose (*nisrīn*), *Rosa moschata* Herrm. See Bedevian, no. 2995; Sontheimer, 2:553–554; Issa, p. 157, no. 10. Red rose (*al-ward al-aḥmar*), *Rosa gallica* L., see Bedevian, no. 2993.

Rose-honey or rose-preserve (*julanjabīn*), *Mel rosarum*. See ath-Tha'alibī, p. 128, n. 70; Sontheimer, 1:255.

Rose jam (*al-ward al-murabbā*).

Rose water (*mā' al-ward*). See Sontheimer, 2:482.

Rue (*sadhāb*), *Ruta graveolens* L. See Bedevian, no. 3020; Sontheimer, 2:6–8; Issa, p. 159, no. 9; Graziani, p. 322.

Saffron (*za'farān*), *Crocus sativus* L. See Isḥāq, p. 202, no. 67; Bedevian, no. 1233; Maimonides, p. 44; Sontheimer, 1:530–532; Darby, p. 805f.; Graziani, p. 330.

Salt (*milḥ*).

Saltwort (*ushnān*), *Salsola kali* L. See Bedevian, no. 3042; Lane and Dozy, s.v. "ashnān"; Sontheimer, 1:53; Issa, p. 161, no. 6.

Sand (*raml*).

Sandalwood (*ṣandal*), *Santalum*. Maimonides, p. 44: The yellowish, fragrant wood obtained from several species of the genus *Santalum*, especially the parasitic Indo-Malayan tree *S. album*. See also Sontheimer, 2:138–139; Graziani, p. 323. White Sandalwood (*ṣandal abyaḍ*), *S. album* L. See Bedevian, no. 3064; Sontheimer, 2:138–139; Issa, p. 162, no. 13.

Sandarac (*sandarūs*), *Callitris quadrivalvis* Vent. See Bedevian, no. 799; Sontheimer, 2:61–62; Issa, p. 37, no. 1.

Sapphire (*yāqūt*), see Maimonides, p. 42; Sontheimer, 2:591–592.

Sawīq. See chap. 12, n. 17.

Schoenanthum or camel's hay (*idhkar*). *Andropogon Schoenanthus* L. See Bedevian, no. 349; Sontheimer, 1:19–21; Anawati, *Drogues*, p. 90; Lane and Dozy, s.v. "idhkhir." Flower of the schoenanthum (*fuqqāḥ al-idhkhir*), see Lane, s.v. "fuqqāḥun."

Scorpion (*'aqārib*). See Lane, s.v. " 'aqrabun."

Sea buckthorn (*ghāsūl*), *Hippophae rhamnoides* L.

Seed (*ḥabb*, *bizr*).

Sesame (*ḥall*). See Isḥāq, p. 200, no. 41; Lane, s.v. "ḥallun"; Sontheimer, 1:460; Issa, p. 169, no. 1; Darby, p. 497f.

Sheep (*ḍa'n*). See Darby, pp. 85, 211–221.

Silk (*ḥarīr*). Silk brocade (*dībāj*). See Serjeant, *Islamic Textiles*, s.v. "dībādj," Lane, s.v. "Dībāj."

Silver (*fiḍḍah*).

Skins (*julūd*).

Snakes (*tha'ābīn*). See Lane, s.v. "thu'bānun"; Darby, p. 411f.

Soft-haired basil or Frankish musk (*afranjamusk*), *Ocimum pilosum* var. *O. Basilicum* Willd. See Isḥāq, p. 205, no. 104; Maimonides, p. 42; Bedevian, no. 2434; Sontheimer, 2:254; Issa, p. 127, no. 1.

Southernwood (*qayṣūm*), *Artemisia Abrotanum* L. See Bedevian, no. 478; Sontheimer, 2:331–332; Issa, p. 21, no. 20.

Sparrows (*'aṣāfīr*). See Sontheimer, 2:196–197.

Spices (*afāwīh*, s. *afwāh*).

Spikenard (*sunbul*), *Nardus celtica* L. or *Andropogan Nardus* L. An aromatic balsam or ointment manufactured from the fragrant rhizome of *Nardostachys jatamansi* D.C., a small plant found in the alpine Himalayas. The Arabic word is also identified with "hyacinth." See Dozy and Lane, s.v. "sunbul"; al-Kindī, *The Medical Formulary*, s.v. "sunbul"; Isḥāq, p. 203, no. 80; Bedevian, nos. 3549, 2387, 348, 3550; Maimonides, p. 43; Issa, p. 123, nos. 9, 10.

Spinach (*isfānākh*), *Spinacia oleracea* L. See Isḥāq, p. 197, no. 4; Bedevian, no. 3282; Sontheimer, 1:34–35.

Starch (*nashā*). See Sontheimer, 2:554–555.

Sticks (*quḍbān*).

Stones (*fuṣūṣ*).

Storax (*may'ah*), *Styrax officinale* L. See Isḥāq, p. 209, no. 142; Bedevian, no. 3327; Sontheimer, 2:539–541.

Sugar (*sukkar*) and lump sugar (*as-sukkar aṭ-ṭabarzadh*). See chap. 14, nn. 6–8.

Sugarcane (*qaṣab as-sukkar*), *Saccharum officinarum* L. See Bedevian, no. 3023; Sontheimer, 2:304; and chap. 3, n. 18.

Sumac (*summāq*), *Rhus Coriaria* L. See Bedevian, no. 2973; Maimonides, p. 44; Sontheimer, 2:48–49; Issa, p. 159, no. 3; Graziani, p. 326.

Sweetmeats (*ḥalāwah*, s. *ḥalwā*).

Ṭabāshīr. See chap. 12, n. 37.

Ṭamarind (*tamrihindī*), *Tamarindus indica* L. Maimonides, p. 44: The pulp of the fruit of Tamarrindus indica, which was usually preserved in sugar. The English term is a derivative of the Arabic, meaning "Indian date." See also Bedevian, no. 3344; Sontheimer, 1:212–213; Issa, p. 176, no. 16; Graziani, p. 327.

Tamarisk, French (*ṭarfā'*), *Tamarix gallica* L. See Lane, s.v. "ṭarfā' "; Bedevian, no. 3347; Sontheimer, 2:153–155; Issa, p. 177; no. 3; Graziani, p. 327.

Tamarisk, oriental (*athl*), *Tamarix orientalis* Forsk. See Lane, s.v. "athl"; Bedevian, no. 3346; Sontheimer, 1:13–15; Issa, p. 177, no. 2; Graziani, p. 327.

Ṭanāfis. See chap. 12, n. 9.

Tar (*qaṭrān*). See Dozy, s.v. "qaṭrana"; Graziani, p. 320.

Taranjubīn. See chap. 13, n. 2.

Tents (*buyūt*).

Theriac (*tiryāq*). See chap. 13, n. 4.

Thyme, wild (*nammām*, *ṣa'tar*), *Thymus glaber* Mill. and *T. serpyllum* L. See Isḥāq, p. 209, no. 148; Bedevian, nos. 3414, 3416; Sontheimer, 2:128–131, 559–60; Issa, p. 181, nos. 2, 4; Graziani, pp. 317f., 323.

Tubs (*ijjānāt*). See Lane, s.v. "ijjānatun."

Turnip (*lift*), *Brassica Rapa* L. See Bedevian, no. 703; Sontheimer, 2:440; Darby, p. 665.

Vessels (*āniyah*, *ẓurūf*). See Lane s.v. "inā'un," "ẓarfun."

Vinegar (*khall*). See Sontheimer, 1:377–380; Darby, p. 617. Wine vinegar (*khall al-khamr*).

Violets (*banafsaj*), *Viola odorata* L. See Isḥāq, p. 198, no. 22; Bedevian, no. 4605; Sontheimer, 1:170–172; de Sacy, p. 36; Graziani, p. 301. Oil of violets, see Sontheimer, 1:442–443.

Walnuts (*jawz*), *Juglans regia* L. See Bedevian, no. 1975; Sontheimer, 1:266–269; Darby, p. 753; Graziani, p. 310f.

Water moss (*ṭuḥlub*), *Lemna minor* L. See Bedevian, nos. 2063, 1173;

Sontheimer, 2:152–153; de Sacy, p. 333, n. 15.

Waterskins (*asqān*, *qirabāt*).

Wax (*sham'*). See Graziani, p. 324.

Wheat (*ḥinṭah*), *Triticum aestivum* L. See Bedevian, no. 3483; Sontheimer, 1:334–335; Darby, pp. 460–465, 482–492.

Whey (*maṣl*), see Sontheimer, 2:522.

Willow (*ṣafṣāf*), *Salix safsaf* Forsk. See Bedevian, no. 3038; Issa, p. 160, no. 13. Egyptian willow (*khilāf*), *S. aegyptiaca* L., var. *S. safsaf* Forsk. See Bedevian, no. 3032; Sontheimer, 1:381–382; Issa, p. 160, no. 5.

Wine (*khamr*, *sharāb*, *nabīdh*). See Sontheimer, 1:383–393; 2:548–550; Lane, s.v. "nabīdhun," "mizrun"; *EI*[1], s.v. "nabīd̲" (Wensinck). Date wine (*an-nabīdh at-tamrī*).

Wool (*ṣūf*).

Worms (*dūd*).

Wormwood (*shīḥ*), *Artemisia herba alba* Asso. See Bedevian, no. 486; Sontheimer, 2:116–117; Issa, p. 22, no. 6; Graziani, p. 325.

· INDEXES ·

Index to Introduction

Index to Text and Translation
Arabic*

*The pagination of the indexes refers to the folios of the edited Arabic text.

English

كتاب

دفع مضار الأبدان

لعلي بن رضوان الطبيب المصري

(١)

بســــم اللــه الرحمن الرحيم (١)

كتاب عليّ بن رضوان في حيلة دَفْع مَضارّ الأبدان في مصر. قال[٢] عليّ بن رضوان : قَصْدنا أن نلخّص الحيلة فى دفع مضارّ الأبدان بأرض مصر. ويجب ضرورة أن نقدّم أسباب هذه المضارّ وما هي ،كيما يتهيّألنا (٣) الوقوف على الحيلة في دفعها (٤). ونسأل الله العونَ والتوفيق فيما نلتمسه فهو وليّ الاجابة بمنّه وطَوْله (٥).

وقد كان أحمد بن إبراهيم الطبيب المغربي (٦) المعروف بابن الجَزّار وضع في ذلك مقالة مُفْرَدة (٧) لم يَسْتقص فيها ما يُحتاج إليه مِن تلخيص القول ،واستيفاء الوصف في ذكر الأسباب البَلَديّة ،وما يُحدِث عنها ،وما يُدْفَع به ضررُها. وَخليق أن يكون قد عرَض له النُقْصان مِن قِبَل(٨) أنه رجل من أهل المغرب ،لم يُعايِن مصر معاينة اختبار وامتحان ،ولكن سمِع بها سماعا (٩). وكتابنا هذا يَزيد على كتابه بمقدار فضل قوّتنا على قوّته في أنواع الفلسفة ،وبمقدار اختبارنا /٢أ/ أرض مصر بالمشاهدة دون الخبَر سنينا كثيرة متوالية . ومَن أحبّ (١٠) الإنصاف وآثَر العدلَ فسيَقف على صدق هذا القول إذا جمع بين الكتابين وتأمّلهما (١١) من غير مَيْل مع الهوى الذي من شأنه أن يَعْمِي عَيْن النفس - أعني العَقل (١٢) ويَطْفِيء نورها. وإذا كان كِتابنا بهذا الحال ،فحاجة الخاصّ والعامّ مِن ساكنِي مصر (١٣) ومَن يصير إليها من الغرباء إليه ضروريّة في صِحّة أبدانهم وإزالة (١٤) أسْقامها ،واشدّهم إليه اضطرارا الأطباء ،إذ كان لا يُوقف على ما يُحْتاج إليه في المداواة دون الوقوف على مِزاج البلد وما يحدث فيه خاصّة . وقد جعلته خمسة عشر فصلا ،في كل فصل معنى مُفْرَد كيما يخِفّ على الإنسان تناوُلُ كل معنى فيه :

الفصل الأول : في صفة أرض مصر ومِزاجها.
الفصل الثاني : في صفة اختلاف هواء أرض مصر وما يتولّد فيها.
الفصل الثالث : في الأسباب الستة المحيطة بالصحّة والمرض بأرض مصر.
الفصل الرابع : في فصول السنة بأرض مصر /٢ب/.
الفصل الخامس : في أنّ أكثر ما أعطاه ابن الجزار من أسباب وخم أرض مصر ليس بصحيح .
الفصل السادس : في اختصاص المدينة الكبرى اليوم بمصر في هوائها وجميع أحوالها.
الفصل السابع : في الوقوف على أسباب الوباء وسائر الأمراض الوافدة .
الفصل الثامن : في إعادة ما تقدّم على سبيل الجملة ،وشَرْح أمْر الأسباب الستة المحيطة بالصحّة والمرض.

الفصل التاسع : في الحيلة الكُلّيّة في حفظ الصحّة ومُداواة الأمراض.
الفصل العاشر : فيما ينبغي للطبيب أن يفعله في الأبدان بأرض مصر (١٥).
الفصل الحادي عشر : في صفة تدبير الأبدان في مصر .
الفصل الثاني عشر : فيما يُصْلِح رداءة الهواء والماء والغذاء بأرض مصر.
الفصل الثالث عشر : فيما يُدْفَع به ضرر الأمراض الوافدة بمصر.
الفصل الرابع عشر : في نسخ أدوية تُسْتَعمل في دَفْع المضارّ وحِفْظ الأبدان.
الفصل الخامس عشر : في أنه ينبغي (١٦) أن تُختار السُكْنَى بمصر، وإن كانت تفعل في الأبدان رداءة /٣أ/ (١٧) .

(٢)

الفصل الأول
في صِفة أرض مصر ومِزاجها

مصر اسم (١٨) نقلت الرُواة أنّه يدلّ على أحد أولاه نْوح (١٩) عليه السلام، فإنهم ذكروا أنّ مصر هذا نزل بهذه الأرض فأنْسَل (٢٠) فيها وعمرها فسميت باسمه . والذى يدلّ عليه هذا الاسم اليوم هو الأرض التي يُفيض عليها النيل (٢١) ويحيط بها حدود أربعة .

الحدّ الشرقيّ (٢٢) هو أنّ الشمس تشرق على أقصى العِمارة بالمشرق قبْل شروقها على هذه الأرض بثماني ساعات وثلث . والحدّ الغربيّ (٢٣): هو أن تغيب عن آخر العمارة (٢٤) بالمغرب بثلاث ساعات وثلثيْ ساعة . فيجب من ذلك أن تكون هذه الأرض في النصف الغربيّ من الربع العامر على ما قال أبْقراط وبطليموس . وهو أقل حرارة وأكثر رطوبة من النصف الشرقيّ لأنه في قسم كوكب القمر. والنصف الشرقيّ في قسم كوكب الشمس (٢٥) . وذلك أن الشمس تشرق على النصف الشرقيّ قبل شروقها على النصف الغربي /٣ب/، والقمر يهلّ (٢٦) على النصف الغربيّ قبل النصف الشرقيّ . وقد زعم قوم من القدماء (٢٧) أن أرض مصر في وسط الربع المعمور من الأرض بالطبع. فأما بالقياس فعلى ما قدّمنا وَصْفه من أنها في النصف الغربيّ . والحد الثالث: وهو الجنوبيّ ،هو أول بُعْد هذه الأرض عن خطّ الاستواء في جهة الشمال ،وهو المدينة المعروفة من أرض (مصر ب) (٢٨) أسوان . وبُعْد هذه المدينة عن خط الاستواء اثنتان وعشرون درجة ونصف بالأجزاء التي بها أعظم دائرة تقع على الأرض ،ثلاثمائة وستون جزءا . فمن البيّن أن الشمس تَسامت رُءوسَ أهل هذه البلدة ـ أعني أسوان (٢٩) ـ مرتيْن في السنة ،أعني كوْنها في آخر الجَوزاء (و) في أول السَرَطان . وفي هذين الوقتيْن لا يكون للقائم ـ في هذه البلدة نصفَ النهار ـ ظلّ أصلاً . والحرارة واليُبْس والاحتراق إذن غالب على مِزاج هذه البلدة ،لأن الشمس تنشف رطوبتها . ولذلك صارت ألوانهم سُوداء وشعورهم /٤أ/ جَعْدة لاحتراق أرضهم . والحد الرابع : وهو الشماليّ (٣٠) هو آخر بُعْد مصر عن خط الاستواء في جهة الشمال ،طرف (٣١) بحْر الرُوم ،وعليه من أرض مصر بُلْدان كثيرة كالإسكندرية ،ورَشِيد ،ودمْياط،وتِنيس ،والفَرَما.وبعدتنّيس عن خطالاستواء في الشمال إحدى وثلاثون درجة وثلث بالأجزاء التي بها أعظم دائرة تقع على كرة الأرض ،ثلاثمائة وستون جزءا . وهذا التعْد هو آخر الإقليم الثالث وأول الرابع . فالشمس إذن لا تبعْد عنهم كلّ البعد ،ولا تقرب منهم كل القُرْب . والغالب عليهم الاعتدال مع ميْل يسير نحو الحرارة ،اذ الموضع (٣٢) المعتدل على الصحة في البلدان العامرة هو وسط الإقليم الرابع . ومُجاورة (٣٣) هذه البلدة البحرَ وإحاطته بها مِمّا يجعلها معتدلة بين الحرّ والبرد،خارجةً عن الاعتدال إلى الرطوبة ،فيكون الغالب عليها المِزاج الرطب الذي ليس بحارّ ولا بارد . ولذلك صارت ألوانهم سُمْرا ؛ وأخلاقهم سهلة (٣٤) وشعورهم سَبْطة .

وإذا كان أول (٣٥) مصر من جهة الجنوب الغالب عليه الاحتراق/٤ب/وآخرها من جهة الشمال الغالب عليه الاعتدال ،فما بين هذين الموضعين من أرض مصر الغالب عليه إذن الحرارة . وتكون قوة حرارته بقَدْر بُعْده عن أسوان وقُرْبه من بحر الرُوم . ومن أجل هذا قال أبْقراط وجالِينوس إنّ المِزاج الغالب على أرض مصر : الحرارة .

وإذ قد حدّدناها وذكرنا مِزاجها ،فلنأخذ في صِفتها ،فنقول (٣٦) :

(٣)

هذه الأرض محصورة بين جبلين آخذين من الجنوب إلى الشمال ،قليليْ الارتفاع وأحدهما أعظم من الأخر . والأعظم منهما هو الشرقيّ المعروف بالمُقَطَّم (٣٧). وأما الغربيّ فصغير ،وبعضه غير متّصل ببعض ،والمسافة بينهما تَضيق في بعض المواضع وتتّسع في بعضها ،وأوسع ما تكون بأسفل أرض مصر . وهذان الجبلان أقرعان لا يَنْبت فيهما النبات كما يكون في جبال البلدان الاخرى.

وعِلّة ذلك أنهما بُوْرَقّيان مالحان (٣٨) لأنّ قوّة طين مصر قوّة تجذب منها الرطوبة الموافِقة في التكوّن ،ولأنّ /٥أ/ قوّة الحرارة تخلّل منهما الجَوْهَر اللطيف العَذْب ،ولا يَرْتقِي إليهما من الأمطار ما يُخْلف عليهما هذا الجوهر العذب ،(٣٩) . ولذلك مياه الآبار فيهما مالحة ويُحْرِقان (٤٠)مايُدْفَن فيهما من الحيوان وغيره ،فإنّ أرض مصر بالطبع قليلة الأمطار ،وجبل المقطم في مشرق (٤١) هذه الأرض يَعُوق عنها ريح الصَبا ،فإنه لم يرَ أحد قطّ بفُسْطاط مصر صَبا خالصة . ولكم متى هبّت الصبا عندهم كانت نَكْباء بين(٤٢) الشرق والشمال، أو الشرق والجنوب . وهذه الريح حارّة رطبة ،وهي أعْدل الرياح وأفضلها لمُشاكلتها مِزاج بدن الحيوان (٤٣)فقدعدمت مصرهذه الفضيلة ،ومن أجل ذلك صارت المواضع التي تهبّ فيها هذه الريح من هذه الأرض أحسن حالا من غيرها كالإسكندرية وتنيس (٤٤) ودمياط(٤٥). ويعوق أيضا هذان الجبلان إشراقَ الشمس على هذه الأرض إذا كانت على الأفق . فيكون زمان لُبْث (٤٦) شعاع الشمس على هذه الأرض أقل من اللُبْث الطبيعيّ . ومثل هذه الحال سَبَبُ /٥ ب / ركود (٤٧) الهواء وغِلَظه .

وأرض مصر كثيرة الحيوان والنبات جدا . فإنك لا تكاد تجد منها موضعا خِلْوا من النبات والحيوان . وهي أرض مُخَلْخَلَة ،كما قال أفورُس . والدليل على تَخَلْخُلها (٤٨) أنك ترها عند انصراف النيل بمنزلة الحَمْأة ، فإذا حلّلت الحرارةُ ما فيها من الرطوبة تشقّقت شُقوقا عِظاما . ومن الظاهر عند الأوائل أن المواضع الكثيرة الحيوان والنبات ، هي أيضا كثيرة العفونة . وقد اجتمع أيضا على هذه الأرض حرارة ومزاجها وسخافتها (٤٩) وكثرة ما فيها من الحيوان والنبات مما يوجب ضرورة احتراقها. ومن أجل ذلك اسودّ طينها من الاحتراق،وصارت أرضا سوداء ،وما قرب من الجبل يسبخ (٥٠) ،وصار بورقيا أو مالحا . ويظهر في هذه الأرض أيضا بالعشيّات بخار اسود واغبر ،وخاصة في أيام الصيف .

وأرض مصر ذات أجزاء كثيرة ،يختصّ كلّ واحد منها بشيْدون شيْ. وعلّة ذلك ضيق عرضها ، واشتمال (٥١) طولها /٦أ/ على عرض الاقليم الثاني والثالث،فإنّ الصعيد فيه من النخيل والسنط وآجام القصب والبرديّ ومواضع إحراق الفحم وغير ذلك شيْكثيرا جدا . والفيوم أيضا فيه من النقائع وآجام القصب والأرز ومواضع تعفن الكتان شيْكثير. وأسفل أرض مصر فيه من النبات أنواع كالقلقاس والموز ونحو ذلك . وبالجملة ،فكلّ بقعة من أرض مصر لها أشياء تختصّ بها وتفضل عن غيرها.

والنيل يمرّ بامم كثيرة من السودان ،ثم يصير الى أرض (٥٢) مصر وقد غسل ما في بلاد السودان من العفونات والأوساخ ،ويشقّمارّا بأرض مصر في وسطها من الجنوب إلى الشمال، إلى أن يصبّ في بحر الروم . ومبدأزيادة هذا النهر في فصل الصيف ،ومنتهى زيادته في فصل الخريف . ويرتقي منه في أوقات عدّة ،رطوبات كثيرة بالتحليل الخفيّ ، فيرطب لذلك يبس الصيف والخريف . وإذا مدّهذا النهر فاض على أرض مصر فغسل ما فيها من الأوساخ نحو الجيف الحيوانية (٥٣) /٦ب / وأزبالها ،وفضول الأجام والنبات ومياه النقائع . وأحدر جميع ذلك معه ،وخالطه من تراب هذه الأرض وطينها مقدار كثير من أجل سخافتها. وباض فيه السمك الذي تربّى في هذه النقائع (٥٤) ومن قبل (٥٥) ذلك نراه في أول مدّه يخضرّ لونه بكثرة ما يخالطه من مياه النقائع العفنة التي قد اجتمع اليها العرمض والطحلب ،واخضرّ لونها من عفنها ،ثم يتعكّر حتى يصير أخر أمره بمنزلة الحمأة . وإذا صفا اجتمع

(٤)

في الإناء طين كثير ،ورطوبة سهكة ،لها لزوجة (٥٦) ورائحة منكرة . وهذا من أوكد الأشياء في ظهور رداءة هذا الماء وعفنه. وبيّن أبقراط وجالينوس أنّ أسرع المياه إلى العفن ما لطّفته الشمس كمياه الأمطار. ومن شأن هذا الماء أن يصل إلى أرض مصر وهو في الغاية من اللطافة من شدّة حرارة بلد السودان ،فإذا اختلطت به عفونات أرض مصر زاد ذلك في استحالته . ولذلك يتولّد فيه من أنواع السمك شئ كثير جدا ،فإنّ فضول الحيوان / ٧أ/ والنبات ، وعفونة هذا (٥٧) الماء ،وبيض السمك تصير جميعها موادّا في تكوّن هذه السموك كما قال أرسطوطاليس في كتاب الحيوان،وذلك أيضا شئ ظاهر للحسّ . فإنّ كلّ شئ يتعفّن ،يتولّد من عفونته الحيوان. ولهذا صار ما يتولّد من الفأر والدود والثعابين والعقارب والزنابير وغيرها بأرض مصر كثيرا.

وقد استبان أنّ المزاج الغالب على أرض مصر الحرارة والرطوبة الفضليّة ، وأنها ذات أجزاء كثيرة ،وأنّ هواءها وماءها رديئان (٥٨).

(٥)

الفصـل الثـانـي
في صفة اختلاف هواء مصر وما يتولّد فيها

قد تبيّن فيما تقدّم أنّ الغالب على مزاج أرض مصر الحرارة التي معها عفونة (٥٩) . وقد بيّن الأوائل أنّ المواضع الكثيرة العفَن (٦٠) ينحلّ (٦١) منها في الهواء فضول كثيرة ،ولا تدَعه يستقرّ على حال ،لاختلاف تَصاعُدها . وقد كان استبان أيضا أنّ هواء أرض مصر يُسرع إليه التغيّر لأنّ /٧ب/ الشمس لا يَلْبث (٦٢) عليه شعاعُها المدّة الطبيعية . فمن أجل هذين كثُر اختلاف هواء أرض مصر (٦٣) ، فصار يوجد في اليوم الواحد على حالات مختلفة : مرّة حارا (٦٤) وأخرى باردا ،ومرّة يابسا ،وأخرى رطبا ،ومرّة متحركا ،وأخرى ساكنا. ومرّة الشمس ضاحيَة ،ومرّة قد ستَرها الغَيم . وبالجملة هواء (٦٥) أرض مصر كثير الاختلاف من أجل ما قلنا ،واختلافه غير لازم لطريقة واحدة ،فيلزم ضرورة أن يكون الروح الحيوانيّ الذي فينا بمُواصلته (٦٦) لهذا الهواء غيرَ لازم أيضا لطريقة واحدة ،فيصير من أجل ذلك ما في الأوعية والعروق من أخلاط البدن لا يَلْزَم حدّا واحدا .

والسبب(٦٧) في قلّة الأمطار بأرض مصر هو ما يتحلّل كل يوم من البخار الرطب بهذه الأرض ،يَعُوقه اختلاف الهواء وقلّة سَمْك الجبال وحرارة الأرض من الاجتماع في الجوّ . فإذا بَرَد الهواء ببَرْد الليل ،وانحدر هذا البخار على وجه الأرض ، فتولّد منه الضباب الذى يَحْدُث عنه الطلّ (٦٨) والندى/٨أ/وربما تحلّل هذا البخار بالتحلّل الخَفيّ ،فإذا يتحلّل في كل يوم ما كان اجتمع من البخار في اليوم الذي قبله ،فمن أجل ذلك لا يجتمع الغَيم المُمْطر بأرض مصر إلا في النُدْرَة . فظاهر من ذلك أيضا أنّ أرض مصر يترطّب هواءها في كلّ يوم بما يَترقّى (٦٩) إليه من البخار الرطب وما يتحلّل . وقد قال بعض الناس إنّ الضباب يتكوّن من استحالة الهواء إلى طبيعة الماء ،فإذا انضاف هذا إلى ما قلناه فيما تقدّم كان أزْيَد في بَيان (٧٠) سرعة تغيّر هواء أرض مصر ،وكثرة العُفونة فيها .

فقد استبان أن أرض مصر كثيرة الاختلاف ،كثيرة الرطوبة (٧١) التي يُسْرع إليها العَفَن . والعلّة القُصْوَى في جميع ذلك هو أنّ أخصّ الأوقات بالجَفاف في الأرض كلّها تكثُر فيه بمصر الرطوبة ،لأنها تترطّب في الصيف والخريف بمَدّ النيل وفَيْضه ، وهذا خلاف ما عليه البلدان الأخرى . وقد عَلّمَنا (٧٢) أبْقراط أن رطوبة الصيف والخريف فَضْليّة ،يعني (٧٣) خارجة عن المَجْرَى الطبيعي كالمطر الحادث في الصيف /٨ب/ . ومن أجل هذا قلنا إن رطوبة أرض مصر فَضْليّة ، وذلك أنّ الحرارة واليُبْس هما بالحقيقة (٧٤) مِزاجُ مِصر الطبيعي ، وإنما عَرَض ما أخرجه عن اليُبْس إلى الرطوبة الفَضْليه ، وهو مَدّ النيل (٧٥) . ولذلك (٧٦) كثُرت العُفونات بهذه الأرض . فهذا هو السبب الأول والأعظم في أن صارت أرض مصر على ما هي عليه من سَخافة الأرض وكثرة العَفَن ورداءة الهواء والماء . إلّا أنّ هذه الأشياء ليست تُحْدِث في أبدان المصريين استحالة مَحْسُوسَة إذا جَرَت على عادتها من أجل إلْف المصريين لهذه الحال ومُشاكَلة أبدانهم لها . فإنّ كلّ ما يتولّد بأرض مصر من النبات والحيوان مُشابه (٧٧) لما عليه مِزاج مصر في سَخافة الأجسام وضَعف القُوَى وكثرة التغيّر وسرعة الوقوع في الأمراض (٧٨) وقِصَر المُدَد ،كالحِنْطة التي بمصر ،فإنها وَشيكة (٧٩) الزوال ،وسريع إليها

(٦)

العُفُنُ في المدّة اليسيرة . ولا تظنّ أنّ أبدان الناس وغيرهم تُخالِف ما عليه الحِنْطَة مِن سرعة الاستحالة ، وكيف لا يكون الأمر /٩أ/ كذلك وأبدانهم (٨٠) مَبْنيّة من هذه الأشياء . فحال إذن ما يَتولّد من النبات بأرض مصر والحيوان فيَ السخافة وكثرة الفُضُول والعُفَن وسرعة الوقوع في الأمراض ،حال سَخافَة أرضها وعَفَنها وفُضُولها وسرعة استحالتها ،لأنّ النسبة واحدة . ولذلك أمكن حياة الحيوان فيها ونباتُ النبات ، فإنّ هذه الأشياء حيث ناسبتها ولم تَبْعُد عن مُشاكَلَتها ،أمكنت حياتُها. فأمّا الأشياء (٨١) الغريبة فإنّها إذا دخلت مصر تغيّرت في أوّل لقاء (٨٢) بها لهذا الهواء ،حتى إذا استقرت وإلِفت الهواء واستمرت عليه ، صحّت صحّةَ مُشاكَلَة لأرض مصر .

(٧)

الفصل الثالث

في الأسباب الستة المحيطة بالصحة والمرض بأرض مصر

إنّ الله عزّ وجلّ لمّا خلق الأشياء جعل بعضها مُرْتبطا ببعض فجعَل للصحة والمرض أسبابا كثيرة • منها ما يتّفق اتّفاقا كالردم والضرب (٨٣) والحَرْق والغَرَق ونحو ذلك • وليس من هذه الأشياء شيء يَنظر فيه الأطباء • ومنها ما هو ضروري /٩ب/ موجود أبدا للإنسان ، وهي على ما عَدّه الأوائل ستة ، الأول منها: الهواء المُحيط بأبدان الناس • والثاني : ما يُؤْكَل ويُشْرَب • والثالث : الحَرَكة والسكون • والرابع : النوْم واليَقَظة • والخامس: الاحتِقان والاستفراغ • والسادس : الأحداث النفسانية •

وقد لخّصنا أمر الهواء المحيط بأرض مصر فيما تقدّم • ومن البيّن عند الأوائل • أنّ الهواء إذا لزم ما جرت به عادته لم يُحْدِث مرضا ، اللهمّ إلا أن يكون بعض الأبدان قد خرج عن مُشاكلته بأمر آخر ،وهو مستعدّ لقَبول المرض • فيَعْرِض له المرض بخروجه عن المُشاكلة واستعداده •

وكذلك القول في باقي الأسباب ، إذا هي لزمت عادتها لم تُحْدِث مرضا • وإذا كان الأمر كما ذكرنا (٨٤) فَلْنقُل الأن (٨٥) في هذه • أمّا ما يُؤكل ويُشْرَب بأرض مصر ، فإنّ الغلاتّ سريعة التغيّر ، سَخِيفة مُتَخَلْخِلَة ، تَفْسُد في الزمن اليسير كالحِنْطَة والشعير والعَدَس والحِمّص والباقِلّي / ١٠أ/ والجُلُبّان ، فإنّ هذه تُسَوِّس في المدّة اليسيرة ، وليس لشيء من الأغذية التي تُعْمَل منها لَذاذَة ما لنَظِيره (٨٦) في البلدان الأخرى ، وذلك أنّ اخبز المعمول من الحِنْطَة المعمولة بمصر متى لبث يوما وليلة (٨٧) لا يُؤكَل ولا يُوجَد له بعد ذلك لذاذة ، ولا تَماسُك لبعضه ببعض ، ولا يُوجَد فيه علُوكة ، ولكنه يَتكَرّج في الزمن (٨٨) اليسير ، وكذلك الدقيق • وهذا خِلافُ أخْباز البلدان الاخرى • وكذلك الحال في جميع غلّات مصر وفواكهها وما يُعْمَل منها ، فإنها وَشيكة الزوال ، سريعة الاسْتِحالة والتغيّر. فأمّا ما يُحْمَل مِن هذه إلى أرض مصر ، فظاهِر (٨٩) أنّ مِزاجها يتبدّل باختلاف الهواء عليها ، وتستحيل عمّا كانت عليه إلى مشاكلة أرض مصرَ ، إلا ما كان مِن هذه حديثا قريبَ العهد بالسفر فقد بقِيَتْ فيه من جَوْدته بقايا صالحة ، فهذا حال الغلّات • فأما الحيوان الذي يأكله الناسُ ، فالبَلَدِيّ منه مِزاجه مُشاكِل لمِزاج الناس بهذه الأرض من السخافة /١٠ب/ وسُرعة الاسْتِحالَة ، فهوَ على هذا مُلائم لطبائعهم • والمَجْلُوب منه كالكِباش البَرْقيّة ، فالسفر يُحْدِث في أبدانهم قَحَلا (٩٠) ويبْسا وأخلاطا لا تُشاكِل مِزاج المصريين • ولهذا إذا دخلتْ مصرَ مرِض أكثرها ، فإذا استقرت بها زمانا صالحا تَبدّل مِزاجُها ووافق مِزاج المصريين •

وأهل مصر يشرب الجمهور منهم من النيل (٩١) ، وقد قُلْنا في النيل ما فيه الكفاية • وبعضهم يشرب مياه الآبار ، وهذه أيضا قريبة من مُشاكلتهم • فأمّا المياه المخزونة ومياه الأمطار (٩٢) فقَلّ مَن يشربها بهذه الأرض • وأجْود الأشربة عندهم الشمْسِيّ ، لأنّ العَسَل الذي فيه يحفظ قوّته ، ولا يَدَعُه يتغيّر بسرعة • والزمان الذي يُعْمَل فيه خالص الحَرّ ، فهو يُنْضِجه • والزبيب الذي يُعْمَل منه مَجْلُوب من بلاد أجود هواء • وأمّا الخمر ، فقلّ مَن يَعْتَصِرها إلا ويُلْقِى معها عَسَلا • ولأنّها (٩٣) معتصرة مِن كُرُومِهم تكون مُشاكِلة أيضا (لهم) (٩٤) ولهذا (٩٥)

(٨)

يختارون الشمس عليها . وأمّا ما عدا الشمسي والخمر من الشراب بأرض /١١أ/
مصر فرديء لا خَيْر فيه لسرعة استحالته وفساد مادّته ،كالنبيذ التمري
والمطبوخ والمِزْر المعمول من الحِنْطَة . وأغذيةُ أهل مصرِ مختلفة . فإن
أهل الصعيد يغتذون كثيرا بتَمْر النخل والحَلاوة المَعْمُولَة من قصَب السكر،
ويحملونها إلى الفُسْطاط وغيرها فتُباع هناك وتُؤْكل . وأهل أسْفَل الأرض (٩٦)
يغتذون (٩٧) بالقُلْقاس والجُلُبّان ، ويحملون ذلك إلى الفسطاط وغيرها فتُباع
هناك وتُؤ كل . وكثير (٩٨) مِن أهل مصر يُكْثِرون أكل السمك طَريّا ومالِحا،
وكثير يُكْثِرون أكل الألبان وما يُعْمَل منها . وعند فلاحيهم نَوْعٌ (٩٩) من الخبز
يُدْعَى كَعْكاً ،يُعْمَل مِن جَرِيش الحِنْطَة ويُجَفّف ،وهو (١٠٠) أكلهم السنةَ كلها.
وبالجملة فكلّ قوم منهم أنْبَتَت أبدانهم مِن أشياء بأعيانها فألِفَتْها ونَشَأت
عليها (١٠١) إلا أنّ الغالبَ بالجملة على أهل مصر الاغذيةالرديئة .وليست تغير
مزاجهم ما دامت جارية على العادة .وهذا أيضاممايؤكّد أمرهم في السخافة وسرعة
الوقوع في الأمراض /١١ب/ وأيضافأهل الريف أكثر حركة ورياضة مِن أهل المدن،
ولذلك(١٠٢) هم أصحّ أبدانا ،لأنّ الرياضة تصلّب أعضاءهم (١٠٣)وتقوّيها . وأهل
الصعيد أخلاطهم أرقّ وأكثر دخانية وتحلّلا(١٠٤)وسخافة لشدّة حرارة أرضهم من
أهل أسفل الأرض (١٠٥) . وأهل أسفل الأرض يكون أكثر
استفراغ فضولهم بالبراز والبول،لفتور الحرارة في أرضهم (١٠٦) واستعمالهم
الآشياء الباردة الغَلِيظة كالقُلْقاس . فأما أخلاق المصريين فبعضها شبيهة (١٠٧)
ببعض . ولأن قُوَى النفس تابعة لمِزاج البدن ، وأبدانُهم سَخِيفة ،سريعةُ التغير
قليلةُ الصبر والجلد،كذلك أخلاقُهم يغلب عليها الاستِحالة والتنقّل من شئ إلى
شئ والرعد(١٠٨) ،والجُبْن ،والقُنوط،والشك (١٠٩) وقلةُ الصبر والرغبةِ في
العلم (١١٠)وسرعةِ الحزم (١١١) والحسدُ،والنميمةُ (١١٢) والكذبُ،والسَعْي إلى
السلطان (١١٣) ،وذم الناس (١١٤) وبالجملة الشرور الدنيّةُ التي تكون مِن
دَناءة النفس . وليست هذه الشرور عامّة فيهم ، ولكنها (١١٥) موجودة في
أكثرهم . ومنهم مَن حَصّنة (١١٦) الله تعالى /١٢أ/ بالفضل وحُسْنِ الخُلُق وبراءةٍ
(١١٧) مِن الشرّ.

ومن أجْل توليد أرضِ مصر الجبنَ والشرورَ الدنيّة في النفس لم تسكُنْها الأسْد(١١٨)
وإذا دخلتها ذَلّت ولم تَتناسَل . وكلابُها أيضا أقلّ حِدّة مِن كلاب غيرها
من البلدان الأخرى . وكذلك سائر ما فيها هو أضعف مِن نُظيرة في البلدان الأخرى
ما خلا ماكان منهافي طبيعة (١١٩) تلائم هذه الحال ،كالحِمار والأرنب .

الفصل الرابع

في فصول السنة بأرض مصر

إنّ جالينُوس يرى ويعتقد أنّ فصل الربيع طَبْعُه (١٢٠) الاعتدال ،ويُناقِض- في كتابه في المِزاج - مَن ظنّ أنه حارّ رَطْب (١٢١) . ومن شأن هذا الفصل أن تِصحّ فيه الأبدانُ ،ويَجُود هَضْمُها ،وتنتشِرُ (١٢٢) الحرارةُ الغريزية فيها ويصفُو الروحُ الحيوانيّ لاعتدال الهواء (١٢٣) ومساواة ليلة لنهاره ،وغَلَبة الدم . والهواءُ المعتدل (١٢٤) هو الذي لا يُحَسّ فيه بِبَرْد ظاهِر ولا حَرّ ولاَ رطوبة ولا يُبْس (١٢٥) ويكون في نَفْسه صافيا نَقيّا ،ويَقْوَى فيه الروحُ /١٢ب/ الحيوانيّ ،وتصِحّ الأبدانُ ،ويكثُر نشَاطُ (١٢٦) الحيوان(١٢٧) وتَنْمِي الأشياءُ وتتولد.وإذا اطلبنا (١٢٨)بأرض مصر مثل هذا الهواء لم نجدْه في وَقت مِن السنة إلا في أَمْشِير وبَرَمْهات وبَرْمُودَة وبَشَنْس ،وذلك عندماتكون الشمس في النصف الأخير من الدَلْو والحُوت الحَمَل والثور. فإنّا نجد في هذا الزمان بأرض مصر أياما معتدلة نَقِيّة صافية ،لا يُحَسّ فيها بحَرّ ظاهِر ،ولا ببرد ولا برطوبة ولا بيُبوسة ،وهي الأيام التى تكون الشمس فيها نقيّةً من الغيوم ،والهواء ساكنا لَا يتحرك . إلا (١٢٩) أن ذلك في بُرْمُودَة وبَشَنْس يحتاج إلى أن تهبّ ريحُ الشمال لتعدِل (١٣٠) ببردها كثرةَ حَرّ الشمس . وفي هذا الزمان تكثُرَ حركة الحِيوان ويَسْفَد (١٣١) ويتحسّن صوتُه ،وتُورِق الأشجار ،ويَعْقِد الزهْر ،وتَقْوَى القُوَى المُوَلِّدة ،ويَغلِب كَيْمُوس الدم . وظاهِر أنّ هذا الفصل يتقدّم (١٣٢) زمانه الطبيعيّ بمقدار ما ينقُص عن آخره ،وعِلّة ذلك قوّة حرارة هذه الأرض .وقد يعرِض في أوّل هذا الفصل أيامٌ شديدة البرد/١٣أ/ وذلك في أمْشِير إذا هبّت ريح الشمال ،وكانت الشمس غير نَقيّة من الغيوم ،وعِلّة ذلك دُخولُ فصل الربيع في فصل الشتاء فإذا هبّت ريحُ الشمال برّدت ببَرْدِها الهواءَ ،فأعادته بعد الاعتدال إلى البرْد. ولكثرة ما يصعَد من الأرض في هذا الزمان من البخار الرطب ،يترطّب الهواءُ ، ويعود إلى حاله في فصل الشتاء . وربّما بَرُد هذا الهواءُ من هبوب رياح أخَر ،فإن ريح الجنوب - التي هي أشدّ الرياح حرارة - إذا هبّت في هذا الزمان اكتسبت برودةً من الأرض والماء اللذيْن قد برّدهما هواءُ الشتاء ،فإذا مرّت بشيء برّدته ببرودتها العَرَضِيّة ،حتى إذا دام هبوبُها أياما كثيرة متوالية ،عادت إلى حرارتها فأسخَنت (١٣٣) الهواءَ وأحدثت فيه يُبْسا. والدليل على أنّ بَرْدَ ريح الجنوب - ويعرفها المصريون باسم المريس -يتولّد مِن بَرْد مياه مصر وأرضها ،لا شيء (١٣٤) طبيعيّ لها ،أنه لا يجتمع في الجو في أيام هبوب الضباب الذي يجتمع من تحليل الحرارة /١٣ب / للبخار الرطب بالنهار وجَمْع البرودة له بالليل . فحرارة ريح الجنوب تعوق البرودةَ عن جَمْعِة وتُبَدِّدُه في الهواء . ولو دام هبوب هذه الريح لسخّنت الماء والارض ، وعادت إلى طبيعتها في الحَرّ . وإذا كان فصل الربيع يتقدّم زمانه الطبيعيّ ويختلف هذا الاختلاف ،وهو في الأصل بمصر يختلف بكثرة استحالته ،وما يَرْقَى(١٣٥) إليه من البخار،فما ظنّك بغَيره من الفصول . ولذلك كثُرت فيه الرياح ،وأخّرَ الأطباءُ فيه سَقْيَ (١٣٦) الأدوية المُسْهِلة إلى أن يستقرّ أمْرُه في شمس الحَمَل مع الثور . ثم يدخل فصلُ الصيف من آخر بَشَنْس وبَؤُونَة وأبيب وبعض مِسْرَى عندما تكون الشمس بالجَوْزاء والسرَطان والأسد وبعض السنبلة ،فيشتدّ الحَرَ واليُبْس في هذا الزمان وتجِف الغلّات وتنضَج الثمار،ويجتمع مِن أكلها في الأبدان كَيْمُوسات كثيرة (١٣٧) . وإذا نزلت الشمسُ السرطانَ أخَذ النيلُ في الزيادة والفيض على الأرض ،فيتغير مزاج الصيف الطبيعي بكثرة ما يتولد (١٣٨) في الهواء من بخار الماء /١٤أ/ .

(١٠)

ويُوجد في (أول) (١٣٩) هذا الفصل ـ عندما تكون الشمس في الجَوْزاء ـ أيامٌ يُشاكِل (١٤٠) هواؤُها هواءَ الربيع، عندما تكون الشمس مستُورة بالغيوم أو تكون ريحُ الشمال هابّة. ولهذا يغلَط كثير من الأطباء فيسقي الأدويةَ المُسْهِلَة في هذا الزمان لظنّه أنّ فصل الربيع لم يَخرُج، إلا أنّ مَن كان منهم أحْذَق فهو يختار ما كان مِن هذه الأيام أسْكن (١٤١) حرارة. والأكثرون لا يشعرون البتّةَ بهذه الحال، ولكن يُعطون الأدوية بجَهْل وسَخافة عقل، ويتعلّقون بكَوْن الشمس في الجَوْزاء ويتركون قول الفاضِل جالِينوس: إن الربيع معتدل. وفي آخر الصيف يكثر فَيْضُ النيل.

وظاهر أنّ هذا الفصل يتقدّم دخوله الزمان الطبيعي بقدر ما يتقدّم آخره وأنّه كثير الاضطراب بكَثْرة ما يَرْقى إليه من بخار الماء. ولولا استمرار أبدانهم على هذا الاختلاف ومُشاكَلتهم لهذه الحال لحَدثت فيهم الأمراضُ التي ذكر أبقراط أنها تَحْدُث إذا كان الصيف رَطْبا.

ثم يدخل فصل الخريف، وطبيعته /١٤ب/ يابسة، من النصف الأخير من مِسْرَى ثم توت وبابة وبعض أيام من هَتُور، وذلك عندما تكون الشمس في آخر السنبلة والميزانَ والعَقْرَب، فتكمُل زيادةُ النيل في أول هذا الفصل، فيطلق (١٤٢) فيُطَبِّق (١٤٣) مصر الماءُ، ويرتفع منه في الجو بخار كثير، فينقل مِزاج الخريف عن اليُبس إلى الرطوبة حتى أنه ربّما وقع فيه المطر وكَثُر الغيمُ في الجو. ويوجد في أول هذا الفصل أيام شديدة الحرّ، لأنها على الحقيقة صيفيّة، فإذا نَقي الجوّ من البخار الرطْب، عادت إلى طبيعتها من الحرارة. وفيه أيضا أيامَ شديدة الشبَه بأيام الربيع، تكون عندما يساوي الليلُ النهارَ ورطوبةُ الماء يُبْسَ الهواء. ويشتدّ في هذا الفصل اضطرابُ الهواء بكثْرة ما يَرْتَقِي إليه من البخار الرطب، فيكون مَرة حارا (١٤٤) ومرة باردا، ومرة يابسا. وأكثر أوقاته تغلب عليه الرطوبة، ولا يزال كذلك يتموّج (١٤٥) حتى تغلب عليه رطوبة الماء في آخر الأمر.

ويُصاد أيام الخريف من النيل أسماك /١٥أ/ كثيرة جدا، يُولّد أكلُها في الأبدان أخلاطا لَزِجَة، وكثيرا ما تَسْتَحيل إلى الصفراء إذا صادفتْ في البدن خِلْطا صَفراويّا. فمن أجل هذه الأشياء تضطرب في الأبدان (١٤٦) الروحُ الحيوانيّ وتَهيجُ الأخلاطُ، ويفسُد الهضْمُ في البطون والأوعية والعروق، ويتولّد عن ذلك كَيْمُوسات رديئة كثيرة الاختلاف، بعضها مِرّة صَفْراء، وبعضها مِرّة سوداء، وبعضها بَلْغم لَزِج، وبعضها خِلْط خام، وبعضها مِرّة مُحْتَرِقَة. وكثيرا ما يتركّب من هذه الأشياء فتكثُر الأمراض. حتى إذا انصرف النيلُ في آخر الخريف وانكشفت الأرضُ وبَرُدَ الهواء وكثُرت الأسماكُ واحتَقن البخارُ وكثُر ما يرتفع من الأرض من العفونة، استَحْكَم عند ذلك فسادُ النظم (١٤٧) وتزايدت الأمراضُ. ولولا إلف (أهل) (١٤٨) هذه الأرض لهذه الأشياء لكان ما يَحْدُث فيهم من الأمراض أكثر.

ثم يدخل فصلُ الشتاء، وطبيعتُه باردة، من النصف الأخير من هَتُور ثم كيهك وطوبة وذلك عندما تكون الشمس في القَوْس والجَدْي/١٥ب/ وبعض الدلو، وذلك (أقل) (١٤٩) من ثلاثة أشهر. والعلّة في هذا قوّةُ حرارة هذه الأرض والأبدان مضطربة (١٥٠).

ويتمّ انكشاف الأرض في أوّل هذا الفصل، فتُحْرَث (١٥١)، وتَعْفَن بالجملة بكثرة ما يُلْقى (١٥٢) فيها مِن أزْبال الحيوان وفضولها. لأنها سَخِيفة وهي كالحمأة

(١١)

في هذا الزمان ، يتولّد فيها من أنواع الفأر والدود والنبات والعُشْب
وغير ذلك ما لا يُحْصَى كثرة . وينحلّ منها في الجوّ أبخِرةٌ كثيرة حتى يصير
الضبابُ بالغدوات ساترا للأبصار عن الألوان القريبة . ويُصاد أيضا من الأسماك
المحبوسة في المياهَ المَخْزونة شيءٌ كثير ،وقدداخلها العَفَنُ لِقلّة جَرْيها (١٥٣)
وحِركتها ،فيولّد أكلُها في الأبدان فضولا كثيرة لَزِجة ،شديدة الاستعداد للعَفَن
فتَقْوَى الأمراضُ في أوّل هذا الفصل . حتى إذا اشتدّ البردُ ،وقَوِيَ الهضمُ في
الأبدان واستقرّ الهواء على شيء واحد ،وعادت الحرارةُ الغريزيّة إلى داخل
وتطبّقت الأرضُ بالنبات ،وسكَنَت عفونتُها ،صحّت عند ذلك الأبدان . وهذا يكون
في /١٦أ/ آخر كِيهَك وفي طُوبَة . فقد استبان بما قُلْنا إنّ الفصول بأرض مصر
هي أيضا كثيرة الاختلاف (١٥٤) ،وأنّ أرْدأ أوقات السنة كلّها عندهم وأكثرها
أمراضا هي آخر الخريف وأوّل الشتاء ،وذلك في شهريْ هَتُور وكِيهَك.
فإذا كان اختلاف الفصول مُشاكِلا لما عليه أرضهم من الرداءة ، فمَضرّة إذن
الفصولِ الأبدانَ أقلُّ منها في البلدان الأخَر ،إذا اختلفت هذا الاختلاف .
واستبان أيضا أنّ السبب الأول في ذلك هو مَدّ النيل في أيام الصيف وتَطْبِيقه
الأرضَ في أيامِ الخريف ،بخلاف ما عليه مياه الأنهار في المَعْمُورة (١٥٥)
كلّها ، فإنّ هذه إنّما تَمُدّ في أخصّ الأوقات بالرطوبة وهي الشتاء والربيع.

ولما كان النيل هو السبب الأعظم في عِمارة أرض مصر وجميع (١٥٦) ما فيها
رَأَي (١٥٧) المصريون القُدُم ،وخاصّة الذين كانوا على عهد دقلطيانوس الملك
أن يجعلوا أوّل السنة الخريفَ ، عند استكمال النيل الحاجة في الأمر
الأكثر ،فجعلوا أول شهورهم / ١٦ب / تُوت ثم بابِهَ هَتُور ،على هذا الوِلاء
بحسب الشهور من ترتيب هذه الشهور.

(١٢)

الفصل الخامس

في أنّ أكثر ما أعطاه ابن الجزّار في وخوم هذه الأرض ليس بصحيح.

ذكر (١٥٨) ابن الجزّار في الباب الأوّل من كتابه أنّ العلّة في مرض الذين وفدوا من المغرب إلى مصر هو كثرة إختلاف هذا الهواء، وقد أنهكها (١٥٩) السفر، فصارت بالسفر مستعدة نحو المرض. فلما تغيّر عليها الهواء وقع أصحابها في المرض والموت السريع. وهذا القول – وإن كان صادقا – فليس يلزم عنه أن يعرض لأهل مصر ما عرض لهذا الوفد مِن قبل إلف أبدان المصريين لما هم عليه من اختلاف الهواء، ولأنّهم لم ينهكهم السفر. وقال في الباب الثاني إنّ هواء أرض مصر في أكثر أيام السنة مشاكل لهواء (١٦٠) الخريف في البرد واليبس والاختلاف/١٧أ/وهذا خلاف ما عليه المحسوس في السنة كلها. فإن هواء مصر يرطب (١٦١) كثيرا في فصل الخريف فضلا عن غيره. إلا أنه قد احتجّ على قوله بأقاويل توهم السامع صدق قوله، منها قول أبقراط: متى كان في أى وقت من أوقات السنة، في يوم واحد، مرّة حرا (١٦٢) ومرّة بردا فتوقّعْ حدوثَ (١٦٣) أمراض خريفية. وقال ابن الجزّار في هذا الباب: فأكثر أمراض أهل مصر خريفية. وهذا غلط، فإن هواء أرض مصر ليس (١٦٤) يتغيّر في اليوم الواحد الى البرد والحرّ فقط، بل وإلى اليبس. وأكثر أوقاته رطب، حتى إنّ الندى يوجد كثيرا في غدوات أيام الصيف، وذلك أنّ الحاصدين أهل الفلاحة لا يمكنهم حصد (١٦٦) الغلّة في أيام الصيف إلا في الأيام النديّة. وأيضا فليس أكثر أمراض المصريين هي أمراض المرّة السوداء، بل هذه الأمراض هي أقلّ أمراضهم، حتى إنّ الكلاب الكلبة قليلة الوجود في هذه الأرض. وخليق (١٦٧) أن يكون دخل عليه هذا الخطأ/١٧ب/ من حيث لم يشاهد مصر، فلما ذكر له الوفد ما حدث بهم من الأمراض واختلاف الهواء، ذكر ذلك ظنّا منه بأنّه هو العلّة في وقوع الوباء. وقد كان استبان فيما تقدم أنّ الرطوبة الفضليّة بأرض مصر كثيرة، فظاهر أن أمراضهم البلديّة من نوع هذه الرطوبة، وإنّى أنا أقلّ (١٦٨) ما رأيت أمراضهم البلديّة هذه كلّها لا يشوبها في أوّل أمرها البلغم والخلط الخام. وحسبك بالمرض الوافد الذي كان في أخر خريف السنة وأوّل شتائها، فإنّ حميّاته كلّها كانت شطر غبّ، والمجانبة للغبّ. على أنّه قد عرض فيه لكثير من الناس السكات والصرع والذبحة والموت فجأة. ومنهم من احترق دمه في أخر الأمر لطول زمان حمّاة (فحدث به الجرب، ومنهم من انتقلت حمّاه) (١٦٩) إلى الرّبع بانتقال أخلاطه إلى المرّة في آخر أمره. وهوءلاء خاصّة أقلّهم عددا. فالأمراض (تحدث عندهم في الأوقات) (١٧٠) كلها كما قال أبقراط وأكثر أمراضهم هي الفضليّة أعني /١٨أ/ الأمراض العفنة التى أكثرها عن أخلاط صفراوية وبلغمية، على ما يشاكل مزاج أرضهم. ثم قال ابن الجزار في الباب الخامس من كتابه: إنّ العلّة في الوباء بمصر هو الضباب الكائن في الهواء وهذا القول ليس بصحيح، فإنّ أكثر تولّد هذا الضباب بأرض مصر عند صحّة الأبدان في آخر كيهك ثم طوبة وأمشير. ومن شأن الشتاء أن يكون كثير الرطوبة. وإذا كان الفصل لازما لنظامه الطبيعي بالبلد (١٧١) فليس يحدث مرضا. وكثرة الضباب في الشتاء بأرض مصر ممّا يرطّب الهواء عوضا عن ماء (١٧٢) المطر. فأمّا قول أبقراط: قلّة المطر أصحّ من كثرته، وأقلّ موتا، فإنما عنى به ما خرج عن الطبع والعادة، فإنّ المطر الخارج عن العادة قلّته أصحّ من كثرته (١٧٣) وأقلّ موتا. فإن كنت لا تقبل هذا على كثرة ما قال فيه جالينوس فاسمع الأن قول أبقراط: إن انقلاب أوقات السنة ممّا يعمل في تولّد الأمراض. أراد بذلك /١٨ب/ أنّ أوقات السنة إذا لم تلزم نظامها الطبيعي أحدثت الأمراض. فالشتاء إذن الرطوبة فيه أحمد وأجود. فالضباب إذن في الشتاء بمصر ليس برديء (١٧٤) لأنه يرطّب الهواء عوضا من المطر.

وقد قال أبقراط: إذا كانت أوقات السنة لازمةً لنظامها، وكان في كل وقت منها ما ينبغي أن يكون فيه، كان ما يحدث فيه من الأمراض حسن الثبات، والنظام، حسن البحران. وإذا كانت أوقات السنة غير لازمة لنظامها، كان

ما يَحْدُث فيها من الأمراض غير مُنْتظم ،سَمِج البُحْران ،فقد صَحّ (١٧٥) مِن كلام أبقراط نفسه أن الضباب الكائن في الشتاء بأرض مصر غيرُ رديء ،فضلاً عن يكون وَبِيّا كما قال ابن الجزّار ،إذ كان عِوضا من المطر في غير مصر . واستبان من قوله (١٧٦) أنّ لزوم أوقات السنة لما هي عليه بمصر ليس بمكروه لأهل مصر لأنه جارٍ على العادة ،وطريقة واحدة مستمرة الدهرَ كلّه .

وقد بيّن جالينوس ومن قبله أبقراط/١٩أ / أنّ الأبدان إذا شاكلت الهواءَ والماءَ والغذاء والأرض والتربة ،كان عند ذلك الصحّةُ . ولولا هذا المعنى لما أمكن السُّكْنَى بمصر لرداءة هوائها ،ولا في أرض السودان لِفَرْط حَرّها ولا في أرض الصقالبة لشدّة برودتها . فمن أين ليت شعري لابن الجَزّار أن يكون اختلاف هواء مصر والضباب الكائن بها سببين لوقوع الوباء فيها ،وهما لا يَخرُجان (١٧٧) عن العادة . ثم قال بعد ذلك إن ماء النيل بمصر مضرّ بكلّ مَن سكَن مصر ضررا محسوسا . وليت شعري كيف يكون ذلك النيل (١٧٨) السببُ الأعظم في سُكْنَى هذه الأرض ،وأبدانهم قد أَلِفَته فهواؤها غير مُضِرّ ،وإن كان بالحقيقة رديئا .

وهذه الأشياء التي غَلِط فيها ابن الجزّار هي التي اعتمد عليها في كتابه . ولو كان ما ذكره صادقا (١٧٩) لوجب ضرورة دوامُ الوباء بهذه الأرض ، لأنّ هذه الأشياء هي دائمة لاتتقطع ،فكانت هذه أرضٌ تَخْرَب ويهلَك جميعُ أهلها . فأقاويل ابن الجزّار تخالف قولَ الأوائل ويلزمها/١٩ب/المَحال (١٨٠) وأيضا فلسنا نجد ابنَ الجزّار في شئ (١٨١) مِن كتابه فرّق بين الأمراض البَلَدية وبين الأمراض الوافدة ،ولكنه جعَل جميعَها شيئا واحدا ،وهذا يُضيع غرضَ (١٨٢) كتابه . والذى أوقع ابن الجزّار في هذا الغلط إهمالُه أمرَ المُشاكَلة التى بين أبدان المصريين وبين هذه الأشياء . وهاأنا قد أقمتُ بمصر سنين كثيرة ما رأيتُ الوباء حدَث فيها من نحو عشرين سنة إلا خمس دفعات وأعظمهن دُفْعة واحدة ،وأما الباقية فكانت أمراضا سليمة . فإن قيل قد ذكرتْ أنا (١٨٣) أيضا مِن أمْر عَفَن هذه الأرض واستحالتها وغير ذلك مما يوجب كثرة الأمراض فالجواب هو أنه كلّ ما ذكرنا فيما تَقدّم يوجب حدوث الأمراض كثيراً ، إلا أنّ مُشاكَلة هذه تعضها بعضا ،واتّفاقَها في نسبة واحدة منَع أن تكون هي نفسها مُمْرِضة متى لزمت العادة . فأما إذا خرجت عن عادتها (١٨٤) فهى تُحْدِث مرضا . وخروجها عن عادتها بأرض مصر /٢٠أ/هو الذي أعدّه أنا (١٨٥) اختلافا مُمْرِضا ،لا الاختلاف الموجود فيها دائما . فإنّ النيل ليَس يُحْدِث في الأبدان في كلّ سنة مرضا ،ولكنّه إنْ أفرطت زيادته أو قَصُر (١٨٦) عن العادة كان ذلك سببا لحدوث المرض الوافِد . وهذا أمر ذهبَ عن ابن الجزّار حتى أغفله ،وهو عُمْدة ما يُحتاج إليه في هذا الفن .

على أنّ كلّ معنى ذكرنا في هذا الكتاب ليس لابن الجزّار فيه شئ ،وكتابُه موجود في أيدي الناس ،وأنت تقف منه على صِدْق هذا القول (١٨٧) إذا تأمّلته بتُؤَدة (١٨٨) ورفْق .

فإن قيل (١٨٩) : إذا كانت أبدان الناس بأرض مصر (١٩٠) من السخافَة (١٩١) على ما ذكرتَ فلعلّها في مرض دائم (١٩٢) . فالجواب : لسنا نُبالي في هذا كيف كان ،لأنّ المرض عند جالينوس والأطباء مِن قَبْله ومن بَعْده هو ما يضرّ بالفعْل ضررا محسوسا مِن غير توسّط . فمن أجل ذلك ليست أبدان المصريين في مرَض دائم ،لكنها كثيرة الاستعداد نحو المرض / ٢٠ب/.

(١٤)

الفصل السادس (١٩٣)

في اختصاص (١٩٤) المدينة الكبرى بمصر في هوائها وجميع أحوالها

أمّا أرض مصر في الهواء والغذاء والماء والتربة فقد قلنا في ذلك على طريق العموم ما فيه كفاية . فأمّا الآن فإنّا نقول في المدينة الكبرى في هذه الأرض خصوصا، ليكون ذلك مثلا يُهْتَدي عليه في غيرها. والمدينة الكبرى بأرض مصر ذات أربعة أجزاء: الفُسْاط، والقَرافَة ، والقاهرة ، والجيزة (١٩٥). وبُعْد هذه المدينة عن خطّ الاستواء ثلاثون درجة ، وجبل المُقَطّم في مشرقها (١٩٦) ، وبينه وبينها مقابرُ المدينة. وقد قالت الأطباء إنّ أردأ (١٩٧) المواضع ما كان الجبل في مشرقها يعوق عنها ريحَ الصبا . وأعظم أجزائها هو الفسطاط ، ويلي الفسطاط من المغرب النيلُ. وعلى شطّ النيل الغربي أشجارُه كثيرة ، طِوال وقِصار. وأعظم (١٩٨) أجزاء الفسطاط موضع (١٩٩) في غَوْر /٢١أ/، فإنه يعلوه من المشرق المقطّمُ ، ومن الجنوب الشرفُ /٢٠٠/ ومن الشمال الموضعُ العالي مِن عَمَل فَوْق ، أعني المَوْقِفَ والعَسْكر وجامع ابن طولون . ومتى نظرتَ إلى الفسطاط من الشرف (٢٠٠) أو من مكانٍ آخر مرتفع (٢٠١) رأيتَ وضْعَها في غَوْر. وقد بيّن أبقراط أن المواضع المُتَسَفّلة أسْخَن (٢٠٢) من المواضع المرتفعةِ وأردأ هواءً لاحْتِقانِ البخار فيها ، ولأنّ ما حولها من المواضع العالية يَعُوق تخلّل الرياح لها. وأزِقّة الفسطاط وشوارعها ضيّقة وأبنيتها عالية . وقد قال روفس : إذا دخلتَ مدينة فرأيتها ضيقةَ الأزقّة ، مرتفعة البناء ، فاهْرُبْ (٢٠٣) منها فإنّها وَبِيّة ، أراد أن البخار لا يتحلّل منها على ما ينبغي لضيق الازقة وارتفاع البناء . ومن شأن أهل الفسطاط أنْ يَرْمُوا ما يموت في دُوَرِهم مِن السنانير والكلاب ونحوها من الحيوان الذي يَألف الناسَ في شوارعهم وأزقتهم فتتعفّن وتُخالِط عفونتُها الهواء. ومن شأنِهم أيضا أن يَرْمُوا في /٢١ب/ النيل الذي يشربون منه فضولَ حيواناتهم وجِيَفهم ، ومَجاري (٢٠٤) كُنُفهم تصبّ فيه . وربّما انقطع جَرْيُ الماء فيشربون هذه العفونة باختلاطها بالماء.

وفي خلال الفسطاط مُسْتَوْقدات عِظام ، يصعَد منهم في الهواء دُخَان مُفْرِط . وهي أيضا كثيرة الغبار لسَخافَة الأرض، حتى أنك ترى في الهواء في أيام الصيف كَدَرا يأخذ بالنفس ، ويتّسِخ الثوبُ النظيفُ في اليوم الواحد (٢٠٥) . وإذا مرّ الإنسان في حاجة لم يرجع إلا وقد اجتمع في وجهه ولحيته غبارٌ كثير ويعلو (٢٠٦) بها في العِشاء (٢٠٧) وخاصّة في أيام الصيف بخارٌ كَدِر وأغبر ، ولا سيّما إذا كان الهواء سليما من الرياح.

فإذا كانت هذه الأشياء كما وصفنا ، فإنها تضرّ (٢٠٨) الروح الحيواني الذي فينا حاله هذه (٢٠٩) الحال، فيتولّد إذن في البدَن من هذه الأمور فضولٌ كثيرة واستعدادات نحو العَفَن (٢١٠) . إلا أنّ إلْفَ أهل الفسطاط لهذه الحال وأنْسَهم بها يعوق عنهم أكثرَ شرّها /٢٢أ/ إن كانوا (٢١١) على حال أسرع (٢١٢) أهل أرض مصر وقوعا في الأمراض .

وما يلي النيل من الفسطاط يجب أن يكون أرطب ممّا يلي الصحراء . وأهل الشرف أصلحُ حالا لِتخرّق الرياح لدُورِهم. وكذلك عَمَل فَوْق والحَمْراء. إلا أنّ أهل الشرف ماؤهم الذي يشربونه أجْوَد لأنه يُسْتقَي قبل أن تُخالِطه عُفونة الفسطاط.

فأمّا القَرافه فأجودُ هذه المواضع لأنّ المُقَطَّم يعوق بخار الفسطاط من المرور بها. وإذا هبّت ريح الشمال مرّت بأجزاء كثيرة من بخار الفسطاط والقاهرة على الشرف فغيّرت حالَه . وظاهر أنّ الموضع المكشوف (٢١٣) في هذه المدينة هو أصحّ هواء ، وكذلك حال المواضع العالية .

(١٥)

ويلي الفسطاط في العظم وكثرة الناس القاهرةُ ،وهي في شمال الفسطاط،وفي شرقها (٢١٤) أيضا المُقَطَّم (٢١٥) يعوق عنها ريح الصبا.والنيلمنها أبعد قليلا . وجميعها مكشوف للهواء ،وإن كان عَمَل فَوْق ربّما عاق عن بعض ذلك. وليس لرتفاع الأبنية /٢٢ب/بها كارتفاع أبنية الفسطاط ،لكن دُونَها كثيرا. وأزِقّتها وشوارعُها أوسع (٢١٦) وأنظفُ وأقلّ وَسَخا وأبعد من العَفَن . وأكثر شُرْبَ أهلها من مياه الآبار. وإذا هبّت الريح تَخرّقتها ،وإذا هبّت ريح الجنوب أحْدَرَت من بخار الفسطاط على القاهرة شيئا كثيراً . وقُرْب مياه آبار القاهرة من وَجْه الأرض مع سَخافَتها يُوجِب ضرورة أن يكون يصل إليها بالرشْح من عُفونة الكُنُف شيءٌ ما . وبين القاهرةَ والفسطاط بَطائِح تمتلئ من رَشْح الأرض في أيام فَيْض النيل،ويصبّ فيها بعض خَرَارات القاهرة . ومياه هذه البطائع رديئة لِوُقُوفها (٢١٧) وسَبَخ أرضها ،ولِما يُصَبُّ فيها العُفُونة. والبخار المرتفعُ منها على القاهرة والفسطاط زائِدٌ في رداءة الهواء بِهما.

ويُطْرَح (٢١٨) في جنوب القاهرة هذه (قَذَر) (٢١٩)كثير نحو حارة الباطِليّة وكذلك أيضا يُطْرَح في وسط حارة العَبيد، إلا أنه إذا تأمّلنا حال القاهرة كانت بالإضافة (٢٢٠) إلى الفسطاط أعْدل وأجود هواءً وأصْلحُ حالا ،لأنّ أكثر /٢٣أ/عفوناتهم تُرْمَى خارجَ المدينة ،والبخار يَنحَلّ منها أكثر. وكثير أيضا من أهل القاهرة يَشرب من ماء النيل ،وخاصّة في أيام دخوله الخَليج . وهذا الماء يُسْتَقَى بعد مروره بالفسطاط واختلاطه بعُفونتها.

وأمّا الجيزة فهي (٢٢١) غربيّ النيل ،وهي صغيرة . وموضعُها في سَمْت الموضع الغائر(٢٢٢) من الفسطاط. وحَوْلَها من الأشجار والنبات شيٌ كثير. ومن شأن المواضع الكثيرة الأشجار أن يَكْثُر فيها العَفَنُ كما قال القُدَماء. وعِلّة (٢٢٣) ذلك ما يَنحَلّ من الأشجار من الفضول وما يَحْتَقِن بينها (٢٢٤) من البخار.والماءُ الذي يشربه هؤلاء من النيل يُسْتَقَى من غير مُخالَطة لِعَفَن الفسطاط ،لأن مَصَبّ النيل نحو الجيزة أكثر،وما يليهم (٢٢٥) منه لا يمرّ بالفسطاط، إلا أن ينقطع مَصَبّ النيل من جِهة الفسطاط فتبلغ العفونة إلى الجيزة . ولشدّة مُجاورة الجيزة للنيل تكون أرطب .

وأمّا الجَزيرة فأصغرُ من الجيزة ،وهي في وسط النيل بين الجيزة والفسطاط وفيها أيضا أشجار كثيرة /٢٣ب/ وهي على حال أرْطبُ هذه المَواضع لأنّ النيل مُحيط بها من كل جانب .

فظاهر أن أصحّ أجزاء المدينة الكبرى: القَرافَة ،ثم القاهرة ،والشرف وعَمَل فَوْق مع الحَمْراء (٢٢٦) ،والجيزة . وشمالُ القاهرة أصحّ من جميع هذه لبُعْده عن بخار الفسطاط وقُرْبه من الشمال. وأرْدأ موضع في المدينة الكبرى هو ما كان من الفسطاط حول الجامع العَتيق إلى ما يلي النيل والسواحل.

وإلى جانب القاهرة من الشمال: الخَنْدَق ،وهو في غَوْر . وهواؤه يتغيّر لهذا السبب فأمّا المَقْس(٢٢٧)فمُجاورته للنيل(تجعله) (٢٢٨) أرطب . وإذا كان في الشتاء وأوّل الربيع حُمِل من البحر المالح سَمَك كثير فيصل إلى هذه المدينة وقد عَفِن وصارت له رائحة مُنْكَرة جدا فيُباع في القاهرة ويأكلُه أهلُها وأهل الفسطاط ،فتجتمع في أبدانهم منه فضول كثيرة عَفِنة . فلولا اعتدال أمزجتهم وصحّةُ أبدانِهم في هذا الزمان ،لكان (٢٢٩) ذلك يُوَلّد فيهم أمراضا كثيرة قاتلة ، إلا أنّ قوّة الاستمرار (٢٣٠) /٢٤أ/تعوق عن ذلك،وربما انقطع النيلُ في آخر الربيع وأوّل الصيف (٢٣١) من جهة الفسطاط فيَعْفَن ما (٢٣٢) يَبْقَى من الماء بِكثرة ما يُلْقَي فيه ، إلى أن يبلغ عَفَنُه أن يصير له رائحة مُنْكَرة مَحْسوسة . وظاهر أنّ هذا الماء إذا صار على هذه الحال غيّر مِزاج الناس تغييرا محسوسا .

(١٦)

وفي جنوب هذه المدينة على مسافة بعيدة موضع يُدعى الفيّوم يخزن فيه ماء النيل ويزرع عليه مرّات في السنة ،حتى إنك ترى هذا الماء إذا خلّى تغيّر لون النيل وطعمه . وأكثر (٢٣٣) ما يحسّ منه هذا الحال البحيرة التي تكون في أيام النيل بسفط ونهيا وصاعدا إلى ما يلى الفيّوم . وهذه حال تزيد في رداءة حال أهل المدينة ولا سيّما إذا هبّت ريح الجنوب . ومن أجل شدّة تجاور (٢٣٤) الفسطاط والقاهرة والجزيرة والجيزة ،تشترك جميعا في الهواء والغذاء والماء والأمراض الوافدة ،وإن كان ذلك في بعضها أيسر منه في بعض (٢٣٥) . فمن البين أنّ أهل المدينة الكبرى بأرض مصر أسرع/٢٤ب / وقوعا في الأمراض من جميع اهل هذه الأرض ما خلا الفيّوم (٢٣٦) فإنها أيضا وبيّة بسبب ما ذكرنا. وأردأما ؤي المدينة الكبرى الموضع الغائر(٢٣٧) من الفسطاط. ولذلك (٢٣٨) غلب على أهله الجبن وقلّة الكرم . فإنه ليس منهم أحد يغيث الآخر ،ولا يضيف الغريب إلا في النادر . ويغلب عليهم الحسد ،وصاروا من أهل السعاية والاغتياب على أمر عظيم . وقد بلغ (٢٣٩) بهم الجبن إلى أن خمسة أعوان تسوق منهم مائة رجل وأكثر ،ويسوق الخمسة أعوان رجلا واحدا من أهل البلدان الأخرى ممّن تدرّب في الحرب .

فقد استبان إذن أنّ العلّة والسبب في أن صار (٢٤٠) أهل المدينة المدينة الكبرى بأرض مصر أسرع وقوعا في الأمراض وأضعف أنفسا . ولعلّ بهذا السبب (٢٤١) اختار القدماء إيجاد(٢٤٢) المدينة في غير هذا الموضع، فمنهم من جعلها بمَنْف ، وهي مصر القديمة (٢٤٣) ،ومنهم من جعلها بعين شمس (٢٤٤) ،ومنهم من جعلها بالاسكندرية ، ومنهم من جعلها في غير هذه المواضع ،ويدلّ على ذلك آثارهم (٢٤٥).

(١٧)

الفصل السابع
في أسباب الوباء

أمّا (٢٤٦) أمراض/٢٥أ/مصر البلديّة فقدْ ذكرنا مِن أصْلها (٢٤٧) ومن أسبابها ما فيه كِفايَة، وظهر من ذلك أن أكثرَها هي الأمراض الفَضْليّة التي تَشُوبها صَفْراء وخام. على أنّ باقي الامراض تَحْدُثُ عندهم بسرعة وقُرْب، وبخاصة في آخر الخريف وأوّل الشتاء. وأمّا الأمراض الوافِدَة فإلى الآن لم نذكر شيئا من أمرها.

ومعنى المرض الوافِد أن يعُمّ خَلْقا كثيراً في بلد واحد وزمان واحد، ومنه نَوْع يُقال له المَوْتَان، وهو الذى يكثُر معه الموت. وحدوث الأمراض الوافِدَة يكون عن أسباب كثيرة تجتمع في الجُمْلة في أربعة أجْناس (٢٤٨) : تغيّر كيفيّةِ الهواء، وتغيّرُ كيفيةِ الماء، وتغيّر كيفية الغِذاء، وتغيّر كيفية الأحداث النفسانيّة.

والهواءُ تتغيّر كيفيتُه على ضَرْبين، أحدهما تَغَيُّرُه الذى جَرَت به العادةُ، وهذا لا يُحْدِث مرضا وافِدا، ولستُ أسَمِّيه تغيُّرا مُمْرِضا /٢٥ب/. والثاني تغيُّرُه الخارج عن مَجْرى العادة، وهذا هو الذي يُحْدِث المرضَ الوافِد. وكذلك الحال في الباقية، فإنها إمّا أن تتغيَّر على العادة فلا تُحْدِث مرضا، وإمّا أن يكون تغيُّرها خارجا عن العادة فيُحدِثُ المرضُ الوافِد.

وخروجُ تغيُّر الهواء عن عادة يكون إمّا (٢٤٩) يسخَن أكثر أو يَبْرُد أو يترطَّب أو يجِفّ أو يُخالِطه (حال) (٢٥٠) عَفَينة (٢٥١). والحال العفنية إمّا أن تكون قريبةً أو بعيدةً. فإنّ أبقراط وجالينوس يقولان أن ليس يمنع (٢٥٢) مانعٌ مِن أن يَحْدُث ببلاد اليونانيين مرضٌ وافِد عن عُفُونة اجتمعت في بلاد الحَبَشَة وتَراقَت إلى الجَوّ وانْحدَرت على اليونانيين واحدثت فيهم المرضَ الوافِد. وقد يتغيّر أيضا مِزاجُ الهواء عن العادة بأن يصِل وَفْد كثير قد أنْهك أبدانَهم طولُ السفرِ وساءت أخلاطُهم (٢٥٣)، فيُخالِط الهواءَ منهم شيء كثير، ويقع الإعْداءُ في الناس، فيَظهَر المرضُ الوافد. والماء أيضا قد يُحْدِث المرضَ الوافد، إمّا بأن يَفرُط مقدارُه / ٢٦أ/في الزيادة أو النُقْصان، أو يُخالِطه حال عفنيّة، ويضطرّ الناس إلى شربه، ويتعفن به أيضا الهواء المحيط بأبدانهم. وهذه الحال تخالطه إمّا قريبا أو بعيدا بمنزلة ما يمرّفي جريانه بموضع حرب(٢٥٤) قد اجتمع فيها من جيف القتلى(٢٥٥) شيْكثير، وبمياه نقائع عفنة فيحدرها معه ويخالطها جسمه.

والأغذية تحدث المرض الوافد. إمّا إذا لحقها اليرقان وارتفعت أسعارها واضطر أكثر الناس إلى تغيير مأكله، وإمّا إذا أكثر الناس منها في وقت واحد كالذي يكون في الأعياد، فيكثر منها (٢٥٦) التخم (٢٥٧)، ويمرضون مرضا متشابها. وإمّا من قبل فساد مرعى الحيوان الذي يؤكل، أو فساد الماء الذي يشربه هذا الحيوان. والأحداث النفسانية تحدث المرض الوافد.

متى حدث في الناس خوف عام من بعض الملوك، فيطول سهرهم (٢٥٨) وتفكّرهم في الخلاص، وفي وقوع البلاء، فيسوء هضم أجوافهم، وتتغيّر حرارتهم الغريزيّه وربّما اضطروا إلى حركة عنيفة / ٢٦ب/في مثل هذه الحال. أو يتوقعون قحط (٢٥٩) بعض السنين، فيكثرون الحركة والاجتهاد في ادّخار الأشياء ويشتدّ غمّهم ممّا (٢٦٠) سيحدث. فجميع هذه الأشياء تحدث في أبدان الناس المرض الوافد متى كان المتعرّض لها خلقا كثيرا في بلد واحد ووقت واحد.

(١٨)

فظاهر أنه إذا كَثُر في وقت واحد المرضُ (٢٦١) في مدينة واحدة ارتفع من أبدانهم (٢٦٢) بخار كثر فيُغيِّر أيضا مِزاجَ الهواء ،فإذا صادف ذلك بدناً مستعِدًّا أمْرَضَه (٢٦٣) ،وإن كان صاحِبُه لم يتعرّض لما تَعرَّض إليه الناسُ في هذه الحال. مِثاله أن يكون قد حدَث في الناس مرض وافد مِن قِبَل ارتفاع السعر وعَدَم الطعام ،ويكون فيهم مَن لم يُغيِّر عادتَه فيما يَأكُل ويَشرَب فإذا ارتفع إلى بدنه بخارُ عفونةِ المَرْضَ وكان بدنُه مستعدًّا ،وَقَع هو أيضا في المرض.

فإذا قد قدّمتُ هذه الأشياء (٢٦٤) ،فالأمراض الوافدةُ إذن تَحدُث بأرضِ مصر إمّا عن فَساد لم تَجْرِ به العادةُ ، يَعْرِض للهواء سواء كان مادّة /٢٧أ/ هذا الفساد مِن نفس أرض مَصر أو من البلاد التي تُجاورها كالسودان والحجاز والشام وبَرْقة . أو يَعْرِض (٢٦٥) للنيل أن تَفْرُط زيادته فتكثُر زيادةُ الرطوبة والعفن ،أو تقِلّ زيادتُه جدا فيجف الهواءُ عن مقدار العادة ،ويضطر الناس إلى شرْب مياه رديئة ،أو تُخالِطه عُفونة تُحْدُث عن حَرْب(٢٦٦) تكون بمصر أو ببلاد السودان أو غيرها يموت فيها خَلْقٌ كثير ،ويرتفع بخارُجيَفِهم في الهواء فيعفنه ،ويتصل عفنُه إليهم ،أو يَسِيل الماءُ ويَحمِل معه العَفنَ. أو يَغْلو السعر. أو يَلْحَق الغَلّات (٢٦٧) آفة . أو يَدْخُل على الكِباش (٢٦٨) مُضَرّة. أو يلحَق الناسَ خوف عامّ أو قُنُوط . فكلّ واحد من هذه الأسباب يُحْدِث في أرض مصر مرضا وافِدا ،تكون قوّتُه بمقدار السبب المُحْدِثِ له . (وإن كان المُحْدِث(٢٦٩) له) أكثرَ مِن سبب واحد ،كان ذلك المرضُ أشدَّ وأقوى وأسرعَ في القَتْل،كما عرض بمصر منذ سنين. فإنّه وقع فيها حربٌ عظيمة ،قُتِل فيها من رجال العدوّ وخَلْق كثير،وعرض لأهل مصر خوف كثير من العدوّ ومن الغَلاء. /٢٧ب/ ثم كانت زيادةُ النيل خارجةً عن العادة في الزيادة والنقصان (٢٧٠) معا،واختلط به مِن عُفونة المَوْتَى شيءٌ كثير،وتعفّن الهواء المحيط بهم من عفن هذه الأشياء،وكثر انقحط،فحدث فيهم الموتان،ومات به نحو ثلث الناس.

وهذا المعنى الذي ذكرناه ـ أَعني خروج هذه الأشياء عن مَجاريها في كل سنة ـ ذَهَبَ (٢٧١) عن ابن الجزّار ،حتى جَعَل نَفسَ ما يُوافِق مِزاج مصر سبباً لوقوع المرض الوافد (٢٧٢).

الفصل الثامن

في إعادة ما تقدَّم على طريق الجُملة (٢٧٣) وزيادة في شَرْح أمر الأسباب الستة المُحيطة بالصحّة والمرض .

مِزاج أرض مصر حار ورَطْب بالرطوبة الفَضْليّة ،وما قَرُب من الجنوب من أرض مصر كان أسْخَن وأقلّ عُفونة في ماء النيل مما كان منها في الشمال،ولا سيما في شمال الفسطاط مثل أهل البَشْمُور ،فإنّ طَبْعهم أغْلَظ والبَلة (٢٧٤) عليهم أغلب وذلك أنهم يستعملون أغذية غليظة جدا ٢٨\أويشربون من الماء الرديء.فأما الاسكندرية وتِنّيس وأمثال هذه (٢٧٥) فقُرْبها من البحر وسكونُ الحرارة والبردُ عندهم وظهورُ الصبا (٢٧٦) فيهم ،مما يُصْلح أمْرَهم وطباعَهم (٢٧٧) ويرفع هِمَمهم (٢٧٨) . فليس يَعْرِض لهم ما يعرض لأهل البَشْمُور من غِلَظ الطبع والحماريّة وإحاطةُ البحر بمدينة تِنّيس يوجب غَلَبة الرطوبة عليها وتَأْنِيث أخلاق أهْلها .

واستبان أيضا أن أرض مصر ذات أجزاء كثيرة ،يختصّ كل جزء منها بحُكْم غير حُكْم الأخر. وأنّ ما ذكَره ابن الجزّار من أسباب وباء أرض مصر ليس بصحيح. وأنّ سبب ذلك خروجُ ما ذكرنا عن العادة ،وأنّ أبدان المصريين وسائرَ ما عندهم (٢٧٩) سَخِيفَة سريعةُ الوقوع في الأمراض . وأن آخر الخريف وأوّل الشتاء شرّ أوقات السنة وأكثرُها مرضا. وأنّ المدينة الكبرى هى أرْدأ حالا من غيرها في سرعة الوقوع في الأمراض . وأنّ أمراضهم البلديّة كثيرة ،وأكثرُها الأمراض الفَضْلِيّة والعفونيّة/٢٨ب / التي معها صَفْراء وبَلْغَم .

وإذا كانت هذه الأشياء كما وصفنا (٢٨٠) فينبغي أن نزيد في الأسباب الستة تلخيصا ،فنقول :

إنّ الهواء المعتدل يَحسُن فيه حال مزاج البدن ويجُود (٢٨١) الهَضْمُ لأن الروح الحيوانيّ الصيائيّ الذي فيه (٢٨٢) تَصْفو ،وتنتشر الحرارةُ الغَريزية (٢٨٣) في البدن على اعتدال. والهواء الذي خرج عن الاعتدال يُغيّر (٢٨٤) الأبدان التي لم تَعتده ،ولا يضرّ الأبدانَ التي قد اعتادته ،إلا أن يُفْرُط استعدادُها نحو المرض أو يفرُط خروجُه (٢٨٥) عن الاِعتدال.

وكذلك القول فيما يُأْكل ويُشْرَب ،فإنّ كان قوم قد ألِفوا أغذية بأَعْيانها ونشأت عليها أبدانُهم ،فإنْ عرَض لهم ما يَقطعُهم (عنها ٢٨٦) وَقعوا في الأمراض .

وأيضا فالرياضة المُعتادَة قد تكون سببا للصحة بتحليلها ما يجتمع في الأبدان من الفُضول والبخار الدخاني. ومَن قد اعتادت أعضاؤُه الرياضةَ(٢٨٧) أصلبُ وأشدّ قوّة . ولذلك الفلاحون وسائر (٢٨٨) الفَعَلَة أشدّ قوّة وأقوى أنْفُسا من أهل الدعة والترف/ ٢٩أ/وفضولُ أبدانِهم أيضا أقلّ . فأما السكونُ فإنّ المعتدل منه يفعل (٢٨٩) أيضا في الأبدان [(٢٩٠) صحّة وقوة ،والسكونُ الكثير لا يدع البخارَ ينحلّ ،فتحتقِن الفضولُ وتُحْدِث في البدن) رداءة ،وهذا يجعل الأبدانِ أكثرَ استعداد لقَبول الأمراض .
وإنّ أهْل السكون والدعة مِن ساكني مصر أسرعُ وقوعا في الأمراض . والرياضةُ المُفْرِطَة أيضا تضرّ بالأبدان لِتَسْخِيفها إيّاها وتوليدِها الفضول الدخانيةَ فيها.
وأمّا النوم واليقَظة فإنهما إذا اعتدلا أحدثا الصحة وحفِظاها ،إذ النوم (٢٩١) يجود به الهضم لغور الحرارة إلى داخل ،واليقظةُ تَنحلّ بها فضولُ الهضم لظهور الحرارة إلي الخارج . والنوم المُفْرِطُ يَبْرُد البدنَ فتكثُر فيه الفضولُ ،واليقظةُ المُفْرِطة تُجفّف البدنَ وتُسيء هضمَه . والقولُ في الاحتقان والاستفراغ كذلك (٢٩٢) فإنّه إذا كان ما يَحْتقِن في البدن من الفضول شيئا كثيرا أفسد (٢٩٣) فيها الهضمَ ،وأسرع إليها العفنُ. وإن كان الذى يستفرغ أكثرَ مما يَحْتَقِن وجب ضرورة أن تكون تلك

الزيادة من نفس أخلاط البدن لا بدله من/ ٢٩ ب/ وإذا أُخرِجت (٢٩٤) منه حَدث فيه (٢٩٥) المرضُ . فسبيل إذن ما يحتقن يكون مساويا لما يُستَفرَغ. إلا أنّ جالينوس والأطباء يقولون إنه يجتمع في فصل الشتاء في الأبدان رطوباتٌ كثيرة لَزِجَة بَلغميّه وأوساخ تَلَجُّج (٢٩٦) في نفس المعدة والأوعية والعروق كما تتلجّج مِن جُرَيان الماء فى القناة والبَرابِخ رطوبة" (٢٩٧) لَزِجة وَسِخَة . فإذا دخل الربيع ذابت تلك الأخلاط البلغمية اللزِجَة فزادت في كميّة الدم وعفنتها (٢٩٨) الأوساخُ التي معها ،فتحتاج من أجل ذلك أن تُستَفرَغ هذه قبل أن تُحِيل الدمَ ،وتُغسَل الأوعيةُ والعروق من الأوساخ اللاجِجَة (٢٩٩) فيها بالأدوية المُسْهلَة . وكذلك يجتمع في البدن ويلج في قَعْر المعدة والأوعية والعروق فَي الصيف أخلاط"حارّة وأوساخ رديئة الكيفية . فإذا دخل الخريف وتغيّر الهواء ،هاجت هذه واحترق كثير منها فيحتاج مِن أجل ذلك أيضا أن تُستَفرَغ هذه/٣٠أ/قبل أن تُحدِث في البدن رداءة. فوجب مِن هذا أن تستفرِغ الأبدانُ في فصليْ الربيع والخريف في كلّ سنة كيما تُنَظَّف الأوعيةَ وأوساخَها ،وتغسِلها من الآشياء الرديئة التى قد لَجِجَت فيها. ويجب أن يكون نوع الأدوية التي يستفرَغ بها (في الربيع غيرَ النوع الذي يُستفرَغ به في (٣٠٠)) الخريفه فإنّ الآدوية التي ينبغي أن يُستفرَغ بها في الربيع يحتاج أن تكون تُسْهِل مقدارا كثيرا من البلغم والرطوبات اللزِجَة ،والتي يُستفرَغ بها في الخريف يحتاج أن تكون تُسهِل مقدارا كثيرا من المِرّة الصفراء والأوساخ الحارّة (٣٠١) مِن أجل ما قدّمنا ذِكْره . ويجب أن تكون أدوية الخريف أيضا تَستَفرِغ الرطوبةَ بأرض مصر خاصة ،لكثرة ما يتولّد في هذا الزمان من الرطوبات في أبدان الناس (٣٠٢). فهذان الاستفراغان اللذان أحدهما في الربيع والأخر في الخريف يُسْهِلان (٣٠٣) ما يحتقن في الأبدان من الأوساخ فيما بينهما.

وأما الأحداث النفسانية كالغضب والحُزن / ٣٠ب/ والسرور ،فإنها إذا لم تفرط لا تحدث مرضا. وينبغي أن يكثر أهل مصر الفرح والسرور فإنّ ذلك يقوّي حرارة أبدانهم الغريزيّة ،فيجود الهضم (٣٠٤) ويقلّ ما يحتقن فيها.

فقد ظهر ممّا قلنا أنّ كل واحد من الأسباب الستة يحدِث الصحّة ويحفظها إذا كان على ما ينبغي في كميّة وكيفيته . وإذا خرجتَ عما ينبغي (٣٠٥) أُحدث (٣٠٦) المرَض . فإذن أمراض مصر البَلَديّة والوافِدَة وغيرها تزيد وتنقص بحسب تعرّض الانسان لهذه الأسباب ،وإهماله إياها ،وتفقّده لها. وذلك أنّ مَن يُكْثِر أكلَ الأغذية المُولّدة للسوداء يستعدّ بدنُه للأمراض السوداوية . وكذلك القَول في الباقية .

وقد تُغيّر هذه الأسبابُ الستة مِزاجَ الانسات وبنيَته (٣٠٧) وسِحْنَته (٣٠٨) وعادته ،والوقتَ الحاضر من أوقات الستة ،ومزاجَ الذكر والانثى . ففي ما قلنا من الأشياء التي احتجنا إلى تقديمها كفاية .

(٢١)

الفصـل التاســع

في الحِيلة الكلية في حِفْظ الصّحة ومُداواة الأمـــراض

/٣١أ/قد عَلَّمنا (٣٠٩) الفلاسفة والأطباء هذه الحِيلةَ بأن أمروا (٣١٠) أن يحتذي (٣١١) بالطبيعة في أفعالها في البدن ،مِن ذلك قولِ أبقراط(٣١٢) : إن كان ما يُستفرَغ من البدن عند اسْتِطلاق البَطْن والقَئْ اللذيْن يكونان طَوْعا من النوع الذي ينبغي أن يُنقّي منه البدنُ ،نَفَعَ ذلك وسَهُل احتمالُه ،وإن لم يكن كذلك كان الأمر بالضدّ(٣١٣). فينبغي (٣١٤) أن تَنظرُ أيضا في الوقت الحاضر من أوقات السنة وفي البلد وفي السنّ وفي الأمراض: هل تُوجب استفراغ ما هممتَ باستفراغه أم لا . وقال أيضا : إن ما ينبغي أنْ يُشْقَىَ من الدواء ما يُستفرَغ مِن تِلقاء نفْسه نفَع استفراغُه (٣١٥). فأمّا ما كان استفراغُه (٣١٦) على خلاف ذلك فينبغي أن تقطَعَه . وقال أيضا: الأشياءُ التي ينبغي أن تُستفرَغ يجب أن تُستفرَغ من المواضع التى هي إليها أمْيل ،بالأعضاء التي تَصلُح لاستفراغها. وقال: ما كان من الأمراض يَحدُث عن الامتلاء فشفاؤه يكون بالاستفراغ ،/٣١ب/وما كان منها يحدُث من الاستفراغ فشفاؤه يكون بالامتلاء . وشفاءُ سائر الأمراض يكون بالمُضادّة. وقال(٣١٧)في حفظ الصحّة: ينبغي أنْ يُحْفَظ كلّ شئ على ما هو عليه .وإذا تأمّلنا جميعَ ما سمِعناه مِن أبقراط في هذه وغيرها ،وما سمعناه من جالينوس فيها وفي غيرها (٣١٨) وجَدْناه يشتمل على ما اجتمع عليه الفلاسفةُ وفِرقة أصحاب القِياس من الأطباء من أنه ينبغي أن يُحْتَذَي-فيما نُورده على الأبدان - بما تفعله الطبيعةُ فيها. فكما أن الطبيعة التى جعلها الله عزّ وجل قائمةً بتَدْبيرِ البدن بإذْنه ،تحفَظ على البدن صِحّته بما تُغذّيه به من الأغذية، وبما تُخرِج عنه مِن فُضول(٣١٩) في كلّ يوم بالتنفّس والعَرَق والبول والقَيْ والبُصاق والرعاف ودم الحيْض والبَواسِير،من العُضو(٣٢٠) المُوافق بحسب مِزاج البدن والوقتِ الحاضر من أوقات السنة والبلد والسنّ والسحنة والعادة ،فذلك سبيلنا أن نفعل فيما نُورده البدنَ من الأغذية والأدوية، وسائر/٣٢أ/ ضروب العلاج. وكما أن الطبيعة أيضا تستفرغ الخلط المؤذي من العضو المُوافق،كالذي يكون في البُحْران ،كذلك سبيلنا (٣٢١) أن نستفرغ ما يجتمع (٣٢٢) في البدن من الخِلْط المؤذي من العضو المُوافق. وذلك أنّه إن نظَرْنا في حال العليل ومزاجه وسِحْنته ومزاج بَلَده والوقت الحاضر وطبيعة المرض وأسبابه وأعْراضه ،وتخيّرنا من الأدوية والأغذية الشيَ المُوافق،وتأملنا جميعَ ما يَحْتاج إليه ،تَهَيّألنا حِفْظ صحته وإزالةُ المؤذي ولذلك اضطررنا إلى معرفة طبائع (٣٢٣) الأغذية والأدوية والتشريح وسائر ما يَنْظرُ فيه أصحاب القياس من الأطباء .

والذي يحتاج أن يُحْصِيه الطبيبُ ويحفَظَه ويعرفه (٣٢٤) في مُداواة كل مرض وفي حِفْظ الصحة خمسة وعشرون شيئا ،بعد جزيئات أخر(٣٢٥) :

١ - مزاج البلد(٣٢٦)   ٢- الأمراض البلديّة   ٣- الوقت الحاضر

٤- مزاج ذلك الوقت .   ٥- المرض الوافِد   ٦- المرض الموجودفي البدن وفي أي عضو هو.

٧- سبب المرض .   ٨- مقدار قوة الأرض

٩- أعراض المرض .   ١٠- قوّة الأعراض .   ١١- قوّة العليل(٣٢٧).

(٢٢)

١٢ – مزاج /٣٢ب/العليل ١٣ – سِنّ العليل ١٤ – مزاج العضو الذي فيه المرض وفعلُه وشَكْلُه ووَضْعُه . ١٥ – سِحْنَة العليل ١٦ – طبيعة العليل من الذكور والإناث . ١٧ – عادته في أيام الصحّة . ١٨ – طبيعة الأغذية والأدوية ١٩ – عادته منها في أيام صحته ومرضه . ٢٠ – ما ينبغي للطبيب أن يختار منها في أوقات الصحّة وفي أوقات المرض . ٢١ – كيف ينبغي أن يكون العلاج .

٢٢ – (أيّ وقت مُوافق للعلاج (٣٢٨). ٢٣ – أيّ عضو موافق في إيراد العلاج ٢٤ – أن يكون المريض ومَن يُحْضِره على وِفاق الطبيب . ٢٥ – أن يكون ما يَعْرِض من خارج مُوافقا .

فهذه الأشياء هي التي يَقْتَدِر(٣٢٩) بها الطبيب على معونة الطبيعة والقيام بخدمتها في حفْظ الصحّة ومداواة المرض . والوقوفُ عليها والعملُ بها ليس بِسَهْل ،والإحاطةُ بها صعبة عَسِرة ،تَحتاج إلى تعب كثير وَعناء ودُرْبَةٍ طويلة في طَلَبها (٣٣٠) ،والرياضة فيها ،وتَرْك التشاغُل عنها والإهمالِ لشيء منها : كبيرها وصغيرها ،دقيقها وجليلها . فإني أنا إلى اليوم لستُ أعرف /٣٣أ/مَن تقدّم بهذه الضمانات من الأطباء . ولا أعرف في هذه المدينة العظيمة مَن يقوم بمعرفة مزاج أهل (٣٣١) مصر ،فضلا عن غيره . وهذا أمْر لا يمكن المُداواة بدونه .وحَسْبُكَ بابن الجزّار – على تقدُّمه في هذه الصناعة – وضَع في أرض مصر كتابا مُفْـرَدا لم يُبيِّن فيه مزاجها ولا شرَح حالَها ،وعَرَض له–مع ذلك (٣٣٢)- سَهْوٌ في مواضع كثيرة من كلامه . وإذا كانت هذه الأشياء على ما وصفنا من الصعوبة ،فليس يَتهيّألِلإنسان إدراكُها إلا بعد السهر الطويل في قراءة كُتب الأوائل للتفكير في مَعانيها ،ومُعاناة ذلك بالنفْس والبدن ليلا ونهارا بقَدْر استطاعة الإنسان ،وقد وصَف أبقراط وجالينوس صعوبة هذا الأمر ، فقال أبقراط : العمر قصير ،والصناعة طويلة ،والوقت ضيّق ،والتجربة خطر ،والقضاء عَسِر . وجالينوس يصف صعوبة الأمر في كثير مِن كُتبه . فمتى أهمل الإنسانُ الأشياء التى لا بدّ منها ،وتوكّل على الأماني / ٣٣ب / والأباطيل ،وأثر (٣٣٣) الراحةَ ،وأدركه الموتُ ،فاتَه طيِّبُ ثَمَرها وحُسْن عاقبتها ،وصار في الآخرة إلى الخُسْران وأليم العذاب . وإذا اجتهد فيما يَحتاج إليه ، حصل له حظّ الدنيا والآخرة ،فإن فاته حظُّ الدنيا لم يفتْه حظّ الآخرة (٣٣٤) .وليست عقوبة الجاهل في الآخرة بصغيرة ،لكثرة ما يُدْخِل على الناس (٣٣٥) من المَضارّ ،بل عذابُه أزْيَد كثيرا مِن عَذاب غيره من اللصوص وقَتَلَة الأنفس .

(٢٣)

فإيّاكَ أيُّها الطبيب إيّاك الاشتغالَ عن صناعتك بلذّات البهائم من الأكل والشرب والنكاح وجَمْع المال والمُفاخرة (٣٣٦) وحُبّ الصلف والمركوبِ والملبوس وغير ذلك من الأشياء التي يُتفاخَر بها، وتُموِّه على العَوام بُمخالطة ذوي اليسار وتطويلِ اللحية والشيْب . فإنّ الاشتغال بذلك كله يعوقكَ عن التخرّج في صناعة الطب . فإنّ هذه الأشياء هي التي يذُمّها (٣٣٧) جالينوس وغيره من الفلاسفة والأطباء . ولقد صارت بحيث يرغب أطباءُ مصر اليوم أكثر من كل شيء ، فإنّ عهدي بهم وقد قَصَدني رجلُ / ٣٤ أ/ منهم في بعض الأوقات وسألني عن أدوية تُطيل شَعرَ لحيته وتُولّد فيها الشيْب . فتعجّبتُ منه وسألته أن يَصْدُقَني عن حاله . فقال : إنّ النافع اليوم بمصر في صناعة الطب طُولُ اللحية (٣٣٨) مع الشيْب، وحُسْنُ الملبوس والمركوب والمُفاخَرة (٣٣٩) بذلك . ألا ترى أن الناس يُعظّمون (٣٤٠) مَن اجتمعت له هذه الخِصال ولا ينظرن في شئ آخر . فقلت له: صدقتَ ، وهذا الذي صيّر باعَة الأدوية أحذقَ من الأطباء بها وأعْرَفَ (٣٤١) وجماعة منهم صاروا مِن وُجُوه أطباء هذه المدينة . ثم أوصيتُه بما ينبغي وحذّرتُه الجهلَ وعرّفته ما قال جالينوس من أنّ الطبيب الجاهلَ شَرّ على الأبدان من الوباء الحاضر ومن اللصوص ، أن اللصوص إنما يرغبون في الأموال ، والطبيبَ الجاهل يأخذ الروح بالواحدة . وما أظنه قَبِلَ – مع هذا – الوصيةَ . ولقيَني أيضا منذ أيام بعضُ أطباء الفسطاط المشهورين ، وأَخَذ بيدي ولامَني على تأخيري عن الرؤساء وجمع المال، وجمع المال، واشتغالي/٣٤ب/عن ذلك بقراءة كتب الأوائل والعمل بها والدربة فيها ، وإهمالي أمْر ما الناس عليه مِن مَحبّة الدنيا (٣٤٢) والدراهِم (٣٤٣) . فقلت له : إنّ جالينوس ليس يَرْضَى أن يُسَمّى هؤلاء الأطباء الذين يُواظبون على أبواب الرؤساء بَوّابين للأبواب (٣٤٤) ولكن أَخَسّ (٣٤٥) مِن ذلك . ولستُ أرضى لنفس بهذه الحال . فانتهرني وقال : هذه مَنْحَسَة ما أظنها تَتخلّى عنكَ ، ومَرَضٌ لا يَنْجَلي . ومضَى وتركني . وقال (٣٤٦) آخَر : إذا رأيتَ إنسانا ينظر في كتاب فهو منحوس . ولقيَني أيضا منذ أيام شيخٌ منهم، فأخذ يسألني عن البُحْران. فإذا به لا يَعرف ذلك ولا يَفهم منه سِوَى اسمه . ولقد أقام معي بعضَ يوم وأنا أفهّمه معنى البُحْران ، وما أظنّه فَهِم . ودخلتُ إلى بعض الأعْلام (٣٤٧) ، فوجدتُ به سوء نَفَس مِن ضَغْط في رئَتيه فقال لي بعضُ أهله : ذَكَر فلانٌ – وسَمَّوْه لي ، وهو مِن وجوه أطباء البلد وأحْسَنِهم (٣٤٨) – بعَليلكم هذا شَوْصَة . فعجبتُ من ذلك ، وقلت لهم : اعلموا أن الشوصة يكون معا حُمّى دائمة ووَخز (٣٤٩) وسُعال ، وهي / ٣٥ أ/ ذات جَنْب خالصة . وليس بعَليلكم شئ من هذا .

وأنا أقصُّ عليكَ من أخبارهم بعضَ ما هم عليه من التمويه والجهْل (٣٥٠) كيما تَحْذَرَهم . ولعلّ السلطان ينظرُ في أمْرهم ،فلا يُمَكّن أحدَهم من التكَسُّب بهذه الصناعة إلا أن يكوُن حاذِقا ،ويعرف عليهم (٣٥١) أفضَلهم ليَقتَدِي به الباقون فيكون ذلك سببا لزوال هذه المِحْنة (٣٥٢) . فمن ذلك أن رجلا من وجوه أطباء الفسطاط صار له صِيت بأن كان يركب ويجعل تحته مخَدّة في السرج ،ولا ينظر في عِلّة أحد حتى يُخرِج اسْطَرْلابا من كُمّه فينظر فيه ،فظنّ العَوامُ (٣٥٣) عند ذلك أنه حكيم بارع . وهذا الرجل - أقسِمُ بالله - ما أعرفُ (٣٥٤) أنه يفْهَم شيئا من صناعة الطب . ومنهم شيخ عظيم اللحية ،ليس يُحْسِنَ الاستِخرْاج ولا الكتابة فَضْلا عن غيرهما ،دخل على الناس بأن كان (٣٥٥) يُخاطِب النساء بما يَليق بهنّ من أمْر النكاح (٣٥٦) ،وكذلك الرجال ،ويُلِين كلامَه ويَهَشّ إليهم ،ويجعلَ ذلك على سبيل الدعابة والمزَح معهم ،فتَواصَفُوه / ٣٥ب / وصار له ذِكْر عظيم ومَكْسب حَسَن (٣٥٧) . وإني لأعرِفُ شيخاآخرمنهم (٣٥٨) ،لستُ أعلمُ أنّ في العالم رجلا آخر أجْهَل منه في سائر الوجوه كلّها ،وهذه صِفَة خِلْقته : هو رجل تام الخَلْق غليظ(٣٥٩) العِظام ،قليل اللحم ،صغير الرأس ،طويل اللحية . هذا الرجل موَّه على الناس والأكابر بإظهار العجب والغضب ، فقام له بذلك سوق كبير (٣٦٠) بإظهار خِدْمَة السلطان (٣٦١) . ولقد حدّثني بعض إخواننا (٣٦٢) أنه استأذن عليه في وقت صائِف شديد الحَرّ ،فلم يأذَن حتى لِبس خمس جبّات ،وتعمّم بعَمائم طِوال ،والتفّ بأرْدِيَة كثيرة . قال صديقي : فلمادخلتُ عليه وهو في هذه الحال رأيت رجلا مجنونا ،فلم يَتهيأله أن يكلّمني مِن شدّة الحَرّ الذى هو فيه . فانْتَهَرني ،وقال لي : اخرُجْ عني ،فاني مشغول بمُداواة نفسي واستفراغ بدني بالعَرَق . فظنّ أنّ ذلك شيء يَجُوزني ويموه عليّ . فقلت له :قد كان لك في الحَمّام ما هو أصْلح من هذا . واجتمعت أنا مع هذا الطبيب (٣٦٣) عند بعض الأعلام (٣٦٤) ،ورأيته وقد جلس / ٣٦أ/ عند رجلِ العَليل ،وأمَر العليلَ بالقيام إليه ،وهو شديد الكَرْب ثم أخذ نَبْضه بعد ذلك . ورأيته أيضا وقد دخل إلى رجل شيخ مَفْلُوح ،فوصف له حَلْب اللبن على رَأْسه في يوم شديدِ البرد. وأمّا الجَرّاحون والكَحّالون منهم ،فإنهم يُداوون الشيخ الكبير والصَبيّ الصغير والرجل والمرأة (٣٦٥) والمدنيّ والقَروىّ(٣٦٦) بأدوية واحدة بأعيانَها . فهذا حال أطباء مصر اليوم (٣٦٧) ،وليس منهم مَن تُحْمَد طريقتَه إلا أربعة نَفَر أو خمسة (٣٦٨).

وأنا الآن أقطع ذكرَهم وأعودُ إلى ما كنتُ فيه ،فأقول : أمّا الحِيلة في حِفْظ الأصِحّاء ومُداواة المرضَى فقدْ قُلنا فيها بالقول المُطْلَق ما فيه كفاية. وأمّا تلخيص ذلك شيئا (٣٦٩) ،فأمر قد لخّصه أبقراط واستقصاه جالينوس .

الفصل العاشر
فيما ينبغي للطبيب أن يفعله بأرض مصر

لمّا كانت أرض مصر وجميع ما فيها سَخيفَة الأجسام / ٣٦ب / سريعا إليها التغيُّر والتعفُّن (٣٧٠)، وجب على الطَبيب أن يختار من الأغذية والأدوية ما كان قريب العهد حديثا، لأن قوّته بَعْدُ باقية عليه لم تتغيّر كل التغيُّر وأن (يجعل) (٣٧١) علاجَه ملائما لما عليه الأبدان بأرض مصر، ويجتهدَ في أن يجعل ذلك إلى الجهة المُضادّة أمْيَل قليلا، ويَتجنّب الآدويةَ القويّة الإسْهال، وكلّ ما له قوّة مُفرِطَة، فإن نِكايَة هذه في الأبدان سريعة لا سيّما أبدان المصريين سريعة الوقوع في النكايات . ويختار ما كان من الأدوية المُسْهِلَة وغيرها ألْيَن قوّة حتى لا تكون على طبيعة المصريين فيها كُلْفَة ولا يَلْحَق أبدانهم منها مَضَرّة . ولا يُقْدِم على الأدوية الموجودة في كُتب الأطباء اليونانيين والفرس فإن أكثرها عُمِلَت الأبدان قويّة البِنْيَة غليظة الأخْلاط . وهذه الأشياء قلّ ما توجد بأرض مصر، لذلك يجب علَيه أن يتوقّف في هذه الأدوية، ويختار ألْيَنها، ويَنْقص من مقدار شربها، ويُبدّل كثيرا منها بما يقوم مقامَه، ويكون ألْيَن منه، فيتّخذ السكنجبين السكّريّ /٣٧أ/ بدلا من العَسَليّ، والجُلّاب بدلا من العسل، وأيضا ينبغي أن يعلم أنّ هواء مصر يعمَل فيَ المَعْجُونات وسائرِ الأدوية ضَعْفا في قوّتها .

وإذا كان الأمر على ما ذكرْنا، فأعْمار الأدوية المُفْرَدة والمُرَكَّبَة : المَعْجُون منها وغير المعجون بمصر أقصرُمن أعمارها في (٣٧٢) غير مصر . فيحتاج الطبيبُ إلى تقدير ذلك وتمييزه حتى لا يَشُذّ عنه منه شئ مما يحتاج إليه . وإذا لم يكتفِ في تَنْقِيَة البدن بالدواء المُسْهِل دفعة واحدة، فلا بَأْس بإعادتها بعد أيام، فإنّ ذلك أحْمد مِن إيراد الدواء الشديد القوة في دفعة واحدة . ألا ترى أنّ الثقل إذا قُسّم وحُمِل جزءا كان أسهل وأخفّ على القوّة مِن حَمْله في دفْعَة واحدة . فلهذا ينبغي أن تُخْرِج الأخلاطَ اللاحِجَة (٣٧٣) في الأعضاء في أكثرِ من دفْعَة واحدة، إذْ كان خروجُ هذه بالدواء الليّن الإسهال يَعْسُر في أوّل دفعة .

وأيضا فلا تغتر (٣٧٤) بهذه الأشياء، ولكن قايِس بينها وبيْن كل ما يُحْتاج إليه، فإن الأدوية إن كثُرَت على البدن أخْلَقتْه كما يُخْلِقُ كثرةُ الغَسْل /٣٧ب/ الثوبَ الصحيح . وأعْطِ في كل فصْل من الأغذية والأدوية ما يُوافق بحسب مزاج ذلك الفصل وما يتولّد فيه في الأبدان . وأجْر (٣٧٥) الناس على عاداتهم ولا تمنعْهم منها إلا أن يعوق عن ذلك شئ آخر . وأمُرْ بالرياضة الدائمة كيما (٣٧٦) تُقَوّي بها الأعضاء، ولا يُسْرِع إليها المرض . وتلطّفْ لكل إنسان بما يُوافقه . والقولُ المُطْلَق هو أنّ سَبيلك أن تَقيس في كل وقت ما يحتاج إليه، وتَمْزج بعضَه ببعض حتى تَقِف من الجميع على الصواب فتفعله . فهذا ما يجب عليكَ (٣٧٧) .

(٢٦)

الفصل الحادي عشر
في صفة تدبير الأبدان بمصر

الأبدان كلّها خمسة : بدن هيئته الهيئة الفاضلة ،وهذا هو قانون صناعة الطب وبدن هيئته الهيئة المضادّة للهيئة الفاضلة وهو البدن المريض،وبدن هيئته الهيئة القريبة من الهيئة الفاضلة وهو البدن الصحيح والمصحّح ، وبدن هيئته الهيئة القريبة من المرض/٣٨أ/ وهو البدن المسقام (٣٧٨) وبدن هيئته الهيئة الوسطى بين الصحّة والمرض.

ولأنّ (٣٧٩) أرض مصر تولّد في الأبدان سخافة وسرعة القبول للمرض (٣٨٠) وجب أن تكون الأبدان التي في الهيئة الفاضلة بأرض مصر قليلة جدا . فأما الأبدان الباقية فكثيرة ،وأن تكون الصحة التامة عندهم على الأمر الأكثر هي القريبة من الهيئة الفاضلة . وظاهر (٣٨١) عند الأوائل - أعني أطباء القياس - أنّ مداواة كل واحد من هذه الأبدان غير مداواة الأخر لأنها وإن كانت كذلك تجتمع في أربع طرق من المداواة . إحداهن أن تجعل جميع الأشياء على غاية الاعتدال لمن هيئته الهيئة الفاضلة . والثاني أن تحفظ جميع الأشياء على مشاكلة الأبدان الصحيحة . والثالث أن تجعل جميع الأشياء إلى الاعتدال أميل في الأبدان المسقامة والتي ليست صحيحة (٣٨٢) ولا مريضة . والرابع أن تجعل جميع الأشياء مضادّة لما عليه الأبدان المريضة . والطريقة الأولى التي تدبّر بها (٣٨٣) الأبدان / ٣٨ب/ التي في الهيئة الفاضلة يحتاج فيها بأرض مصر إلى تدبير الهواء والماء والغذاء وسائر الأشياء تدبيرا تصيّرة (٣٨٤) في غاية الاعتدال . والطرق الباقية يحتاج فيها إلى مقايسة ونظر فيما يحتاج إليه منها .
وهذه الأشياء التي ذكرتها هي العمدة والأصل الأعظم في حفظ الصحة ومداواة المرض . وما رأيت أحدا من أطباء مصر ولا سمعت عنه أنه يفهم هذا الأمر فضلا أن يعمل به .
ولأنّ الهضم كثيرا ما يسوء بأرض مصر ،وكذلك حال الروح الحيوانيّ (٣٨٥) ،وجب عليك أن تصرف العناية (٣٨٦) إلى مراعاة أمر القلب والدماغ والكبد والمعدة والعروق والأوراد (٣٨٧) وسائر الأعضاء الباطنة في تجويد الهضم وإصلاح أمر الروح الحيواني وتنظيف الأوساخ اللاحجة .

وأعلم أيضا أن الاعتدال في كل شيء لا يؤثّر أصلا (٣٨٨) ضررا في أمر من الأمور. فإن لم تقدر على ما يجب فاقصد قصد الاعتدال على كلّ حال ،وأصلح الهواء والماء والغذاء بحسب ما يليق بمزاج كل إنسان وعادته ،ويوافق استطاعته . ولا تغفل عن شيءمن ذلك /٣٩أ/ (٣٨٩) .

(٢٧)

الفصل الثاني عشر

فيما يُصْلِح رداءة الهواء والماء والغذاء بأرض مصر

أوّل شئ يحتاج في هذا هو أن تكون المساكن والمجالس فَسيحة ليَنحلّ منها من البخار مِقدارًا وافر، ويكون لها مَخاريقُ ينحلّ منها البخارُ ويدخُل منها شعاعُ الشمس. وينبغي أن تكون هذه المساكن والمجالس مُرخّمَة أو مُبلّطَة أو معمولة بالجصّ والجبْس (٣٩٠) ويُتعاهَد تنظيفُها، وتُفْرَش في الأوقات الحارة بالحُصُر الباردِة والفُرُش الباردة مثل السامان (٣٩١) والطبريّ والعباداني. وفي الأوقات الباردة بالبُسُط الحُمْرانيّة (٣٩٢) والميسانِي والطنافِس واللّبُود وأنواع الديباج والصوف. فمَن لا يُمْكنه ذلك (٣٩٣)، فالحُصُر الخبّ وفِراء الكِباش. وصِفْ لكل إنسان على قدْر استطاعته حتى تصِف لبعضهم الرمْل والحَشائشَ المُباحة الباردة، بدلاً من الرخام والفرش الباردة، ولبعضهم الحشائشَ الحارة المُباحة، بدلاً من الفرش الحارة. وقَدِّر لكل إنسان ما يحتاج إليه بحسب استطاعته/٣٩ب/ومزاجه وعادته. وإذا كان الهواء حارا أمرتَ برش المياه الباردة والفوّارات وصَبّ المياه في البِرك والأسقان والقصارى والاجّانات الفِضّة والصيني والرصاص والخزف والفخّار وخاصة ما عُمِل منه في شهر طُوبَة، وكثرةِ المَراوح والجلوس في بيوت الخَيْش، وتكون المجالس شمالية، وافرِشْها بالرياحين الباردة كالبنفسج والورد والنيلوفر والريْحان الرقيق الصعتريّ واللفّاح (٣٩٤) وما شاكَل ذلك. واجعل الطيب: الكافورَ وماء الورد والصندل. والأدْهان (٣٩٥): دُهْن الورد ودُهْن البنفسج ودهن النيلوفر. فإن لم تُمْكِن هذه فافرشْ المجلس بوَرَق الآسِ وأغصان الكرْم ورقه والخِلاف وجميع أنواع الصفصاف وحَيّ العالَم والعرْمَض والطحلب وعِنَب الثعلب. فإذا لم يُوجد شئ من هذا رطباً، أخذت يابسَه وتَنْضَح عليه الماءَ في كل قليل (٣٩٦). واجعل الأغذيةَ لحمَ الجَدْي والحُمْلان والقَطَف والاسْفاناخ والرجلة والهِنْدِباء والخَسّ والريباس والسمّاق (٣٩٧) والخَشْخاش الأبيض (٣٩٨) والخِيار والقَرَع /٤٠أ/ والبِطّيخ والفقّوس والقِثّا، وما عُمِل من الشعير كالكشك والسويق. واجعل اللباس خليعَ الدبيقيّ والغلائل وسائر الثياب الخفيفة الخلِيعَة النظيفة، وضَمّخْها بالكافورَ والصندل وماء الورد. واسق الألبان الحامضة والحِصْرِم (٣٩٩). واطبخ الحُماضِيات والمخللات مثل المَصْل وماء الحصرم وماء الليْمون الحامِض وماء التمْرهِنْدي والألبان الحامِضة. والغاسُول (٤٠٠): دقيق الشعير ودقيق الباقلاّء والورد المَطْحون والصندل المطحون. واجعل الفاكهة: التفاح والسفرجل والإجّاص والرمان والخوْخ والنبق. والحَلْوَى: ما عُمِل بالكافور وماء الورد والسكر والجُلّاب والنشا. والأدوية: السكنجبين وحِساء الشعير ونقوع الفاكهة وماء الإجّاص وسائر الأشياء المُبَرِّدَة. وللشراب: الخمر الأبيض الصافي والعَفِص القريب العهد (٤٠١). وبالجملة اجعلْ الأشياء كلها إلى البرد أمْيل. فإن كان الهواء باردا، جعلت في المجالس كوانين النار وفرشتها بالأغصان والأوراق والأزهار الحارّة (٤٠٢) مثل النرْجس والخيريّ والريْحان والنمّام/٤٠ب/والأترجّ وورق البابُونَج (٤٠٣) والمَرْزَنْجُوش وقضْبان البَلَسان وورقه، والسوْسَن والياسمين والنسرِين وأغصانه وورقه وورق شجرة إبراهيم والإفرَنْجمُشْك (٤٠٤) والشيح والقَيْصوم والأقحُوان والبابُونَج والفوذَنْج. وبخّرْ بالندّ والعَنْبر والعُود (٤٠٥) والأفاوِيه المعمولة من الهال والأفلَنْجَة والفاغِرة والقُسْط والسكّ (٤٠٦) والكندرَ والمَصْطَكاء وقشار الكندر والمَيْعَة. والطيب: المسْك والعنبر والغالِيَة والزعْفران واللخالِخ الحارة والعود وماء القرنفل وماء

(٢٨)

زَهْر البابُونَج (٤٠٧) . والأَدْهان : دُهن المَحْلَب ودهن البان (٤٠٨) ودهن النرجس (٤٠٩) ودهن الحَلّ ودهن النارْدِين ودهن القُسْط ودهن المُصْطَكِي ودهن الفجْل ودهن الخِرْوَع . واللباس : الحرير والقطن والصوف . والأغذية : لحوم الضأن والعصافير والحِمِّص السلْق والهَلْيُون الجزَر واللفْت والنعناع والرازيانج والكرفس والثوْم والبصَل والكُرّاث والسذاب والخردل والزنْجَبيل /٤١أ/ والراسَن. ويُلقى في الأطعمة الفلفل والدار فلفل والدار صِيني والقِرْفة والخُولَنْجان والكروياء والأنيسون . والغاسُول : الإذخر والسعْد والحندقوق والأشْنان الذي يُباع بمصر ودقيق الحمّص ودقيق الترمس . والفاكهة : التين (٤١٠) والزبيب والعسل والسكر والجوْز وللوْز والبُنْدق والفُسْتق وسائر الحلاوات (٤١١). والأدوية : الجَلَنْجِبين والجوارشات وسائر ما يسخّن الأعضاءَ. والشراب : الشمسْ (٤١٢) والخمر العتيق. وقدّرْ لكل إنسان ما يُمْكنه حتى تصف لبعضهم وَسَخ الكِباش الموجود في أفخاذها، وهو الزوفاء الرطب . وإن كان الهواء يابسا رطّبتَه بتواتُر (٤١٣) صبّ المياه ورشّها، واتّخذتَ من الأشياء المُجَفّفة مثل الدخن التي من العُود والندّ والعنبر والكندر وقشورة والمَيْعَة والسندروس . وإن كان الهواء ساكنا حرّكتَه بالمراوح ، وإن كان متحركا سكّنتَه بالستور وغَلْق الأبواب . وإن كان الهواء عَفِنا جفّفتَه وقبضته بوقيد الطرفاء والاثل والكرم والبلوط والسدرو السنط وقشور /٤١ب/ اللبان. فعلى هذا جَرَى إصلاح الهواء (٤١٤) وأما الماء فينبغي أن يُسْقى ماءُ النيل من المواضع التي فيها جَرْيه أشدّ، والعفونة فيها أقلّ، مثاله بالفسطاط من محاذاة الموضع المعروف بالكُوم الأحْمر مما يلي الجيزة . ويُصفّى كل إنسان هذا الماءَ بقدر ما يُوافق مزاجه (٤١٥) . أما المَحْرُورون (٤١٦) ففي أيام الصيف بالطباشير والطين الأرمني والمغرة والنبق المَرْضوض والزعرور المرضوض والخلّ. وأمّا المبرّدون (٤١٧) ففي أيام الشتاء باللوز المرود اخل نوى المشمش والصعتر والشبّت . وينبغي (٤١٨) ان يقطف ما يُرَوّق ويُشْرَب ، وأن (٤١٩) تُصَفّيه بأن تجعله في آنية الخزف أو الفخّار أو في الجلود، وتأخذ ما يَحصُل منه بالرشْح . وإن شئتَ أسْخَنْتَه (٤٢٠) بالنار وجعلتَه في هواء الليل حتى يَرُوق ثم قطفت منه ما راق. وإذا ظهرتْ لك فيه كَيْفية (٤٢١) رديئة محسوسة فاطبُخْه بالنار ثم بَرِّدْه تحت السماء في برودة الليل وصَفِّه بأحد الأدوية (٤٢٢) التي ذكرتُها . /٤٢أ/ وأجوَدُ ما اتُّخِذ هذا الماء أن يصفّى مرارا وذلك بأن تسخنه أو تَطبُخه ثم تُبرّده في هواءَ الليل، وتطبخ ما يُرُوق منه وتُصفّيه أيضا ببعض الأدوية ، ثم تأخذ ما يروق فتجعله في آنية تَمَصّل في برد الليلَ، فتأخذ الرشحَ فتشربه . واجعل آنيةَ هذا الماء في الصيف الخزف والفخّار المعمولين في طُوبَة (٤٢٣) ، والظروف الحجازيّة (٤٢٤) والقِرَب الحجازية وغيرهذا ممّا يُبرِّده . وأما في الشتاء فالآنية الزجاجُ المدهون وما يُعْمَل في الصيف من الفخّار والخزف . وتكون مواضعه في الصيف تحت الأسْراب وفي مخاريق ريح الشمال. وفي الشتاء الواضع الحارّة (٤٢٥) . وتُبرِّده (٤٢٦) في الصيف بأن تَخْلِط معه ماءَ الورد، أو تأخذ نظيفةً (٤٢٧) وتشدّ فيها طباشيرَ أو بزر رجلة أو خشخاش أبيض أو طين أرْمني أو مغرة ، وتُلْقَى فيه كيما يَأخُذ من بردها ولا يُخالِطه جِسْمُها. وتُغْسَل أوعيتُه في الصيف بالخزف المدقوق وبدقيق الشعير والباقلاء والصندل (٤٢٨) وتُبَخَّر بالكافور /٤٢ب/ والصندل . وفي الشتاء تُغْسَل بالأشنان (٤٢٩) والسعْد ، وتُبَخّر بالمصطكى والعود. وأمّا مياه الأبار فينبغي أن تُسخّن (٤٣٠) ثم تُبرّد في الليل وتشرب . وأردأ ما يكون النيل بمصر عند فَيْضِه وعند وقوف حركته ، فعند ذلك ينبغي أن يُطبَخ ويُبالَغ في تَصْفِيته بقلوب نوى المشمش وسائر ما يَقطع لُزوجتَه . وأجود ما يكون في طُوبَة (٤٣١) عند تكامُل البرد. ومن أجل هذا عرف المصريون بالتجربة أن ماء طوبة أجودُ المياه ، حتى صار كثير منهم يَخْزُنه في القِربات (٤٣٢) الزجاج والصيني ويشربه السنةَ كلّها ويزُعم أنه لا يتغيّر ، وصاروا أيضا لا يُصَفّونه في هذا الزمان لظنّهم أنه على غاية الخلاص . فأمّا أنتَ فلا تَسكُن لذلك (٤٣٣) ، وصفّه على أيّة حالة كان ، فإن الماء المخزون لا بدّ أن يتغيّر .

فأما الأغذية فأكثر (٤٣٤) منها ما كان حديثا قريبَ العهد صَلْبا مُلَزّزا . فإن صلابتها وتلزّزها بمصر هو بمنزلة رخاوتها وسخافتها بغيْر /٤٣أ/ أرض مصر.

واجعل أفضلَها لمِن مزاجه أفضل ،وله قدرة على إيجاد (٤٣٥) الأجود كالخبز المحكم الصنعة ،َأعني الذي ذُلِك في عجينة دَلْك بالغا ،وقُدِّر (٤٣٦) مِلْحه وخميره ،وخُبِز في تنّور بنار ليّنة ،وقد نفذت في جميع أجزاءه بالسواء ، والحنطة التى عُمِل منها مختارة ،ودقيقه قريب العهد بالطحْن . ثم (٤٣٧) يُؤكل عندما يَبْرُد قليلا ،وبعد ثُلثيْ يوم مِن طبْخه فما دُون ذلك . وذلك أنّ الخبْز بمصر إذا بات لم يَطِب . وأطعِمْهم خصَّ الديوك والفراريج والدرّاج والطيهوج (٤٣٨) والقنابروِمُحاح البَيْض . ونزّل (٤٣٩) الناس من هذه المنزلِة إلى ما دونَها على قَدْر استطاعة كل إنسان. واطرَحْ في الخبْز من الأبازير ما يُعِين على هَضْمه ويطيّب طعمَه . وحَذِّرْ الناس من التخم وسوء الاستمراء وأمّا اللحمُ فينبغي أن يكون من حيوانات فتيّة قد رعت حشائشَ مُوافقة وهي صحيحة الأبدان . قد جُعلت قبل الذبح في مواضع (٤٤٠) فَسيحة /٤٣ب/جَيّدة الهواء ،تَسْرَح فيها كيمَا تتحلّل الفضول المجتمعةُ في أبدَانها. وما كان من اللحم أقْرب عهدا بالذبح فهو أجودُ . واخترْ من السمك أقْربه عهدا بالصيْد ،وتجنّبْ ما أفْرَط كبره . ولمّا كان أكثر الناس يأخذون اللحمَ من السوق (٤٤١) وجب عليهم أن يختاروا أجودَه وأطْراه ثم يُصلِحونه عند الطبْخ والشيّ بما يُضِيفونه إليه من الأبازيز وغيرها. إن أرادوا إصلاح أبدانِهم وسلامةَ صحتها.

وسبيل (٤٤٢) ما يُفْعَل في هذا الفَنّ يكون مُوافقا لبدن الأكل واللوْن الذي يُتّخَذ منه . وسبيل الشراب أن يتّخذ من كروم عتيقة وزَبيب قريبِ العهد بالجمْع . جيّد العَسَل (٤٤٣).

وعلى هذا المثال ينبغي أن تُصْلِح جميعَ ما يُؤْكَل ويُشْرَب . والقول في ذلك يطول . وقد وضع كثير من الأطباء فيه كتبا مُفْرَدَة (٤٤٤) كالكتاب الذى عمله أبو بكر الرازي في دفع مضار الأغذية ،فيعرف هناك ما يحتاج اليه . /٤٤أ/ ولعلنا (٤٤٥) نضع في هذا المعنى كتابا نافعا إن وهب الله عزّوجلّ (٤٤٦) عمرا وفراغا.

(٣٠)

الفصل الثالث عشر

فيما يدفع به ضرر الأمراض الوافدة بمصر

ينبغي (٤٤٧) ههنا أن تَسمع ما وَصّى به أبقراط وجالينوس . أما أبقراط فقال: ينبغي أن تحفظ التدبير على حاله متى لم يكن هو نفسُه السببَ في المرض وأمرا أن يُنْقَص من مِقدار الأغذية والأشربة التي جَرَت بها العادةُ قليلا على تدريج ورفق وأن يُمالَ بعده (٤٤٨) مَيْلا يسيرا نحو مضادّة السبب المُمْرِض . واحذرْ (٤٤٩) أن تَبْلُغ من ذلك إلى إضعاف البدن . وأمر أن يُحْتال (٤٥٠) في تَغيير (٤٥١) السبب المُمْرِض ما أمْكَن حتى يكون ما يصل منه إلى البدن في غاية المضادّة لما كان عليه قبل أن يتغيّر . فأما جالينوس فقال: إنه ينبغي أن يُتْرَك التعبُ وتحذر العطش والتخم والاكثار من الشراب . وأنتَ إن كنتَ /٤٤ب/ ذاكرا لما قلناه أولاً ، فقد تقف بسهولة على الأسباب المحدثة بأرض مصر للمرض الوافد ، وتعرف (٤٥٢) ما يَدْفَع مضرّتها فإنّ الهواء إذا تغيَّر إلى الحرارة فينبغي أن تجلس (٤٥٣) في المجالس البعيدة عن وَهَج (٤٥٤) الشمس وبالضدّ (٤٥٥) . وبالجملة فإنه إذا خَرَج عن العادة إلى الحرّ أو البرد أو الرطوبة أو اليبوسة (٤٥٦) أو العفن ، فزوالُ (مَضرَّتِه (٤٥٧)) هو أن تلزم البيوتَ والمجالس التى قد فُرِشَت بما يُضادّ حاله بلك . وكذلك سبيل الماء إذا خَرج عن العادة أن لا تتعرّض له كثيراً (٤٥٨) . وإصلاحُ الماء إذا تعفّن أو خالطته عفونة كثيرة يكون بأن يُطبَخ ثم يُصَفّى بما يُضادّ بلك العفونة ، ثم يُغَطّى من الهواء العفن ، وتُبَخّر آنية (٤٥٩) بالمُصْطَكى ، ويُغسّل بالسعد والصندل ويُطرَح في الماء نفسه الطين الأرمني والطباشير إذا كان المزاج حارا ، وإن كان باردا لطّخت شِفاف الاتية بالقطران ، وأُلقيت فيه الثُوم فإنه نافع من شرب المياه الرديئة . وإن كان حدوث المرض الوافد عن /٤٥أ/ مآكل رديئةٍ فاحذر تلك المآكِل . وإن كان خوف عام فينبغي أن يشجِّع الناس بعضهم بعضا ، ويتواصون بترك الخوف والقنوط . وإذا حدث المرضُ الوافد عن أكثر من أمريْن من هذه (٤٦٠) ، جعلت التدبيرَ مركبّا بحسب ذلك .

ومن البيّين أنّ الهواء تتغيّر معه (٤٦١) الأشياء التي تحيط بها ، وأنّ الماء إذا تغيّر وكان كثيرا كماء النيل غيّر الهواء . وكذلك أنفاس الناس تُغَيِّر الهواءَ إذا كثر فيهم المرض . فمن أجل هذه الحال ينبغي أن تَصْرِف العنايةُ في كل مرض وافد إلى إصلاح الهواء . وقد قلنا إن الهواء إذا استحال الى الحرارة المُفْرِطة فإصلاحه يكون بصَبّ المياه الباردة وفرش المجالس بالورد والبنفسج والآس والخلاف وشرب السكنجبين السكّري والنيلوفر والخلاف والإجّاص وماء الورد وماء الرمان الحامض والحلو ونقوع التَمر هِنْدي والاجاص (٤٦٢) ، وشمّ الأدْهان الباردة كدهن الورد والنيلوفر والبنفسج وكذلك الكافور والصندل وماء الورد/٤٥ب/ واستعمال القَوابض مثل التفاح والسفرْجَل وقَقاع الأشجار والحشائش الباردة واستعمال الأضمدة المُتّخَذة بدهن البَنَفسج وماء الورد والصندل (٤٦٣) على الصدر . واجعل الأغذية سَويقَ الشعير بالسكّر وسائر المبرّدات والطبيخ بحَبّ الرمان الحامض وماء الحِصرم والخَلّ والسمّاق وماء التمرهندي (٤٦٤) وماء الليمون أو حمّاض الأترجّ ، وأمثال هذه (٤٦٥) .

(٣١)

ويُتجنّب في (٤٦٦) مثل هذه الحال ما كان من الأغذية وغيرها حارّ المزاج. ويتوقّى الجماع والصوم. ويتعرّض لريح الشمال . ويجلس في الأسراب . وإذا رأيتَ البدن ممتلئا استفرغْه بأدوية ليّنة الاسْهال كالتمر هندي والترنجبين والخيارشنبر . وإن احتاج إلى الفصد ،فافْصِدْ من ساعتك على المكان . وإن لم يتهيأ الفصدُ لصغر السنّ أو للشيخوخة ،فالحِجامَة . واجتهدْ في أن يكون جميع ما يُؤكل ويُشْرَب باردا مُقبِضا . واحذرِ الرياضةَ والحمّامَ في مثل هذه الحال . وإن كان الهواء قد أفرَط بَرْدُه وقدْتَ النيران/٤٦أ/ وفرشتَ المجالس بالريحان والنرجس والنارنج والمرزنجوش والخيريّ والياسمين والنمّام ،واستعملتَ المسك والعنبر والعود والزعفران والمصطكى والكندر والقسط وسائر الأفاويه الحارّة . وأكثِرِ الأدويةَ (٤٦٧) اللطيفةَ الجوهر الحارّة ليقاوم حرّها برد الهواء، ولطافة جوهرها ما يُحْدِثه الهواء من الكثافة (٤٦٨) . واستعمل الورد المربىّ والجوارشات والعسل ،والشراب ، والرياضة (٤٦٩) ،والتعرّق في الحمّام ،وسائر ما يفتح مسامّ البدن ويَنْقُض من برد الهواء . وإن كانت رطوبة الهواء قد أفرْطت فقد يَكفيكَ في هذه الحال استعمالُ النيران والأغذيةِ المنشّفة كالقلايا والمطجّن. واستعمل العنبرَ والمسك والنرجس والمرزنجوش . وإن كان الهواء قد أفرْط يُبْسُه ،فصبّ المياهِ المتواترة ،واستعمالُ الأشياءِ الرطبة . وإن كان الهواء قد تعفّن - وهذا النوع أكثر ما يُحْدِث (٤٧٠) المرضَ الوافد - فاقْصِدْ إلى تَجْفيف (٤٧١) البدن قليلا قليلا بُنْقصانَ الأغذية والأشربة والاستفراغ الليّن . /٤٦ب/ واجتهدْ في تجويد الهَضْم ،وامنَعْ من الحركة في الهواءِ ،وامُرْ بلزوم البيوت التي يوقد فيها الطرفاء والأثل والكرم (٤٧٢) قد فُرِشت بالآس والخِلاف والوَرد وأغصان الكرم (٤٧٣) وورقهِ . ورُشّ البيوتَ بالخلّ الممزوج بالماء. واجعْلِ الأغذيةَ إلى البرد والقبض أميل ،فإن هذه كلّها تضادّ العفن . وتَعاهَدْ التَرباق والمثرود يطوس ونحو ذلك . وشمّ القطران والبخور بالمصطكى والعود واللاذن والميعة والمرّ وللبان وقشُوره نافعُ في هذا الحال. كذلك لباس الجوهر (٤٧٤) كالياقوت والزمرّد والدرّ والذهب (٤٧٥) والفضّة والعَقيق المرتِفع وسائر الفصوص الثمينة . وبالجملة سائر الأشياء الجالِبة للسرور ،وأجْودُها ما كان معه برد وقبضٌ فإن البرد والقبض يُضادّان حالَة العَفَن ،لأنها إنما تكون عن الحرارة والرطوبة الفضليّة التى قد عفنت (٤٧٦) .

وقد حكى جالينوس أنه شاهد في وباء قوما كانوا يشربون في كل يوم من الطيّن الأرمني مع الخلّ الممزوج /٤٧أ/ بالماء ،فتخلّصوا بذلك من مَضرّة الوباء ، وأن الذين لم يتعالجوا (٤٧٧) به هلك (٤٧٨) جميعهم .

وذكر بعض الأوائل أنه أُخذ من الصبر جزءا ،ومن المُرّ والزَعفران من كل واحد مثله ،وسحق الكلّ ،وشَرب منه في كلّ يوم نصف مثقال ،مع أوقية شرَاب ممزوج ،انتفع به جيدا . قالَ : وليس أحد تناول (٤٧٩) من هذا الدواء في الوباء إلا وتخلّص من مضرّته . وينبغي أن يلقي (٤٨٠) في الماء المشروب في أوقات الوباء الطين الأرمَني والطباشير والمَغَرَة وتُغطّيه من الهواء العفن وتحذرَ كل الحَذرَ الجِماعَ والتَعبَ المفرطَينَ ،وكذلك الصوم والعطش (٤٨١) ،وسائر ما يولّد في الأبدان فضُولا رديئة كالفواكِه كلها وسائر الأطعمة العسرة الاستمراء فإن هذه الأشياء كلّها لا ينبغي أن يُكثَر منها في هذه الحال(٤٨٢) . وإن احتجت إلى الفصْد ،فافصد . وتَعاهَدْ تقويةَ الصدرِ وآلات الغذاء والأعضاء الرئيسية بضمّادات متّخذة من دَقيق الشعير والورد والصندل وماء الورد وماء السفرجل وماء التفاح . / ٤٧ب/ وأعطِ من الأدوية ما كان كذلك مبرّدا مُقبضا مانعا من عفَنَ الأخلاط وما كان منها أيضا باردا (٤٨٣) مدّرا للبول كالبُزور ،ومُليّنا للطبع كشراب الاجّاص وماء البقل فهو نافع في هذه الحال. واجتهد في حفظ المزاج ومُضادّة السبب الممرض بغاية (٤٨٤) ما تقدر عليه وأتمه إن شاء الله تعالى .

الفصل الرابع عشر

في نسخ أُدوية مركّبة ينتفع بها في ما تقدّم ذكره (٤٨٥)

قد يُحتاج في هذا الموضع أن يُختار من هذه الأدوية ومن غيرها الأوفق فالأوفق . فانظرْ كيف حالك فيها (٤٨٦).

نُسْخَة دواء يقوّى الكبد والمعدة (٤٨٧) على الهضْمِ ألَّفْتُه : يُؤْخَذ من ماء السفرجل الحامض والتفاح الحامض رطل ،ومن الخمرَ العفن مثلُه ،ومن الرمان الحامض والحلو أربعةُ أرطال ،ويُحْمَل على النار. ويُشَدّ في خرقةَ نظيفة زنجبيل ومصطكى وسنبل ومسك وزعفران شعر،مِن كل واحد نصف درهم ويُطبَخ حتى يصير في قوام الشراب (٤٨٨) .

نسخة شراب ذكر الساهر أنه يفعل مثل فعل الأوّل : /٤٨أ/يوْخذ من الورد العراقيّ جزء ،ويُنْقَع في أربعة أمثاله ماءٍ حارّ ثلاثة (٤٨٩) أيام ،ثم يُطْبَخ في مائه حتى يرجع الماءُ إلى النصف ،ويُصَفّى ،ويُلْقَى على الماء جزء مِن سُكرّ وجزء من عسل منزوع الرغوة ،ويُطْبَخ ثانية حتي يَثْخُن ،ويُوْخذ ريمه ،ويُرْفَع . نُسْخة شراب ذكر الساهر أنه أصلح به معدة عُبَيْد الله بن طاهِر : يوْخذ من ماء السفرجل ومن ماء التفاح ومن ماء الورد ،من كل واحد جزء ،ومن السكر ومن العسل ،ومن كلّ واحد نصف جزء ،ومن الخمر ستة أجزاء ،ويُطبَخ الجميع حتى يَنْعَقِد ،ويُرْفع (٤٩٠).

نسخة شراب ألّفْتُه (٤٩١) يَحْفَظ الأبدان (٤٩٢) في أيام الوباء: يُوْخذ ماء ورد وماء سفرجل حامض وماء تُفّاح حامض (٤٩٣) وماء حُمّاض الاترّج وماء الرمان الحلو(٤٩٤) وماء الرمان الحامض،من كلّ واحد جزء ،وشراب أبيض أو ريحان (٤٩٥) عصير لم يعتّق جدا مثلُ الجميع ،ويُطبَخ الجميعُ حتى يَصير له قوام الأشربة (٤٩٦) ،ويُتَناوَل بالجلّاب فإنه نافع .

صِفة سكنجبين ألّفْتُه (نافِع) (٤٩٧) في هذه الحال ،وهو يَفتَح السدد(٤٩٨) ويُدِرّ البول: يوْخذ بزر هندباء وبزر كشوت أبيض ،وبزر رازيانج وبزر كرفس ،من كل واحد/٤٨ب/سبعة دراهم ،يُنْقَع في أربعة أرطال من خلّ خمر(٤٩٩) أربعة أيام ثم يُوْخذ جزء من ماء السفرجل العفن ،وجزء من ماء الحصرم ،ويُغْلَي مع عشرة أرطال ماء ،ومثلها سُكّر،حتى إذا صار في قوام الجلّاب ألقِي عليه الخلّ ،وعقد حتى يَسْتَوِي .

نسخة شراب ألّفه ابن ماسويْه (٥٠٠) نافع من الحميّات الحادّة الوبائية ويَفْتَح السدد(٥٠١) ،وهو عجيب الفعل : يوْخذ من خلّ الخمر خمسة أرطال،ومن قشر الكرفس والرازياج ،ومن كل واحد أُوقيتان ،وأسارون وفقّاع الاذخر وبزر الكرفس (٥٠٢) من كل واحد أوقية ،أنيسون وسنبل من كل واحد نصف أوقية ،يُجْمَع ذلك ويُنْقَع في الخلّ يوما وليلة ،ثم يُطْبَخ حتى يَرْجِع إلى النصف ،ثم يوْخذ من ماء الرمان الحامض وماء السفرجل والمطبوخ ويُخْلَط الجميعُ مع مثله عسل السكر،ويُطْبَخ الجميعُ ثانية حتى يعتدل ،ويُصَفّى ويُرْفَع . الشربةُ (٥٠٣) أُوقية بالماء البارد . نُسْخةُ شراب الإجّاص ،ذَكَرَ الرازي أنه يَنْفَع من القولنج ومن وجع المفاصل ،وأنه يُلَيِّن الطبع : يوْخذ من الإجّاص (٥٠٤)/٤٩أ/ السمين (٥٠٥) العلك ،فيُلْقَي في برمة غير دسمة ،ويُصَبّ (٥٠٦) عليه غمره

من الماء (٥٠٧) بأربع أصابع مضمومة ،ويُغْلَي على نار لَيِّنة رقيقة ، ويُحْفَظ مقدارُ الماء والنارُ عليه (٥٠٨) ويُزاد الماء متى نقص بماء مَغْلِيّ (٥٠٩) حتى يَتَهرّأ الإجّاص ،ثم يُصَفّى بعد أن يُمْرَس ويُعْصَر (٥١٠)ويترك ليلة حتى يرسب فيه مايرسب (٥١١) ،ويُصَفّى التفل الراسب (٥١٢) ويُطْرَح عليه مع الماء وزن الجميع من السكر الطبرزد،ويُطْبَخ وتُوخذ رغوته حتى يدور ،ويُحْمَل (٥١٣) في زجاجة إذا برد ويكون قوامه مثل الجلّاب • فإن أريد تَلْيين البطن شُرِب منه رطل بمثله ماء قليلا قليلا ،كما يَشْرَب أصحابُ النبيذ ،ويُشرب في الصيف بالغدوات فيُطْفِئ الحرارة ويُبَرِد ويَقْطَع العطش ويُليّن البطن ويُحَدِّر الصفراء•

نسخة شراب التين ،ذَكَر الرازي أنه يُسْتَعمل في الشتاء يُلَيّن البطن ويُسَمّن الكلى ويُخْصِب الجسم ويَنْفَع صاحب البواسير إلا من خطر (٥١٤) عظيم : يُوخذ من التين الأصفر العلك الكثير العسل ،فيُعْمَل على صِفَة الإجّاص،ويُلْقَى ماؤه المصفّى على مثله فانيد سكريّ(٥١٥) / ٤٩ب/وأنا أقول : إذا لم يوجد هذا الفانيد فينبغي أن يوءخذ عوضه من السكر السليمانيّ• قال الرازي : وإن احْتِيج فيه إلى فضل إسْخان فاجعلْ في كل رطل من الشراب درهما (٥١٦) من الدارصيني ودرهما من خولنجان ودرهما من الفلفل ودرهما زنجبيل • اسْحَق الكلّ(٥١٧) ،وصيِّره في خِرْقَة (٥١٨)تُلْقى فيه عند الطبخ وتُماث فيه إماثَة جيّدة ، فإنه حينئذ يفعل تلك الأفاعيل ،ويَهضِم الطعامَ ويَصْلُح أن يستعمله مَن لا يشرب النبيذ ،والشيوخُ ،ومَن يحتاج إلى تَسْخِين (٥١٩) معدته وبدنه •

صِفةُ شراب ألّفَه ابن الجزّار ،و ذكر أنه عجيب الفعل في زمن الوباء والورشكين والجدري والحصبة ،قال : ما علمتُ أحدا (٥٢٠) من الناس استعمله إلا ودفع عنه فسادَ الهواء والأمراض الحادّة : يوخذ من ماء الرمان الحامض رطل ،ومن ماء السفرجل وماء التفاح الحامض وماء الحصرم وماء الهندباء المنزوع الرغوة من كل أحد رطل ونصف رطل ،وماءُ ورد،وتُجْعَل جميعُ ذلك في قدر بِرام (٥٢١) مع ثلاثة أرطال سكر طبرزد ،ويُطْبَخ بنار ليّنة حتى يصير له/٥٠أ/قوام ويفتق(٥٢٢) فيه من الكافور دانق ،ويُرْفَع ويُسْتَعمل (٥٢٣) • نسخة شراب ألّفَه ابن الجزّار ،وذكر أنه جرّبه فوجده نافعا في إدْرار البول وتَنْقِيَة العروق وتَفْتيح السدد ودَفْع مضارّ الهواء عن آلات التنفس ،وأنّ له منافع كثيرة : يوخذ من لحاء أصل الرازيانج ،ولحاء أصل الكرفس ،من كل أحدعشرون درهما ،وأصْل السوس المجرود الأعلى ،وفقّاح الاذخر ،وزهر الورد الأحمر ،وكشوت أبيض ،من كلّ أحد عشرة دراهم ،وبزر هندباء و رازيانج وكزبرة بير (٥٢٤) ،من كلّ أحد أربعة دراهم ، أميرُ باريس وطباشيرُ وصندل أبيض ومصطكى ،من كل أحد درهم•

تُجْمَع هذه الأدوية (٥٢٥) وتُنْقَع في اثنىْ عشر رطلا ماء عذبا مغليّا ليلةً واحدة ،ثم تُطْبَخ بنار ليّنة حتى تبقى أربعة أرطال،ويُمْرَس ويُصَفّى ،ثم يُمْرَس في صَفْوِه أربعون درهم تَرَنْجُبين مرسا جيدا،ويُصَفّى ثانية ،ويُعاد إلى القدر ،ويُلْقَي عليه في أيام الحرّ رطل مَن ماء الرمان الحامض أو ماء التفاح الحامض أو ماءحمّاض الأترجّ •
فإن تعذّر ذلك فرطل من خلّ خمر ثَقِيف(٥٢٦) ،وأربعة أرطال /٥٠ب/من السكر الطبرزد يُعْقَد بنار ليّنة حتى يصير في قوام الجلّاب ويُبَرّد ويُشْرَب ،فإنّ فيه استدامة الصحّة ويُفَتح السدد،ويَمْنَع أسباب الوباء •

نسخة جوارش يُقوّي المعدة ويُشَهّي الطعام ويُمْرِيْ،ذكره الساهر :يوخذ تفّاح شاميّ منقّى رطلين ،ويُنْقَع في مثله من الشراب العفص يومين ،ويُغْلَي حتى يَنضج ،ثم يُدَقّ (٥٢٧) ويُلْقَى عليه زنجبيل وقاقلّة وقرفة ونارمشك ،من كلّ أحد مثقال دارصيني

وعود ،من كلّ أحد (٥٢٨) نصف مثقال ،زعفران درهم مسك دانق.

نسخة جوارش (٥٢٩) يُقوّي المعدة : يُؤخذ سفرجل وتُفّاح شاميّ مقشّرين ، يُغليان بشراب حتى يَنْضَجا ،ثم يُجْعَل معهما عسلٌ منزوع الرغوة قدر الحاجة ،ويُطبَخ الجميع بنار ليّنة حتى يَنْعَقِد ، ويُنْزَل عن النار ،ويُلْقَى فيه زنجبيل مسحوق ،ودار فلفل مصطكى وزعفران . الشربة مثقال .

نسخةُ سفرجل مربّى يُقَوّي المعدة والكبد والقلب ألّفتُه . يؤخذ السفرجل فيُقْشَر / ٥١ أ/ويُشقّق ويُنْقَع في شراب عفص مع قليل من لسان الثور أربعة أيام ،ثم يؤخذ الشراب ويُصَبّ عليه عسل منزوع الرغوة قدر الحاجة (٥٣٠) ويُغْلَى بنار ليّنة حتى ينعقد ،ثم يُطْرَح فيه السفرجل ، ويُطَيَّب بمسك (٥٣١).

نسخةُ قيرُوطِي (٥٣٢) يَنقع من شدّة الحرّ ومن لهيب القلب والمعدة وسائر الأحشاء: يوخذ شمع أبيض مصفّى ،ويُذوّب بدهن ورد ثم يُربّب في الهاون بماء القرع وماء الحيّ عالم وماء البقلة وماء الخسّ وماء الخيار أو ماء عنب الثعلب ،أيّ شئ اتّفق منهما ،مع شئ مِن كافور وصندل أبيض وماء ورد ،ويُستَعْمل (٥٣٣) .

(٣٥)

الفصل الخامس عشر

في أنه ينبغي أن تختار السكنى بمصر، وإن كانت تفعل في الأبدان رداءة

أما (٥٣٤) أرض مصر فينبغي أن تُؤْثَر (٥٣٥) السكنى بها لأمر (٥٣٦) يُتَبَيَّن على هذا النحو: قد قلنا إن الأمراض التي تعرض للأبدان بمصر يمكن زوالها / ٥١ب/ وظاهر أيضا أنّ أخلاق النفس يُمكن مداواتها، كما قيل في كتب الأخلاق . على أنّ شرور نفس المصريين سريعة القبول للعلاج لأنّ شرورهم ضعيفة دنيّة غير مستصعبة . فما يُكْرَه إذن من أجله السكنى بمصر سهل الزوال (٥٣٧)، وأيضا فلأنّ مصر كثيرة العمارة والناس . والمواضع التي هذا حالها هي أكثر (٥٣٨) تمدّنا . والانسانُ بالطبع مدنيّ، فسُكْناه إذن في المواضع التي تُلائِمُه (٥٣٩) أوْفق وأفضلُ (٥٤٠)، لكثرة ما يَجِد فيها من الأشياء التي يَضْطرّ إليها في قِوام حياتِه . وأيضا (٥٤١) فأرَض قليلة الفتن والحرب لسكون أنفس أهلها إلى مَن يَسُوسهم وضعفهم عن الجهاد (٥٤٢) فالسكنى إذن بمصر ينبغي أن تُؤْثَر . (٥٤٣) وإن كانت أسعارُها مرتفعة، فالمكاسبُ فيها كثيرة .

تمّ الكتاب والحمد لله كثيرا /٥٢أ

قال(٥٤٤) عليّ بن رضوان : بعد أن أتممتُ هذا الكتاب سمِعه منّي بعضُ أهل البلدان البعيدة ،فأخذ يطبق على مصر وأهلها (٥٤٥) ،وظنّ أني ذمَمْتُهم حيث وصفت أخلاقهم . فقلتُ : ليس الأمر على ما ظننتَ ،وذلك أن شرور المصريين دنيّة خمسة ،فعلاجُها سهل وعاقبةُ أمرِها على الأكثر محمودة .

وليس يُوقِع أهلَها في المهالك العظام . وأما شرور أنفس غير المصريين فرديئة خبيثة غير مأمونة العواقب ،وذلك يُوقِع أهلَها في المهالك العظام والحروب الطويلة والبلاء والقتل . وعِلاجُها صعْب عَسِر ،وإن كان الغالب على الناس الشرور ما خلا الشاذّ منهم . فالشرور الدنيّةُ التي تَقْبَل العلاج بسرعة وسهولة أحْمَدُ وأفضل من الشرور الخبيثة التي يَعْسُر علاجُها ،ولا سيما وعاقِبتُها آمَن (٥٤٦) .

فأهل مصر إذن أفضلُ أخلاقا وأجودُ طريقة* . ورسَمْتُ ذلك ههنا ليُلْحَق بما تَقدّم إن شاء الله تعالى .

الاختصارات والرموز للنسخ

الأصل : نسخة دار الكتب

دك : دار الكتب

رد : Roy Dobbin

دط : دار الكتب (طب)

مع : المتحف العراقي

شب : Chester Beatty

ف : الفاتيكان

ملاحظات

(١) زاد في دك بعد البسلمة : " وصلّى الله على سيّدنا محمّد، أمّا بعد ،فهذا" . وزاد في شب : " ربّ يسّر وأعن " . وجاء في رد . " حمدا لمن رفع السموات ،وبسط الأرضين . وصلاة وسلاما دائمين على أشرف المرسلين وعلى آله وصحبه أجمعين . وبعد ،فهذا مختصر لطيف ،جمعت فيه ما لخصه علي بن رضوان في دفع مضارّ الأبدان بأرض مصر . وزدت عليه فوائد نافعة وفوائد جامعة . ويجب أن أقدم أسباب هذه المضارّ وما هي " .

(٢) في مع : قال الشيخ .... رحمه الله تعالى ،آمين . ثم زاد قبل هذا الكلام ما يلي : " الحمد لله .الذي شهد بوجوده جميع الكائنات ،والصلاة والسلام على سيّدنا محمّد المبعوث بالأيات الواضحات ،وعلى آله وصحبه التابعين له في المكرمات " . وفي دط :" الحمد لله ربّ العالمين ،صلّى الله على سيّدنا محمّد وعلى آله وصحبه . قال العبد الفقير، المعترف بالذنب والتقصير ،بعد حمد الله القويّ القدير ،والصلاة والسلام على نبيّه البشير النذير،وعلى آله وصحبه ذوى المقام الأثيل الأشيع ".

(٣) ليس في دك .

(٤) زاد في دك : " إن شاء الله تعالي" .

(٥) في رد : وكرمه .

(٦) في مع : " الحكيم " ،مكان قوله "أحمد" . وقوله : " المغربي " ،ليس في دك . وقوله " الطبيب المغربي " ،ليس في شب ،دط،رد .

(٧) قوله : " ذلك مقالة مفردة " ،سقط من مع .

(٨) قوله : " قبل "،سقط من مع .

(٩) زاد في سائر النسخ : " فذكر ما سمع به فقط بحسب ما تضمنه كلامه" .

(١٠) سقط من دك .

(١١) في الأصل : وتأملها ،خطأظاهر ،والصواب في باقي النسخ .

(١٢) ليس في رد .

(١٣) زاد في دك : " وما يليها" ،بعد قوله : " مصر" .

(١٤) هنا ينتهي الخرم الموجود في ف .

(١٥) قوله : " بأرض مصر" ،لم يرد في شب ،دط ،رد .

(١٦) في الأصل : ينبغ ،خطأظاهر ،والصواب في سائر النسخ.

(١٧) زاد في شب ،دط : " تمت فصول هذا الكتاب ".

(١٨) زاد بعده في ف : " فيما " .

(١٩) في ف : أولاد بنى نوح النبي . وفي مع،رد : نوح النبي عليه الصلاة والسلام . وفي شب : نوح النبي .

(٢٠) في الأصل : فانل ،خطأظاهر ،والصواب في باقي النسخ .

(٢١) في دك : الظل ،خطأواضح ،والصواب في باقي النسخ .

(٢٢) سقط من ف .

(٢٣) قوله :"والحد الغربي هو أن الشمس" ،سقط من مع ،دط ،رد .

(٢٤) في رد : العامر .

(٢٥) قوله : "والنصف الشرقي في قسم كوكب الشمس" ،سقط من ف .

(٢٦) في الأصل : يصل ،خطأواضح ،والصواب في سائر النسخ .

(٢٧) قوله :"وقد زعم قوم من القدماء " ،سقط من ف ،وكان في الأصل يوم من القدماء

(٢٨) الزيادة من سائر النسخ .

(٢٩) قوله :"أعني أسوان " ، لم يرد في باقي النسخ .

(٣٠) قوله :"وهو الشمالي " ،لم يرد في ف .

(٣١) في مع : وجهة طرف . ...

(٣٢) سقط من ف : .

(٣٣) زاد قيلة ف : " وأيضا" .

(٣٤) كان في الأصل : واحدا فهم شهلة . والتصويب من باقي النسخ .

(٣٥) سقط من دك .

(٣٦) قوله :"وإذ قد حددناها وذكرنا مزاجها ،فلنأخذ في صفتها" ،لم يرد في رد ،وجاء مكانه : " ثم نقول ".

(٣٧) في دك ،دط : بجبل المقطم . وفي رد ،شب : بجبل ألوقا في الصورة ، ولم نجد هذا الاسم فيما بين يدينا من مصادر.

(٣٨) قوله : " مالحان" ،ليس في رد . وفي دط : ما كان ،تحريف .

(٣٩) قوله :"ولا يرتقي ..... العذب " ،ليس في رد ،شب .

(٤٠) في رد: وتجفف ،خطأ. وفي شب : وتجففان ،ورواية سائر النسخ أفضل .

(٤١) في رد : وجبل ألوقا في شرقي .

(٤٢) قوله :"نكباء بين " ،سقط من رد.

(٤٣) قوله : " حارة .... الحيوان " ،لم يرد في رد ،شب ،دط . وجاء مكانه: " يابسة مانعة من التعفن " .

(٤٤) في شب ،دط : بيبس ،تحريف .

(٤٥) قوله : " دمياط " لم يرد في شب ،دط .

(٤٦) في شب ،دط : ليت ،وكتب بجانبها : " كذا " ، أي لم يستطع الناسخ أن يقرأها .

(٤٧) في شب ،دط : ركوب الهواء ،وهي رواية جيدة .

(٤٨) أصل التخلخل : عدم التضام والتماسك .

(٤٩) أصل السخافة : الرقة في كل شيء ،كرقة الثوب والسحاب ،وتكاد لا تستعمل إلا في العقل خاصة ،ومنه أرض مسخفة : أي قليلة الكلأ.

(٥٠) في رد ،شب،دط : يسيح ،وكتب أمامها " كذا" أي أن الناسخ لم يستطع قراءتها . وسبخت الأرض : صارت مالحة .

(٥١) في رد : استمالة ،خطأ.

(٥٢) لم يرد في دك .

(٥٣) في شب ،دط ،ف : جيف الحيوان .

(٥٤) في رد ،شب ،ف : وباض فيه السمك الذي تربي فيه مياه النقائع .

(٥٥) في مع : ومن أجل ذلك .

(٥٦) في سائر النسخ : رطوبة لزجة ،لها سهوكة . والسهوكة : الرائحة القبيحة

(٥٧) من بعد قوله " عفونة" مطموس في دط ،حتى قوله " طبيعة الماء، فإذا النضاف إلى ما قلنا ...."

(٥٨) جاء في رد في ختام هذا الفصل : الزنابير وغير ذلك بأرض مصر للحرارة والرطوبة الفضلية ،وأنها ذات أجزاء كثيرة ،وأن هواءها وماءها رديئان.

(٥٩) في رد : رطوبة · ورواية الأصل ،وسائر النسخ أصح ·

(٦٠) في رد : التعفن ·

(٦١) في رد : يحلل فيها الهواء فضولا ·

(٦٢) في رد : لا يثبت ·

(٦٣) من هنا حتى نهاية هذا الفصل سقط من دك ،ولم يبق منه إلا سطر واحد تقريبا في ختامه أوله " لقاءها لهذا الهواء ....." ·

(٦٤) في رد ،شب ،ف :حرّو أخرى برد " ،وبقية الكلمات بالرفع ·

(٦٥) ليس في رد ،وفيها : اختلافها ،والضمير يعود على أرض مصر ·

(٦٦) في رد ،شب : أصلية ،خطأ·

(٦٧) في رد،ف : " أيضا" ،قبل قوله :" السبب " ·

(٦٨) في رد ،شب ،ف : الظل ،خطأظاهر ·

(٦٩) في رد ،شب ،ف : يتراقى ،ولم نجد صيغة " تفاعل " من هذا الفعل ·

(٧٠) في رد : في ثبات ،ليست جيدة ·

(٧١) زاد في در بعده " الفضلية " ·

(٧٢) في رد : أعلمنا ·

(٧٣) في رد ،ف : أعنى ·

(٧٤) في رد : هونا تجفيف ،مكان قوله " هما بالحقيقة " ،تحريف شديد·

(٧٥) زاد في رد ،ف : " في الصيف والخريف " بعد قوله : " النيل "·

(٧٦) في رد ،دط : وكذلك ،خطأ·

(٧٧) في الأصل ،در : ما به عليه ،خطأ،والتصويب من باقي النسخ ·

(٧٨) في ف : الانقراض ،تحريف ·

(٧٩) في رد : وسيلة للزوال ،تحريف ·

(٨٠) من بعد قوله :" أبدانهم " مطموس في دط ،حتى قوله : " المدة اليسيرة "·

(٨١) في رد ،شب : الأسباب ·

(٨٢) في شب ،ف : لقائها·

(٨٣) في رد ،شب ،ف : كالضرب والردم .

(٨٤) في دك ،ف : كما وصفنا .

(٨٥) قوله : " الأن "،لم يرد في شب .

(٨٦) كان في الأصل ،دك : بالنظيرة ،والتصويب من باقي النسخ .

(٨٧) في دط ،شب : بليلته .

(٨٨) في دك ،ف : الزمان .

(٨٩) في رد : فالظاهر .

(٩٠) ليس في رد .

(٩١) في رد : وأما ماء النيل فأكثر المصريين يشربون منه .

(٩٢) قوله : " مياه الأمطار" ،ليس في رد ، شب .

(٩٣) في ف : وكونها .

(٩٤) زياده يستقيم بها السياق ،عن ف ،وزاد بعدها في ف ،دك : " أيضا ".

(٩٥) زاد بعده في كل النسخ ما عدا ف : صاروا .

(٩٦) ليس في رد ،مع ،دط ،شب ،ف .

(٩٧) في رد ،ف : يتغذّون .

(٩٨) في رد : ومِن أهل مصر مَن يكثر ...... ومنهم مَن يكثر مِن ....

(٩٩) في دط : نوعا ،خطأ .

(١٠٠) في ف : أكثر أكلهم .

(١٠١) في دط : نشست ،مع سقوط حرف الجر " عليها" ،تحريف .

(١٠٢) في دط : كذلك ،والأصل وباقي النسخ أصح .

(١٠٣) في رد ،شب : أبدانهم .

(١٠٤) في دط ،در ،شب : وتخلف ،خطأ.

(١٠٥) في دط : أسفل أرض مصر . في رد : أهل أسفل .

(١٠٦) في كل النسخ : حرارة أرضهم .

(١٠٧) في دط ، شب : سببا ،خطأ .

(١٠٨) وهذا المصدر ليس موجودا في المعاجم . وفي دك ،شب ،ف : الدعة .

(١٠٩) في دك ،دط ،شب ،مع ،ف : الشح .

(١١٠) في رد ،شب : العمل .

(١١١) في رد ،شب ،ف : الخوف .

(١١٢) في رد : الحقد .

(١١٣) في رد : والسعي في المفاسد .

(١١٤) قوله : " ذم الناس " ليس في رد .

(١١٥) قوله :"وهذه الشرور ليست عامة فيهم ولكنها " ،ليس في رد .

(١١٦) في سائر النسخ : خصّه .

(١١٧) في رد ،دك : برّأه .

(١١٨) في رد : لم يسكن بها الأسد ،وإذا دخلها ذل ولم يتناسل .

(١١٩) في مع ،دك ،ف : في طبعه ملائم لهذه .

(١٢٠) في رد : طبيعته ،وفي ف : طبيعته طبعه .

(١٢١) قوله : "ويناقض " إلى " رطب " ،لم يرد في رد .

(١٢٢)في رد ،دط : تتيسّر .

(١٢٣) زاد بعده في كل النسخ : " وصفائه " .

(١٢٤) مطموس في دط .

(١٢٥) قوله : " ولا يبس " ،ليس في دط ،رد .

(١٢٦) في دط : نسل .

(١٢٧) في رد : ولهذا السبب تنضج فيه الأبدان ويكثر النسل . وفي شب : ويقوى فيه الروح الحيواني لهذا السبب .

(١٢٨) في دط : طلبت .

(١٢٩) في رد ،شب ،ف : إلا أن يكون ذلك في برموده وبشنس فإنه يحتاج ...

(١٣٠) في رد ،مع : فتعدل .

(١٣١) في دط ،شب ،ف : وشبقه ،وفي رد : وسعيه .

(١٣٢) في ف : يقدر ،تجريف .

(١٣٣) في دط ،رد ،شب : سخنت : (بتشديد الخاء) ،وهما سواء

(١٣٤) في ف : لا لشيء .

(١٣٥) كان في الأصل : يرمي ،خطأظاهر .

(١٣٦) ليس في دط .

(١٣٧) زاد بعده في دك ،مع ،ف : رديئة .

(١٣٨) في رد،ف : يتراقى ،والمعروف في هذا الفعل تفعّل (كتعلّم)

(١٣٩) زيادة من باقي النسخ .

(١٤٠) في رد : من الأيام ما يشاكل .

(١٤١) في الأصل ،دك : أسخن ،خطأ،والتصويب من باقي النسخ .

(١٤٢) زاد في دط ،شب ،ف : " على الأرض " ،بعد قوله : فيطلق . وفي رد: ويفيض على الأراض .

(١٤٣) زاد بعده في دط ،ف : أرض .

(١٤٤) في ف : حرّ ... برد ... يابس (بالرفع) ،والصواب والنصب .

(١٤٥) في الأصل ،دك : ينمزج ،والتصويب من سائر النسخ .

(١٤٦) في رد،شب : ما في الأبدان من .

(١٤٧) في ف : الهضم،وهي رواية جيدة . وزاد بعدها في دط : " ووجود العفن".

(١٤٨) الزيادة عن سائر النسخ .

(١٤٩) الزيادة عن سائر النسخ .

(١٥٠) قوله : " والأبدان مضطربة " جملة حالية . وسياق الكلام : ثم يدخل فصل الشتاء والأبدان مضطربة .

(١٥١) كان في الأصل : وتحدث ،والصواب في باقي النسخ .

(١٥٢) في دط ،رد شب : ما يلقي فيها من البذور وأزبال ...

(١٥٣) ليس في دط ،رد، ف .

(١٥٤) تكرر بعد هذه العبارة الفصلُ الثاني كله في نسخة دك ،ما عدا الأسطر الخمسة الأولى .

(١٥٥) في رد : وتغطيته .

(١٥٦) قوله :" جميع ما فيها" ،سقط من دط ،رد .

(١٥٧) في رد ،مع : اضطر .

(١٥٨) في رد : اعلم أن ابن الجزّار ذكر ...

(١٥٩) يعني : الأبدان ،ولعل هذه الكلمة سقطت من الأصل ،فقد جاء قبلها في النسخ : ونعم ما قال ،لأن أبدانهم لم تألف هذا الهواء .

(١٦٠) في شب ،ف : يشاكل هواء .

(١٦١) في رد ،شب ،ف : هواء أرض مصر يترطب .

(١٦٢) في دك : حر ... برد ،بالرفع .

(١٦٣) في دك : وقيع ،والصواب : وقوع .

(١٦٤) في الأصل ،دك ،ف : ليس إنما يتغير ،وكتب الناسخ في" الأصل " : كذا ، أي لم يفهم السياق ،والكلام يستقيم بحذف كلمة " إنما " .

(١٦٥) زاد قبله في رد : ولكن .

(١٦٦) في رد ،شب ،ف:جمع .

(١٦٧) في الأصل : خليف ،وفي ف : حليق ،والصواب في سائر النسخ .

(١٦٨) في الأصل وكل النسخ : وإني لناقل ،فاستظهرنا الصولب .

(١٦٩) الزيادة من سائر النسخ .

(١٧٠) الزيادة من سائر النسخ ما عدا ف ،حيث يوجد خرم بمقدار صفحة يبدأ عقب قوله " أقلهم عددا ،فالأمراض".

(١٧١) في الأصل ،دك : والبلد ،والتصويب من سائر النسخ .

(١٧٢) ليس في باقي النيخ .

(١٧٣) في شب : قلتها أصح من كثرتها . وذلك لا يستقيم ،فالمطر مذكر .

(١٧٤) في دط : يؤذي ،والأصل وسائر النسخ أوفق .

(١٧٥) في دك : وضح . وفي رد : صرح أبقراط نفسه أنّ ....

(١٧٦) يعني قول أبقراط .

(١٧٧) في رد ،شب : لم يخرجان ،والصواب إسقاط النون ،كما في دك،ف .

(١٧٨) في ف : ونيل مصر .

(١٧٩) في رد : صدقا .

(١٨٠) في رد : مخالف لقول الأفاضل من الأطباء ،ويلزم عليه المحال .

(١٨١) في رد : محل .

(١٨٢) في رد ،دط ،شب : تضييع .

(١٨٣) في رد ،دط ،ف : ذكرت أنت . وفي دك : ذكرت فقط .

(١٨٤) زاد في دك :"بأرض مصر " ،بعد قوله : " عاداتها " ،ثم أسقط " خروجها عن عاداتها بأرض مصر" .

(١٨٥) كان في الأصل : أعدنا ،والتصويب من سائر النسخ .

(١٨٦) في رد ،شب : ودام مدة .

(١٧٨) في رد : ومن تأمل كتابه وقف على صحة هذا القول .

(١٨٨) في دط : تودد ،وكتب الناسخ أمامها " كذا" أي لم يستطع قراءتها.

(١٨٩) في مع : فإن قال قائل .

(١٩٠) قوله :"بأرض مصر " ،ليس في شب .

(١٩١) في الأصل : النحافة ،والصواب في ف ،مع . وهذه الكلمة لم تزد في دك .

(١٩٢) في رد : " فإن قيل : إذا كان الضباب يولّد في أبدان الناس الأمراض فحينئذ تكون الأبدان في مرض دائم . فالجواب : هذا ليس بصحيح " .

(١٩٣) جاء في دط ،شب : " الفصل السادس من هذا الكتاب يجب أن يزال منه بالواحدة ، لأني رأيت في عمرى تغيّرا كثيرا في هذه المدينة ".وهذا كلام الناسخ أوبمعنى أصح المختصِر.

(١٩٤) في رد ،ف : اقتصاص ،خطأواضح .

(١٩٥) قوله " القرافة ... والجزيرة " سقط من ف ،ومكانه : الجيزة .

(١٩٦) في رد : شرقيها .

(١٩٧) في رد : أردى ،أفعل من الرّدى.

(١٩٨) قوله : " أعظم " إلى قوله : " المقطم " ، سقط من رد .

(١٩٩) في شب: موضوع .

(٢٠٠) في الأصل ،وكل النسخ ما عدا مع : الشرق . والصواب ما في مع .

(٢٠١) في ف ،مع : عال .

(٢٠٢) قوله : أن المواضع المغلة أسخن " ،سقط من رد .

(٢٠٣) قوله : " فاهرب " إلى " البناء" ،سقط من دك .

(٢٠٤) في رد ،دط ،شب ،ف : خرّارات .

(٢٠٥) في رد : من ساعته.

(٢٠٦) قوله : " يعلو " إلى قوله " أغبر" ،لم يرد في رد . وجاء مكانه :" وكل ذلك خاصة في أيام الصيف".

(٢٠٧) في دك ،دط ،ف : العشيات .

(٢٠٨) في رد : تصير الروح الحيواني مضطربة فيتولد .....

(٢٠٩) سقط من دك .

(٢١٠) في رد : " أخلاط " ،مكان قوله : " واستعدادات نحو العفن ".

(٢١١) قوله : " وإن كانوا " إلى آخر العبارة ،سقط من رد .

(٢١٢) في كل النسخ : يسرع ،والتصويب من شب وحدها .

(٢١٣) في رد ،ف : المواضع المكشوفة .... هى .

(٢١٤) في دك : مشرقها .

(٢١٥) في رد: جبل المقطم .

(٢١٦) ليس في رد ،دط ،شب .

(٢١٧) في رد ،مع : لِسَبَخ .

(٢١٨) قوله : " ويطرح" إلى " أيضا" سقط من رد .

(٢١٩) الزيادة عن دك ،ليستقيم السياق .

(٢٢٠) كذا في كل النسخ ،يريد :"بالمقارنة إلى القاهرة".

(٢٢١) في رد ،مع : " صغيرة واقعة" ،بعد قوله : " هي " .

(٢٢٢) في دك ،رد ،دط ،شب ،ف : العامر ،خطأ. وما في الأصل ،مع هو الصواب .

(٢٢٣) كان في الأصل : وقلة . خطأواضح ،والصواب في باقي النسخ .

(٢٢٤) في رد : بين الأشجار .

(٢٢٥) في رد : وما يليها .

(٢٢٦) في رد : الحمل ،خطأ.

(٢٢٧) في الأصل ،دك ،دط ،شب ،ف : المقسم ،والتصويب من رد .

(٢٢٨) الزيادة من سائر النسخ .

(٢٢٩) في رد : " لولّد" ،مكان : " لكان ذلك يولّد " . وفي رد : " لكان تولّد".

(٢٣٠) يعني استمرار أبدانهم في إلْف ذلك والتعوّد عليه .

(٢٣١) قوله : " في آخر الربيع وأول الصيف " ليس في رد .

(٢٣٢) قوله :"ما يبقى من الماء " ،لم يرد في شب .

(٢٣٣) قوله :"وأكثر ما يحس منه هذا الحال " ليس في رد .

(٢٣٤) في رد ،شب : مجاورة .

(٢٣٥) في رد: بعضها الآخر .

(٢٣٦) في شب : أهل الفيوم .

(٢٣٧) في رد ،دط ،شب : العامر ،تحريف .

(٢٣٨) في رد : " والغالب على أهلها الجبن وعدم الإغاثة لبعضهم " ،مكان قوله " ولذلك غلب " إلى " أمر عظيم" .

(٢٣٩) في رد : " حتى قيل إن الخمسة رجال من رجال البلدان الأخرى تسوق مائة رجل من رجالها " ،مكان قوله : " وقد بلغ بهم " ،الى قوله: " في الحرب " .

(٢٤٠) في رد : صيرورة ،مكان : أن صار .

(٢٤١) زاد بعده في رد : " وهوما تقدم ذكره".

(٢٤٢) في سائر النسخ : اتخاذ . والمدينة هنا يعني العاصمة .

(٢٤٣) قوله : " وهي مصر القديمة " ،لم يرد في رد .

(٢٤٤) في رد : بتنّيس . خطأفليس من المعروف في تاريخ هذه البلدة أنها كانت عاصمة لمصر القديمة أوغيرهافي أي زمن.راجع كتاب أنيس الجليس في أخبار تنيس لابن بسام المحتسب ،تحقيق جمال الدين الشيال .

(٢٤٥) زاد بعده في رد : الموجودة الآن . وفي دك : والله أعلم .

(٢٤٦) يبدأ الفصل السابع في رد بقوله : " وسائر الأمراض الوافدة"، ثم كلمة " اعلم " ،مكان كلمة : " أمّا " .

(٢٤٧) في دك : أهلها ،خطأ . وفي شب ،ف : أمرها .

(٢٤٨) في رد : أشياء .

(٢٤٩) في رد : إما بأن تشتد سخونته أو برودته أو رطوبته أو جفافه .

(٢٥٠) زيادة عن باقي النسخ .

(٢٥١) في رد : عقبية ،وهي كذلك في كل المواضع التى وردت فيها في هذا الفصل ،وذلك خطأظاهر .

(٢٥٢) في رد : هناك .

(٢٥٣) في شب : أخلاقهم ،تحريف .

(٢٥٤) في رد ،دط ،شب : خرب ،خطأ.

(٢٥٥) في رد ،دط ،شب : الموتى .

(٢٥٦) في رد ،شب ،ف : فيهم .

(٢٥٧) في رد ،دط : التخمة .

(٢٥٨) في رد : غَمّهم .

(٢٥٩) في رد أو توقعوا قحطا في .

(٢٦٠) في دط : بما .

(٢٦١) في دط : المرض .

(٢٦٢) في رد : أبدان المرض .

(٢٦٣) في الأصل : لمرض ،والتصويب من باقي النسخ .

(٢٦٤) قوله : " فإذ قد قدمت هذه الأشياء " ،لم يرد في رد ،وجاء مكانه : " حينذاك ". وفي ف : الأسباب .

(٢٦٥) في رد : أو يعرض للنيل فرط زيادة ... أو يعرض له قلّة الزيادة .

(٢٦٦) في دط : جرب ،تحريف .

(٢٦٧) في رد : الغلال .

(٢٦٨) زاد بعده في رد ،شب ،ف : ونحوها .

(٢٦٩) زيادة عن باقي النسخ .

(٢٧٠) قوله :"الزيادة والنقصان معا " ،لم يرد في رد .

(٢٧١) في رد ،دط : لم يتأمله .

(٢٧٢) زاد بعد في دك : والله تعالى أعلم .

(٢٧٣) في رد : الإجمال .

(٢٧٤) في رد : والبلادة .

(٢٧٥) في رد : وأمثالها فللقرب .

(٢٧٦) في رد ، دط : الضياء ،خطأ.

(٢٧٧) زاد قبله في دك ،رد ،شب ،ف : وترق .

(٢٧٨) في شب : همتهم .

(٢٧٩) زاد بعده في رد : من الحيوان .

(٢٨٠) في رد ،دط : كما ذكرنا.

(٢٨١) في دط : ويجوز ،تحريف .

(٢٨٢) فيه : أي في البدن ،وفي دك ،ف : فينا .

(٢٨٣) في رد ،دط : وتنشأ الغريزة ،مكان : وتنتشر الحرارة الغريزية ،خطأ.

(٢٨٤) قوله : " بغير" حتى نهاية الفقرة سقط من ف .

(٢٨٥) في الأصل ،دك : خروجها ،والصواب ما في باقي النسخ .

(٢٨٦) الزيادة من سائر النسخ .

(٢٨٧) في رد ،دط ،شب : ومن اعتاد الرياضة أعضاؤه .

(٢٧٨) قوله : سائر الفعلة ،لم يرد في رد دط .

(٢٨٩) في رد : يورث .

(٢٩٠) ما بين القوسين زيادة من كل النسخ .

(٢٩١) في دط : النجوم ،خطأواضح .

(٢٩٢) فى دك : لذلك ،خطأ.

(٢٩٣) في باقي النسخ : فسـد .

(٢٩٤) في رد : خرجت .

(٢٩٥) في الأصل ،دك : فيها ،والصواب في باقي النسخ .

(٢٩٦) المعروف ـ في هذا المعنى ـ الفعل الرباعي .

(٢٩٧) زاد بعده في رد ،دط : عظيمة .

(٢٩٨) قوله : وعفنتها الأوساخ التى معها ،ليس في رد .

(٢٩٩) في رد ،دط : التي .

(٣٠٠) الزيادة من باقي النسخ .

(٣٠١) في دك : الحادة .

(٣٠٢) قوله : في أبدان الناس ،جاءت في رد قبل قوله : من الرطوبات.

(٣٠٣) في الأصل : يسويّان . وفي دك ،دط ،شب ،ف : يساويان ،والصواب في مـع ، رد.

(٣٠٤) في دط : الهم ،خطأ.

(٣٠٥) زاد في دك بعده : لها .

(٣٠٦) أي كل واحد من الأسباب الستة .

(٣٠٧) في الأصل وكل النسخ : سنة ،وأثبتنا ما في ف .

(٣٠٨) في دط : وسَجِيته .

(٣٠٩) في رد : اعلم (أن) الفلاسفة والأطباء قالوا : إن الحيلة في حفظ الصحة ومداواة الأمراض هو اقتفاء أثر الطبيعة في أفعالها في البدن

(٣١٠) في دط ،ق : أمرونا .

(٣١١) في دط : نختفي ،والصواب : نحتفي ، أى نهتمّ . ورواية سائر النسخ أُجود.

(٣١٢) في رد : بعضهم .

(٣١٣) في رد : على العكس . وفي دط ،شب،ف : على الضد .

(٣١٤) زاد في دط قبل قوله " ينبغي " ما يلي : كذلك خلاء العروق ،فإنها إن خلت من النوع الذي ينبغي أن تخلو منه نفع ذلك وسهل احتماله ،وإن لم يكن كذلك كان الأمر على الضد .

(٣١٥) زاد بعده في رد : بعضهم .

(٣١٦) قوله :"فأما ما كان استفراغه " ،سقط من رد .

(٣١٧) في رد : نقل عن أبقراط في هذه المواضع .

(٣١٨) قوله :"وما سمعناه عن جالينوس فيها ،وفي غيرها " ،ليس في رد ،ف.

(٣١٩) في دك ،ف : فضوله .

(٣٢٠) سقط من دك ،وزاد فيها ،وفي شب ،رد : " في الوقت الموافق "،بعد قوله : " العضو الموافق " .

(٣٢١) كان في الأصل : سبيلها .

(٣٢٢) في رد : اجتمع في الأبدان .

(٣٢٣) قوله " وتأملنا " إلى " طبائع " لم يرد في دك . وجاء مكانه : وتخيرنا من الأغذية ...

(٣٢٤) قوله :"ويحفظه ويعرفه " ،ليس في رد . وقوله : " يحفظه " ،ليس في ف .

(٣٢٥) زاد في ف : كثيرة ،بعد قوله : " أخر" .

(٣٢٦) في رد : أمزجة البدن . وما في سائر النسخ أصح .

(٣٢٧) في رد ،دط ،ف : مقدار قوة العليل .

(٣٢٨) زيادة عن بقية النسخ ،يتم بها الكلام .

(٣٢٩) في الأصل ،دك : يقتدي ،وأثبتنا ما في سائر النسخ .

(٣٣٠) كان في الأصل : وعناد ومدة طويلة في ميلها،وأثبتنا ما في سائر النسخ.

(٣٣١) ليس في رد . وفي ف : أرض .

(٣٣٢) مع ذلك : يعني مع تقدمه .

(٣٣٣) في ف : وإيثار .

(٣٣٤) قوله : " فإن فاته " إلى " الآخرة " ،لم يرد في دط .

(٣٣٥) في دط : على النار ،خطأ.

(٣٣٦) في دط : التفاخر.

(٣٣٧) في ف : بيّنها .

(٣٣٨) في سائر النسخ : طول اللحى .

(٣٣٩) في رد : التفاخـــر .

(٣٤٠) في شب : يطعمون ،ليست جيـــدة .

(٣٤١) كذا في كل النسخ . والأجود أن تكون " جماعة " مفعولا به الفعل "أعرف "، وتسقط الواو .

(٣٤٢) قوله : ما الناس عليه من محبة الدنيا ،ليس في شب .

(٣٤٣) في رد ،شب ،ف : الدرهم .

(٣٤٤) ليس في رد .

(٣٤٥) في دط ،شب : أحصن ،خطأ .

(٣٤٦) زاد بعده في دط : لى .

(٣٤٧) في رد ،ف : الأعِلّاء ،وهي أجـود .

(٣٤٨) زاد بعده في دط :لا .

(٣٤٩) رد ،دط : وحرّ .

(٣٥٠) رد : من الجهل والتموه .

(٣٥١) ليس في دط .

(٣٥٢) في شب : المحن .

(٣٥٣) في رد ،دط : القوم .

(٣٥٤) دط ،شب : عرفت .

(٣٥٥) في رد : بكونه التزم أن . و قوله : " بأن كان " ،جاء بدله " بما"، في دك .

(٣٥٦) زاد بعده في رد : ودواعيه .

(٣٥٧) رد : جسيم .

(٣٥٨) قوله :"وإني لأعرف شيخا آخر منهم " ،ليس في رد .

(٣٥٩) في رد ،شب : عظيم .

(٣٦٠) جاء في رد : " فنال بذلك ما نال " ،بدلا من قوله " فقام له بذلك سوق كبير " .

(٣٦١) قوله :"بإظهار خدمة السلطان " جاء في سائر النسخ إلا دك بعد قوله " موّه على الناس " ،وذلك أجود للمعنى .

(٣٦٢) في رد ،دط ،شب: إخواني .

(٣٦٣) زاد في رد بعده : المجنون.

(٣٦٤) فى رد : الأعِلّاء .

(٣٦٥)قوله " الرجل والمرأة " ليس في ف ،وجاء مكانه : " والترف والشقى".

(٣٦٦)قوله : " رجل" إلى " القروى"،ليس في دك .

(٣٦٧) زاد بعده في رد : وهذا ما كان من وصف أطباء مصر . وزاد قبله: وكحّاليها .

(٣٦٨) في رد " القليل " ،مكان قوله :" أربعة نفر أو خمسة".

(٣٦٩) في دط ،شب : شيئا شيئا .

(٣٧٠) في ف : والعَفَن .

(٣٧١) زيادة من : دط ،شب ،يستقيم بها الكلام .

(٣٧٢) قوله : " في " إلى " بالدواء " سقط من رد .

(٣٧٣) قوله : اللاحجة " إلى " إذ كان " ليس في رد ،وجاء مكانه : من الأعضاء بالتدريج .

(٣٧٤) في رد : ولا ينبغي تغييرها ،بل المقايسة بينها.

(٣٧٥) قوله : " وأجر الناس" ،لم يرد في رد .

(٣٧٦) في رد : لأجل أن .

(٣٧٧) زاد في دك بعده : والله سبحانه وتعالى أعلم . وزاد في رد ،دط،شب : فاعرفه .

(٣٧٦) في رد : المستقام ،خطأواضح .

(٣٧٩) في رد : لما كانت .

(٣٨٠) في رد : قبول الأمراض .

(٥٨١) في رد : ومعلوم .

(٣٨٢) في رد ،ف : بصيحة .

((٣٨٣) كان في الأصل : تدبرتها .

(٣٨٤) في رد : يصير به .

(٣٨٥) ليس في رد .

(٣٨٦) العناية في .

(٣٨٧) المعروف في جمع وريد : أَوْردة ،وُرُود .

(٣٨٨) ليس في دط ،شب .

(٣٨٩) زاد في دك بعده : والله تعالى أُعلم .

(٣٩٠) في ف : والجير .

(٣٩١) في دك ،مع : الشامان .

(٣٩٢) في رد ،دط ،شب : الجهرمانية .

(٣٩٣) جاء في رد " لمن لا يمكنه ذلك " ،مكان :"فمن .... الكباش " .

(٣٩٤) في رد : التفاح ،خطأ

(٣٩٥) زاد قبلها في رد ،دط ،شب : ومن .

(٣٩٦) زاد بعده في رد : الزمن .

(٣٩٧) قوله " الريباس والسماق " ،لم يرد في رد ،وكاء مكانه : الكزبرة .

(٣٩٨) زاد بعد ،في دط : وعنب الثعلب .

(٣٩٩) لم يرد في دط .

(٤٠٠) زاد قبله في رد : واجعل .

(٤٠١) في سائر النسخ : الخمر البيضاء الصافية العفصة القريبة العهد .

(٤٠٢) قوله : " الأزهار الحارة " ،لم يرد في رد ،دط .

(٤٠٣) في در ،دط ،ف : والأترج وورقة والنارنج وورقه .

(٤٠٤) في رد : الفرنجسك .

(٤٠٥) زاد بعده في : اللاذن .

(٤٠٦) في ف : النبك .

(٤٠٧) في رد ،دط : نوار زهر النارج .

(٤٠٨) ليس في دط ،مع .

(٤٠٩) زاد بعده في دط : ودهن الخيري .

(٤١٠) زاد بعده في دط ،ف : والعنب .

(٤١١) في رد : أنواع الحلوى .

(٤١٢) في الأصل ،دك : السمسى ،والصواب من سائر النسخ .

(٤١٣) في رد ،ف : يرش المياه ،واتخذ من الأشياء أرطبها . وإن كان الهواء رطبا ، اتخذ الأشياء المجففة من الدخن .... وفي دك فقط : " واتخذت من الأشياء أرطبها " ،بعد قوله : " ورشها " .

(٤١٤) في رد : " وعلى هذا فقس " ،مكان :" فعلى هذا جرى إصلاح الهواء".

(٤١٥) زاد بعده في رد : صيفا وشتاء .

(٤١٦) في رد : فإذا كان محرورا فيصفيه ....

(٤١٧) في رد : وإن كان مبرودا .

(٤١٨) في رد : وينبغي أن ينتظر عليه مدة بعد الترويق والتصفية حتى ينظف ويروق ،ثم يشرب منه . وإن شئت أن تصفيه فاجعله ...

(٤١٩) في دط : وإن شئت أن تصفيه .

(٤٢٠) في دط ،ف : طبخته .

(٤٢١) في رد،دط : كيفيات ... محسوسات .

(٤٢٢) في رد ،دط : الأخلاط التى تقدم ذكرها .

(٤٣٣) في رد : شهر طوبة .

(٤٢٤) قوله " الظروف الحجارية " ،ليس في رد .

(٤٢٥) في دط : اتخاذه ،خطأ.

(٤٢٦) في رد : ويكون تبريده في الصيف .

(٤٢٧)في دك : لطيفة .

(٤٢٨) زاد في رد بعده : وفي زمن الشتاء بالأشنان والسعد .

(٤٢٩) لم يرد في رد .

(٤٣٠) في رد : تغلي بالنار .

(٤٣١) في رد : شهر طوبة .

(٤٣٢) في رد : القوارير ،وهي أفضل ،لأن القربة لا تعمل إلا من الجِلْد .

(٤٣٣) في رد : فلا تركن إلى ذلك .

(٤٣٤) في رد : فالمختار . وفي دط ،ف : فاختر .

(٤٣٥) في رد ،دط : اتخاذها ،مكان قوله : إيجاد الأجود .

(٤٣٦) في رد : واحكم .

(٤٣٧) قوله : " ثم يؤكل" إلى " لم يطب " ،لم يرد في رد .

(٤٣٨) في كل النسخ : الطبهوج ،والصواب ما أثبتنا .

(٤٣٩) في رد : واترك ،خطأ،والصواب : وأَنْزِل .

(٤٤٠) في شب : أماكن .

(٤٤١) في رد : الأسواق .

(٤٤٢) قوله : " وسبيل " إلى قوله " يتخذ منه " لم يرد في رد .

(٤٤٣) في رد : الغسل .

(٤٤٤) ليس في دك .

(٤٤٥) قوله " لعلنا" ،حتى آخر الفصل لم يرد في رد .

(٤٤٦) في دط : تعالى .

(٤٤٧) في رد : " اعلم أن أبقراط قد أوصى فقال " ،بدلا من افتتاح الكلام حتى قوله : جالينوس .

(٤٤٨) في شب ،ف : وأن يمال بهذه .

(٤٤٩) في دط : وحذر من أن يبلغ ذلك إلى .

(٤٥٠) في رد : أن يختار .

(٤٥١) في رد ،دط : تقليل .

(٤٥٢) في رد ،دط : وتكون عارفا ... به .

(٤٥٣) في رد : الجلوس .

(٤٥٤) في رد : حَرّ . وفي دط : أذى .

(٤٥٥) في رد : وبالعكس .

(٤٥٦) في ف : اليبس .

(٤٥٧) زيادة عن باقي النسخ ليصح الكلام .

(٤٥٨) قوله :"أن لا تتعرض له كثيرا " ،لم يرد في رد .

(٤٥٩) في الأصل ،دك ،مع : بيته ،والتصويب من باقي النسخ .

(٤٦٠) زاد بعده في رد : الأمور المذكورة .

(٤٦١) زاد بعده في رد : سـائر .

(٤٦٢) ليس في رد .

(٤٦٣) زاد بعده في رد ،ف : والكافور.

(٤٦٤) ليس في رد .

(٤٦٥) في رد : وما يماثل ذلك .

(٤٦٦) قوله : " في مثل " إلى " والصوم " ،لم يرد في رد ،وجاء مكانه : " من مثل هذه الأغذية ما كان فيه إساءة للمزاج " . والأفعال الواردة في هذه الفقرة كلها أفعال أمر : تجنبْ توّقَ ،تعرّضْ ، اجلِسْ .

(٤٦٧) في دك ،رد ،دط ،ف : اختر الأغذية .

(٤٦٨) زاده بعد في رد ،ف : في الأجسـام .

(٤٦٩) لم يرد في رد .

(٤٧٠) في رد : حدوثا للمرض . والصواب إحداثا .

(٤٧١) في رد : إلى الأبدان ما يخف وذلك ....

(٤٧٢) قوله : " والكرم " إلى " أغصان الكرم" ،ليس فى رد ،دط .

(٤٧٣) في ف : الكروم .

(٤٧٤) في رد : والتختم بالجوهـر .

(٤٧٥) ليس في رد .

(٤٧٦) في رد ،مع : تعفنت .

(٤٧٧) في دط : يستعملوه • وفي شب : ينتفعوا • وفي ف : يشربوه •

(٤٧٨) في شب : هلكوا •

(٤٧٩) في دط : يتناول •

(٤٨٠) في رد : يبقى •

(٤٨١) زاد بعده في دك ،ف : المفرطين •

(٤٨٢) زادبعده فيرد:" بل عدم تناولها أَوْلَى " •

(٤٨٣) في شب،ف : بارد المزاج •

(٤٨٤) في رد ،دط ،شب،ف : بما تقدر عليه • مكان : بغاية ...

(٤٨٥) في سائر النسخ : وصفه •

(٤٨٦) في سائر النسخ ما عدا دك ،زاد بعده : ولا تُجازِف •

(٤٨٧) زاد بعده في شب : ويعين •

(٤٨٨) في رد ،دط جاءت نسخة هذا الدواء مختلطة مع نسخة شراب الساهر الآتية بعدُ هكذا : نسخة دواء يقوى الكبد والمعدة على الهضم : يُؤْخَذ من ماء السفرجل الحامض أو التفاح الحامض رطل ،ومن الخمر رطل ،ومن ماء الرمان الحامض والحلو أربعة أمثاله ،ومن الماء الحار مثل الجميع ،ويُترَك ثلاثة أيام ثم يطبخ حتى يرجع إلى النصف ،ويُصَفّى، ويُلْقَى عليه جزء سكر وجزء عسل منزوع الرغوة ،ثم يُطْبَخ ثانية حتى يثخن ،ويؤخذ ريمه ، ويرفع •

(٤٨٩) قوله : " ثلاثة " إلى قوله : " ويصفى " ،لم يرد في شب•

(٤٩٠) ليس في رد •

(٤٩١) ليس في رد ،دط •

(٤٩٢) في رد : البدن •

(٤٩٣) قوله : " وماء تفاح حامض " ،لم يرد في رد •

(٤٩٤) ليس في رد•

(٤٩٥) في دط ،ف : ريحاني عصير •

(٤٩٦) لم يرد في ف • وفي دط : الجلاب •

(٤٩٧) الزيادة عن رد ،شب ،ف •

(٤٩٨) كذا في جميع النسخ ،والمعروف في جمعه سُدُود ،وأَسِدّة ،والأخيرة جمع شاذ .

(٤٩٩) في رد : وينقع في خل خمر قدر أُربعة أرطال ويترك فيه .

(٥٠٠) ليس في رد .

(٥٠١) لم يرد في رد .

(٥٠٢) قوله : فُقّاع الإذْخَر وبزر الكرفس ،لم يرد في رد .

(٥٠٣) زاد بعده في رد : منه .

(٥٠٤) زاد بعده في شب ،ف : الحلو .

(٥٠٥) قوله " السمين العلك " ،لم يرد في رد ،وجاء مكانه : قدر الطلب .

(٥٠٦) في ف : يصيـــر .

(٥٠٧) في رد : من الماء حتى يغمره .

(٥٠٨) قوله : " والنار عليه" ،لم يرد في رد .

(٥٠٩) في رد : ومتى نقص يزاد عليه ماء مغليّ .

(٥١٠) كان في الأصل : ويصفى ،والتصويب من سائر النسخ .

(٥١١) في شب : يتفل فيه ما يتفل .

(٥١٢) مكان هذه الكلمة في دط ،شب : ثانية .

(٥١٣) في سائر النسخ : ويجعل .

(٥١٤) كان في الأصل : خطأ ،وأثبتنا ما في باقي النسخ ،فهو أجود .

(٥١٥) في شب : شجرى ،وفي ف : سحرى ،تحريف .

(٥١٦) جاءت هذه العبارة وما بعدها حتى نهاية الجملة بالاضافة ،أى : درهم دار صيني ... الخ .

(٥١٧) في رد ،شب : مثل الكحل .

(٥١٨) في رد ،ف : صُرّة .

(٥١٩) في دك ،شب ،ف : إسخان .

(٥٢٠) في شب : واحدا ،وكذلك في بقية المواضع في صفة هذا الشراب والذي يليه ·

(٥٢١) البرام : جمع بُرْمة ،وهي القدر المعمولة من الحجارة ·

(٥٢٢) في رد ويضاف إليه ·

(٥٢٣) زاد بعده في رد : وقت الحاجة ·

(٥٢٤) في دك ،ف : البير ·

(٥٢٥) لم ترد في ف · وفي رد : العقاقير ·

(٥٢٦) قوله:"من خل خمر ثقيف" ،لم يرد في رد ·

(٥٢٧) في رد : يرق ·

(٥٢٨) تنتهي هذا نسخة ف ،فهي تنقص حوالي ثلاث صفحات ·

(٥٢٩) زاد بعده في دط ،شب : سفرجل طيب ·

(٥٣٠) في شب : قدر الشراب ·

(٥٣١) زاد في رد بعده : ثم يستعمل ،فإنه ينفع من لهب القلب والمعدة وسائر الأحشاء ·

(٥٣٢) نسخة القيروطي لم ترد في رد ،دط ·

(٥٣٣) زاد بعده في دك : والله أعلم ·

(٥٣٤) في رد : اعلم أنّ ·

(٥٣٥) في رد : إيثار ·

(٥٣٦) في رد : لأمرين ، الأول : أن المضار التي تعرض للأبدان فيها يمكن زوالها · وأخلاق النفس تسهل مداواتها ····

(٥٣٧) في رد : كذلك لا تكره السكنى من أُجله ،لسهولة زواله ·

(٥٣٨) في رد : أشدّ ·

(٥٣٩) في رد : في الموضع الذي يلائمه ·

(٥٤٠) في رد : أولى وأنسب ·

(٥٤١) جاء في رد مكانه : والأمر الثاني : إن مصر ...

(٥٤٢) قوله : " وضعفهم عن الجهاد" ،لم يرد في رد .

(٥٤٣) في دط : فإن قيل إن أسعارها مرتفعة ،فالجواب أن المكاسب ......
ونسخة شب تختم بهذه العبارة : فإن قيل إن أسعارها . وجاء في
رد بدلا من هذه العبارة حتى آخر هذا الفصل ما يلي : وهذا آخر
ما تيسر لي من جمع هذه الفوائد ،و لله الحمد وصلى الله على
سيدنا محمد النبي الأمي وعلى آله وصحبه وسلم تسليما كثيرا إلى
يوم الدين . آمين .

(٥٤٤) هذه الخاتمة جائت في رد فقط .

(٥٤٥) في الأصل : وغيرها . وأثبتنا ما في دك .

(٥٤٦) يعني الشرور الدنية التي تقبل العلاج .